LOVE AND SEX

Cross-Cultural Perspectives

Elaine Hatfield
Richard L. Rapson

University Press of America,® Inc.
Lanham · Boulder · New York · Toronto · Oxford

Contents

Preface

Love among the Global Villagers

The global village is upon us. No longer a utopian vision, we can see it materializing through the mist. Regardless of how we may feel about it, the revolution in communications and information stands as one of this century's monumental transformations. Our century, as it careens toward its close, is practically defined by globalization.

In the most remote village in India are farm communities gathered around the settlement's television set to watch programs brought down to earth by satellite. In Paris or Jerusalem or Beijing, people turn on their televisions and see wars being fought in Somalia, Bosnia, or Northern Ireland. Laptop computers, modems, FAX machines, electronic mail, interactive television, and palm-held telephones clearly represent only the beginning of the global shrinking to come.

The implications for our intellectual and personal lives are enormous and nowhere are they greater than in the intensely private spheres of love and sex. The ways in which we think about love and sex are no more immune from change than the ways we organize our political lives, dress, eat, or hear music. West is meeting East and East is meeting West (and North and South).

In the West—by which we mean Western Europe, the United States, and British dominions such as Canada, Australia, and New Zealand—there has been a strong tendency to see nearly everything from a Western point of view. Social science research, including that into love and sex, has generally been conducted by Western scientists, from a Western perspective, with Western subjects—as though this perspective were universal. Clearly that will not do any longer, and one purpose for our writing this book is to contribute to the development of a larger and richer perspective, one that is more in accord with today's world realities.

The Multidisciplinary Strategy and Its Pitfalls

We are interested in looking at passionate love and sexuality from every vantage point possible. We wish to bring to bear on these topics some of the best research, expression, and thinking from a wide variety of intellectual disciplines: anthropology and sociology, molecular biology, sociobiology, primatology, chemistry, literature and art, and, of course, from our two disciplines—psychology and history. We employ examples from our psychotherapy practice, from our lives, from everything we know.

This sort of synthesis is infrequently attempted in academia, and many oppose such attempts. This is partly because intellectual life has evolved over the past century into hundreds of specialized disciplines, all speaking their own languages, adopting their own definitions and methodologies, asking their separate questions, and rarely addressing one another, not to speak of the general public. This specialization has produced a wealth of new knowledge about practically everything. Despite our interest in multidisciplinary work, we ourselves have willingly been card-carrying members of and engaged in the arcane rituals of our specialties.

In trying to see our large topic whole, to bring together a variety of disparate insights and works, there are several things our work here cannot be. We cannot satisfy the demands for precision, linguistic purity, exact definitions, bibliographic references, or knowledge of any one of the disciplines represented, including our own. Cultural anthropologists, scholars of homosexuality, researchers on primate behavior, and so forth will be painfully aware of what we have left out or oversimplified.

And they will be right. Multidisciplinary syntheses, even without treading into the treacherous arena of multiculturalism, are new. They are, in our opinion, desperately needed and will prove to be immensely rewarding. But the enterprise is only beginning, and there is no well-laid out or safe path. So our words, simple, nontechnical, and plain-spoken, are invitations to thought, discourse, and exploration, and, above all, to much more research.

An Overview of the Text

Relationships unfold over time. In this volume, we plan to focus on the passionate beginnings of relationships: how people meet, mate, fall in love, make love, and fall out of love, usually only to risk it all over again. We plan to compare the way cultures try to set rules for these incendiary matters. We ask: What seems to be biological and universal? What seems to be socially constructed and transient? And, taking a historical perspective, we ask: Where are the different societies (and the world itself) headed?

This book does not deal with the later stages of relationships, with issues of companionate love, commitment, intimacy, power, or communication, except for a final chapter on the breakup of relationships. As yet, there is simply not much cross-cultural research on these deeper aspects of love. A wealth of exciting research remains to be done; throughout the book we will try to provide some roadmaps for those future explorations.

In Chapter 1, "The Many Paths to Love," we find that recently, theorists from a variety of disciplines—anthropology, history, and cross-cultural psychology—have begun to speculate about the impact that culture and ethnicity have on love and sexuality. Theorists have raised a variety of questions: What aspects of passionate love and sexuality are biologically mandated and/or universal? What aspects are limited to certain historical eras or specific cultures? Is the world rapidly becoming one? Or, will traditional customs prove to be surprisingly tenacious? Do some cultural practices work better than others? In Chapter 1, we provide an overview of the answers the different disciplines offer.

We turn to more specific matters in Chapter 2, "The Romantic, Sexual, and Marital Ideal." In all societies, young men and women fall in love, feel sexual desire, and live together or marry. We begin this chapter by discussing what men and women in a variety of cultures desire in romantic partners, sexual partners, and/or mates. We target the controversy between evolutionary psychologists and feminist scholars as to whether existing gender differences in preferences are "writ in our genes" or a consequence of sociocultural differences in the opportunities tradition-ally available to men and women. Then, we chart the revolution that is occurring in the ways young people select their partners. We will see that parental power is crumbling. The tradition of arranged marriages is quickly being replaced by the ideal of marriage for love. Finally, we will test how well traditional arranged mar-riages work out versus modern marriage for love. Our explorations will take us to the United States, Europe, Russia, China, Japan, India, Africa, as well as other places.

In Chapter 3, "Falling in Love," we begin by exploring cultural differences in the meaning of passionate love. Is love a delight or a tragedy? Other questions quickly appear: Who is the most vulnerable to passionate love? Why are they so vulnerable to passion? What sorts of people spark other people's passionate fanta-sies? When are people especially vulnerable to love's tender discoveries, sudden torments, and consuming desires? We wade into the swirl of contradictory desires that seem to fuel this intense emotion: the pleasure and the pain, the wish for closeness and separation, the longing for both security and excitement.

In Chapter 4, "Sexuality: Then and There" we examine the evolutionary, histori-cal, and cross-cultural underpinnings of sexuality. We discuss the array of sexual attitudes, feelings, and behaviors that have been considered "natural" in different times and places. We hope this will allow us to view our own time and our own attitudes and behavior from a wiser perspective. Chapter 5, "Sex: Now and Every-where," continues the discussion with a hard look at our sexual world today. We will find that people in different countries often possess very different attitudes toward homosexual, bisexual, and heterosexual experimentation. They also differ in how likely they are to engage in a variety of premarital, marital, and extramarital sexual activities.

In Chapter 6, "Passion—For Better or Worse," we discuss the gossamer delights and the thorny problems of passionate love. Hollywood films and television tend to glamorize love relationships. The realities of love are more fascinating, complex, and unexpected than the Hollywood romances. We end by asking: Who falls out of love and why? Can lovers do anything to prevent an incandescent, passionate affair from burning itself out, ending in ashes?

Finally, in Chapter 7, "Breaking Up and Starting Over," we discuss the end of love affairs and marriages. We catalog people's efforts to survive their dashed hopes, pick themselves up, and start over, intending to be wiser the next time.

We end by trying to guess, with help from the historical record, what the future may hold for lovers in a world of rapid and accelerating change. We do not love today as did the ancient Greeks or Chinese, the medieval troubadours of France, or the pre-Columbian Sioux of North America. To see into the future, we need more than a static collection of daguerrotypes from the past or a collection of snapshots of where things stand at this single instant in time. In this text we have tried to provide a moving picture, which has recorded where various societies have been, where we are now, and guesses at where we may be heading—in a world that has witnessed astounding changes in the way humankind loves and makes love.

About the Authors

Elaine Hatfield   My mother's (Eileen Kalahar's) family were immigrants—from Ireland, to Canada, and then to the United States. My mother (like the rest of her family), was an Irish Catholic. My father's (Charles Hatfield's) family arrived in America from England long before the American Revolution. The family was reluctant to talk about its "notorious" past in American history (they were the Hatfields of Hatfield and McCoy fame.) The Hatfield's were mostly English, but there was a sprinkling of Irish, Scottish, and French or American Indian thrown in.

We were definitely poor. I grew up in a segregated low-income housing project in Detroit. I had little experience with other cultures or ethnic groups.

My graduate research in psychology took me into forbidden territories: love, physical attraction, and the emotions. I was interested in trying to apply scientific rigor to topics which were traditionally left to poets, philosophers, and celibate priests. Early on, most of my colleagues thought these research interests were vaguely amusing. I have hung around long enough to see the tide turn.

Nonetheless my knowledge of and contact with other cultures were limited. I traveled, but having spent most of my life until age 45 in the Midwest, nearly all of my students, colleagues, and friends were European Americans. And it seemed quite enough to study how they and others similar to them loved, made love, fell out of love, cursed love, and embraced it all over again. My post-graduate education in cultural diversity was to come.

Richard L. Rapson   I am a historian of the United States. My books have dealt with what were once "unorthodox" areas of historical inquiry—families, women, children, love, and sex—rather than presidents, kings, and wars. I have no particular scholarly expertise in cross-cultural work. For much of my life I had no particular interest in the rest of the world, particularly beyond the boundaries of the United States and Western Europe. To compound the matter, I spent my first 18 years on a very provincial and isolated island: Manhattan Island.

Since 1966 I have lived on another little island, this time in the middle of the Pacific Ocean, 2300 miles from the nearest mainland. Oahu, one of the Hawaiian Islands, felt to me as though it were in the middle of nowhere when I first arrived. But I did begin to meet, to teach, and to learn from people who were very different from me. Four voyages around the world teaching on a ship formed the core of a life of travel, and forced me to reappraise my youthful cultural blind spots.

The Hawaii Factor   For both of us, our respective moves to Hawaii increased our fascination with, and our realization of, the importance of cultural and ethnic variety. Hawaii is a multicultural society—approximately 28 percent European American, 26 percent Japanese American, 16 percent part-Hawaiian, 12 percent Filipino American, 6 percent Chinese American, and sizable numbers of African Americans, Samoans, Korean Americans, Tongans, southeast Asians, and so forth.

Sixty percent of the marriages performed in Hawaii in the past 15 years have been interracial. This compares to less than 4 percent on the American mainland! Families are often so mixed in their ethnic expectations that the younger generation has a great deal of trouble answering questions as to their ethnic identity. In Hawaii one often notices the striking combinations of the cosmopolitan names one routinely hears: Farouk Wang, Tennyson Yamasaki, Kenji Klein, and so forth. Each individual may represent a brief truce among surprisingly juxtaposed cultures, peoples who would never have crossed paths in previous ages.

In Hawaii, when students are asked to identify their ethnic heritage they often (and proudly) recite "Portuguese, Chinese, Swedish, Hawaiian, and Irish." When asked to "check one" on a demographic questionnaire, they can be at a total loss. Soon, survey researchers in Hawaii learn to repeat the mantra: "If you don't know what to check, just check the ethnic group with which you identify the most." (If people were to check "Other," almost everyone would fall into that category.) As a consequence, it is not unusual for one child in a family to claim to be European American while his brother checks off Chinese American.

As co-psychotherapists (we are also husband and wife), we have gotten to know clients from a variety of cultural and ethnic groups extremely well. We have seen three generations of Japanese, Chinese, and Pacific Islanders; adherents of every religious group . . . or none; couples who had arranged marriages and who had married for love; and couples who formed a single, nuclear family or who congregated in large extended families.

In writing this book we hope to increase the reader's knowledge of and interest in the different ways cultures love and make love—the ways they think about sex and love, the ways they allow themselves to feel about sex and love, and the ways they behave.

Acknowledgments

We would like to thank our literary editor Cynthia Clement, who blended an elegant sensibility with dogged determination in helping us to write and rewrite our text. We are also indebted to Richard Brislin, The East–West Center, Honolulu, HI; Ayse

Carden, Agnes Scott College; Janet Hyde, University of Wisconsin; Cigdem Kâğitçibaşi, Bogaziçi University; Uichol Kim, University of Hawaii; Shinobu Kitayama, Kyoto University; Wei-Hung Lin, University of Hawaii; Cookie and Walter Stephan, University of New Mexico; Harry Triandis, University of Illinois; Stephen and Joan Uhalley, Jr., University of Hawaii; Susumu Yamaguchi, University of Tokyo; and Gail Wyatt, UCLA; who painstakingly reviewed portions of the manuscript. Thanks also to Korey Sato, our editorial assistant, who was relentless in ferreting out elusive source material. Finally, we would like to express our appreciation to Ann Weber, University of North Carolina, at Asheville; Beverly Drinnin, Des Moines Area Community College; Deborah R. Winters, New Mexico State University; and Susan Sprecher (Illinois State University), who reviewed early versions of the manuscript.

Chapter *1*

The Many Paths to Love

She took his right hand and placed it against hers, palms touching. He didn't get the point at first. Then he realized that she was comparing the size of their hands. The difference made her laugh.

"What's funny?"

She told him his hand was funny.

"Why mine? Why not yours?" he said. "If the difference is great, maybe you're the funny one, not me."

"You're the funny one," Lu Wan said.

She matched left hands now and fell sideways to the bed laughing. Maybe she thought they were two different species. One of them was exotic and it wasn't her.

—Don DeLillo (1988, p. 219),
describing an interracial love affair

Beyond Narrow Boundaries

In all cultures, people are ethnocentric. It is natural to assume that the way *we* think, feel, and behave is the only sensible way to be. Those who are different are assumed to be at best exotic and at worst pitiable, sinister, or detestable. Here are two classical examples of such chauvinism—one from the West, the other from the East. In the fifth century B.C., the Greek historian Herodotus (1942) observed, "The Greeks have been from very ancient times distinguished from the barbarians by superior sagacity and freedom from foolish simpleness" (p. 25). In 1793, the Chinese Emperor Ch'ien Lung issued a withering Imperial mandate to King George III of England, whose ministers had dared to propose that Imperial China and the British Empire might establish a trading partnership:

You, O King, from afar have yearned after the blessings of our civilisation, and in your eagerness to come into touch with our converting influence have sent an Embassy across the sea bearing a memorial.

> *Swaying the wide world, I have but one aim in view, namely to maintain a perfect governance and to fulfill the duties of the State: strange and costly objects do not interest me. . . . As your Ambassador can see for himself, we possess all things. I set no value on objects strange or ingenious, and have no use for your country's manufactures (Backhouse & Bland, 1914, pp. 324–326).*

Sad to say, until very recently the social sciences have been guilty of similar blind ethnocentrism. In psychology, America has dominated the scene since the end of World War II (Smith & Bond, 1994). Researchers have interviewed hundreds of thousands of American college students about their romantic and sexual experiences. They have generally assumed that their findings would generalize not only to America or to the West, but even to the world beyond. But the West is not the world. The next stage in social science research requires scientists to push the extraordinary pioneering scholarship of the West forward. We must begin to learn more about other cultures and to initiate truly collaborative work with scientists around the globe. Such a strategy would enable us to answer a number of critical questions:

What aspects of passionate love and sexuality are universal? What aspects are social constructions, limited to certain historical eras or to specific cultures?

Is the world rapidly becoming one, or are traditional cultural practices more tenacious and impervious to this sort of deep transformation than some have supposed (Axtell, 1981; Kâğitçibaşi, 1990; Moore, 1966)? Does the arrival in Japan, for instance, of such Western icons as McDonald's fast food, rock 'n roll, blue jeans, Mozart, and baseball represent a trivial alteration in a fiercely unchanging Land of the Rising Sun? Or are such changes harbingers of the more profound and double-edged Western inroads of popular democracy, individualism, freedom, women's rights, crime, drugs, material greed, egalitarian families, and the desire for personal happiness into the traditional ideals of duty, obedience, and collective responsibility?

Do some cultural practices work better than others?

To answer such questions, we need to conduct open-minded, comparative cultural research.

Recently, theorists from a variety of disciplines have begun to speculate about the impact of culture and ethnicity on love and sex. Better yet, many of these scholars have begun to collaborate in their research. In the history of science, such collaborations have often yielded exciting intellectual discoveries. In this chapter, we try to illuminate some of the rich possibilities offered by synthesis. We try to allow theorists from very different disciplines to talk across the specialized (and somewhat artificial) intellectual barriers of their disciplines. Let us begin by reviewing what anthropologists and evolutionary theorists, historians, and cross-cultural theorists have to tell psychologists about the nature of love and sexual desire.

Definitions

First, we define the powerful emotions with which this book is concerned—passionate love and sexual desire—and distinguish them from their cooler counterpart, companionate love.

Passionate Love and Sexual Desire

[He manifested] all Sappho's famous signs—his voice faltered, his face flushed up, his eyes glanced steathily, a sudden sweat broke out on his skin, the beatings of his heart were irregular and violent.

—Plutarch

Passionate love is a "hot," intense emotion, sometimes called a crush, obsessive love, lovesickness, head-over-heels in love, infatuation, or being in love. We define it this way:

A state of intense longing for union with another. Passionate love is a complex functional whole including appraisals or appreciations, subjective feelings, expressions, patterned physiological processes, action tendencies, and instrumental behaviors. Reciprocated love (union with the other) is associated with fulfillment and ecstasy. Unrequited love (separation) is associated with emptiness, anxiety, or despair. (Hatfield & Rapson, 1993b, p. 5)

Sex researchers tend to use the terms *passionate love* and *sexual desire* almost interchangeably. Perhaps this is not surprising. Passionate love has been defined as a "longing for union." (In various societies, that longing for union may or may not include a desire for sexual union.) Sexual desire has been defined as a "longing for *sexual* union" (Hatfield & Rapson, 1987b, p. 259).

Companionate Love

In romantic love you want the other person. In real love you want the other person's good.

—Margaret Anderson

By contrast, companionate love (sometimes called true love or marital love) is a "warm," far less intense emotion. It combines feelings of deep attachment, commitment, and intimacy. We define it this way:

The affection and tenderness we feel for those with whom our lives are deeply entwined. Companionate love is a complex functional whole including appraisals or appreciations, subjective feelings, expressions, patterned physiological processes, action tendencies, and instrumental behaviors. (Hatfield & Rapson, 1993b, p. 9)

It is with the passionate *beginnings* (and sometimes unsettling endings) of love affairs that this book is primarily concerned. The complexities of serious companionate relations are beyond the scope of this brief introductory text.

Anthropological and Evolutionary Perspectives

Social psychologists, anthropologists, and evolutionary psychologists have studied people in a wide variety of societies. They find clear evidence that passionate love and sexual desire *are* cultural universals, feelings that seem to have existed at all times and in all places (Brown, 1991; Buss, 1988a and b; Hatfield & Rapson, 1993b).

Many theorists have argued that, in the course of evolution, our prehistoric ancestors' brains developed the ability to feel passionate love and sexual desire. Robert Plutchik (1980), for example, pointed out that at every phylogenetic level (from the lowest single-celled organisms to the highest primates), living beings faced many of the same problems. They had to survive and reproduce. First reptiles, then mammals, and finally primates were forced to evolve a set of emotional "programs" to allow them to deal quickly and effectively with recurrent "adaptive situations—fighting, falling in love, escaping predators, confronting sexual infidelity, and so on, each [of which] recurred innumerable times in evolutionary history" (Toobey & Cosmides, 1990, pp. 407–408). Many of these neo-Darwinians believe that passionate love and sexual desire are built on the ancient circuitry evolved to ensure that mothers and infants remain closely attached to one another and that adults mate and reproduce (Hatfield & Rapson, 1993b).

Anthropologists have begun to document the universality of passionate feelings. (Sometimes, they attempt to distinguish between "romantic passion" and "simple lust.") William Jankowiak and Edward Fischer (1992) tried to find out whether or not men and women in a sampling of tribal societies fell passionately in love. They selected 166 hunting, foraging, and agricultural societies from the *Standard Cross-Cultural Sample*, which provides comprehensive information on 186 cultures from 6 distinct geographical regions. In only one of the 166 societies did the resident anthropologist state that there was no evidence of passionate love. The scientists could find no evidence one way or another as to whether or not passionate love existed in 18 of the societies. In 147 of the 166 societies, people showed definite scars from Cupid's arrows. In all of these far-flung societies, young lovers talked about passionate love, recounted tales of love, sang love songs, and talked about the longings and anguish of infatuation. When the adolescents' passionate affections clashed with their parents' or elders' wishes, they eloped.

Here is an example of one confirming report.[1] In this early report, the explorer Basil Thomson (1908), self-righteously commented on passionate love in Fiji.

The nervous system of the Fijian is curiously contradictory. . . . In sexual matters they are certainly neurotic. I have met with several cases of what is called ndongai, *which corresponds with what is called "broken heart" in Europeans. Two young people who have come together once or twice, and who have been suddenly separated, sicken and pine away, and unless their intrigue can be resumed, they do not recover. It is not regarded as a psychological or interesting malady, as love-sickness is with us, but as a physical ailment for which but one remedy is known.*

The causes of the growing laxity of morals lie too deep for the efforts of the Wesleyan missionaries to check it. (p. 241)

Clearly, passionate love existed in Fiji. Jankowiak and Fischer (1992) concluded that romantic love may well be a universal characteristic. They admitted that there may well be cultural variability in how common such heart-pounding, sweaty-palmed feelings are, however.

Anthropologists have also been interested in the kinds of societies in which our primate ancestors lived. Volker Sommer (1993), for example, asked a challenging question: Did our ancient *Homo sapiens* ancestors live in monogamous, polygynous, polyandrous, or polygynandrous communities? (For a definition of these terms, see Table 1.1.)

After observing many kinds of primates, Volker discovered that it was easy to predict what sort of sexual mating arrangements a primate species would possess. All he needed to know were four facts: (1) In that species, which was bigger—the males or the females? (2) How much did the males' testes weigh? (3) Did the females have sexual swellings (which signal sexual receptivity and fertility)? (4) How long did sexual intercourse last? The scientists found, for example, that in monogamous species such as gibbons, males and females were generally about the same size. In polygynous species such as orangutans, where successful males must physically dominate their rivals, males were much larger than their mates. In polyandrous species such as chimpanzees, where successful females must dominate their rivals, females were much larger than their mates.

When Sommer classified *Homo sapiens* based on these four characteristics, his calculations led him to conclude that there is no chance that our human forebears

TABLE 1.1 Types of Mating/Marital Arrangements

Monogamy	Men and women are permitted to have only one regular sexual partner or marry only one person at a time.
Polygamy	Men or women are allowed to have more than one regular sexual partner or mate at a time.
Polygyny	Men are allowed more than one regular sexual partner or wife at a time.
Polyandry	Women are allowed more than one regular sexual partner or husband at a time.
Polygynandry	Both men and women can have as many sexual and/or marital partners as they desire.

were either polyandrous or polygynandrous. They *may* have been monogamous. It is most likely, however, that they were polygynous.

What about our more immediate ancestors? How did they live? Helen Fisher (1989), on the basis of her calculations, concluded that throughout the world, although in theory most societies are polygynous, in fact the overwhelming majority of married men and women are actually in monogamous marriages. Fisher studied the marital arrangements of the 853 societies sampled in the *Ethnographic Atlas*. (The *Atlas* contains anthropological information on more than 1,000 representative pre-industrial societies throughout the world.) She found that although almost all societies (84 percent) permitted polygyny, men rarely exercised this option. Only about 10 percent of men had more than one wife. Most had just one wife. A few were unmarried. In 16 percent of societies, monogamy was prescribed. Polyandry was extremely rare. Only 0.5 percent of societies permitted polyandry.

Thus far we have discussed cultural universals. Now we turn to the work of historians and cross-cultural researchers, who stress not cultural universals but cultural variability in love and desire. They remind us that culture can have a powerful impact on how easily and how deeply people fall in love and how they try to deal with these tumultuous feelings.

Historical Perspectives

> *The past is a foreign country: they do things differently there.*
> —L. P. Hartley

The historical record tends to confirm the hypothesis that passionate love and sexual desire have always existed—in all times and in all places. The earliest Western literature, bound up as it is between myth and reality, abounds in stories of lovers caught up in a swell of passion and violence: Odysseus and Penelope, Orpheus and Eurydice, Daphnis and Chloe, Pelleas and Melisande, Dido and Aeneas, Abelard and Eloise, Dante and Beatrice, and Romeo and Juliet. And not only Europe. For more than 4,000 years China's history and art have been filled with tales of the anguish of people torn between romantic desire and filial duty. In the Song Dynasty (960–1279 A.D.), the *Jade Goddess* recounted the story of a passionate young couple who defied their parents' wishes, challenged convention, and eloped, only to fall into desperate straits (Ruan, 1991). Almost all of the ancient societies—China, Egypt, India, Japan, Korea, Persia, and the other Arab countries—possess a similar collection of love stories and erotic art (Jankowiak, 1993; Kakar & Ross, 1986; Ruan, 1991).

The main message of historical research, however, is not the universality of passionate love, but its fragility. Generally, political and religious authorities have been the enemies of the pleasures of romantic love and the body. Throughout most of recorded history, until about 1500, in most cultures, passionate lovers' elemental and powerful feelings were viewed as a threat to the social, political, and religious order and were harshly suppressed. In the West, during the early Christian era, for example, suppression was especially harsh. For 1,500 years—from the earliest days of the Roman Catholic Church in the second century A.D. up to the sixteenth-century Protestant Reformation and Catholic Counter-Reformation—the Church proclaimed passionate love and sex (even marital sex) to be inherently evil and shameful. Abstinence was the ideal. Sex for any purpose other than procreation was a mortal sin, punishable by eternal damnation (Gay, 1984). St. Jerome, in the fifth century, for example, wrote:

> *It is disgraceful to love another man's wife at all, or one's own too much. A wise man ought to love his wife with judgment not with passion. Let a man govern his voluptuous impulses, and not rush headlong into intercourse . . . . He who too ardently loves his own wife is an adulterer. (cited in Hunt, 1959, p. 115)*

The effects of those pronouncements, still being made—though in milder form—caused millions of people to feel guilty for even harboring pleasurable *fantasies* about sex. In his richly textured work on sex and love in nineteenth century England and America, Peter Gay (1986) wrote:

> *The Catholic cult of virginity and praise of monasticism, the Protestant constriction of love to the sober performance of lawful procreative tasks, and the insistence of both that lust is a sin, left deposits of guilt and depression on many nineteenth-century minds. There was a general sense that respectable love is the very antithesis of libertine, and no hesitation in affirming that Christian civilization had tamed Eros. (p. 50)*

For most of Western history until the eighteenth-century "Age of Reason," love was not expected to end well. Romeo and Juliet, Ophelia and Hamlet, Abelard and Eloise did not make love, get married, have two children, and live happily ever after. Juliet stabbed herself. Romeo quaffed a dram of poison. Ophelia went mad and drowned. Hamlet was felled by a poison sword point. Peter Abelard (a real person) was castrated and his beloved Eloise retired to a nunnery. Passion was assumed to end in shame, humiliation, dishonor, suicide, and ruin in almost every early society (Kakar & Ross, 1986; Mace & Mace, 1980).

> *It was Rousseau who first started the cult of passion for passion's sake. Before his time, the great passions, such as that of Paris for Helen, of Dido for Aeneas, of Paolo and Francesca for one another, had been regarded as disastrous maladies rather than as enviable states of soul. Rousseau, followed by all the romantic poets of France and England, transformed the grand passion from what it had been in the Middle Ages—a demonic possession—into a social obligation, and promoted it from the rank of a disease to that of the only true and natural form of love.*
> —*Aldous Huxley*

The assumption that passionate affairs should end so dismally may sound strange to the modern reader. And so it should. In the realms of love and sex, a profound revolution has taken place in the last three centuries, and it is still happening (for better or for worse, depending on one's beliefs). It started in Europe, spread to the United States, and now appears to be reaching deep into the traditions of many non-Western societies. It is part of the dominant tendency of modern history in all phases of life, a tendency given the name of "Westernization." It is important to describe, however briefly, the general nature of this ongoing revolution because, from the point of view of world historians, it underlies practically everything we see going on about us (McNeill, 1963; Rapson, 1988; Roberts, 1976). A description of the historical model that most scholars interested in world history use follows.

Throughout the centuries, four cultures possessed the most political and economic power and the most influential cultural traditions. These four were the *East Asia* area (today's China, Japan, Korea, Southeast Asia); *South Asia* (India, Pakistan, Afghanistan, Sri Lanka); the *"Middle East"* or *West Asia* (Egypt, Persia [Iran], Mesopotamia [Iraq], Palestine, Syria, and other Arab countries); and *Western* civilization (Europe and, recently, Canada and the United States). There have been other strong, original cultures—in Africa, North and South America, the steppes of Asia, Polynesia, Oceania and other places—but none of them could match the power and influence of those four. Until 1500, the four major groups were, by and large, separate and independent cultural units. They tended to move on parallel tracks, intersecting at times, but generally swerving away from one another. There barely existed even the *concept* of one world. In the realms of passionate love and sexual desire, different cultural groups possessed somewhat different ideas about social rules governing them (Braudel, 1984; Stavrianos, 1981).

All that changed after 1500. Large transformations followed in the wake of the Renaissance, the Scientific Revolution, and the Industrial Revolution. By the late eighteenth century, the West began to alter its view of love and almost everything else. Western culture began to "invent" a number of unique and modern ideas. In the *material sphere*, "Westernization" has meant the rapid expansion of urbanization, industrialization, and technology. In the *economic and political spheres*, it has meant a move toward democratic, capitalistic, socialist, and/or totalitarian systems. In the *philosophical sphere*, it has meant an increasing faith first in Christianity and then in humanism, secularism, and science. And, perhaps most important for our purposes, in the *psychological sphere*, it has meant an increasing insistence on individualism, the desirability of the goal of personal happiness and the reduction of pain, accompanied by personal and artistic freedom and more fluid class systems. Looming large in the psychological arena has been a metamorphosis in European–American approaches to love and sex, many of which are being emulated in corners of the non-Western world (McNeill, 1963; Roberts, 1976; Stavrianos, 1981; Toynbee, 1962; Wallerstein, 1974). We will be discussing these throughout this book.

The West initiated such ideas and practices as: a high value placed on romantic and passionate love; marriage for love (as opposed to arranged marriage); egalitarian families (as opposed to patriarchal, hierarchical arrangements); sexual freedom for men *and* women; a movement toward equality for women; sexual permissiveness; and childhood considered as a separate phase of the life cycle with children deserving special treatment (as opposed to treating very young children as miniature adults sent out to farm the fields as soon as they could walk) (Ariès, 1962; Coontz, 1988; Ladurie, 1979; Stone, 1990). By 1800, the West had been transformed by these ideas.

Have India, China, Japan, Egypt, Iran, and the nations of Africa and Latin America escaped these revolutions? Not completely. In his travel diary, Indian journalist, Pico Iyer (1988) illustrates this process of Westernization (see Box 1.1 on page 10). We might expect that, to some extent, Western views of passionate love and sexual desire have been swept to the far corners of the globe in the carrying cases of transistor radios, record players, and VCRs.

One particularly intriguing and important phenomenon: it took the West over 500 years to embrace (though still not unanimously) "modern" ideas of love, sex, and intimacy. In some non-Western cultures, however, many of these same changes are occurring in less than fifty years (Bendix, 1964; Dunn, 1989; Wittfogel, 1957). It looks as though history is hurtling through these societies at an ever-accelerating pace.

Recently, of course, there has begun to be a backlash against Western ideas and hegemony. Non-Western ethnic groups have begun to celebrate their own cultures and to resist wholesale Western cultural imperialism. Throughout the world, people have begun to speculate about the possibilities of taking only the best that the West has to offer and integrating it with the cultural traditions that are uniquely their own (Axtell, 1981; Kâğitçibaşi, 1990; Skocpol, 1979). Some feel it is best to reject Westernization entirely (which many associate with racism, drugs, crime, licentiousness, divorce, and greed) and try to turn back the clock. The dialectic between Westernization and resistance to it defines much of international life today.

Among historians, there is as yet no substantial disagreement with the contention that since 1800, the West has greatly expanded its influence on the rest of the world (Braudel, 1984; McNeill, 1963; Roberts, 1976; Stavrianos, 1981). There *is* serious debate, however, about how deep those influences go. Are they fundamental or cosmetic (Axtell, 1981; Moore, 1966; Skocpol, 1979; Wittfogel, 1957)? And there is heated controversy about whether Western cultural expansion has been largely constructive or malignant (Bendix, 1964; Dunn, 1989; Rapson, 1988; Toynbee, 1962; Wallerstein, 1974).

Historians, then, remind us that, although throughout history people may have longed for passionate and sexual experiences as fervently as we do, most of them were never allowed to indulge in the pleasures of passion and sensuality. Now, however, times are changing. If existing historical trends continue, people throughout the world may be increasingly expected to embrace three powerful ideas: a belief in the equality of women and other minority group members, a belief which validates the pursuit of happiness and the avoidance of pain, and a belief that life should be and can be improved. The adoption of such beliefs should have a powerful impact on people's attitudes and behaviors. People may, for example, become increasingly intolerant of a double standard of sexual behavior and more tolerant of sexual permissiveness and diversity.

BOX 1.1   Rambo's Conquest of Asia

Rambo had conquered Asia.

. . . As I crisscrossed Asia in the fall of 1985, every cinema that I visited for ten straight weeks featured a Stallone extravaganza. In Chengdu, I heard John Rambo mumble his *First Blood* truisms in sullen, machine-gun Mandarin and saw the audience break into tut-tuts of head shaking admiration as our hero kerpowed seven cops in a single scene. In Jogjakarta, I went to *Rambo* on the same night as the *Ramayana* (though the modern divinity was watched by hosts of young couples, stately ladies in sarongs and bright-eyed little scamps, many of whom had paid the equivalent of two months' salary for their seats, while, on the other side of town, the replaying of the ancient myth remained virtually unvisited). Just five days later, I took an overnight bus across Java, and, soon enough, the video screen next to the driver crackled into life and there—who else?—was the Italian Stallion, reasserting his Dionysian beliefs against Apollo Creed. As the final credits began to roll, my neighbour, a soldier just returned from putting down rebels in the jungles of East Timor, sat back with a satisfied sigh. "That," he pronounced aptly, "was very fantastic."

. . . Rambo had also, I knew, shattered box-office records everywhere from Beirut to San Salvador. But there seemed a particular justice in his capturing of Asian hearts and minds. For Rambo's great mission, after all, was to reverse the course of history and, single-fisted, to redress America's military losses in the theaters of Asia. And in a way, of course, the movie's revisionism had done exactly that, succeeding where the American army had failed, and winning over an entire continent. . . . Our clothes, our language, our movies and our music—our way of life—are far more powerful than our bombs.

. . . This contest for cultural sovereignty was nothing new, of course. . . . In recent years, however, the takeover had radically intensified and rapidly accelerated. For one thing, satellites were now beaming images of America across the globe faster than a speeding bullet; the explosion of video had sent history spinning like the wheels of an overturned bicycle. For another, as the world grew smaller and ever smaller, so too did its props: not only had distances in time and space been shrunk, but the latest weapons of cultural warfare—videos, cassettes and computer disks—were far more portable than the big screens and heavy instruments of a decade before. They could be smuggled through border checkpoints, under barbed-wire fences and into distant homes as easily, almost, as a whim. In the cultural campaign, the equivalent of germ warfare had replaced that of heavy-tank assaults.

Suddenly, then, America could be found uncensored in even the world's most closed societies, intact in even its most distant corners. Peasants in China or the Soviet Union could now enjoy images of swimming pools, shopping malls and the other star-spangled pleasures of the Affluent Society inside their own living rooms.

. . . More important, the video revolution was bringing home the power of the Pax Americana home with greater allure and immediacy than even the most cunning propaganda (Iyer, 1988, pp. 3–6).

Cross-Cultural Perspectives

What do we mean by "culture"? In his classic definition, Edward Burnett Tylor (1871/1958) defined culture as "that complex whole which includes knowledge, beliefs, art, morals, law, custom, and any other capabilities and habits acquired by man as a member of society" (p. 1). But cross-cultural scholars have offered many definitions of the term. Recently, John Berry and his colleagues (1992) proposed this simple definition of culture: "the shared way of life of a group of people" (p. 1). Some have argued that culture consists of three major elements: ideas, beliefs, and values; patterns of behavior; and products of behavior (e.g., tools and art) (Jahoda, 1980; Swartz & Jordan, 1980).

Cross-cultural psychologists have been interested in cross-cultural similarities and differences, cross-national comparisons (comparisons between groups that are culturally similar—say, Scots and Britons); and in ethnic differences (differences between groups within a single culture—for example, African Americans and Hispanic Americans).

Cross-cultural research contributes to our understanding of passionate love and sexual desire in two different ways. First, it provides some sense of the social structures and processes that are found throughout the human family. Second, it furnishes some sense of how variable social arrangements can be. Researchers find that culture exerts a profound influence on how people view love, how susceptible they are to falling in love, and how their passionate affairs work out. Below we discuss some of this research.

A View from the West

Societies are almost infinite in their variety. Societies differ in their physical environment and resources; in their subsistence systems (are they hunting and gathering, agricultural, or industrial societies?); in their social institutions; in the ways people perceive the world, in what motivates them, in how they learn; and in their childrearing methods and patterns of social behavior (Triandis, 1980, p. 9). All these factors could, conceivably, have an impact on the way people view passionate love and sexual desire. Most cross-culturalists, however, have zeroed in on a single cluster of factors when attempting to explain such cultural differences. They point to the contrast between modern versus traditional, or urban versus rural, or affluent versus poor, or independent versus interdependent, or individualistic versus collectivist societies. Theorists may use somewhat different words in identifying the dichotomies they think are important, but all of the preceding distinctions belong to the same conceptual family—and for simplicity's sake, we call that cluster of factors "individualism versus collectivism" (see Markus & Kitayama, 1991; Schwartz, 1993, 1994; Triandis, 1994). Let us see why theorists, West and East, identify these differences as important.

Hazel Markus and Shinobu Kitayama (1991) argued that culture has an important impact on people's self-construals (on the way they see themselves and others). Culture affects cognitions, emotions, and motivations. In most Western, *independent* cultures, there is a belief in the inherent separateness of people. These cultures value individuality, uniqueness, and independence. Most non-Western, *interdependent* cultures, on the other hand, insist on the fundamental connectedness of human beings. The self is defined in relation to ancestors, family, and friends, and workmates. These cultures emphasize conformity, harmonious interdependence, and attending to and fitting in with others. Markus and Kitayama observed that although Americans, especially American men, tend to possess independent self-construals, throughout history most men and women possessed an interdependent view of the self. Kazuo Kato and Hazel Markus (1992) developed a scale to measure individual differences in these self-construals (see Box 1.2). You might want to complete the scale to see where you stand on these dimensions.

Markus and Kitayama (1991) contended that culture has an important impact on the way an individual relates to others. Independents, they argued, focus most on their own thoughts and feelings. Interdependents, who are primarily concerned with maintaining a connection with others, are constantly aware of others' needs, desires, and goals.

Other theorists, such as the Greek–American Harry Triandis and his colleagues (1990) have highlighted the difference between individualistic and collectivist cul-

---

BOX 1.2 Independence/Interdependence Scale

Please rate how well the following statements describe you, using the following 10-point scale.

0	1	2	3	4	5	6	7	8	9

Doesn't describe me at all

Describes me very much

Independence

(On this scale, independence is assessed by two kinds of items. Some items assess the extent to which people differentiate themselves from others. Other items assess how much self-knowledge people possess). The scale includes items such as these:

_____ 1. I am special.
_____ 2. Nothing can keep me from doing something if I want to do it.
_____ 3. I have planned my future.
_____ 4. I always know what I want.

The higher the score, the more the cultural group or person is said to value independence.

Interdependence

(Interdependence is assessed by two kinds of items. Some items assess people's concern with the evaluations of others. Other items assess people's concern with maintaining tight bonds between themselves and others.)

_____ 1. I automatically tune myself into other people's expectations of me.
_____ 2. It is important to me to maintain a good relationship with everybody.
_____ 3. It is important to maintain harmony in the group.
_____ 4. It is better to follow tradition or authority than to try to do something in my way.

The higher the score, the more the cultural group or person is said to value interdependence.

Based on Kato & Markus (1992).

tures. Individualistic cultures such as the United States, Britain, Australia, Canada, and the countries of northern and western Europe tend to focus on personal goals. Collectivist cultures such as China, many African and Latin American nations, Greece, southern Italy, and the Pacific Islands, on the other hand, press their members to subordinate their personal interests to those of the group: the family, the clan, or the tribe.

Triandis and coworkers (1990) pointed out that in individualistic cultures, people are expected to put their own needs first. In collectivist cultures, they are pressed to subordinate their needs to those of the group. Individualist cultures stress rights over duties; collectivists stress duties over rights. Individualist behavior is shaped primarily by one's attitudes and preferences, by private cost-benefit analyses of what will work for them and what won't. Collectivists are expected to conform to social norms.

Individualists are good at meeting strangers, forming new groups, and getting along with a wide range of people. They are less good at managing long-term relationships. Collectivists, on the other hand, make a sharp distinction between in-group and out-group members. With family and friends, they are warm and cooperative. With out-group members, they are formal and non-cooperative.

Triandis and his colleagues acknowledged (1990): "In collectivist cultures there is much emphasis on hierarchy. Usually, the father is the boss and men subordinate women. This is not nearly as much the case in individualistic cultures" (p. 1007). Triandis and his co-workers went on to develop a scale to classify *cultures* as individualist or collectivist. Within a given culture, of course, individuals' philosophies can vary. Thus, the scale also indicates the extent to which *individuals* are idiocentric (individualistic) or allocentric (collectivist).

Geert Hofstede (1983) ranked fifty countries on an index of individualism/collectivism. Table 1.2 on page 14 shows how countries ranked on his *Individualism Index*.

Hofstede discovered that wealthy countries—the United States, Australia, and Britain—were the most individualistic. Japan (a wealthy, but not consumer-oriented country) and India (a poor one) were in the middle, and the poor countries of Africa, Latin America, and Asia were the most collectivist.

With a few exceptions, most of the scholars we have cited live and work in North America or Europe. But Asian scholars have also begun to speculate about cultural differences in passionate love and sexual desire.

A View from the East

> Fall in love, fall into disgrace.
> —Chinese proverb

Japanese psychiatrist L. Takeo Doi (1973) contended that a key to understanding the Japanese cultural perspective is to understand the concept of *amae*. The verb *amaeru* can be translated as "to depend and presume upon another's love" or "to indulge in another's kindness" (Doi, 1963, p. 266). This word describes the attach-

TABLE 1.2 How Individualistic Are Various Countries?

Rank	Country or Region	Rank	County or Region
1	U.S.A.	28	Turkey
2	Australia	29	Uruguay
3	Great Britain	30	Greece
4/5	Canada	31	Philippines
4/5	Netherlands	32	Mexico
6	New Zealand	33/35	East Africa
7	Italy	33/35	Yugoslavia
8	Belgium	33/35	Portugal
9	Denmark	36	Malaysia
10/11	Sweden	37	Hong Kong
10/11	France	38	Chile
12	Ireland	39/41	West Africa
13	Norway	39/41	Singapore
14	Switzerland	39/41	Thailand
15	Germany	42	Salvador
16	South Africa	43	South Korea
17	Finland	44	Taiwan
18	Austria	45	Peru
19	Israel	46	Costa Rica
20	Spain	47/48	Pakistan
21	India	47/48	Indonesia
22/23	Japan	49	Colombia
22/23	Argentina	50	Venezuela
24	Iran	51	Panama
25	Jamaica	52	Equador
26/27	Brazil	53	Guatemala
26/27	Arab countries		

Based on Hofstede (1983), p. 299.

ment infants and small children feel for their mothers: a wish to cling to her; a desire for infantile dependency; to have someone attend to one's every need; to resist being cast into the cold world of objective reality. In adulthood, Doi (1973) argued, "*amae, generally speaking, is an inseparable concomitant of love (koi)*" (p. 118). When people's desire for such indulgence is thwarted, they often behave like resentful children: they may sulk, be resentful and defiant, or feign indifference. They may behave irresponsibly. According to Doi, the Japanese assume that *amae* will continue to cement their most intimate of relationships throughout their lives.

Godwin Chu (1985) contrasted the traditional American and Chinese views of self:

The American self seems to be characterized by individualism. It tends to assert one's self rather than accommodate others and to strive for a high degree of self-

reliance and independence. . . . The traditional Chinese self exists primarily in relation to significant others. Thus, a male Chinese would consider himself a son, a brother, a husband, a father, but hardly himself. It seems as if . . . there was very little independent self left for the Chinese. This point can be further illustrated by the position of women in traditional China. Before marriage, a woman followed her father. After marriage, she followed her husband. After the death of her husband, she followed her son. The self had little meaning outside these rigidly defined social contexts. The idea that a woman could stand on her own, and be herself, simply did not seem possible. A person, in this case a woman, measured the worth of herself not by what she had personally achieved, but by the extent to which she had lived up to the behavioral expectations of the significant others as defined by the predominant cultural ideas. (pp. 257–258)

As a consequence, Chu observed, American and traditional Chinese men and women desired very different qualities in a mate. For most North Americans and Europeans since the end of the eighteenth century, love and compatibility have been the first priority. Not so in China:

In traditional China the selection of a marital partner was made by parents, who relied on go-betweens. The main criteria were known as men tang hu tui, *that is, the doors of the two families should be of similar texture and the houses must face each other. In other words, comparability of family social status was of paramount importance. Whether the young couple were compatible and could get along with each other was of little consequence. (p. 264)*

Chu expressed considerable alarm that in the wake of the Cultural revolution of the 1970s, modern Chinese men and women seemed to have lost their traditional anchorage and to have become increasingly self-centered and materialistic. To cement his argument, Chu reproduced a list, circulated among young women in China, of what one should look for in a prospective mate. We and the young Chinese women who have taken our classes assumed that young women composed this list tongue-in-cheek. Chu, however took a different view—he saw it as evidence of modern young women's selfishness. You can be the judge (see Box 1.3 on page 16).

Chu believed that this list underscores all that is wrong with modern young Chinese men and women. He asked, "How can one explain this change from the past"? He postulated that the Cultural Revolution caused this "decline," but held on to the hope that this trend would be reversed. Some, of course, might see such changes more neutrally, as evidence of the embryonic "Westernization" or modernization of China. They would suspect that China's transformation is a more permanent one. There remains the additional irony that Mao's Cultural Revolution was designed to purge China of all Western influences.

Anthropologist Francis Hsu (1985) contrasted Western and Chinese values concerning passionate love and intimacy. American culture, he argued, is interested in personality; it is individual-centered. It attaches great importance to emotional expression. Chinese culture is situation-centered. Individuals are caught up in "a

---

BOX 1.3   Ten Criteria for Choosing a Husband

These criteria are recited in verse form and are rhymed in Chinese.

(1) *One* **Son of the Family**
There are no brothers or sisters-in-law to bother with. In the past, unmarried sisters-in-law often picked on the bride, who was considered an intruder.

(2) *Two* **Parents Have Gone to Heaven**
In the past, the bride was supposed to serve her husband's parents, especially the mother, in a totally submissive manner. Mistreatment of the daughter-in-law by the mother-in-law was common.

(3) *Three* **Things That Turn and One Thing That Has a Voice**
These refer to dowry, including a watch, a bicycle, and a sewing machine, which all have some moving parts, and a radio. Only a man of some means can afford all of these.

(4) *Forty*-**eight Meters**
Housing is in short supply in China. This criterion requires the groom to provide a living space of forty-eight square meters, or 432 square feet, which is considered to be first-rate accommodation.

(5) *Five* **Facial Features Are Well Balanced**

(6) *Six* **Categories of Kinship Relations Are Totally Ignored**
The Chinese generally use the term *six categories* to refer to a broad range of relatives by blood and by marriage. This particular criterion was an old saying in the past to refer to someone who had no regard whatever for the important Chinese value of honoring kinship obligations.

(7) *Seven*ty-**two Yuan**
A good wage in China.

(8) *Eight* **Sides All Smooth and Slippery**
This is another phrase taken from the traditional repertory of Chinese sayings. It means that the person is a wheeler-dealer.

(9) **Wine** (which is pronounced the same way as *nine* in Chinese) **and Cigarettes Are Taboo**

(10) *Ten*-**degree (Fully) Satisfied to Have Me Run the House**
The bride should be the boss.

Based on Chu (1985), p. 264–266.

web of interpersonal relationships" (p. 33). Group members are required to conform to "the interpersonal standards of the society" (1971, p. 29). Chinese men and women tend to "underplay all matters of the heart" (1971, p. 12). Hsu (1953) maintained that such differences have a critical impact on how romantic love is viewed in each society. The concept of romantic love fits in well with a North American cultural perspective but *not* with a Chinese cultural orientation, where one is expected to consider not just one's own personal feelings, but obligations to others, especially one's parents. Hsu wrote: "An American asks, 'How does my heart feel?' A Chinese asks, 'What will other people say?'" (p. 50). Hsu claimed that the Western idea of romantic love has almost no appeal for young adults in China. He pointed out that the Chinese generally use the word *love* to describe not a respectable, socially sanctioned relationship, but an *illicit* liaison between a man and a woman.

Hsu (1971, 1985) also noted that culture has a profound impact on where people seek intimacy and how likely they are to find it as well. In the West, people focus on romantic love; it is in passionate affairs that they expect to find intimacy. People are considered to be immature if they remain dependent on their parents for too long. In Chinese society, men and women expect less from marriage. Parents and kin are the source of intimacy. Men and women assume they will be tied to their families throughout life. Love may fail, but families do not. Hsu (1985) remarked:

> *Most parents are like dogs; one can kick them in the teeth and they will still come back for more. No one can take his peers for granted to that extent. He and they are likely to compete for the same things. His desire for mastery over them is matched by theirs over him. He has to satisfy his peers as much as they have to satisfy him. (p. 38)*

Cross-cultural models of considerable ingenuity abound. The usefulness of these models, of course, depends on how well they predict the ways in which real women and men actually experience and handle the powerful emotion of love. We suggest, as a prelude to moving from the abstract to the specific, several guidelines to help enrich the journey.

From Our Perspective

> *We are all more human than otherwise.*
> —Harry Stack Sullivan

From our own work as psychotherapists in Hawaii with clients from a variety of cultures, from our work as teachers of history and of social psychology, and from our own cross-cultural research, here are some observations designed to temper the preceding theoretical statements:

1. *The major cultural groups are more similar in their views of love and sex than the stereotypes suggest.* In making theoretical distinctions, it sometimes helps to caricature, to exaggerate the distinctions among "ideal" types. In today's reality, however, none of the major cultures—North American, European, Japanese, Indian, Chinese, African, or South American—can accurately be portrayed as purely individualistic or purely collectivist. In *all* cultures, people must often put themselves first. In *all* cultures, people must sometimes sacrifice themselves for others if the marriage, family, or community is to survive. Often, when students—from the East or West, independent or interdependent, individualistic or collectivist—have looked at the theoretical literature, they have felt that the theorists didn't have it quite right. One American woman, for example, admitted she knew some people ("mostly men," she claimed) who were totally narcissistic and unwilling to sacrifice anything for anybody. Yet, most of the young people she knew spent an inordinate amount of time passionately in love, willing to sacrifice anything to make a relationship work. In fact, she mused, many women went too far; they were willing to sacrifice everything by clinging to destructive relationships. "My family sounds *Japanese*," one Irish girl said. "My parents take it for granted that they are entitled to receive respect and obedience from us. And we aren't even supposed to THINK about sex!" One Japanese man snorted at descriptions of Japanese men and women, who supposedly keep a tight reign on their emotions, rarely showing anger. "That certainly doesn't sound like my father!" he observed. "He blows his top if we even breathe wrong."

Real people in all cultures are, of course, always engaged in a balancing act. They must balance their own personal concerns against the needs and desires of the group. Roger and Terri Joseph (1987) observed the nomadic Aith Waryaghar in Morocco, for example. Their "double pull" sounds like the dilemma we all face.

> *Within the cultural life of the Aith Waryaghar and the Ibuqquyen there is a double pull toward two dissimilar poles. One impulse is toward an ad hoc, individualizing, self-interested, agonistic direction, and the other is toward social unity, collectivism, alliance, and the submergence of the individual to communal interests. . . . the two potentials exist simultaneously and are in constant dialectal interplay. (p. 26)*

Differences exist, but we must be careful not to overdo them for the sake of simplicity, drama, or ideology.

Japanese psychologist Susumu Yamaguchi (1994) suggested that self-interest may underlie both individualist and collectivist sentiments. People probably learn to focus on their own needs or to sacrifice themselves for others, depending on the costs and benefits of various courses of action in a given "individualist" or "collectivist" society. Perhaps the two aren't so very different after all.

2. *Cultural influences* can *last a lifetime, but sometimes people assimilate rapidly to new circumstances.* Sometimes, cross-cultural researchers write as though once people have been socialized by their cultures, their personalities and characters are fixed forever. Of course, sometimes cultural habits do last a lifetime. Some of us may have grandparents who are still speaking and thinking in Romanian, or German, or Chinese, even though they have lived in America for half a century. Nonetheless, some of us have been startled to discover how rapidly others can assimilate, especially if a new culture proves more rewarding than the old. We once viewed an interview with a young Iraqi jet pilot who had been recruited for the military from a nomadic tribe because of his intelligence, keen eyesight, and quick reflexes. Much of the time he lived in a condominium in Baghdad. By day he flew the latest jets. By night, he drank, flirted with women, and danced at a local disco. Once a month he visited with his nomadic family in the desert (if he could find them!), riding a camel across the sands, and settling in to all the centuries-old traditions of his wandering tribe. Then back to the discos again. He seemed to find nothing incompatible with these vastly different ways of life: the camel-driving nomad who flew jet planes.

As societies change, and different things come to be rewarded and punished, the relative emphasis on individualism–collectivism can change. Today, for example, much of the non-Western world is coming to accept the Western notions of individualism, progress, science, and democracy. At the same time, many Americans are recognizing that among some, individualism has edged into selfish narcissism and that, for all of us, more collective concern would make life infinitely richer. Given the wildly rapid pace of change in today's world, we will likely see the unexpected all around (and perhaps within) us.

3. *Individual personality differences may be more powerful than cultural differences in shaping behavior.* Culture exerts a profound impact on behavior. Nonetheless, we are often struck by the extent to which personality seem to clash with the dictates of culture. Within a single Spanish family, one daughter can be quiet and reserved; another raised in exactly the same way will be fierce and energetic. We all know Americans who are self-effacing and deferential or Asians who are self-centered and rude. When we deal with real people, cultural stereotypes often shatter. In Chapter 2, for example, we will find that, in theory, a culture may ordain that it is parents or kin (or the young people themselves) who have the right to pick a mate. When we deal with real parents and real children, however, we often find that in every society some people are so willful that others bow before their dictates, regardless of the official "rules."

Nonetheless the influence that varying cultures do have on love, sex, and intimacy is as real and fascinating as the more unifying effects of biology and the infinitely differentiated outcomes of personality.

4. *One must not be ideological, but ruthlessly truthful about the advantages/disadvantages of various cultures.* The ideas of some cross-cultural theorists verge on propaganda. They are either relentlessly chauvinistic, finding fantastic ways to praise their own society's most appalling failures, or they are endlessly accommodating—ready to explain away the most repulsive behavior of some other society in the name of "cultural sensitivity." In cross-cultural commentaries and social action we must try to be more even-handed. An objective observer must admit that assets and liabilities are to be found in all cultures. A fair-minded observer can easily understand that it is possible to be attracted by Western energy and repelled by Western insensitivity; to be attracted by Asian order and stability, but enraged at the role women are forced to play in many traditional societies. Triandis and his colleagues (1990), for instance, when tallying the advantages of communal societies, claimed that such societies are bastions of both hierarchy *and* harmony.

> *In collectivist cultures there is much emphasis on hierarchy. Usually, the father is the boss and men subordinate women. This is not nearly as much the case in individualistic cultures. Furthermore, harmony and saving face are important attributes in collectivist cultures. The in-group is supposed to be homogeneous in opinion, and no disagreements should be known to outgroups. In*

individualistic cultures confrontations within the in-group are acceptable and are supposed to be desirable because they "clear the air." Thus, hierarchy *and* harmony *are important defining attributes of collectivists. (p. 1007)*

But whence the coupling of hierarchy with harmony? Is such an equation applicable when one is at the bottom of the pecking order? In traditional societies, where women are frequently at the bottom, is the so-called harmony a bit overrated for women? Is it men who tend to equate hierarchy with harmony? How far shall we take "cultural sensitivity" at the expense, perhaps, of the concept of universal human rights (a repulsion against torture or infanticide, for example, wherever it may occur)? In these days of intensely charged political feelings, these questions are not easily answered, but they do need to be faced.

As we write this, Orlando Ganal, Sr. of Honolulu has been charged with first-degree murder in a 1991 firebombing and shooting spree. Ganal and his wife Mabel had long had a rocky marriage. When Ganal discovered that his wife had fallen in love with David Touchette and planned to divorce him, he went berserk. He went to her parents' home and shot them to death. Then he returned home and shot his wife and son Orlando, Jr. He set fire to the laundry in which he worked. Then he torched the home of Touchette's brother. Wendy Touchette was disfigured. Her husband, Michael and their two children—Kalah, two years old, and Joshua, ten months of age—died in the blaze. Ganal had gone on a terrifying rampage of revenge.

Ricardo Trimillos, chairman of Asian studies at the School of Hawaiian, Asian and Pacific Studies at the University of Hawaii testified on Ganal's behalf. Ganal's lawyer, Keith Shigetomi, summarized Trimillos testimony:

Shigetomi said the expert's testimony will be that "it is an understandable pattern of behavior. . . . [The] Filipino male has a strong ego. In that culture, the husband is supposed to control the wife, and the husband, but not the wife, is supposed to "cheat and have affairs."

. . . Shigetomi said the testimony will be that the release of the tension through "amok," in which the person appears to be on "auto-pilot," is "not right, but it happens. (Kobayashi, 1993, pp. 1–2)

The Ganal case is not yet settled. Yet, we would bet that the "traditional" defense sounds inappropriate not just to our Western ears but to traditional Filipino ears as well. We suspect that the "cultural defense" will not be enough to justify the murder of five innocent people.

A second, less violent example: A visitor to Hawaii, a Japanese woman who is a stockbroker in Tokyo, read Takeo Doi's (1963) observation that "Japanese mothers are in almost constant attendance on their babies and are likely to pick them up or otherwise divert them as soon as they cry" (p. 268). She also noted his contention that men and women want to be able to "depend and presume upon another's love," to behave as badly as they like and still be loved (p. 266). The visitor was skeptical. "He's not talking about *amae*," she said, "he's talking about power. And men have it all. When he talks about 'people,' mentally substitute 'sons,' especially oldest sons and you'll have it. Mothers indulge their *sons'* every whim, not their daughters. It is mothers, not fathers, who can get 'kicked in the teeth' and still come back for more. It is husbands who presume that they can stay out all night, come home drunk, and still be met with a loving welcome by their wives. Just let their wives try that and they'll see how far the spirit of *amae* gets them." We see, then, that within a culture, there may be gender (as well as racial and class) differences in how appealing various cultural practices are.

What about harmony? Are collectivist cultures necessarily more harmonious? It depends. We once saw a Sikh businessman and his family in therapy. He was the undoubted head of the family. When it came time to make a decision, he said, "I go in my room and ask God for the answer. He tells me what is right, and I tell my wife and daughters." What if they didn't like his decision? "How could they go against God?" he asked, horrified. He assumed the family was entering therapy because of the disobedience of his most beloved younger daughter. Her biggest sin, according to her father, was that she wanted to cut her hair. In fact, separate meetings with her revealed that her problems ran much deeper. At the age of twelve, she was involved in drugs, shoplifting, and promiscuous sex. He thought he could read his wife's and daughter's minds, that he knew everything they thought. One thing they knew: they couldn't talk to him. Hierarchy? Yes. Harmony? Only its illusion. Hierarchy works well if you have power; it works better in most cultures if you are a man. It is not so good for women or for the powerless, chafing under the demands of the top dogs.

Theorists and researchers have a relatively easy time of it. They need only describe "what is." Politically minded cultural activists have a harder time of it. They must balance an appreciation of multiculturalism with a sensitivity to gender differences, kindness, justice, exploitation, and human rights before they decide how to take action.

The Future: Conclusions

Since about 1500, as it came to dominate the world, the West has assumed itself superior to all other cultures. Since the late nineteenth century, when the West invented the social sciences, social scientists have sometimes been equally ethnocentric.

Today, however, in American universities and other corners of the West (let alone the non-West), we have sometimes seen, in spasms of guilt, self-hate, and heightened cultural sensitivity, a nearly opposite reaction. To many, all evils are attributable to the West, or at least to European-American white males. Now, everything non-Western is seen as superior and harmonious.

Neither view is truthful. As we now turn to look at passionate love and sexual desire in various cultures, we will strive, as best we can, to tell a more complicated and hence more interesting love story. It is one in which heroes, villains, and straw people are replaced by imperfect human beings of all colors and shapes trying, as they and their society see it, to make the best out of life. For such a grand story, propaganda is inappropriate.

Finally we must note that which, more than anything else, may force us to be wary about all cross-cultural generalizations: the amazing pace of change on our planet. What seemed true and eternal yesterday may seem dated tomorrow. In our presentations, we must endeavor to factor in something social scientists are usually not forced to consider—the possibilities of change over time. In cross-cultural analyses, the temporal element, combined with some historical consciousness, should help to enrich our understanding.

What might that future look like? We can only guess, of course. If the global trends we have charted throughout this chapter continue, visionaries might predict that in the arenas of love, sex, and intimacy, "Westernization," or "modernization," call it what you will, may well prevail. Earlier, we recounted the great debate between historians and cross-cultural theorists. Many historians (probably most Western theorists) assume that the world has been becoming increasingly "Westernized" for 500 years and that there is every reason to anticipate that such Westernization may continue, though not without zigs and zags.

The world does not have to choose between Westernization *or* traditionalism, of course. For many, the most appealing alternative is to take the best that the West and other cultures of the world have to offer (Western scientific medicine, the Chinese tradition of scholarship, Middle East religious scholarship, and African art, for example), and integrate it with one's own unique cultural traditions (Levine, 1968; Smith & Bond, 1994; Yang, 1988). We must remember that the West has stood not only for marriage for love and increasing gender equality (which many of us might applaud), but also for material greed, colonial exploitation and murder, and destruction of the environment (Guisinger & Blatt, 1994). Yet, it also leads in the movement to save the environment. "Westernization" is no simple phenomenon, morally or technically.

Nevertheless, whether for better or worse, we can hazard some tentative speculations about future global tendencies that seem possible. In the material sphere, we would bet that industrialization, technology, and urbanization will continue to expand. In the political and economic spheres, democracy, free markets, and mixed economies may very well prosper. In the philosophical sphere, the faith in science, in the long run, will likely flourish. And, in the psychological sphere, with which we are most concerned, we would guess that although America can well afford to temper its brash individualism with a bit more communitarianism (and may well do so), throughout most of the rest of the developing, communal world, the trend toward individualism will advance. When given the choice, will women prefer to be assigned a spouse or will she prefer to marry for love? Will citizens of the world prefer an ascribed inferior status to one of equality of opportunity? Will people who love prefer to express those feelings or to suppress them, to enjoy sexual experiences or keep them tightly reigned in? In those areas, we would expect that personal freedom, once experienced, may be difficult to surrender. But no one knows the future for certain, and the tempestuous story of passionate love and sexual desire remains to be written—on the global scale as well as in our personal lives.

In Chapter 1 we provided a general overview of the contribution that scholars from a variety of disciplines have made to the study of passionate love and sexual desire. Let us now consider the particulars of love and passion—beginning with that age-old question: "What do men and women desire in a romantic, sexual, and marital partner, anyway."

Endnote

1. Scientists tend to assume that the more up to date research is, the better. Here, however, the scientists were interested in whether or not passionate love was observed in tribal societies before the idea had been introduced through Western media. So in this case, the older the observation, the better.

C h a p t e r *2*

The Romantic, Sexual, and Marital Ideal

The eleventh century Persian poet Fakhr-ud-din Gurgani recounted the legend of King Moubad, his brother Ramin, and the King's reluctant bride-to-be, Vis. King Moubad commissioned Ramin to fetch Vis. Vis was a haughty and beautiful young woman. Her nature embodied "the hardness of a diamond, the sweetness of honey, the cruelty of a tiger, the warm brightness of a fire, and the coolness of snow" (Kakar & Ross, 1986, p. 110). Ramin took one look at Vis and that was that. He was ablaze with erotic passion.

> *He fell from his horse as mighty as a mountain, like a leaf that the wind rips from the tree. The brain in his head had begun to boil from the fire in his heart; heart had fled from body and sense from head. . . . The rosy cheeks had turned the colour of saffron; his wine-coloured lips blue as the sky. The hue of life had deserted his face, the insignia of love appeared there in its stead. (Evola, 1983, p. 60)*

It is clear what inflamed Ramin. But what is it that makes most people fall passionately in love? What combination of face, form, scent, hardness, and honey do people look for in romantic, sexual, and marital partners? In this chapter, we begin by discussing cultural universals and differences in what men and women desire in romantic and sexual partners and/or mates. Then, we discuss cultural differences in how marriages are negotiated—whether couples' marriages are arranged or whether individuals are allowed to chose their own mates. Finally, we investigate which form of marriage seems to work best—arranged marriages or marriage for love.

What Men and Women Desire in Romantic Partners, Sexual Partners, and Mates

Cultural Universals in What Is Desired

In most societies, men and women desire many of the same things in a mate. In an impressive cross-cultural study, David Buss (1989) asked over 10,000 men and women, from thirty-seven countries, located on six continents and five islands (Box 2.1), to indicate what characteristics they valued in potential mates. The thirty-seven

The Ideal Man

Jennifer Berman, 1989.

BOX 2.1   Countries Participating in the Mate Selection Study

African	*European-Eastern*	*North American*
Nigeria	Bulgaria	Canada (English)
South Africa (Whites)	Estonia S.S.R.	Canada (French)
South Africa (Zulu)	Poland	United States (Mainland)
Zambia	Yugoslavia	United States (Hawaii)

Asian	*European-Western*	*Oceanian*
China	Belgium	Australia
India	France	New Zealand
Indonesia	Finland	
Iran	West Germany	*South American*
Israel (Jewish)	Great Britain	
Israel (Palestinian)	Greece	Brazil
Japan	Ireland	Columbia
Taiwan	Italy	Venezuela
	Netherlands	
	Norway	
	Spain	
	Sweden	

Based on Buss (1989), p. 4.

---

cultures represent a tremendous diversity of geographic, cultural, political, ethnic, religious, racial, economic, and linguistic groups.

As you might expect, it was extraordinarily difficult to interview people in so many countries. Questionnaires had to be translated into thirty-seven languages. Even then, cross-cultural researchers worried that in different societies the same word (say, *love*) might mean very different things. If people could not read, anthropologists had to read the questions aloud and record the answers themselves. In Nigeria, where polygyny is practiced, questions had to be added about men's preferences in multiple wives. In South Africa, data collection was "a rather frightening experience" (p. 5). Researchers were swept up in political and racial turmoil and violence. In many countries, permission to interview people had to be secured from central government committees, which often took months. In one country, after the data were collected, officials changed their minds and the project had to be terminated. Nonetheless, the team of researchers completed the study.

The authors asked men and women to look over eighteen traits and to rate the desirability or importance of each trait in choosing a mate. They rated their preferences on a four-point scale ranging from three (indispensable) to zero (irrelevant or unimportant). Buss found that, in general, men and women throughout the world desired much the same things (Table 2.1 on page 28). Of utmost importance was love!

TABLE 2.1 The Importance of Various Traits in Mate Selection throughout the World

Men's Ranking of Various Traits[1]	Women's Ranking of Various Traits[1]
1. Mutual attraction—Love	1. Mutual attraction—Love
2. Dependable character	2. Dependable character
3. Emotional stability and maturity	3. Emotional stability and maturity
4. Pleasing disposition	4. Pleasing disposition
5. Good health	5. Education and intelligence
6. Education and intelligence	6. Sociability
7. Sociability	7. Good health
8. Desire for home and children	8. Desire for home and children
9. Refinement, neatness	9. Ambition and industrious
10. Good looks	10. Refinement, neatness
11. Ambition and industrious	11. Similar education
12. Good cook and housekeeper	12. Good financial prospect
13. Good financial prospect	13. Good looks
14. Similar education	14. Favorable social status or rating
15. Favorable social status or rating	15. Good cook and housekeeper
16. Chastity (no previous experience in sexual intercourse)	16. Similar religious background
17. Similar religious background	17. Similar political background
18. Similar political background	18. Chastity (no previous experience in sexual intercourse)

[1]The lower the number, the more important men and women throughout the world consider this trait to be (on the average).
Based on Buss et al. (1990), p. 19.

Elaine Hatfield and Susan Sprecher (in press) selected three nations from the Buss group's sample for further study—the United States, Russia, and Japan. They chose the "big three" because, although all three were powerful, modern, influential industrial societies, culturally they are very different. The United States is a Western, individualistic culture. Russia is a "mixed" culture, influenced by East and West and valuing individualism *and* collectivism. Japan is a traditional, Eastern, collectivist culture. The scientists posed two questions: (1) Would young people from these three very different societies desire different things in a love affair or marriage? (2) Would those from a Western individualistic culture expect *more* from a love affair or marriage than would those from an Eastern collectivist society? (In Western, individualistic societies, after all, men and women are "supposed" to focus on personal fulfillment, whereas in collectivist societies, they are "supposed" to have more modest aspirations: they are supposed to subordinate their needs to those of the group.) To answer these questions, Hatfield and co-workers surveyed more than 1,500 men and women from five universities in the United States (Illinois State University, Southern Methodist University, the University of Hawaii, Bradley University, and Millikin College), one in Russia (Vladimir Poly-Technical Institute), and two in Japan (Nanzan University and Tohoku University). They asked students to consider twelve items (similar to those Buss used) and to indicate how important they thought each item was in a marriage partner. Students indicated their requirements on a five-point scale, ranging from one (*It does not matter to me if my partner has this characteristic*) to five (*This would be a necessity; I would not even consider a person as a mate if he/she did not have this characteristic*).

Students in the three nations were surprisingly similar in the traits they desired in a mate. Generally, students thought that such traits as kindness and understanding, a sense of humor, expressiveness and openness, intelligence, and being a good conversationalist (in that order) were most critical. It was moderately important to have a mate who was outgoing and sociable, ambitious, and physically attractive. Relatively unimportant were such traits as skill as a lover; potential for success; money, status, and position; and athletic ability.

Although students in the three nations did not differ in the kinds of things about which they cared most they did differ in the extent to which they assumed that, in love, they could "have it all." American students were the most insistent that they had to "have it all" in a mate. (They considered more traits to be "indispensable" or at least very important than did people in the other two countries.) Japanese students were the least demanding.

Now that we have surveyed existing research exploring what men and women throughout the world desire most in romantic, sexual, and marital partners, let us focus in on a few of the traits Buss and his colleagues identified.

Mutual Attraction and Love
Throughout the world, young couples are gaining increasing power to marry someone they love. In the Buss (1989) study, which surveyed people from thirty-seven different countries, researchers found that today, throughout the world, most men and women considered mutual attraction–love to be indispensable in settling on a mate.

There is yet other evidence that young people are coming to consider passionate love, or at least some kind of love, to be a prerequisite for marriage. In an early study, William Kephart (1967) asked 1,000 American college students: "If a boy (girl) had all the other qualities you desired, would you marry this person if you were not in love with him (her)?" In the 1960s, American men and women differed considerably in how important they considered romantic love to be. Most men insisted that, for them, the right "chemistry" was a prerequisite for marriage (12 percent said they would marry, 24 percent were undecided, and 65 percent said they would *not* marry a woman they did not love, even if she had everything else they desired). Women were generally more practical (4 percent said they would marry, 72 percent were undecided, and only 24 percent said they would not marry a man they did not love). Presumably, American men had the luxury of holding out for love, while women did not. Kephart speculated that this was probably because, in the 1960s, although American men could make it on their own, an American woman's social and economic status depended on her husband's. Thus, women had to take a suitor's family background, professional status, and income into account when making a marital decision.

Since the 1960s, social psychologists have continued to ask generations of young American men and women whether or not they consider love to be a prerequisite for marriage. They find that, year by year, young American men *and* women have become increasingly determined to have it all. By the 1990s, for example, Elizabeth Allgeier and Michael Wiederman (1991) found that 86 percent of American men and 91 percent of American women would not even consider marrying someone they did not love. Jeffry Simpson and his colleagues (1986) remind us that American society has changed since the 1960s. Women have more social, legal, and economic independence than ever before. As a consequence, they can afford to put their romantic desires before pragmatic considerations in choosing a mate.

Having the right "chemistry" is now seen as so important for a marriage that some young people claim that if they fell out of love they would not even consider *staying* married. Jeffry Simpson and his colleagues (1986) asked students the extent to which they agreed, were neutral, or disagreed with two statements: "If love has completely disappeared from a marriage, I think it is probably best for the couple to make a clean break and start new lives," and "In my opinion, the disappearance of love is not a sufficient reason for ending a marriage, and should not be viewed as such." They found that 57 percent of men and 62 percent of women agreed that if love was gone, couples should separate; 61 percent of men and 65 percent of women insisted that the disappearance of love was a sufficient justification for ending a marriage. Of course, with more experience young people might find that they are willing to settle for less than they once thought.

How do young men and women in other countries feel about this issue? As you may recall, cross-cultural researchers have generally insisted that it is only in the West that men and women insist on love *and* marriage. Young people in Eastern, collectivist societies have been assumed to be more practical. Alas, it appears that the researchers' crystal ball was somewhat fogged. Robert Levine and his colleagues (1994) tried to determine the impact of West versus East, individualism versus collectivism, and affluence versus poverty on young people's insistence that they would marry for love or not at all. They asked college students in eleven different nations if they would be willing to marry someone they did not love, if that person had all the other qualities they desired. Students could answer "yes" or "no" or admit that they were "undecided." In the four affluent Western nations, young people were the most insistent on love as a prerequisite for marriage. In the United States, Brazil, Australia, and England, only a tiny percentage of young people said they would be willing to say "Yes" to a loveless marriage; (Table 2.2). College students in Eastern, affluent nations tended to vote for love as well. In Japan, Hong Kong, and Mexico (all of which have a fairly high standard of living), most insisted on love as well. Only a few college students in these countries said they would be willing to marry someone they did not love. It was only in the four Eastern, collectivist, underdeveloped nations that students were the most willing to compromise. In the Philippines, Thailand, India, and Pakistan, a somewhat higher percentage of college students said they would be willing to marry someone they did not love. In these four societies, of course, the extended family is still extremely important. (Similar results were secured by Sprecher & Chandak, 1992.)

TABLE 2.2 **If a Man (Woman) Had All the Other Qualities You Desired, Would You Marry This Person If You Were Not in Love with Him (Her)?**

	Response		
Country	Yes	Undecided	No
Australia	4.8%	15.2%	80.0%
Brazil	4.3%	10.0%	85.7%
England	7.3%	9.1%	83.6%
Hong Kong	5.8%	16.7%	77.6%
India	49.0%	26.9%	24.0%
Japan	2.3%	35.7%	62.0%
Mexico	10.2%	9.3%	80.5%
Pakistan	50.4%	10.4%	39.1%
Philippines	11.4%	25.0%	63.6%
Thailand	18.8%	47.5%	33.8%
United States	3.5%	10.6%	85.9%

Based on Levine et al. (1994).

Research, then, suggests that today young men and women throughout the world generally consider love to be a prerequisite for courtship and marriage. It is only in a few Eastern, collectivist, and poorer countries that passionate love remains a bit of a luxury.

Education and Intelligence

Worldwide, both men and women seem to prefer mates who are intelligent and educated (Buss, 1989). When Douglas Kenrick and his colleagues (1990), for example, asked American college students about their minimum requirements in a casual date, a sexual partner, a steady date, and a mate, they found that although people might be willing to date or have sexual relations with someone who was good looking but not too bright, most people would consider marrying only someone who was fairly intelligent (Figure 2.1 on page 32). This figure shows that men consider intelligence to be slightly less important than do women, especially in selecting a partner for a casual sexual encounter.

Good Looks

Teenagers are often obsessed with looks; they are well aware of the importance of beauty. Paul Theroux (1983) recorded this snatch of a conversation on a local English train:

> *I took the train to Worthing.*
>   *Irby and Vitchitt, two schoolboys, were talking behind me in low serious voices, on the train. They were both about fifteen years old.*

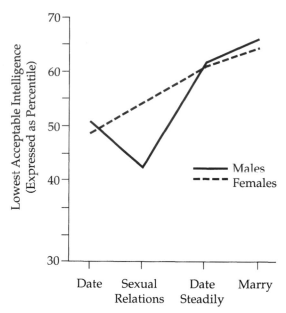

FIGURE 2.1   Minimum Level of Intelligence Required in a Partner

Based on Kenrick, D. T., and Sadalla, E. K., Groth, G. E., & Trost, M. R. (1990). "Evolution, Traits, and the Stages of Human Courtship: Qualifying the Parental Investment Model." *Journal of Personality*, 58, 97–117.

> *Vitchitt said, "If you could change any feature of your body," and he paused, "what would you change?"*
> *"Me fice," Irby said. He had not hesitated.*
> *Vichitt said, "Your 'ole fice?"*
> *"Yeah."*
> *Vitchitt stared at him.*
> *Irby said, "Me 'ole fice."*
> *"What about your oys?"*
> *"Me oys" Irby said. "I dunno."*
> *"What about your 'air?"*
> *"Me 'air." Irby looked stumped. "I dunno."*
> *"What about ya rears?"*
> *"Me years," Irby said. "Smaller anyway."*
> *"What about teef?" Vitchitt said.*
> *"Dunno. I have to fink about vat," Irby said.*
> *And then, as they pushed through the door at Worthing, they began to talk about contraceptive devices (pp. 70–71).*

Artists, philosophers, and scientists have long wondered if there were any universal standards of beauty. In the fifth century B.C., for example, the Greek philosopher Aristotle proposed that the Golden Mean, a perfect balance, was a universal ideal. Others, such as the Romans, spoke out in favor of the rare and exotic. Recently, anthropologists, evolutionary psychologists, and social psychologists, employing more sophisticated sociobiological theories and research techniques, have begun to identify some aesthetic universals.

Judith Langlois and Lori Roggman (1990) found evidence that the Greeks' Golden Mean may, in fact, serve as the gold standard of sex appeal. In the 1800s, Sir Francis Galton found that composite faces of men and of women, created by superimposing many individual photographs of faces on a photographic plate, were more attractive than were any of the individual faces making up the composite (reported in Thornhill & Gangestad, 1993). To test this notion, Langlois and Roggman assembled photographs of the faces of young men and women. Using state-of-the-art video and computer techniques, they generated a series of composite faces (from truly average men and women). They, too, found that composites were far more appealing than were any of the individual faces. The unsettling quirks that mar individual faces or give them distinctiveness—the off-kilter eyes, the ears that are too large, the crooked teeth—were less appealing than the averaged face. The average of many imperfect faces resulted in . . . perfection. Their conclusion? "Attractive faces are only average." This preference for the appealingly mediocre has been found to exist in societies as diverse as those of Brazil and Russia, in Indians in eastern Paraguay, and in several hunting and gathering tribes (Gangestad, Thornhill, & Yeo, 1994; Jones & Hill, 1993).

Evolutionary psychologists contend that men and women prefer faces that, in a sense, have it all—faces that combine the innocence of childhood with the ripe sexuality of the mature. Early ethnologists observed that men and women often experienced a tender rush of feeling when they viewed infantile "kewpie doll" faces—faces with huge eyes, tiny noses and mouths, and adorable little chins (Eibl-Eibesfeldt, 1971). Later researchers (see Gangestad, 1993) have found that men and women are most aroused by faces that signal that a prospective suitor is at a peak of sexual fertility, mature power, and good health (say, women who possess thick, luxuriant hair, dewy skin, full lips, and high cheekbones or men who possess similar assets, with the bonus of a firm jaw and strong chin). Most recent evidence indicates that young people are attracted to faces that hint at both innocence and maturity. The preference is for women with big limpid eyes, tiny noses, and small chins, combined with full sexual lips and high cheekbones and men with big eyes, prominent cheekbones, and a strong jaw and chin (Cunningham et al., 1990). In a variety of cultures, men who possess prominent cheekbones and rugged chins are judged to be especially attractive (Cunningham, 1991; Cunningham, Barbee, & Pike, 1990). Whether these preferences will turn out to be universal is not yet known. In any case, we do know that people who are considered good looking in their own cultures are likely to be considered to be attractive in other cultures as well (Cunningham, Barbee, & Pike, 1990; Jones & Hill, 1993).

Some sociobiologists have argued that men and women prefer good-looking lovers because good looks are a certificate of good health. Good-looking people (who possess average, symmetrical bodies) have been found to be unusually resistant to parasites and to a host of other diseases (Gangestad et al., 1994).

Historians remind us, however, that cultural notions as to what is good looking are always subject to change. Lois Banner (1983), for example, tracked the changing American standards of female beauty over the past 150 years. She found that from 1800 to 1921, the idea as to what was appealing changed radically—four different times. Before the Civil War, the "frail, pale, willowy woman" represented the ideal. After the War, the "buxom, hearty, and heavy" woman prevailed. In the 1890s, the "tall, athletic, patrician Gibson girl" became the vogue. She, in turn, was replaced in the 1920s, by the skinny, waifish "flapper." And on and on . . . (p. 5).

In Hawaii's diverse society, we have been impressed by just how fluid are ideas as to what is good looking. In 1981, one of Elaine Hatfield's Pacific Islander students reported that in a few months, the first Western television shows would be coming to their island. Soon, the island would be bombarded with reruns of the pale-skinned, skinny stars of *Dynasty, Charlie's' Angels*, and *Three's Company*. What effect would this have on the inhabitants' standards of beauty? (On their atoll, dark-skinned, muscular, and extremely fat men and women were considered to be good looking.) A few years later, we had the answer. The islanders had quickly come up with the perfect compromise. If you were light skinned, you were "supposed to be" tiny; if you were dark skinned, fat was beautiful.

Similarity in Education, Religious Background, and Political Affiliation
Most people are romantically attracted to those who are reasonably similar to themselves in background, personality, attitudes, beliefs, feelings, and behaviors (Byrne et al., 1986; Cappella & Palmer, 1990; Hatfield & Rapson, 1992b; Lykken &

Similarity Breeds Content

Jennifer Berman, 1990.

Tellegen, 1993). Donn Byrne and his colleagues (1971) proposed that people find it rewarding when others share their views and challenging when they do not. They found that, as predicted, college students worldwide were most attracted to those whose attitudes were carbon copies of their own. This was true in the United States (where researchers interviewed Chinese American, European American, and Japanese American students) as well as in India, Japan, and Mexico.

Milton Rosenbaum (1986) offered a second explanation for this phenomenon. He argued that it is not so much that we *like* people who are similar to ourselves, but that we *dislike* those who are not, a rather bleak view of the possibilities. Men and women, he contended, tend to be repulsed by potential dates, sexual partners, or mates who disagree with their cherished attitudes, beliefs, and values. They tend to assume that anyone who disagrees with the ideas that seem so reasonable to *them* must be unethical, short-sighted, stupid, or maybe even a little bit crazy.

Whatever the reason—attraction, repulsion, or dire necessity—there is considerable evidence that people end up with lovers and romantic partners who are strikingly similar to themselves. People are most likely to marry those who are similar to themselves in age, ethnic background, socioeconomic status, religion, physical attractiveness, intelligence and education, social attitudes, level of education, family size, intelligence, personality, and personal habits (Buss, 1985; Hatfield & Sprecher, 1986b; Rushton, 1989).

People are also most likely to marry those who confront similar mental and physical problems. People with personality disorders or psychiatric problems or those who are mentally retarded, blind, or deaf tend to marry those who share their difficulties. So do alcoholics, drug abusers, or those with criminal records (Hatfield & Rapson, 1993b; Rushton, 1989).

In one intriguing paper, J. Phillippe Rushton (1989) contended that people are genetically predisposed to look for such similarities. Genetic similarity theory argues that people are programmed to detect genetic similarities in others, so that they may proffer preferential treatment to those who are most similar (a sort of "like likes like" theory). He wrote:

> *It is known that the dimensions on which spouses and friends resemble each other are partly inherited. . . . hence, unless one adopts the implausible idea that humans detecting similarity are responding purely to the environmentally influenced component of a trait, it follows that genetic similarity between partners must occur.*
>
> *More direct evidence is also available. Using blood antigen analyses from nearly 1,000 cases of disputed paternity, [we] found that the degree of genetic similarity predicted: (1) whether a pair was sexually interacting or randomly generated; and (2) whether a pair produced a child together or not. Seven polymorphic marker systems (ABO, Rhesus [Rh], P, MNSs, Duffy [Fy], Kidd [Jk], and HLA) at 10 loci across six chromosomes were examined. Sexually interacting couples were found to share about 50% of measured genetic markers, partway between mothers and their offspring who shared 73%, and randomly paired individuals from the same sample, who shared 43%. . . . Close friends were also found to be genetically similar using the same blood analyses. (p. 31–32)*

These results are arresting. They suggest that when we think we are drawn to someone because of their dusky good looks, love of Vietnamese cuisine or foreign films, or their stand on environmental issues, we might actually be admiring our genetic similars.

Other Assets

What else might men and women throughout the world long for? Hatfield and her students (1984) interviewed over 1,000 dating couples, 100 newlyweds, and 400 elderly women, asking them to note the rewards (or lack thereof) most critical in their relationships. The three groups, very different in age and life experiences, were surprisingly similar in what they thought was most important in a love affair or marriage. The things they said they cared most about are itemized in Table 2.3.

Cultural Differences in What Is Desired

Cross-cultural theorists remind us that in different cultural, national, and ethnic groups, people often desire very different things in a romantic, sexual, or marital partner. Cultural values determine whether people focus first and foremost on power and status, on aesthetic and sexual appeal, or on finding someone who has a sweet and loving nature. Many speculate that such cultural differences will continue to exist into the foreseeable future (Berry et al., 1992; Kâğitçibaşi, 1990).

Earlier, we reported that Buss (1989), in a mammoth cross-cultural study, asked young people in thirty-seven countries what they yearned for in a mate. Buss, of course, was interested in cultural universals. Nonetheless, he could not help but be struck by the powerful impact that culture had on preferences. In China, India, Indonesia, Iran, Israel (the Palestinian Arabs), and Taiwan, for example, young people were insistent that their mate should be "chaste" (never having had sex before marriage). In Finland, France, Norway, the Netherlands, Sweden, and West Germany, on the other hand, most thought chastity was relatively unimportant; a few even jotted a note in the margin of the questionnaire, indicating that, for them, chastity would be a *disadvantage*.

Many societies regard postpubescent chastity as undesirable. At the recent International Academy of Sex Research meetings, for example, colleagues from Sweden and the United States found one another's arguments totally perplexing during an informal debate as to the best tactics for fighting AIDS. Should authorities preach "chastity" or should they "accept reality" and provide high school and college students with condoms and information about AIDS? "But why would teachers want to encourage students to be abstinent?" wondered my Swedish colleague. "How will teenagers ever learn to become loving, considerate sexual partners if they don't practice?" The silence that greeted the question was the sound of two cultures clashing. The "clarifying" notes on the Buss questionnaires probably reflect the same cultural collision.

Kim Wallen (1989) conducted a secondary analysis of Buss's data to determine whether culture or gender had the most important impact on people's romantic

TABLE 2.3   Rewards in Love Relations

Personal Rewards
- Appearance (having mates who are attractive and take care of their appearance)
- Social grace (having mates who are sociable, friendly, and relaxed in social settings)
- Intelligence (having mates who are intelligent and informed)

Emotional Rewards
- Feeling liked and loved
- Feeling understood
- Feeling accepted
- Feeling appreciated
- Physical affection (being kissed and hugged)
- Sex
- Security (knowing partners are committed and there is a future together)
- Plans and goals for the future (being able to dream about your future together)

Day-to-Day Rewards
- Smoothly running daily routine
- Comfortable finances
- Sociability and good communication
- Decision making (having partners who take a fair share of the responsibility for making and carrying out decisions that affect both of you)
- Remembering special occasions

Opportunities Gained and Lost
- "Opportunities gained" include the things that one gets from being married: the chance to become a parent; the chance to be invited, as part of a "married couple," to social events; having someone to count on in old age.
- "Opportunities foregone" include the things that one has to give up to be in a relationship: other possible mates, a career, money, travel, sexual freedom.

preferences. He found that, overall, culture was far more important than gender in shaping preferences. (Gender accounted for only 2 percent of the variation, whereas culture accounted for 14 percent of the variation in mate preferences.) For a few traits—such as good looks and financial prospects—gender was what mattered. (Gender accounted for 40 to 45 percent of the variance; geographical origin for only 8 to 17 percent of the variance.) For most other traits—such as chastity, ambition, and preferred age—culture mattered most. (Here, gender accounted for only 5 to 16 percent of the variance, whereas geographical origin accounted for 38 to 59 percent of the variance.) He concluded that, in general, the cultural perspective is far more powerful than the evolutionary perspective in understanding mate selection.

Other researchers have documented that culture has a critical impact on what people yearn for in a mate. You will recall that Hatfield and Sprecher (in press) studied three powerful, modern, and industrial societies—the United States, Russia, and Japan. They found considerable differences in how important men and women in these cultures considered various traits to be. Culture had a significant impact on how men and women rated eleven of the twelve traits. Men and women in Western, individualistic cultures, such as the United States and to some extent Russia, thought they were entitled to far more in a marriage than did people in a collectivist culture, such as Japan. The Americans and Russians considered all twelve traits to be more important in mate selection than did the Japanese.

Gender Differences in What Is Desired

> *Hoggamous, Higgamous, men are polygamous,*
> *Higgamous, Hoggamous, women are monogamous.*
> —Lois Gould

Sociobiological Theory

Since Darwin's (1871) classic essay on the importance of sexual selection in the evolution of humankind, anthropologists have been interested in how men and women go about selecting sexual partners and mates. Today, sociobiologists have concluded that there *are* some cultural universals in what men and women desire in a mate. Donald Symons (1979) believed that, in the course of evolution, men and women came to be programmed differently from one another and to desire very divergent characteristics in a mate. His argument proceeded as follows: "According to evolutionary biology, an animal's 'fitness' is a measure of the extent to which it succeeds in passing on its genes to the next generation" (p. 6).

It is to both genders' evolutionary advantage to produce as many children, grandchildren, and great-grandchildren as possible. But men and women differ in

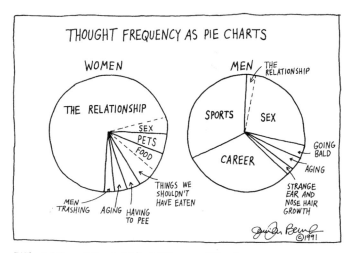

What Men Want; What Women Want

Jennifer Berman, 1991.

one critical respect—how much they are required to invest to ensure the survival of their offspring. Men need invest only a trivial amount of energy in any one child. (One man could conceivably father an almost unlimited number of children. In recent times, Abdul Aziz married more than 300 wives to ensure the loyalty of the desert tribes. His sons now rule Saudi Arabia. One Saudi ruler claims to have more than 5,000 children [Sasson, 1992]). Women, on the other hand, must invest a great deal in their offspring if they are to survive. In tribal societies, most women are lucky to produce even five surviving children (Hrdy, 1981). Nancy Howell (1979), for example, followed the reproductive careers of 166! Kung women over eleven years. She reported that the maximum number of births for any woman was five; the minimum zero. Then, women must usually sacrifice a year or two in nursing, protecting, and teaching children to survive on their own. Thus, it is to women's advantage to be choosy in selecting sexual partners and mates. It is to their advantage to ensure that the few children they do conceive survive. Symons observed:

> *The enormous sex differences in minimum parental investment and in reproductive opportunities and constraints explain why* Homo sapiens, *a species with only moderate sex differences in structure, exhibits profound sex differences in psyche.* (p. 27)

Recently, David Buss and David Schmitt (1993) proposed a "sexual strategies theory" of human mating. They argued that not only were men and women programmed to desire different traits in a mate, but also that it was to their advantage to employ very different strategies in short-term relationships (such as "one-night stands" or brief affairs) and in a long-term (marital) relationships. Here is a sampling of some of the twenty-two hypotheses derived from their sexual strategies model:

1. *In short-term relationships,* men should tend to be interested in "playing the field." Women's interests should vary—depending on whether they are entirely focused on what's in it for them in the short run or are more focused on what is to their long-term advantage.

It is to *men's* advantage to be sensitive to clues to women's reproductive fitness. They should be "turned on" by women who are easily available and "turned off" by women who are sexually inexperienced, conservative, prudish, or who have a low sex drive. They should care a great deal about good looks, youth, and health. They should be eager to have numerous, fleeting sexual encounters. In the absence of an ideal sexual partner, however, men should be willing to engage in casual sex with almost anyone, under almost any circumstances. They should try to avoid commitment or investing too much in any one relationship.

> La femme moyenne sensuelle . . . *[finds] her* raison d'être *in the love of a male as close to the alpha as she can get.*
>
> —*Norman Rush*

Women in short-term relationships should employ one of two adaptive strategies. Some women may choose to focus on what's in it for them in the short run. Such women can maximize their outcomes by concentrating on getting as much as they can as soon as they can (what Buss and Schmitt politely call "immediate resource extraction"). They should look for men who will give them presents and other resources in return for sex. Other women may chose to take a longer view. Such women can maximize their evolutionary outcomes by spending their time in brief encounters, trying to size up men so that they can identify those who would be willing and able to protect them and their offspring. They should look for professional men with ambition, status, good earning capacity, and a strong career orientation; men who are kind and considerate, understanding, honest, dependable, easy-going and adaptable; men who like children. Women should insist on knowing a man for a fairly long time before they are willing to risk a sexual encounter and/or commit themselves to marriage. (See also Buss & Barnes, 1986; Buss 1988a & b.)

2. In *long-term relationships*, once again men and women confront a different set of problems. Men should still prefer women who are good looking, young, healthy, and of maximum reproductive value. But now they must also be concerned about finding someone who is willing and able to commit herself to a long-term relationship, who is faithful, and who possesses good mothering skills.

Women who are considering a long-term relationship should still prefer mates who seem able and willing to protect them and their children. They should still prefer men who will make a commitment, who are willing and able to invest resources in them and their children, who possess parenting skills, and who are willing and able to protect them from harm. (Most women desire the same thing in short-term and long-term relationships.)

In theory, as men and women's investments converge (as they do in long-term relationships), both should become increasingly choosy about whom they select as a mate.

The Evidence

Evolutionary psychologists have collected considerable evidence in support of the contention that men and women worldwide do desire slightly different things in a mate.

You will recall that Buss (1990) asked more than 10,000 men and women, from thirty-seven countries what they desired in a potential mate. The thirty-seven cultures represented a wide range of geographic, cultural, political, ethnic, religious, racial, economic, and linguistic groups.

Buss found that when men and women were asked what they cared most about, it was evident that both desired the same things. Both desired someone they could love; who was dependable, emotionally stable, and mature; who had a pleasing disposition, and so forth (see Table 2.1). Buss (1989) acknowledged that "species-typical mate preferences may be more potent than sex-linked preferences" (p. 13).

When Buss (1989) moved down the list of valued qualities, however, he found that, as predicted, the sexes did differ slightly in how important they considered various traits to be. Men seemed to care more about traits that signaled *reproductive capacity*. They preferred partners who were two to three years younger than they. They cared more about good looks than women did. In some cultures, men were more likely than women to insist on chastity (i.e., that their mates be sexually inexperienced).

Sometimes, men's obsession with young and beautiful women is a bit funny. One of our close friends is eighty-five years old. He thinks of himself as just a boy; four years ago he served a stint in the Peace Corps. Two years ago he received a Ph.D. Until a few months ago, he had been casually dating a 35-year-old beauty, who flew in from San Francisco now and then to meet him. But the last time she arrived in Hawaii, he was shocked. She had "aged" . . . and all his old attraction to her was gone. "She looked old enough to be my grandmother!" he said. Our friend, who still has all his marbles, couldn't quite understand the general hilarity that engulfed his audience. He couldn't quite grasp that to be *his* grandmother, she would have to be at least 115 years old.

Buss also found that, as predicted, women seemed to care more about cues to *resource acquisition* than did men. Women preferred men who were three to four years older than they. They also valued, more than men, mates who possessed status, who had good financial prospects, and who were ambitious and industrious. (For further evidence in support of these hypotheses, see Buss & Schmitt, 1993 or Ellis & Symons, 1990).

Other researchers, who have studied societies ranging from the most individualistic to the most collectivist have secured similar results. Some examples follow.

The People's Republic of China is, of course, an extremely traditional, collectivist society. The Marriage Law of 1950 stipulated that men and women should base their mate selections on only three things—character, personal compatibility, and the correctness of political attitudes. Nonetheless, William Jankowiak (1993) found that, even in China, men tend to focus on physical appearance, while women tend to focus on their suitors' income and occupation when making marital decisions. Jankowiak reported:

> *The sum of women's images for an ideal husband* (hao zhangfu) *were as follows: a man who is tall, healthy, kind, handsome, strong, intelligent, brave, well-mannered, and one who has status and can provide for a family. The sum of men's images for an ideal wife* (hao qizi) *were as follows: a woman who is beautiful, tall, healthy, soft, kind, well mannered, loyal, virtuous, and one who is skilled in domestic crafts (e.g., sewing, cooking, and so forth) and can take care of children.* (p. 168)

Researchers have found similar gender differences in societies ranging from the most individualist to the most collectivist. Hatfield and Sprecher (in press) asked young men and women in the United States, Russia, and Japan what they desired in a mate. Although (as we reported earlier in this chapter) men and women generally agreed about what was important, there were some differences in their concerns. In all three societies, men tended to more focus on physical attractiveness than did women. Women were more concerned with men's intelligence; ambition; potential for success; money, status, and position; kindness and understanding; and expressiveness and openness. (Evolutionary psychologists, of course, would predict such differences.) Overall, women were more "choosy" in their requirements for a mate. They rated all twelve traits as more important than did men.

Evolutionary psychology challenges us with some arresting ideas. Its adherents soften their message by reminding us that there are enormous individual differences in preferences, that what is true for *most* men and women is not true for *all* men and women, and that men and women are far more similar in their desires than different (Buss & Schmitt, 1993; Simpson & Gangestad, 1992).

The Critics Speak

Feminist scholars have rightly criticized sociobiological theories that attempt to provide a biological justification for the striking differences in men's and women's political, economic, and social positions. Those who wield power almost always take it for granted that anyone who is different from themselves—in gender, race, culture, ethnicity, or religion—is "naturally" inferior. We have to be a bit suspicious of Western, white, male sociobiologists who see existing power imbalances as natural and who assume that it is "writ in the genes" that men will naturally try to dominate women; men will be selfish, ambitious, and ruthless whereas women will be warm and nurturant; that men will be promiscuous while insisting that their mates be chaste and faithful; that men are programmed to rape *and* to try to maim or kill their mates if *they* dare to dally (Bleier, 1984; Collier & Rosaldo, 1981; Quinn, 1977). Ellen Berscheid (1993) stated the feminist critique succinctly:

> *Sociobiological studies of the biological bases of social behavior begin with the assumption that all social behavior does have a biological base and, thus, it is the job of the sociobiologist to guess just what that biological base might be. The result has been that there appear to be very few, if any, sex differences in social behavior that the creative mind of some sociobiologist somewhere has not attributed to the evolutionary forces of natural and sexual selection operating differentially on male and female humans. Unfortunately for sociobiologists, however, Mother Nature did not videotape the evolution of the human species for our analysis—which leaves a great deal of current sociobiological discourse about the genesis of sex differences in behavior on a par with science fiction.*
>
> *Although often as entertaining as science fiction, some sociobiological treatises on the genesis of sex differences in behavior are not as innocuous. Biological determinism is sometimes used both as an explanation and as a justification for the current status and power differences between men and women. Sociobiology, in fact, has earned its reputation for being the psychology of sex, violence, and oppres-*

sion . . . with the presumed differential biological bases of behavior being both the reason ("it's only natural") and the excuse ("they can't help it") for male domination and violence toward women. (p. xii)

The eminent biologist Ruth Bleier (1984) reminded us that those in power have always found such glib explanations for social inequities appealing. In the past, evolutionary theory was used to buttress Western imperialism and male supremacy. The "survival of the fittest" was translated into "grab all you can get." "Man the hunter" was seen as somehow entitled to be dominant, aggressive, and sexual, a protector and provider. Women were seen as naturally passive, weak, and sexually restrained. Their world was that of wife and mother. Bleier warned readers that such scientific appeals to nature over nurture have an insidious effect on political movements designed to right social wrongs. The debate is moved from the political realm, where people can brainstorm about the most effective ways of producing social change, to the scientific realm—"reducing them to inevitable, if regrettable, manifestations of immutable natural laws that can then be used to rationalize and justify sexual oppression" (Smuts, 1991, p. 30).

The Social Learning Perspective
Many historians, anthropologists, sociologists, and psychologists have looked not to ancient genetic codes to explain gender differences in sexual and marital preferences but to different socialization and social opportunities experienced by men and women. This perspective has been variously called the "social argument," "principles of social factors," "social learning theory," the "structural powerlessness hypothesis," and the "socioeconomic explanation." The theorists, who we will call "social learning theorists" contend that, in all cultures, people's choices are shaped by cost-benefit considerations.

In traditional male-dominated societies, they point out, women generally lack the social, educational, and economic means to make it on their own. Thus, it is not surprising that women are generally forced to focus on the ability of potential mates to acquire resources and to be willing to invest them in a relationship. Unlike the sociobiologists, however, social learning theorists would predict that as social conditions change (as, say, casual sex becomes safer and as birth control techniques become increasingly effective, as women's social and economic positions improve, if society begins to subsidize day-care facilities, time-sharing, and parental leaves) men's and women's preferences in sexual partners and mates should become increasingly similar. There is some evidence in support of social learning theorists' contentions. There is also evidence that in different times and places, men and women have readily adapted to very different social realities, and, as a consequence, their preferences in romantic and sexual partners have altered dramatically (Bem, 1993; Bleier, 1984; Griffitt & Hatfield, 1985; Reiss & Lee, 1988; Travis & Yeager, 1991). Researchers have also found that in those societies where women possess a measure of economic independence, they begin to focus more on sex appeal than on practicality in choosing sexual partners (Gangestad, 1993). (However, see Wiederman & Allgeier, 1992, for some conflicting evidence.)

Evolutionary psychologists may be correct in thinking that, to some extent, existing gender differences may be genetically determined. To some extent, genetics may be destiny. However, men and women have always turned out to be more adaptable than people have supposed. If we had to bet, we would guess that many of the gender differences that seem so "natural" today, are about to be swept away by the winds of social change.

Who Decides? From Arranged Marriages to Marriage for Love

In the sweltering summer of 1950, the Hit Parade blared out an insipid ditty: "love and marriage, love and marriage, go together like a horse and carriage." Thousands of Gothic novels, summer movies, and country-and-western laments later, the notion that passionate love, sexual desire, and marriage "go together" has been embedded in the Western psyche as an Eternal Truth.

But it was not ever thus. In the West, before 1700, no society ever equated *le grand passion* with marriage. In the twelfth century, in *The Art of Courtly Love,* for example, Andreas Capellanus (1174/1941) stated:

> . . . *everybody knows that love can have no place between husband and wife. . . . For what is love but an inordinate desire to receive passionately a furtive and hidden embrace? But what embrace between husband and wife can be furtive, I ask you, since they may be said to belong to each other and may satisfy all of each other's desires without fear that anybody will object? (p. 100).*

And Capellanus wasn't even talking about passionate love—just love. To make his argument perfectly clear, he added, "We declare and we hold as firmly established that love cannot exert its powers between two people who are married to each other." (p. 106)

Shakespeare may have written a handful of romantic comedies in which passionately mismatched couples hurtled toward marriage, but these plays were the exception. Until 1600, most courtly love songs, plays, (including most of the Bard's) and stories assumed a darker ending: passionate love was unrequited or unconsummated, or it spun down to family tragedy and the suicide or deaths of the lovers.

As late as 1540, Alessandro Piccolomini could write peremptorily that "love is a reciprocity of soul and has a different end and obeys different laws from marriage. Hence one should not take the loved one to wife" (Hunt, 1959, p. 206). Piccolomini, true to his times, began to change his mind just before he died.

In the great societies of Asia—China, Japan, and India (lands of the arranged marriage)—at least since the end of the seventeenth century, thousands of *haiku* poems, *Noh* plays, and heroic legends later, the notion that passionate love and sexual desire "go together" with thwarted hopes for marriage and suicide has been embedded in the Eastern psyche as an Eternal Truth. Classical tales recount the couple's journey together to the chosen place, leaving forever behind them familiar scenes, agonizing mental conflicts, and the last tender farewells (Mace & Mace, 1980).

In China, lovesick couples, forbidden to marry, often followed the rules even as they chose to defy convention. In early China, couples would ritually drown themselves in the well of the parents who had refused to sanction the marriage. Later, fashionable young romantics affirmed their love by swallowing rat poison. Such poisonings became so common that drugstores were warned not to sell cyanide to young couples. Today, Chinese lovers promised to others jump off a cliff hand in hand or tie themselves together and throw themselves in front of an oncoming train. On some railroad routes, love suicides were so common that young couples were routinely questioned about their intentions if they tried to purchase a one-way ticket (Mace & Mace, 1980).

To today's young individualistic Americans and Europeans, such tales of forbidden romance may seem ridiculous. But to young Asian romantics, who knew that passion had little chance of flowering into marriage, the tales were sublime tragedies.

In traditional cultures, it was the lovers who had to adapt, not the society. Individual happiness mattered little; what was important was the well-being of the family and the maintenance of social order. As one modern Chinese woman asserted: "Marriage is not a relation for personal pleasure, but a contract involving the ancestors, the descendants, and the property" (Mace & Mace, 1980, p. 134).

In contemporary societies, however, most young men and women do meet, fall in love, feel sexual desire, and live together or marry. In this section, we begin by discussing the revolution that is occurring in the ways young men and women (heterosexual and homosexual) currently select their romantic, sexual, and marital partners. We will see that parental power is crumbling and that arranged marriages are being replaced by the ideal of love marriages.

Arranged Marriages

Throughout history, cultures have varied markedly in who possessed the power to select romantic, sexual, and marital partners. In the distant past, in most societies, parents, kin, and the community usually had the power to arrange things as they chose. Marriage was assumed to be an alliance between two *families* (Dion & Dion, 1993; Lee & Stone, 1980). Families might also consult with religious specialists, oracles, and matchmakers (Rosenblatt & Anderson, 1981). When contemplating a union, parents, kin, and their advisors were generally concerned with a number of background questions: What was the young person's caste, status, family background, religion, and economic position? Did their family possess any property? How big was their dowry? Would they fit in with the entire family? In Indian families, for example, men and women said that what their families cared most about in arranging a marriage was religion (whether one was a Hindu, Muslim, Sikh, or Christian), social class, education, and family background (Sprecher & Chandak, 1992).

Some problems are serious enough to rule out any thought of marriage. Sometimes, religious advisors would chart the couples' horoscope. Couples born under the wrong sign may be forbidden to marry (Bumroongsook, 1992). Generally, young people are forbidden to marry anyone who is too closely related (say, a brother or sister or a certain kind of cousin). Sometimes, they are forbidden to marry foreigners. In Thailand, Thais are often forbidden to marry Chinese, Indian, Japanese, Mons, or Malay suitors (Bumroongsook, 1992). Similar assets and liabilities have been found to be important in a variety of countries, such as India (Prakasa & Rao, 1979; Sprecher & Chandak, 1992), Japan (Fukuda, 1991), Morocco (Joseph & Joseph, 1987), and Thailand (Bumroongsook, 1992). If things look promising, parents and go-betweens begin to talk about the exchange of property, dowries, the young couple's future obligations and their living arrangements.

Colombian novelist Gabriel García Márquez (1990) portrayed one arrangement in *Collected Stories*—the betrothal and marriage of Isabel to Martín. Here, the father and son-in-law arranged the marriage in the hopes of cementing a risky business partnership. (When the business failed, so did the marriage.)

> *[The character Isabel recalled that] two days after Martín's arrival in December, my father called my stepmother to the office to tell her that the wedding would take place on Monday. It was Saturday.*
>
> *My dress was finished. Martín had been to the house every day. He spoke to my father and the latter would give us his impressions at mealtime. I didn't know my fiancé. I hadn't been alone with him at any time. Still, Martín seemed to be linked to my father by a deep and solid friendship, and my father spoke of him as if it were he and not I who was going to marry Martín.*
>
> *I felt no emotion over the closeness of the wedding date. I was still wrapped up in that gray cloud which Martín came through, stiff and abstract, moving his arms as he spoke, closing and opening his four-button jacket. He had lunch with us on Sunday. My stepmother assigned the places at the table in such a way that Martín was next to my father, separated from me by three places. During lunch my stepmother and I said very little. My father and Martín talked about their business matter; and I sitting three places away, looked at the man who a year later would be the father of my son and to whom I was not even joined by a superficial friendship.* (pp. 68–69)

Today, in many parts of the world, parents and matchmakers still arrange their children's marriages. Arranged marriages are common in India, in the Muslim countries, in sub-Saharan Africa, and in cultural enclaves throughout the remainder of the world (Rosenblatt & Anderson, 1981). One of our University of Hawaii friends, Jagdish Sharma, a historian, insists on trying to serve as a matchmaker for any hapless student who arrives in the history department unmarried. We have several clients in our psychotherapy practice and friends whose marriages were arranged.

Compromising on Love

More recently, in most of the world, prospective brides and grooms, parents, elders, and the extended family have consulted with one another before arranging a marriage. Even in the most traditional of societies, parents and husbands have generally been forced to balance conflicting interests. The Moroccan tribal world, for example, is definitely a man's world. Men possess absolute authority over their wives and children. They have the power to take several wives. They often promise their sons and daughters to potential allies at very young ages. Yet, if you think of your own family, you will surely observe that things do not always go as they are "supposed" to. Some fathers are impossible. Eventually, family members learn that it is easier to give in than to try to argue. Some aunts are strategic geniuses—they can enlist an army of relatives to plead, threaten, and haggle on their behalf. The same thing is true in Morocco. Roger and Terri Joseph's (1987) vivid descriptions of Moroccan family life make it clear that, even in Morocco, compromise is often required. Hamadi and Fatima, for example, were going along, happily married, when Hamadi decided that it was time to acquire a second wife. Within days, everyone in his immense, extended family was squabbling. Fatima threatened to divorce Hamadi if he married again. She refused to share her house with another woman. Fatima's brothers warned Hamadi that if Hamadi and Fatima got a divorce, they would reclaim all the land she had brought into the marriage. (Hamadi had spent years planting fruit and nut trees on the property.) Fatima threatened to take their twin daughters to her brother's house as well. Technically, Hamadi's family "owned" the infants, but since they were still nursing he would have to wait two years to collect them. In Morocco, twins are considered to be *baraka* (good fortune); if Hamadi's daughters left, people might conclude that good fortune had left Hamadi's house. To add to Hamadi's woes, Fatima issued a final warning. If Hamadi divorced her, she would march bare-breasted to the weekly market. This left him badly shaken. Things got worse. One of Fatima's brothers had married Hamadi's cousin. He announced that if there was to be bad blood between the two families, he would divorce his wife. Hamadi's mother complained that the money Hamadi had saved for a second wife should be spent on Hamadi's son Ali, who had just turned 15. He needed money for *his* wedding. Finally, a tired Hamadi surrendered. He concluded, "Women are to be gotten around, but I guess I won't get around these" (p. 55).

When other "all powerful" Moroccan fathers tried to force their children into unappealing marriages, sympathetic family members employed an avalanche of strategies to thwart them. Young lovers persuaded mothers, uncles, brothers, neighbors, and business partners to plead on their behalf. One fond mother slyly hinted that a prospective bride her son secretly disliked was bad tempered, lazy, and had a bad reputation. When his father forced Abdallah to marry a woman he disliked, Abdallah claimed his wife was a witch. He divorced her and married the woman he had been attracted to in the first place. After that, his poor father's alliances were really in shambles.

One young woman threatened to kill herself if she were forced to marry. Many relied on witchcraft or magical charms to get their way. One woman warned an unappealing suitor (Haddu) that she had visited a *dhazubrith* (witch) and obtained a spell that was guaranteed to make him impotent. The marriage took place, but the hapless Haddu was unable to "become stiff" (p. 49). He tried counter-charms but to no avail. He finally agreed to dissolve the marriage. Sometimes these desperate stratagems worked, sometimes they didn't.

Cross-cultural surveys document the variety of types of mate selection systems that currently exist throughout the world (Goode, 1963; Rosenblatt, 1967; Stephens, 1963). In the majority of systems, however, parents, kin, and young men and women all have some say in choosing prospective mates. In the musical *Fiddler on the Roof*, Tevye's daughters daydreamed about a perfect arranged marriage. For Mama, he must be a scholar, for Papa, someone as rich as a king. What they longed for, however, was a husband "handsome as anything!"

The *Ethnographic Atlas* contains anthropological information on more than 1,000 preindustrial societies throughout the world. When Gwen Broude and Sarah Greene (1983) sampled 186 of these groups, they found that in most societies, parents, kin, and young men and women are supposed to consult with one another in this most important of family decisions. In most societies, men had considerably more power than did women to determine their own fates, however. In only in a minority of societies were men and women allowed complete power in choosing their own mates (Table 2.4).

Within a single society, arrangements often vary from ethnic group to ethnic group, class to class, region to region, and family to family (Bumroongsook, 1992).

TABLE 2.4 Mate Selection Practices throughout the World

	Men	Women
Parents choose partner; individual cannot object	13%	21%
Parents choose partner; individual can object	17	23
Arranged marriages and individual choice are both acceptable alternatives	18	17
Individuals, parents, kin, and others have to agree on an appropriate match	3	3
Individual selects partner: parental, kin, and/or community approval necessary or highly desirable	19	29
Individual selects partner: approval by others unnecessary	31	8

Based on Broude & Green (1983), pp. 273–274.

Love Marriages

In Westernized cultures such as our own, parents often try to persuade their children to make a "sensible" choice. In Amy Tan's book (1989), *The Joy Luck Club*, for example, Waverly Jong was hesitant to tell her mother that she and Rich Schields were engaged. She knew that her mother would begin to tease her, she's resist for a time, but in the end she would submit to her mother's wishes. But in America, no matter how fierce the parents and how timid the children, when push comes to shove, young lovers usually get their way (Cate & Lloyd, 1992). In the end, after all, Waverly Jong did marry Rich Schields, despite her mother's objections. Increasingly, the same thing is becoming true throughout the rest of the world.

More Love Marriages on the Way?

In the far distant past, historians remind us, parents and kin generally had the power to arrange marriages as they chose. Families married families. Later, in most societies, parents and kin began at least to consult with their sons and daughters. Recently, however, the rules have begun to change dramatically. In the West, young people have generally acquired the power to make their own marital decisions. They *may* consult their parents about their romantic, sexual, and marital choices, but sometimes they do not even feel constrained to do that.

This revolutionary view of the "right" way to select partners is spreading throughout the world. Arranged marriages are increasingly surrendering to love matches. Two examples follow.

India is a complex society. Indians possess a plenitude of customs, belong to a variety of castes, speak a cacophony of languages, and live in a multitude of environments Yet, from the Vedic period (4000–1000 B.C.) until very recently, all Indian parents agreed on one thing: it was their privilege and responsibility to arrange the marriages of their children (Prakasa & Rao, 1979). Today, however, the 6,000-year-old tradition of arranged marriages is fast crumbling. More than 43 percent of young Indian men and 37 percent of young Indian women now assume that *they* should be allowed complete freedom in choosing a mate (Prakasa & Rao, 1979; Sprecher & Chandak, 1992).

Xiaohe Xu and Martin Whyte (1990) surveyed 586 women who had gotten married between 1933 and 1987 in Chengdu, People's Republic of China. For centuries, Chinese parents (aided by family councils and hired go-betweens) had the power to determine all marriages. Sometimes they did not even give the young couple a chance to meet before the wedding. In this century, reformers and revolutionaries such as Mao Zedong began to condemn the personal misery and suicides that resulted from these traditional practices (Pa, 1933/1972). When the Communists came to power, they instituted the new Marriage Law of the People's Republic of China in 1950. It denounced the

> . . . *arbitrary and compulsory feudal marriage system . . . which ignores the children's interests [and proclaimed that] marriage shall be based upon the complete*

willingness of the two parties. Neither party shall use compulsion and no third party shall be allowed to interfere. (Yang, 1959, p. 221)

Marriage registration offices began carefully to interview couples to make sure they wished to marry. This campaign changed the Chinese power balance. In the Chengdu study, 69 percent of the people who married before 1949 reported that their parents had arranged things. By 1977, no one reported having a traditional arranged marriage. Reports that parents dominated the proceedings declined from 56 percent in the pre-1949 period to 5 percent today (Table 2.5).

In such traditional societies as those in Africa (Solway, 1990; Timaeus & Graham, 1989), the Arab countries (Davis & Davis, 1994; Shaaban, 1991), China (Chu & Ju, 1993; Honig & Hershatter, 1988; Xu & Whyte, 1990), Egypt (Ahmed, 1992), Japan (DeMente, 1989; Kumagai, 1984), Russia (Kerblay, 1983); Thailand (Bumroongsook, 1992), and Turkey (Duben & Behar, 1991), most young men and women now agree that, although parents should be consulted, they themselves should be free to choose their own mates or at least to have a significant role in the selection.

In such swiftly changing societies, some young people find it difficult to get used to freedom. Paul Rosenblatt and Roxanne Anderson (1981) noted:

Perhaps the greatest tension in moving to a system based on freedom of choice is simply the lack of social skills and of attitudes necessary to cope with such a system.

TABLE 2.5   The Steady Change from Arranged Marriage to Free Choice Marriage in China

	Year of Marriage				
	1933–1948	1949[a]–1957	1958[b]–1965	1966[c]–1976	1977[d]–1987
1. Traditional arranged marriage	69%	22%	1%	0%	0%
2. Type of marriage					
Arranged	68%	27%	0%	1%	2%
Intermediate	15	33	45	40	41
Individual choice	17	40	55	59	57
3. Dominant role in mate choice					
Parents	56%	30%	7%	8%	5%
Mixed	15	11	6	3	6
Respondents	28	59	87	89	89

[a]The Chinese Communist Party comes to power
[b]The launching of the Great Leap Forward
[c]The onset of the Cultural Revolution
[d]The beginning of the post-Mao reform era
Based on Xu & Whyte (1990), p. 715.

> *[Many authors] have written about the uncertainties, insecurities, and bungling of young people, like young Japanese or Chinese, who have lacked models of how to behave, have been raised by kin who were reared under the arranged system, and who lacked confidence in their own criteria of choice. For some people the freedom creates a hunger for films, fiction, and gossip that provide an education in how to cope with freedom. For other people the demands of freedom seem too much and they prefer to have a marriage arranged for them, perhaps with a clear-cut opportunity to veto the selected spouse. Thus one of the fascinating findings of studies of the newly created free marriage systems is the part some young people play in subverting their own freedom. (p. 238)*

Change, then, may be expected to be slow and uneven, but relentless. As we observed in Chapter 1, throughout the world, three beliefs once confined to the West are gaining increasing acceptance—a belief in gender equality, a belief in the value of the pursuit of happiness and the avoidance of pain, and a belief that things can change for the better. Marital arrangements reflect these changes. Today, throughout the world, young people—men and women—are gaining more power to say whom they will marry. Polygamous marriages are surrendering to monogamous ones (Bumroongsook, 1992; DeMente, 1989; Honig & Hershatter, 1988; Shaaban, 1991, Solway, 1990; Timaeus & Graham, 1989; Xu & Whyte, 1990).

How Do Arranged and Love Marriages Work Out?

Which fare the best: arranged marriages or love matches? People have hotly debated this question.

The Debate

Those who cast their vote for love, argue that it is cruel to force young people to marry and live their entire lives with someone they may neither love nor like. Young people, they continue, are the only ones who can know deep in their bones what appeals to them. Parents and outsiders can make only the roughest of guesses. Worse yet, those in power may well be tempted to take their own best interests, not those of the young couple, into account when arranging a marriage. So the argument goes.

Since the twelfth century, legends have recounted the love stories of couples whose passionate, consuming love was extinguished only by death. Romeo and Juliet, and Tristan and Isolde (in the West); Layla and Majnun, Sohni and Mahinwal, and Heer and Ranjha (in the Middle East), and Radha and Krishna as well as couples in the Mahabharata and Ramayana (in India) were willing to sacrifice everything for love. They chose to die rather than marry those their parents had chosen for them.

In real life, young people sometimes protest their fates with equal vehemence (Cohen, 1969; Topley, 1975). In one Kalahari (African) village, for example, Bakgalagadi parents promised their teenage daughter to a man more than fifty years her senior. She was to be his fourth wife. She refused to marry. Nonetheless, she was "dragged kicking and screaming to her marital home." (Solway, 1990, p. 50). Husbands must sometimes force their reluctant brides to have sexual relations.

Some miserable young people commit suicide rather than marry against their will. One of our clients was a cultured, intelligent, and calmly beautiful Indian woman. Her parents arranged a marriage for her (against her strenuous objections) with a man from a politically powerful, landed family. Her mother-in-law had a savage temper and often whipped her until she fell unconscious. Her pampered husband expressed his irritation by burning her with the end of his cigarette. No one would come to her aid. All her parents could do was to say how sorry they were they had made a mistake, but that what was done was done and she must try to make the best of it. It was her job to make the marriage work. Eventually, she tried to kill herself. Only then was the marriage dissolved.

Traditionalists, of course, cast their vote for the arranged marriage. Passionate love, they point out, is a kind of madness. People who are blinded by love are in no position to make a lifetime decision. Parents know a great deal more about what it takes to make a marriage go.

In China, there is a proverb: "Love matches start out hot and grow cold, while arranged marriages start out cold and grow hot." If couples are flushed with love before they marry, the argument goes, their feelings are bound to cool in time. The realities of marriage cannot help but be daunting. In arranged marriages, couples have a chance to fall in love and come to know one another *after* marriage. Because they know they will be married the rest of their lives, they generally do their best to make things go. Some partisans contend that arranged marriages are more likely to last than are marriages for love. This argument loses a bit of its appeal, however, when we realize that in those traditional societies where marriages are still arranged, divorce is often forbidden or at least extremely difficult to secure, especially for women. (Some evidence in support of these notions comes from Gupta & Singh, 1982, and Rosenblatt & Anderson, 1981).

Other traditionalists take a different tack in defending arranged marriages. They point out that it is not really fair to ask if young men and women prefer love matches to arranged marriages. One couple's happiness or unhappiness is not very important in the scheme of things. One should rather ask how pleased the *families* are with the arrangement. Did the marriage bring the families closer together? help them repay old debts? consolidate neighboring farms? It is, they argue, duty and ancestors, the family, and the well-being of generations to come that matter.

Susan Sprecher and Rachita Chandak (1992) interviewed Indian men and women who had observed both arranged marriages and love matches firsthand. They wanted to find out what they saw as the advantages and disadvantages of both kinds of marriages. The Indian men and women they surveyed ranged in age from fourteen to forty-two. A few were married; most were not. Most were of upper-middle or middle class in origin. They were living in India, England, or the United

States. Religiously, they were Hindus, Christians, or Muslims. Traditionally, in almost all of their families, until very recently, marriages had always been arranged. Even today, about half of the respondents (53 percent) took it for granted that *their* marriages would be arranged as well. Some (17 percent) weren't sure how matters would be settled; 30 percent insisted that they would choose their own partners.

Men and women knew full well that both systems had certain advantages and disadvantages. Table 2.6 lists some of the pros and cons of arranged marriages and love matches.

TABLE 2.6   The Advantages and Disadvantages of Arranged Marriages and Love Matches According to Indian Men and Women

Arranged Marriages

Advantages
1. Support from families (23%)
   ("Parents' full support." "Can always fall back on parents when things go wrong.")
2. Quality and stability of the marriage (16%)
   ("Good and long-lasting relationships." "Works because you can't break up for fear of going against tradition.")
3. Compatible or desirable backgrounds (13%)
   ("Same social background, so it's easier to understand each other.")
4. Learning adjustment in marriage (7%)
   ("Adjustment and compromise can be learned.")
5. Happiness of parents and family (6%)
   ("Please my parents.")
6. Approval by society (6%)
   ("Respected in society." "Satisfaction of society.")
7. Ease of meeting a partner (5%)
   ("Easy way to meet decent people." "Saves hassle of looking around.")
8. Excitement of the unknown (5%)
   ("Thrilling experience to get to know the person.")
9. Parents know best (4%)
   ("Parents can select a more suitable match.")

Disadvantages
1. Not knowing each other well (24%)
2. Problems with the dowry (24%)
   ("Ill treatment of bride." "In-laws greedy for dowry." "Groom and parents may harass bride for dowry.")
3. Incompatibility/unhappiness (23%)
   ("Personality clash." "Bride and groom may not like each other." "Conflicts may arise." "May not be compatible.")
4. Limited choice (11%)
   ("Bride/bridegroom do not have much to say." "One cannot select the life partner of one's choice." "Females have mostly no say on the final decision.")
5. Family and in-law problems (11%)
   ("Problems arise for girls because of their in-laws." "The families may quarrel." "Personal time regulated by family." "Conflicts with in-laws.")

Continued

TABLE 2.6 *Continued*

Dating and Love Marriages

Advantages
1. Getting to know the other (35%)
   ("Knowing the person before getting seriously committed.")
2. Stimulation and fun (12%)
   ("Do something you like with someone you like." "Seems exciting.")
3. Socialization concerning the opposite sex (10%)
   ("Better knowledge of the other sex.")
4. Broadening outlook (10%)
   ("Develop a broader outlook." "Become more outgoing.")
5. Sex (5%)
   ("French kissing." "Premarital sex.")
6. Love and romanticism (4%)
   ("Great feeling of being in love.")
7. Freedom of choice (4%)
   ("Gives more freedom to individual." "Females have more say than in the arranged marriage system.")
8. Leads to a good choice (4%)
   ("Learn to choose well, after many dates.")

Disadvantages
1. Sex, pregnancy, and immoral behavior (18%)
2. Disapproval by parents (14%)
   ("Get in trouble at home.")
3. Cause anguish (11%)
   ("Feelings of guilt." "Misunderstandings." "Getting hurt.")
4. Short-lived (10%)
   ("Infatuation." "Short-lived affairs.")
5. Disapproval by society (7%)
6. Negative effect on studies (7%)
   ("Distraction from studies.")
7. Waste of time and money (6%)
8. Bad reputation (6%)
9. Risky (6%)
   ("Might meet the wrong type of person." "Could be dangerous.")
10. Immaturity (4%)
    ("Often it is misunderstood by young.")

Sprecher & Chandak (1992), p. 66–67.

When men and women were asked, given the pros and cons of both, whether they favored traditional arranged marriages or love matches, respondents' opinions depended on their age. The older people tended to favor traditional, arranged marriages. (Even they thought that parents should at least consult with the young couple about such a momentous decision, however.) Most young people, on the other hand, thought that young men and women should be allowed to date and marry whomever they pleased. Men and women were uncertain, however, as to which form of marriage works out the best.

The Data

We were able to find one study that suggests that sometimes in traditional societies such as India arranged marriages *may* work out the best. Usha Gupta and Pushpa Singh (1982) interviewed fifty couples living in Jaipur, India. Some had married for love, while the others' marriages had been arranged. Couples were asked to complete two scales—one assessing how much romantic love they felt for their mate and a second asking how much they liked him or her. At first (during the first five years of marriage), it was couples who had married for love who loved and liked their partners the most. After that, however, the couple's feelings began to change. When couples who had been married five to ten years were interviewed, the researchers found that now it was the couples in arranged marriages who were most in love. Men (but not women) in arranged marriages had also come to like their partners more than before.

Most evidence, however, suggests that arranged marriages generally do not work very well. Robert Blood (1967) asked Japanese men and women, whose marriages had been arranged or who had married for love and who had been married for various lengths of time, how happy their marriages were. Generally, parents had consulted with their sons about their preferences before arranging a marriage; they were far less likely to have consulted with their daughters. Blood found that for men it didn't seem to matter much one way or the other how their mates had been selected. In general, Japanese men were happier in their marriages than were women. Men were equally happy in either arranged marriages or love marriages. Women, on the other hand, seemed to pay a large cost for powerlessness. Overall, women were less happy with their marriages than were men. In arranged marriages, the longer women were married, the more unhappy they were with their marriages. Women who had married for love remained far happier over time.

In a similar study, Xiaohe Xu and Martin Whyte (1990) surveyed 586 women in Chengdu, People's Republic of China, who had married sometime in the period from 1933 to 1987. Some of the marriages had been arranged; others were free-choice marriages. The results were clear. Women were the happiest if they were allowed to choose their own mates (see Figure 2.2 on page 56).

Marriages for love also seemed to be most stable. Divorce is rare in China (only 3.9 percent of first marriages end in this fashion), but Xu and Whyte found that more arranged marriages than free-choice marriages eventually ended in divorce.

Regardless of the pros and cons of the various possibilities, young men and women throughout the world seem to have made their choice. Increasingly, parental power is eroding. Young people, men *and* women, are insisting on marrying for love. In even the most traditional of societies, most young men and women now agree that, although parents should be consulted, they themselves should be free to choose their own mates.

FIGURE 2.2   Marital Satisfaction in Arranged Marriages and Love Matches

Xu & Whyte, 1990, p. 718.

Conclusions: From Front Porch to Back Seat

Some social commentators have objected to the phrase "mate selection." They feel such chilly language robs romance of . . . well, its romance. They prefer "courtship" or "wooing." Such words come closer to affirming a faith in the magic of love, a faith that somewhere out there resides the perfect mate, and that when you see her or him, you will know it instantly. No traits, no careful assessments, few worrisome complications. Others, of course, would argue that such a romantic vision is wildly unrealistic. Marriage should be based on a firmer foundation of tradition, family, and duty.

Regardless of one's views, as this chapter makes clear, a social revolution in wooing, courtship, and marriage (call it what you will), is occurring worldwide. Humans have, for millennia, been falling in love—and hard. But, until very recently, unbridled passion has had powerful enemies. Political tyrants, religious authorities, and the family have long feared love's raptures, its consuming hungers, its instabilities. The powers-that-be (who benefit from maintenance of the status quo) were naturally threatened by the recklessness of love. Families also sometimes had benevolent motives for attempting to rein in passion: they yearned to protect their children from the suffering that sometimes comes from a too-hasty, passionate choice. The modern sentiment: "falling in love with love is falling for make-believe" reminds us of passionate lovers' potential for self-delusion. In any case, for most of recorded history, the powerful prevailed. Love was sharply kept in check. Even today, the "enemies" of love retain some influence (Ariès, 1962; Ladurie, 1979; Phillips, 1988).

This chapter, however, emphasizes the appeal and spread of passionate love and the growing acceptance of the ideal of marriage for love around the world. Today, in most societies, most people do seem to respond to love's tender currents. Arranged marriages are easing into marital compromises; such compromises are, in turn, being thrust aside by love matches. The simple sentence, "Arranged marriages are yielding to marriages for love," is true, but it ignores the fact that the process of change is not a direct, linear one. Many compromises, confusions, and inconsistencies are encountered along the way.

In the West, in the last century, young people have gained increasing power to choose their own dates, sexual partners, and mates. Beth Bailey (1988), in *From Front Porch to Back Seat*, provides a history of courtship in twentieth-century America. She points out that at the start of the twentieth century, in America, couples' wooing took place under the eyes of watchful parents. Then, even that began to change:

> *In twentieth-century America, courtship became more and more a private act conducted in the public world. This intimate business, as it evolved into "dating," increasingly took place in public places removed, by distance and by anonymity, from the sheltering and controlling contexts of home and local community. Keeping company in the family parlor was replaced by dining and dancing, Coke dates, movies, "parking." In the twentieth century, youth increasingly moved from the private to the public sphere. (Bailey, 1988, p. 3)*

Change is occurring in the rest of the world as well. Sometimes it is difficult to recognize just how much things are changing. As shown in Table 2.5, in traditional cultures, arranged marriages come in a variety of shapes and forms. There are variations in who is supposed to propose a match in the first place, who is to be consulted, who has the ultimate say, and so forth. Sometimes it is difficult to realize how significant a seemingly slight alteration in power might be. Nonetheless, when one steps back and takes the long view, change is evident.

Sometimes, people are not sure just how much they like all these changes. When things are in flux, it is only natural to wish now and then for the certainties of the past. Young people's confusion and uncertainty should not be confused with a desire to go back to arranged marriages, however. There is no evidence that, in the end, young people wish to turn back the clock. Such a return to the past is probably no longer possible. Bailey (1988) concluded her book with these observations:

> *The vast uncertainties of contemporary courtship have produced a flood of nostalgia [in America]. We look longingly, in our popular culture, back to the "traditional" courtship of the postwar era—when rules were rules. . . . Even if the rules were*

stifling, it seems, at least we knew what they were—and the consequences of breaking them.

This nostalgia is misplaced. Our past does not contain a golden age of court-ship, and the "security" of the postwar era was bought at great price. Besides, we are not those people. We are too far from their understandings of the world. For all the problems with modern relationships, we have made gains in freedom and equality; for all our fears in facing an uncertain world, we have incorporated the revolution into our ways of seeing. And it is a revolution we are still fighting. (p. 143)

As the old rules break apart, couples—Eastern or Western; uniracial or interracial; heterosexual, bisexual, or homosexual—are being flung into a world where they may sometimes have to forge their own rules. For many this prospect is terrifying. For others it is liberating. For the moment, like it or not, we will all just have to muddle through as best we can. In the long run, things are likely to work themselves out. To some extent, our preferences are shaped by our genetic and biological heritage. Part of that heritage, however, is the ability to adapt to change. We may admire our forebears, but we are not those people. Courtship patterns are part of a story of continuity, but they are also integral to an exciting and unpredictable tale of discontinuity, self-invention, and couples-invention.

Chapter 3

Falling in Love

For more than 2,000 years, elders, poets, and storytellers in every corner of the globe have handed down tales of passionate love (Kakar & Ross, 1986; Trawick, 1990). At different times and in different places, however these weavers of stories have had very different tales to tell.

During the Middle Ages, Western Crusaders, troubadours, and courtiers spun tales of the joys and searing miseries of pure love. Andreas Capellanus (1174/1941), in *The Art of Courtly Love,* set down the cruel rules of chivalry. To be worthy of love, a woman must put herself beyond love; she must be noble, chaste, and so utterly virtuous she was forever unattainable. The true lover must eagerly embrace not his beloved, but the Grail-like quest for love. He must be willing to perform any deed and suffer any torment to attest to the purity of his doomed love (Gay, 1986; Murstein, 1974; Tannahill, 1980).

In the seventh and eighth centuries, Arab storytellers told a more complex, often contradictory, narrative of romantic, erotic love. One source of the tales was the professional storytellers, who flourished in the cities of the Near East. Reay Tannahill (1980) observed:

> *The repertoire of these men, especially the Persians among them, was astonishingly varied. They drew on the Bible and the Vedas, recounted the exploits of Greek heroes, Roman warriors, and Egyptian queens, told of angels and djinns, winged horses and magic carpets, of treasure houses on earth and dancing girls in paradise. Their word pictures had a wild, exotic glamour that took possession of the Arab imagination. (p. 235)*

Often their stories were tales of the purest love. Pure love was a spiritual, romantic, and eternal kind of love. The beloved was usually a dimly glimpsed woman, chaste and forever unattainable. (Generally, the beloved was a devout Muslim wife, imprisoned in a *harām*). This sort of love promised only yearning and exquisite torture.

Seductive slave singers, on the other hand, offered another vision of romance—love-desire. This was a happier, rougher, sexier, and transient kind of love. Here, the woman who caught the lover's eye (for the moment) was generally a slave singer—cultured, exquisite, deceitful, and very sexy. Love-desire was not expected to last forever. Men buzzed from flower to flower, enjoying whichever slave-singer or adolescent boy happened to catch their attention at the moment (Tannahill, 1980).

The Western Crusaders, troubadours, and courtiers and the Arab storytellers and slave singers tended to separate falling in love and making love—tenderness and lust. After 1800 the two grew more tightly connected. In the 1860s, for example, the American social reformer Lester Frank Ward composed a diary of his ongoing love affair. Carl Degler (1980) described it this way:

> *Ward reported that he and "his girl," as he referred to the young woman who later became his wife, kissed and caressed each other until the early morning hours. On a Monday night in 1860, when he was nineteen, he left her only "at half past three . . . amid thousands of kisses." Then on the following Wednesday he escorted her home, not leaving again until 3:00 A.M. During that stay, he reported they spent "an hour embracing, caressing, hugging, and kissing. O bliss! O love! O passion, pure, sweet, and profound! What more do I want than you?"*
>
> *Nor was all the initiative his. On a subsequent visit, after an absence of several days, he found her most captivated by him. "She looked at me so gently and spoke so tenderly. 'I love you,' she said, kissing me on the mouth. 'I love this mouth, I love those dear eyes, I love this head,' and a thousand other little caressing pet-names. (p. 21)*

In this diary entry, courtship and passionate love are inextricably intertwined. And despite the reputation of the Victorian world of England and America for its sexual prudery and hypocrisy (an inaccurate, oversimplified stereotype), we read of two young people in 1860 even engaging in some premarital sexual high jinks. Just how far they went we reserve for the next chapter on sexuality.

In this chapter, we explore contemporary visions of passionate love. We begin by examining cultural differences in the definition of passionate love. Then, we attempt to discover whether or not those in Western, individualist cultures are any more susceptible to its charms than are those in Eastern, collectivist cultures. Finally, we consider the impact of both culture and personality on men's and women's passionate feelings and experiences.

What Is This Thing Called Love and How Can We Measure It?

Kurt Fischer and his colleagues (1990) pointed out that all emotions, including love, possess a number of components. They defined *emotions* as "organised, meaningful, generally adaptive action systems. . . . [they] are complex functional wholes includ-

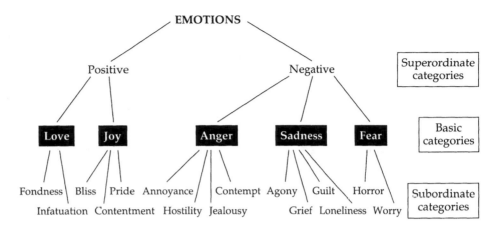

FIGURE 3.1　An Emotion Hierarchy

Fisher et al., (1990), p. 90.

ing appraisals or appreciations, patterned physiological processes, action tendencies, subjective feelings, expressions, and instrumental behaviors" (p. 84–85).

They concluded that there are five basic emotions—two positive emotions (joy and love) and three negative ones (anger, sadness, and fear) (Figure 3.1). There are two major kinds of love: passionate love (which they labeled *infatuation*) and companionate love (which they labeled *fondness*).

Love is a basic emotion. It comes in a variety of forms. Most scientists distinguish between two kinds of love—*passionate love* and *companionate love*. Most of us understand the difference between being "in love" with someone and "loving" them. When besotted lovers hear the dreaded mantra: "I *love* you . . . , but I'm not *in love* with you. Can't we just be friends?" their hearts sink. Researchers find that men and women in a variety of nations, homosexual or heterosexual, single or married, resonate to this distinction (Fehr, 1993).

Assessing Passionate Love

> In between freezing and melting. In between love and despair. In between fear and sex, passion is.
>
> —*Jeanette Winterson*

In Chapter 1, we defined passionate love this way: "A state of intense longing for union with another. . . . Reciprocated love (union with the other) is associated with fulfillment and ecstasy. Unrequited love (separation) is associated with emptiness, anxiety, or despair" (Hatfield & Rapson, 1993b, p. 5).

People in all cultures recognize the power of passionate love. In South Indian Tamil families, a person who fell head-over-heels in love with another was said to

What Is This Thing Called Love?

Howard & MacIntosh (1994).

be suffering from *mayakkam*—dizziness, confusion, intoxication, and delusion. The wild hopes and despairs of love, then, mixed you up (Trawick, 1990).

Elaine Hatfield and Susan Sprecher (1986a) developed the *Passionate Love Scale (PLS)* to tap the cognitive, emotional, and behavioral incidents of such longing for union. The *PLS* is reproduced in Box 3.1.

It is, of course, this kind of love with which this text is primarily concerned. Researchers have often taken great pains to distinguish this kind of love from other, related kinds of love, such as companionate love.

Assessing Companionate Love

> *He loves me, I know that, and I love him, but in a brotherly incestuous way. He touches my heart, but he does not send it shattering through my body.*
> —*Jeanette Winterson*

Companionate love is a gentler emotion. The Welsh philosopher Ilham Dilman (1987) observed: "It seems to me that there are some rare cases where the very passionate love that a husband and wife had for each other at the beginning of their marriage is weathered with age and deepened with the trials it survives. In such cases this love becomes more like friendship, without losing its sexual character" (p. 90). We call that feeling companionate love. Companionate love combines feelings of deep attachment, commitment, and intimacy. In Chapter 1, we defined it this way: "The affection and tenderness we feel for those with whom our lives are deeply entwined. . . ." (Hatfield & Rapson, 1993b, p. 9).

Psychologists have used a variety of scales to measure companionate love. Robert Sternberg (1988), for example, contended that companionate relationships required both commitment and intimacy. Thus, many researchers have assessed companionate love by measuring commitment and intimacy (Box 3.2 on page 64).

BOX 3.1 The Passionate Love Scale

We would like to know how you feel (or once felt) about the person you love, or have loved, most *passionately*. Some common terms for passionate love are *romantic love, infatuation, love sickness,* or *obsessive love.*

Please think of the person whom you love most passionately *right now*. If you are not in love right now, please think of the last person you loved. If you have never been in love, think of the person you came closest to caring for in that way. Try to tell us how you felt at the time when your feelings were the most intense.

Who are you thinking of?
☐ Someone I love *right now.*
☐ Someone I *once* loved.
☐ I have never been in love but am describing how I think I *would* feel if I were in love.

Possible answers range from:

1	2	3	4	5	6	7	8	9
Not at all true				Moderately true				Definitely true

1. I would feel deep despair if _____ left me.

   1 2 3 4 5 6 7 8 9

2. Sometimes I feel I can't control my thoughts; they are obsessively on _____ .

   1 2 3 4 5 6 7 8 9

3. I feel happy when I am doing something to make _____ happy.

   1 2 3 4 5 6 7 8 9

4. I would rather be with _____ than anyone else.

   1 2 3 4 5 6 7 8 9

5. I'd get jealous if I thought _____ were falling in love with someone else.

   1 2 3 4 5 6 7 8 9

6. I yearn to know all about _____ .

   1 2 3 4 5 6 7 8 9

7. I want _____—physically, emotionally, mentally.

   1 2 3 4 5 6 7 8 9

8. I have an endless appetite for affection from _____ .

   1 2 3 4 5 6 7 8 9

9. For me, _____ is the perfect romantic partner.

   1 2 3 4 5 6 7 8 9

10. I sense my body responding when _____ touches me.

    1 2 3 4 5 6 7 8 9

11. _____ always seems to be on my mind.

    1 2 3 4 5 6 7 8 9

12. I want _____ to know me—my thoughts, my fears, and my hopes.

    1 2 3 4 5 6 7 8 9

13. I eagerly look for signs indicating _____'s desire for me.

    1 2 3 4 5 6 7 8 9

14. I possess a powerful attraction for _____ .

    1 2 3 4 5 6 7 8 9

15. I get extremely depressed when things don't go right in my relationship with _____ .

    1 2 3 4 5 6 7 8 9

Hatfield and Sprecher (1986a), p. 391.

BOX 3.2 A Companionate Love Scale

We would also like to know how you feel (or once felt) about the person you love, or have loved, most *companionately*. Some common terms for companionate love are *affectionate love, tender love, true love,* or *marital love.*

Please think of the person whom you love most companionately *right now.* If you are not in love right now, please think of the last person you loved. If you have never been companion- ately in love, think of the person you came clos- est to caring for in that way. Try to tell us how you felt at the time when your feelings were the most intense.

Who are you thinking of?:
☐ Someone I love *right now.*
☐ Someone I *once* loved.
☐ I have never been in love but am describing how I think I would feel if I were in love.

Please indicate your feelings on the following scale:

1	2	3	4	5	6	7	8	9
Not at all true of me		Somewhat true of me		Moderately true of me		Quite true of me		Extremely true of me

Commitment

Sternberg measured commitment by such items as these:

1. I expect my love for _____ to last for the rest of my life.

   1 2 3 4 5 6 7 8 9

2. I can't imagine ending my relationship with _____ .

   1 2 3 4 5 6 7 8 9

3. I am certain of my love for _____ .

   1 2 3 4 5 6 7 8 9

4. I am committed to maintaining my relation- ship with _____ .

   1 2 3 4 5 6 7 8 9

5. I have confidence in the stability of my rela- tionship with _____ .

   1 2 3 4 5 6 7 8 9

Intimacy

Sternberg assessed intimacy by such items as:

1. I have a warm and comfortable relationship with _____ .

   1 2 3 4 5 6 7 8 9

2. I experience intimate communication with _____ .

   1 2 3 4 5 6 7 8 9

3. I have a relationship of mutual under- standing with _____ .

   1 2 3 4 5 6 7 8 9

4. I receive considerable emotional support from _____ .

   1 2 3 4 5 6 7 8 9

5. I give considerable emotional support to _____ .

   1 2 3 4 5 6 7 8 9

6. I experience great happiness with _____ .

   1 2 3 4 5 6 7 8 9

The companionate love score is calculated by adding up scores on the commitment and inti- macy subscales. The higher the score, the more companionately one is assumed to love another.

Based on Sternberg (1986).

Love Lite

Tim Downs (1993).

Other Typologies

Some scientists have proposed that love can be dissected still further:

1. *Love Styles.* John Lee (1973), for example, proposed that when young men and women think of "love," they might be thinking of any of six types of love: *Mania* (possessive, dependent love) or *Eros* (passionate love), both of which sound a bit like passionate love; *Pragma* (logical, "shopping list" love) or *Storge* (friendship love), both of which sound a bit like companionate love; *Ludus* (game-playing love) or *Agape* (all-giving, selfless love). Clyde Hendrick and Susan Hendrick (1989) have developed scales to tap these six varieties of love.

2. *A Triangular Theory of Love.* Robert Sternberg (1988) outlined a triangular model of love. He states that different kinds of love vary in the extent to which they contain the three basic ingredients of love—passion, intimacy, and the decision and commitment to stay together (Figure 3.2).

As you can see from Figure 3.2, three kinds of love offer just one asset: *passionate love,* which Sternberg labeled "infatuation, thrives on passion but promises little commitment or intimacy; *empty love* involves the decision to stay committed but little else; and *liking* provides intimacy alone. *Companionate love* offers more. It may be lacking in passion, but it provides a great deal of intimacy and commitment. *Romantic love* provides both intimacy and passion. *Fatuous love* involves passion and commitment. *Consummate love* is the most complete form of love. It has it all: passion, intimacy, and commitment.

3. *Love Prototypes.* Finally, Beverley Fehr and her colleagues (Davis & Todd, 1982; Fehr, 1988 and 1993; Fehr & Russell, 1991; Fitness & Fletcher, 1993; Mar-

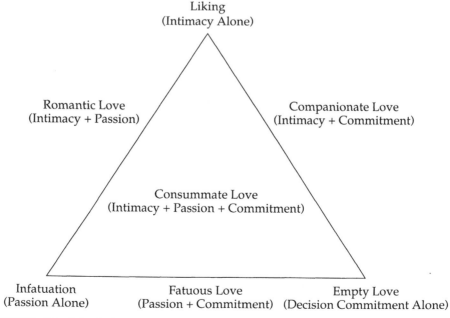

FIGURE 3.2 The Triangular Model of Love

Sternberg (1988), p. 122.

ston, Hecht, & Robers, 1987) have taken a very different, and quite promising, approach to the study of love. First, they simply ask people to list all the kinds of love they can. Typically, people list friendship and sexual, parental, brotherly, sibling, maternal, passionate, romantic, and familial love. In one study, people in Australia and the United States were able to list ninety-three types of love (Fehr & Russell, 1991)! Then, researchers may ask people to list the defining features of love. Typically, people list such things as euphoria, excitement, affection and contentment; laughing, gazing at the other; sacrificing for the other; thinking about the other all the time; seeing only their good qualities; having butterflies in your stomach, sexual passion; feeling free to talk about anything; and, sometimes, feeling uncertain and scared. In a series of studies, Fehr (1993) found that people were able to list sixty-eight features of love. They note that when asked about love, people sometimes think immediately of "passionate" love and its defining features. Much more often, however, companionate love and its defining features spring to mind.

In this book we do not discuss these many typologies of love. Everywhere people seem able to make the simple distinction between "I love you" and "I am in love with you." Less commonly the young men and women we encounter distinguish between the many varieties of love.

Culture and Passionate Love

Some evidence shows that, in different cultures, men and women have somewhat different attitudes toward passionate love. We must be careful not to exaggerate these differences, however.

Passion: Is Something Lost in Translation?

> *My friend, I love you as one ought to love, to excess, in madness, ecstasy, and despair.*
>
> —*Julie De Lespinasse*

Are there currently cultural differences in how men and women view passionate love? Recently, Phillip Shaver, Shelley Wu, and Judith Schwartz (1991) interviewed young people in North America, Italy, and the People's Republic of China about their emotional experiences. In all cultures, men and women identified the same emotions as basic, prototypic emotions. These were joy/happiness, love/attraction, fear, anger/hate, and sadness/depression (see Figure 3.1). They also agreed completely as to whether the various emotions should be labeled as positive experiences (such as joy) or negative ones (such as fear, anger, or sadness). They agreed completely, that is, except about one emotion—love. North American and Italian subjects tended to equate love with happiness; both passionate and companionate love were assumed to be intensely positive experiences. Chinese students, however, had a darker view of love. In Chinese there are few "happy-love" ideographs (printed words). Love is associated with sadness. Chinese men and women associated passionate love with such ideographs as infatuation, unrequited love, nostalgia, and sorrow-love.

Interestingly, equating love with sadness seems to be an ancient Eastern tradition. For example, in *Five Women Who Loved* (Saikaku, 1956), a collection of love stories from seventeenth-century Japan, almost all the love affairs ended sadly. For the heroines, impetuous passion led almost inevitably to ruin, to suicide, or to the execution of the lovers. Phillip Shaver's students (Shaver et al., 1991) from the East and West never came to an agreement as to the nature of love. Each cultural group continued to regard one another's visions of love as "unrealistic."

The Susceptibility to Love

At the turn of the century, Frank Norris (1899/1965) recounted the savage reaction of "Mac" McTeague (a crude, oxlike dentist who is the hero of the story) to the delicate Trina Sieppe:

> *Trina was McTeague's first experience. With her the feminine element suddenly entered his little world. . . . How had he ignored it so long? It was dazzling, delicious, charming beyond all words. His narrow point of view was at once enlarged and confused, and all at once he saw that there was something else in life besides concertinas and steam beer. Everything had to be made over again. His whole rude idea of life had to be changed. The male virile desire in him tardily awakened, aroused itself, strong and brutal. It was resistless, untrained, a thing not to be held in leash an instant.*
>
> *Little by little, by gradual, almost imperceptible degrees, the thought of Trina Sieppe occupied his mind from day to day, from hour to hour. He found himself thinking of her constantly. . . . At night he lay awake for hours under the thick blankets of the bed-lounge, staring upward into the darkness, tormented with the idea of her, exasperated at the delicate, subtle mesh in which he found himself entangled. During the forenoons, while he went about his work, he thought of her. As he made his plaster-of-paris moulds at the washstand in the corner behind the screen he turned over in his mind all that had happened, all that had been said at the previous sitting. . . .*
>
> *At two o'clock on Tuesdays, Thursdays, and Saturdays Trina arrived and took her place in the operating chair. While at his work McTeague was every minute obliged to bend closely over her; his hands touched her face, her cheeks, her adorable little chin; her lips pressed against his fingers. She breathed warmly on his forehead and on his eyelids, while the odor of her hair, a charming feminine perfume, sweet, heavy, enervating, came to his nostrils, so penetrating so delicious, that his flesh pricked and tingled with it; a veritable sensation of faintness passed over this huge, callous fellow, with his enormous bones and corded muscles. He drew a short breath through his nose; his jaws suddenly gripped together vise-like.*

> *But this was only at times—a strange, vexing spasm, that subsided almost*
> *immediately. For the most part, McTeague enjoyed the pleasure of these sittings*
> *with Trina with a certain strong calmness, blindly happy that she was there. This*
> *poor crude dentist of Polk Street, stupid, ignorant, vulgar, with his sham education*
> *and plebeian tastes, whose only relaxations were to eat, to drink steam beer, and to*
> *play upon his concertina, was living through his first romance, his first idyll. It*
> *was delightful. (pp. 20–21)*

It has been claimed that Americans (like poor McTeague), generally are preoccupied with love (Murstein, 1986). When Clyde and Susan Hendrick (1986) asked University of Miami students "Are you in love now?", men and women seemed to differ in their susceptibility to love. Forty-six percent of men and 66 percent of women admitted they were in love at the present time. Eighty-nine percent of students had been in love at least once in their lives. Only 11 percent had *never* been in love.

How about men and women in the rest of the world? Some cross-cultural theorists, as we saw in Chapter 1, have argued that passionate love is a Western phenomenon. They contend that Western, individualistic cultures idealize love's tender yearnings, but that Eastern, collectivist cultures do not (see Ho, 1982; and Doi, 1973).

Early researchers (Goode, 1959; Rosenblatt et al., 1967) also assumed that romantic love would be most highly valued and prevalent in modern, industrialized, countries. The emerging evidence suggests, however, that men and women in a variety of cultures, industrializing as well as industrial, are every bit as romantic as Americans. Let us consider a sampling of this research.

When researchers (Aron & Rodriguez, 1992) asked Mexican American, Chinese American, and Anglo American college students if they had ever been in love, they found that young men and women from a variety of American ethnic groups were very susceptible to falling in love. Ninety-five percent of Anglo Americans, 72 percent of Chinese Americans, and 86 percent of Mexican Americans reported that they had been in love at least once in their lives.

Elaine Hatfield asked her University of Hawaii students if they were in love with anyone *right now.* In Hawaii, students identify with a wide variety of ethnic groups. Their grandparents, parents, and they, themselves, may come from China, Europe, Japan, or the Pacific Islands, including the Philippines, Hawaii, Samoa, Guam, Tonga, Tahiti, and Fiji. She found that it made little difference what students' ethnic backgrounds were, whether or not they possessed individualistic or collectivist values, or how acculturated they were to American culture. All seemed to be quite vulnerable to love. If anything, it was the Pacific Islanders who were the romantics, not the Westerners (Table 3.1 on page 70).

In Chapter 2, we described a study by Susan Sprecher and her colleagues (1994), who interviewed 1667 men and women, all college students in the United States, Russia, or Japan. These three cultures were chosen to represent the extremes in individualism and collectivism. The authors accepted the cultural stereotypes

TABLE 3.1 Are You in Love Right Now?

Ethnic Background	Percent Answering Yes
Pacific Islanders	76%
Chinese Americans	56%
European Americans	53%
Japanese Americans	53%

Based on Doherty et al. (1993).

which say that while American men and women fall in love very easily, those in other cultures, such as Russia and Japan, do not. Passion turned out to be more common worldwide than the researchers had expected. Contrary to their expectations, it was the Russians who were most likely to say they were in love. American men and women were next likely to be in love. The Japanese were least likely to be in love. The percentages of those currently in love, however, was surprisingly high in all three societies (Table 3.2). In all three societies, men were slightly less likely than were women to be in love at the present time.

Researchers from the Family Planning Association of Hong Kong (1987) asked boys and girls and men and women, who ranged in age from 13 to 27, if they had ever been in love with someone they had dated. At 13, not a single teenager reported that he or she had ever fallen in love with a date. (One problem with the study is that only 1 percent of 13 year olds had ever been allowed to date. They may, of course, have fallen in love with someone they yearned for from afar.) By the age of 18, 22 percent of respondents had been in love. By age 22, 60 percent of them had been in love, and by 27, 78 percent of them had fallen in love with one of their dates. By then, 86 percent of men and women had a chance to date someone.

These studies, then, suggest that passionate love is very common, at least throughout the modern, industrial, world.

TABLE 3.2 Are You in Love Right Now?

Cultural Group	Percent Answering Yes	
	Men	Women
Russians	61%	73%
Americans	53%	63%
Japanese	41%	63%

Based on Sprecher et al. (1994).

TABLE 3.3 **Passionate Love Scale Scores of Various Ethnic Groups**

	Men	Women
European Americans (Mainland USA)	97.50	110.25
European Americans (Hawaii)	100.50	105.00
Filipino Americans (Hawaii)	106.50	102.90
Japanese Americans (Hawaii)	99.00	103.95

Based on Hatfield & Rapson (1987a), p. 131.

The Intensity of Passionate Love

What effect does culture have on how passionately young people fall in love? In a second study, Hatfield and her students (Hatfield et al., 1988) asked European American, Filipino American, and Japanese American men and women to complete the *Passionate Love Scale.* Some of these students were newly arrived from the Philippines and Japan; most had lived in Hawaii all their lives. Regardless of how long students had been in America or the extent to which they were assimilated to Western culture, the various ethnic groups seemed to love with equal passion (Table 3.3).

In later research, Hatfield and her students (Doherty et al., 1993) asked University of Hawaii students from Chinese American, European American, Japanese American, and Pacific Islander ethnic backgrounds how passionately and companionately they loved. Students filled out the *Passionate Love* and *Companionate Love* scales.

The folklore, of course, says that it is European Americans who are most "obsessed with love." But, as before, the cultural stereotypes were wrong. Men and women in all of the ethnic groups seemed to have fallen head-over-heels in love with someone, sometime. In fact, in this study, Chinese American, Pacific Islanders, and Japanese Americans all scored higher on the *PLS* than did the "love besotted" European Americans (Table 3.4). Men and women from various ethnic backgrounds seemed to companionately love and like one another to the same extent as well (see Table 3.4).

TABLE 3.4 **Passionate Love and Companionate Love in Various Ethnic Groups in Hawaii**

	PLS Scores	*CLS* Scores
Chinese Americans	108.92	56.84
Pacific Islanders	105.74	59.27
Japanese Americans	105.15	57.76
European Americans	103.69	55.91

Based on Doherty et al. (1993).

Love Schemas and Passionate Love

Habits of the Heart

In our clinical practice, we can't help but observe how different people are in what they hope for from love. Young people's individual views of love may be socially constructed from the love affairs they have seen played out on television, in movies, or read about in books; from the experiences they have had in their own families; and from their own love affairs. In psychology, the word *schema* is used to indicate a person's mental model of the world—what they expect from themselves, those they love, and from their relationships. People possess very different schemas concerning love. Some men and women are quite secure in their love affairs. They prefer to be swept up in a romantic love affair, but they know that, if things fall apart, they will survive. Others are quite clingy. They need to be close to someone. If they are forced to spend much time alone, they are miserable. Still others are quite skittish. They begin to feel pressured when someone they love begins to demand too much from them. They like to spend a lot of time on their own. Some people are impossible. They always want what they don't have. They always seem to fall in love with someone who isn't interested in them. When they finally succeed in capturing that person's interest, they lose interest themselves. Finally, some people are just very casual about relationships or are uninterested in them. It seems as if men and women, both homosexual and heterosexual, fall roughly into one of six categories, depending on how comfortable they are with closeness and/or independence:

1. The *secure* seem comfortable with both closeness and independence.

2. The *clingy* desire a great deal of closeness. They are terrified of being forced to be on their own. We have probably seen slightly more clingy women than clingy men. Probably this is because, to some extent, American society still encourages women to be expert at love, intimacy, and nurturance but neglects to teach them how to be brave and independent.

3. The *skittish* are uneasy when they are pushed to get too close. They start to feel smothered. They often flee. They are very good at being independent. We have probably seen slightly more men than women who are skittish about relationships. Probably this is because, to some extent, American society still focuses on teaching men to be brave and independent, but neglects to teach them how to be close, loving, and nurturant.

4. The *fickle* are never comfortable with what they've got. They are uneasy with either closeness or independence. They often fall passionately in love. As soon as someone reciprocates their love, however, they get bored, irritated, or anxious and bolt. The minute the other begins to forget them and get involved with someone else, however, the inconstant realize they have made a terrible mistake and begin courting, sometimes desperately, the other again. And so on and so

on. The fickle seem particularly turned on by fantasies of conquest, mastery, and ravishment, but once having gained the prize, restlessness sets in. These folks can be trouble!

Finally, there are two groups of people who are simply not much interested in relationships:

5. The *casual* are interested in relationships, but simply don't want to get committed or invest very much in them. Dalliances may be pleasant, but more pleasure may be garnered from playing with one's computer—whose responses one can anticipate—than getting enmeshed in the unpredictable messiness of human closeness. Again, we see more men than women in this category, but it seems entirely likely that as women discover the potential joys of work and the possibilities of financial independence, some may become quite as casual about love as are men.

6. The *uninterested* are simply not interested in having a relationship with *anyone*.

The casual and uninterested are often bypassed by love researchers, but large numbers of people fall in these categories. Nor are such casual or downright unloving people necessarily pathological. It is quite possible to live a rich and valuable life without investing in human relationships; existence may not require them. Such people can compose wonderful music, develop useful computer programs, love nature, invent devices, enjoy sports, or even cherish animals. Some "loners" do suffer serious problems, but most of our forebears were not interested in intimacy; we need to remind ourselves how recently it was that any society placed a high value on personal closeness. Keeping distance may constitute a pathology or a reasonable choice based upon self-knowledge. In any event, these last two types do exist and should not be dismissed or too easily patronized.

In research we have attempted to identify people who possess various love schemas with questions such as these (Box 3.3 on pages 74–75). You will notice that in Box 3.3 we have replaced our terms (i.e., "secure," "clingy," "skittish," and so forth) with terms that, although they may be less picturesque and less accurate are a lot more tactful. Who, after all, is going to admit to being "clingy?" Rate yourself (privately) on this love profile.

Of course, as young lovers mature or have more experience with life, their schemas may change. As people get older, for example, they often become more secure in their abilities to deal with the vicissitudes of relationships. People who are hurt by their love affairs may become increasingly skittish with time.

People may also react differently in different kinds of relationships. Someone who is clingy and smothering may drive even the most secure person crazy with their demands. In such a relationship, a basically secure person may be forced to become a bit "skittish" about getting too close.

BOX 3.3 Romantic Feelings and Experiences

People have different experiences in their romantic relationships. Some people prefer to be involved in a romantic relationship, but deep down they know that, if things fall apart, they will be able to manage on their own. Others need to be close to someone; they are miserable when they are forced to be on their own. Still others need a great deal of time on their own. Some people aren't quite sure what they *do* want. (They *think* they want a relationship, but somehow they always seem to fall in love with someone who isn't interested in them.) Finally, some people are just very casual about relationships or are uninterested in them.

Please take a moment to think of the times you have been romantically and/or passionately in love; it doesn't matter whether or not your feelings were reciprocated. Please read the following six descriptions, and indicate to what extent each describes your feelings and experiences in romantic and passionate love affairs.

1. [Secure] I Am Comfortable with Closeness and/or Independence* I find it easy to get close to others and am comfortable depending on them and having them depend on me. I don't often worry about being abandoned or about someone getting too close to me.

0%	25%	50%	75%	100%
Never true of me		True of me about *50%* of the time		*Always* true of me

2. [Clingy] I Need a Great Deal of Closeness* I find that others are reluctant to get as close as I would like. I often worry that my partner doesn't really love me or won't want to stay with me. I want to merge completely with another person, and this desire sometimes scares people away.

0%	25%	50%	75%	100%
Never true of me		True of me about *50%* of the time		*Always* true of me

3. [Skittish] I Need a Great Deal of Independence* I am somewhat uncomfortable being close to others; I find it difficult to trust them completely. It is difficult to allow myself to depend on them. I am nervous when anyone gets too close, and often love partners want me to be more intimate than I feel comfortable being.

0%	25%	50%	75%	100%
Never true of me		True of me about *50%* of the time		*Always* true of me

4. [Fickle] I Am Not Quite Sure What I Need Sometimes, I don't know *what* I want. When I'm in love, I worry that my partner doesn't really love me or won't want to stay with me. When people get too interested in me, however, I often find that I'm just not interested in them. I end up feeling bored, irritated, or smothered. Either I fall in love and the other person doesn't or the other person falls in love and I don't.

0%	25%	50%	75%	100%
Never true of me		True of me about *50%* of the time		*Always* true of me

5. [Casual] I Am Fairly Casual about Relationships I like having someone, but I don't want to have to get *too* committed or to have to invest *too* much in a relationship.

0%	25%	50%	75%	100%
Never true of me		True of me about *50%* of the time		*Always* true of me

6. [Uninterested] **I Am Uninterested in Relationships** I don't have time for relationships. They are generally not worth the hassle.

0%	25%	50%	75%	100%
Never true of me		True of me about *50%* of the time		*Always* true of me

Love Schemas

In the previous section we described six "love schemas":

1. I am comfortable with closeness and/or independence.
2. I need a great deal of closeness.
3. I need a great deal of independence.
4. I am not quite sure what I need.

5. I am fairly casual about relationships.
6. I am uninterested in relationships.

This time, we are interested in finding out which of the six descriptions sounds *most* like you, which sound somewhat like you, and which sounds *least* like you. Please *rank* these six descriptions from (1), that which sounds most like you and best reflects your experiences in passionate love relationships to (6), that which sounds least like you and least like the experiences you have had. (Just indicate the appropriate number in the box).

☐ 1. Sounds most like me (the best-fitting description).
☐ 2. Second best-fitting description.
☐ 3. Third best-fitting description.
☐ 4. Fourth best-fitting description.
☐ 5. Fifth best-fitting description.
☐ 6. Sounds least like me.

*These three items are based on Hazan & Shaver (1987) p. 515.

How did you rate yourself on the *Love Schemas* scale (see Box 3.3)? Which of the descriptions sounded most like you? Do you think that is your basic personality type? Has your personality changed over time? How? Have different relationships brought out different sides of your personality? To see how your feelings and experiences match those of other young people, you might look back to Box 3.3, and the *Love Schemas* scale, which asked you to indicate which of the six profiles sounded most like you. How do your feelings and experiences compare to those of other college men and women? When Ted Singelis and his colleagues (1995) asked American men and women from a variety of ethnic groups to rate their feelings and experiences, most students (62.2 percent) concluded that generally they were fairly secure. Some admitted that they tended to be clingy (7.6 percent), skittish (10.5 percent), or fickle (12.2 percent). A few reported being casual (6.7 percent) or uninterested (0.8 percent) in relationships.

Not surprisingly, perhaps, most young people reported that they *generally* felt fairly secure in their romantic relationships. Many admitted that they had been clingy, skittish, or fickle in some of their romantic encounters. Only a few students said that they had generally been casual or uninterested in a love affair.

Researchers have found that American men and women from a variety of ethnic backgrounds (Chinese American, European American, Japanese American, and Pacific Islanders) tend to classify themselves in much the same ways on the *Love Schemas* measure (Doherty et al., 1993; Singelis et al., 1995). Other researchers have found that men and women from the United States, Australia, and Israel generally rate themselves and their experiences in much the same way, as well (Feeney & Noller, 1990; Mikulincer, Florian, & Tolmacz, 1990; Shaver & Hazan, 1993). Researchers have, of course, found some cross-cultural differences in young people's *Love Schemas* scores. Researchers found, for example, that American men were more likely to claim to be secure in love than were Russian or Japanese men. American and Japanese women were more likely to identify themselves as secure than were Russian women (Sprecher & Chandak, 1992). But people throughout the world have recognized the variability in lovers and love.

Theoretical Background

There is some justification, both theoretical and empirical, for the love schemas typology we have found to be so useful in a clinical setting. Social psychologists have charted the process by which infants, teenagers, and young adults learn to love and to balance the conflicting desires for closeness and independence. Pioneering scientists such as Sigmund Freud, John Bowlby, Helen Ainsworth, and Cindy Hazan and Phillip Shaver have charted the way infants come to be attached to their caretakers. Erik Erikson has charted the way adolescents and young adults learn to negotiate the delicate balance between independence and interdependence. All assume that these early experiences will have a dramatic impact on what young men and women desire in their love affairs and how competent they will be at satisfying their desires.

Attachment Theory

Social psychologists have argued that passionate love and sexual desire are constructed on the ancient foundations laid down between caretakers and children in infancy. Of course, in different cultures, the nature and intensity of these attachments may differ.

Primatologists, such as Leonard Rosenblum (1985), have pointed out that many primates, such as pigtail macaques, seem to experience a primitive form of passionate love. Sometimes in the mornings as we stroll through the "African Savanna," an attraction at the Honolulu Zoo, we are charmed by the sight of tiny infant monkeys, tightly clinging to their mothers' fur, as the mothers casually execute a series of breathtaking loops and dives on overhanging branches. When the monkeys get to be a little older, they are still careful to stay close enough to their mothers to peek at her now and then as they experiment with their own loops and dives. They are wary of strangers. When other, larger animals come bounding into the play area, the young monkeys quickly rush to their protective mothers' sides. They cling to her as before. Rosenblum commented that it not surprising that primate mothers and infants are so tightly bonded. After all, in the wild, separation is generally lethal. Infants are in continual danger from poisonous plants, insects, reptiles, and predators. They need the constant attention of their caretakers if they are to survive. (See Norikoshi, 1990, for additional data in support of this contention.) Harry and Margaret Harlow (Harlow, 1975; Harlow, Harlow, & Suomi, 1971) studied the development of love in rhesus monkeys. They discovered that, for newborns, contact comfort (snuggling) is more important than food!

Mary Ainsworth (1989) and John Bowlby (1969, 1973, 1980), who were well grounded in evolutionary theory, studied the process of attachment, separation, and loss in human infants. Infants normally progress through four developmental phases during their first year of life (Cohen, 1976):

1. In the first few months of life, they smile, gurgle, and snuggle into almost anyone. Anyone can provide contact comfort.
2. At about three months of age, the infants begin to notice that their mother is someone special and they respond to her with special interest.
3. At about six to nine months, infants become deeply attached to their mothers. They smile, jabber, and stretch out their arms to her. When they are separated their confidence is shaken. They protest. No one else will do. They are frightened of strangers and reject their well-meaning attempts at comfort.
4. After about nine to twelve months, toddlers slowly begin to take an interest in a wider circle of people. Even so, they rush back to their mothers anytime something unsettles them.

Not surprisingly, in all cultures, caretakers and children become deeply attached to one another. Social psychologists have argued that such early attachments are the forerunners of adult passionate attachments and the desire for union (Bowlby, 1979; Hatfield & Rapson, 1993a and b; Hazan & Shaver, 1987). As John Bowlby (1979) observed: "In terms of subjective experience, the formation of a bond is described as falling in love, maintaining a bond as loving someone, and losing a partner as grieving over someone" (p. 69).

In different cultures, mothers, infants, and children differ in the *form* this attachment takes, however. Mary Ainsworth and her colleagues (Ainsworth et al., 1978; Ainsworth, 1989) observed mothers and infants in both home and laboratory settings. First, in an initial home visit, observers coded how mothers treated their infants: Were they responsive? neglectful? inconsistent? Then, observers coded infants' and children's' reactions in a stressful laboratory situation. Mothers were instructed to play with their children until the children had settled down. Then, the mothers were instructed to exit the room, leaving a stranger in charge of their children. After a few minutes the mothers were allowed to return. The psychologists found that although all infants and young children were attached to their caretakers, the nature of that attachment varied dramatically:

1. *The secure.* During the home observations, some mothers were consistently responsive to their infants' needs. They were there when they were needed, but when their children wanted to play quietly, they left them alone. Their infants seemed to be *securely attached* to their mothers. In the laboratory test, when their mothers left the room (on cue), the secure children were naturally somewhat upset, but when she returned, they cuddled up to her and then quickly settled down to play.

2. *The clingy.* During the home observations, some mothers were inconsistent in their reactions to their infants' signals. Sometimes they ignored their infants' signals, while at other times they were bossy and smothering. In the laboratory setting, their children displayed an *anxious/resistant* attachment to their mothers. When their mothers left the room, these infants were anxious and angry. They were equally ambivalent when she returned. One moment they would cling to her and the next they would angrily push her away.

3. *The skittish.* Some mothers had consistently rebuffed their infants' bids for comfort, especially for close bodily contact. Their infants formed an *avoidant* attachment to their mothers. When their mothers left the room, these infants seemed to take their mothers' departure in stride. When she returned, however, they generally studiously avoided her and pointedly directed all their attention toward their toys.

4. *The fickle.* In recent years, child psychologists have identified a fourth pattern (Main & Solomon, 1990). This pattern seems to arise when an infant's primary caregiver is depressed, disturbed, or verbally or physically abusive (Crittenden, 1988; Main & Hesse, 1990). These infants show a *disorganized/disoriented* pattern of attachment. They seem to lack a coherent strategy for managing anxiety. When their mothers leave, they show a mixture of anxious-ambivalent and avoidant behavior (Main & Solomon, 1990).

Researchers have found that in different cultures, parents and children differ in the kinds of attachments they form, that is, in the percentage of infants who are securely attached, clingy, skittish, and so forth. Perhaps these differences are due to "nature" (differences in temperament which exist from the start) or perhaps to "nurture" (to cultural differences in parents' childrearing techniques). Researchers have found that, in different cultures, newborns do seem to possess somewhat different personalities. In some cultures, newborns tend to possess sunny, mellow dispositions. In others, they are a great deal more energetic (Campos et al., 1983; Miyake, Chen, & Campos, 1985). Researchers have also found that, in different cultures, caretakers have very different attitudes about how affectionate and independent infants should be. American mothers, for example, generally are delighted when their babies are independent, talkative, and active (Caudill & Weinstein, 1969). It is common for mothers and infants to be separated for brief periods (Grossmann & Grossmann, 1981). Japanese mothers prefer quiet, contented babies. They prefer to have a close, emotionally intense relationship with them (Caudill & Weinstein, 1969). Japanese mothers are usually very physical with their children and stay in close, constant, physical contact with them. Mothers touch their infants to communicate with them, breast feed, carry them around on their backs, take baths, and sleep with them. Mother and child are rarely separated during the first months of life (Azuma et al., 1981; Lebra, 1976; Vogel, 1963). Typically, they do not even sleep in separate beds (Miyake, et al., 1985).

!Kung (African) children spend their first few years in almost constant close contact with their mothers. During the day, they are carried in a sling, skin-to-skin on the mother's hip, wherever the mother goes, at work or at play. At night, they sleep at her side. When the child is about two and a half years old, it will begin to be drawn into groups of children playing around the village (Shostak, 1981).

Psychiatrists Sudhir Kakar and John Ross (1986) poetically described the tight bonding that exist between Indian mothers and their infants:

> *We know . . . that from the moment of birth the Indian son is greeted and surrounded by direct, sensual body contact, by relentless physical ministrations. Constantly cuddled in the mother's arms, the son's experience of the mother's body is a heady one. When the infant is a few months old and able to rest on his stomach, he may be carried astride the mother's hip, his legs on each side of her body, as she goes about on visits to neighbors, to the market, to the fields and on other errands.*
> *. . . For many years the child will sleep at night with the mother in the same bed. . . . The mother's smell and bodily warmth and the texture of her skin, in a climate which ensures that a minimum or no clothing at all is worn by the young child, pervade the early sensory and sensuous experiences of most Indian men. It is an experience different from the more disengaged, less enveloping and stimulating lot of the Western boy. (pp. 186–187)*

Despite these cultural variations in *amount* of contact, the nature and quality of the contact between primary caregivers and their infants may be quite similar. Mothers in all cultures may be likely to kiss, nuzzle, nurse, comfort, clean, and respond to their children in much the same way (Hazan & Zeifman, in press).

In any case, perhaps as consequence of differences in both "nature" and "nurture," infants' and children's patterns of attachments often differ from culture to culture. In various cultures, differing percentages of children are classified as secure, anxious/resistant, avoidant, or disorganized/disoriented (van IJzendoorn & Kroonenberg, 1988). Researchers have assessed the attachment styles of children in *Africa* (Ainsworth, 1967; Kermoian & Leiderman, 1982; Konner, 1982); *America; China* (Li-Repac, 1982); *Germany* (Beller & Pohl, 1986; Lütkenhaus, Grossmann, & Grossmann, 1985); *Israel* (Sagi, et al., 1985); *Japan* (Miyake, Chen, & Campos, 1995; Takahashi, 1986); *Netherlands* (Goossens, 1986; Smith & Noble, 1987; van den Boom, Broekema, Leonard, & Kellenaers, 1987); and *Sweden* (Lamb, Hwang, Frodi, & Frodi, 1982). They document cultural differences in infants' typical attachment styles.

Social psychologists have argued that infants' early attachments are the forerunners of adult passionate attachments. Phillip Shaver and Cindy Hazan (1993) argued that infant's and toddler's early attachment patterns would be mirrored in their adult romances.

> *We predicted that love in adulthood would be similar to the kind of love an infant feels for his or her caregiver in terms of the importance of seeking and maintaining close physical proximity, relying on the partner's continued availability, turning*

*to the partner for comfort, being distressed by separations or threats to the relation-
ship, and so on. We also predicted that the three patterns of attachment identified
in infancy would be evident in the way adults think, feel, and behave in close
relationships. (p. 31)*

Erikson's Stage Theory

Developmental theorists have pointed out that, important as infancy is, young
people learn even more about passionate love and intimacy in adolescence. Erik
Erikson (1982) wrote that "anything that grows has a ground plan, and out of this
ground plan parts arise, each part having its special time of ascendancy" (p. 92).
Infants, children, adolescents, and adults face a continuing series of developmental
tasks (see Table 3.5). If loved and nurtured, infants develop a basic trust in the
universe. (In the previous section, we considered infants' first developmental task—
attachment (in Ainsworth's terms) or learning to trust (in Erikson's terminology).
But there is more learning to come. In early, middle and late childhood, children
learn to know their own minds, to have a sense of purpose, to take initiative, and
to work hard. The next two stages are those in which we are primarily interested.
In adolescence, teenagers must develop some sense of their own identity. Only when
they have formed a relatively stable, independent identity are they able to tackle the
next developmental task—to learn how to love someone and to become deeply
intimate with them. Mature relationships, then, according to Erikson, involve an
ability to balance intimacy and independence.

Neurophysiologists remind us that passionate love may also be fueled by pu-
bescent sexual and hormonal changes (Gadpaille, 1975; Money, 1980). Puberty and
sexual maturity may well bring a new depth to passion (Meyers & Berscheid, 1995).

Researchers provide some evidence in support of Erikson's theorizing (Bellew-
Smith & Korn, 1986; Orlofsky & Ginsburg, 1981; Tesch & Whitbourne, 1982.)

Erikson (1959) also argued that men and women may differ a bit in how easy
they find it to achieve independence/intimacy. He contended that as men mature,
they find it easy to achieve an independent identity; they experience more difficulty

TABLE 3.5   Major Stages in Psychosocial Development over the Life Span

Stages	Psychosocial Crisis
Infancy	Basic trust vs. basic mistrust
Early childhood	Autonomy vs. shame and doubt
Play age	Initiative vs. guilt
School age	Industry vs. inferiority
Adolescence	Identity vs. identity
Young adulthood	Intimacy vs. isolation
Adulthood	Generativity vs. stagnation
Old age	Integrity vs. despair

Based on Erikson (1982).

in learning to be intimate with those they love. Women have an easy time learning to be close to others; they have more trouble learning how to be independent. Other theorists would agree. Carol Gilligan (1982) pointed out that men are taught to take pride in being independent while women take pride in being close and nurturant. (See also Goleman, 1986; Hodgson & Fischer, 1979; Pollak & Gilligan, 1982; White et al., 1986).

Erikson's model, then, reminds us that if people are to have a close loving relationship with others, they must have learned how to be comfortable with both independence and closeness. Until they learn how to deal with both they are likely to encounter problems in their love affairs.

The Evidence

In this section, we will follow a somewhat unorthodox procedure. In our clinical practice, we have developed a "feel" for the way the secure, clingy, skittish, and so on, think, talk, feel, and behave. Thus, we will begin our discussion of each love schema with a literary quote or two—which we hope will give you the same sense of what the various types are like. Then we will move on to hard evidence. Researchers have found considerable evidence that people's love profiles (their skills at dealing with independence and closeness) are linked to their thoughts, feelings, and experiences in potentially passionate encounters.

The Secure

In Charles Baxter's (1993) novel *Shadow Play*, Ellen Palmer was charmed to discover that her nephew Wyatt had winning ways with women:

> Ellen watched apprehensively as the children grew. She had no feeling for parenthood, for rules or discipline, and all the books claimed that improvisation in parenting brought on seething resentment and ultimate disaster. All the same, improvisation was what the children got.
>
> . . . But as Wyatt grew, he seemed, to Ellen's pleasure and astonishment, to be a sweet and kindhearted kid. He worked in the hardware store, painted canvases on weekends, and brought his girlfriends home to meet his aunt. He was devoted to these girls, and he fell in love easily. He was one of those boys who was not only attracted to young women but who loved them as well. Girls loved how he loved them, and they swarmed around him, putting their hands in his long hair, and making offers to cook for him and to mend his socks. He had a girl named Tracy his junior year and another named Carrie his senior year, and Carrie, in particular, all but moved in with him. The house was full of noise and laughter and shouting and lovemaking and chatter. Ellen hadn't meant to nurture so much uproar, but there it was. These young women Wyatt sought out were proud and strong-willed—what Ellen noticed about them first was the way they stood, as straight as soldiers, and a particular way of looking around a room without fear—and it seemed that perhaps there was, after all, cause for optimism in what had happened between the sexes, at least in this one respect, that perhaps the young men and women liked each other

more than they had in her father's generation. No more angry stoicism, or prideful unexpressed resentment. (pp. 190–191)

Reseachers have found that men and women who are secure do fall passionately in love now and then. A steady personality does not guarantee smooth sailing in romantic waters, of course. Love is difficult for everyone. The vast majority of love affairs fail. Nonetheless, the secure do seem to do better than most at negotiating stable, companionate, intimate love relationships. (See Doherty et al., 1994; Hazan & Shaver, 1987; Mikulincer & Nachshon, 1991; and Singelis et al., 1995 for evidence in support of these contentions).

In one study, Elaine Hatfield and her students (Doherty et al., 1994), interviewed 300 men and women from the University of Hawaii. The students ranged in age from 17 to 62. They were members of four ethnic groups and possessed very different views of *individualism/collectivism*. The European Americans were most individualistic. The Japanese Americans and Pacific Islanders (Filipino, Hawaiian, and Samoan Americans) were intermediate in individualism/collectivism, and the Chinese were most collectivist in their beliefs. The four groups may have had different beliefs in general, but they were strikingly similar when it came to love. What mattered there was not the individual's ethnic group or his or her attitude toward individualism/collectivism, but his or her *Love Schemas* profile. The authors selected students who rated themselves as secure, clingy, or skittish and asked them to fill out the same *Passionate Love* scale and *Companionate Love* scale you filled out earlier (see Boxes 3.1 and 3.2). The authors found, as you might expect, that it was the clingy who generally loved most obsessively. They scored higher on the *PLS* than did any other group. The secure (the group in which we are interested here) were more temperate in their passion. And again, not surprisingly, the skittish were the least likely to have ever felt passionately about another.

A look at men's and women's *Companionate Love* scale scores adds a missing piece to the puzzle. Those who felt secure about love were most likely to companionately love their partners—they were more committed to them and their relationship was more intimate than was that of any other group. The clingy were intermediate in *CL* and, again, not surprisingly, it was the skittish who secured the lowest *CL* scores).

The Clingy

In *Cat's Eye*, the Canadian novelist Margaret Atwood (1989) described Susie's fatal attraction to Mr. Hrbik, her professor:

The teacher is Mr. Hrbik. He is in his mid-thirties, with dark thickly curled hair, a mustache, an eagle nose, and eyes that look almost purple, like mulberries. He has a habit of staring at you without saying anything, and, it seems, without blinking.
. . . Susie came out of Mr. Hrbik's office. "Hi, you guys," she said, trying for cheer. Her eyeshadow was smudged, her eyes pinkish. I'd been reading modern French novels and William Faulkner as well. I knew what love was supposed to be: obsession, with undertones of nausea. Susie was the sort of girl who would go for

this kind of love. She would be abject, she would cling and grovel. She would lie on the floor, moaning, hanging onto Mr. Hrbik's legs, her hair falling like blond seaweed over the black leather of his shoes (he would have his shoes on, being about to stalk out of the door). From this angle, Mr. Hrbik was cut off at the knees and Susie's face was invisible. She would be squashed by passion, obliterated.

I was not sorry for her, however. I was a little envious. (pp. 288 and 312)

Researchers find that those who are clingy are most vulnerable to "neurotic love." The clingy have low self-esteem, but idealize their romantic partners. They obsess about the other's feelings. They criticize their partners for their failure to make a commitment and to take care of them in the way they long to be cared for. They are so focused on what they long for from an affair that they are oblivious that others might have very different feelings and needs. They are addicted to the relationship—dependent. They are on an emotional roller coaster—elated one minute and anxious, frightened, and lonely the next. They have trouble finding a stable, committed, companionate relationship; their insatiable demands seem to drive others away. (For evidence in support of these propositions, see Bartholomew & Horowitz, 1991; Collins & Read, 1990; Daniels & Shaver, 1991; Feeney & Noller, 1990; Hazan & Shaver, 1987; Hindy, Schwartz, & Brodsky, 1989; Kunce & Shaver, 1991; Levy & Davis, 1988; Mikulincer & Nachshon, 1991; Shaver & Hazan, 1993; Simpson, 1990).

In one study, for example, Theodore Singelis and his colleagues (1995) interviewed American college students from a wide variety of ethnic groups. They found that the more clingy men and women acknowledged they were, the more susceptible they were to love's ecstatic heights and agonizing abysses (i.e., the higher their scores were on the *Passionate Love* scale). They experienced a great deal of joy in their love affairs but they suffered too.

The Skittish

In Alice Adams's (1993) novel *Almost Perfect* she described the difficulties Stella Blake, a young Mexican American woman, encountered when she fell in love with Richard Fallon. The first time she needed him, Richard ran:

He [Richard] is sitting at his desk, trying to draw (trying to think of something to draw) and waiting for the phone to ring. Nothing special, he just needs some distraction. Interruption. Although it is just as apt to be bad news.

And it is.

. . . . His answering machine clicks on, and he hears . . . Stella, Stella sobbing, her voice almost unrecognizable. "Richard, it's me. I had this terrible news. It's Prentice, my father. He—he's dead." More sobs. "Call me right away, okay?"

Jesus. All he needs. Stella on his hands like this. Tears, sobbing. Jesus. No control. Women like to cry.

But at the same time that he thinks of her so angrily, Richard's stomach clenches in sympathy for Stella, his Stella. Oh, poor Stella, and her father always such a shit to her, and now dead. Poor Stella! Tears come to his own eyes as he reaches for the phone to call her back.

And then does not. No reason to call her right away; for all she knows, he's out. Out of town, he could be.

. . . . He dials Andrew's number, gets Andrew's jaunty recorded message. Hi! In no mood for jauntiness, Richard hangs up.

He sits there fuming, breathing heavily. His morning ruined, ruined with women. All wanting too much. Oh Christ! their demands! (pp. 70–71)

Researchers have found that the skittish seem to fear romantic intimacy. They are pessimistic about love. They avoid intimate social contact, especially emotional confrontations. They focus their attention on their work or on nonsocial activities instead. They are uncomfortable with partners who disclose too much to them. They prefer uncommitted sexual relationships. Their love relationships rarely go well. Breakups are not terribly upsetting, however. The work of a variety of researchers leads us to these gloomy conclusions (Bartholomew & Horowitz, 1991; Collins & Read, 1990; Daniels & Shaver, 1991; Feeney & Noller, 1990; Hazan & Shaver, 1987; Hindy, Schwartz, & Brodsky, 1989; Kunce & Shaver, 1991; Mikulincer & Nachshon, 1991; Shaver & Hazan, 1993; Simpson, 1990).

Earlier, we mentioned that Singelis and his colleagues (1995) had interviewed American college students from a variety of ethnic groups. As one might expect, they found that men and women who were skittish about love shied away from any

Fear of Intimacy

Jennifer Berman (1990).

kind of passionate or affectionate involvement. They received fairly low scores on both the *Passionate Love* scale and the *Companionate Love* scale.

> *I loved them until they loved me.*
> —Dorothy Parker

The Fickle

The fickle lover—irresistibly drawn to the challenge of the unavailable—is easily recognizable. In this excerpt from *Money*, the English novelist Martin Amis (1984), comments on the sodden John Self's love affair with Selina Street:

> *Intriguingly enough, the only way I can make Selina actually want to go to bed with me is by not wanting to go to bed with her. It never fails. It really puts her in the mood. The trouble is, when I don't want to go to bed with her (and it does happen), I don't want to go to bed with her. When does it happen? When don't I want to go to bed with her? When she wants to go to bed with me. I like going to bed with her when going to bed with me is the last thing she wants. She nearly always does go to bed with me, if I shout at her a lot or threaten her or give her enough money. (pp. 142–143)*

As you might expect, the fickle person's love affairs do not go well. The research of Singelis and his colleagues (1995) makes it clear why fickle people's relationships are such a mess. Sometimes the fickle fall passionately in love. They receive intermediate scores on the *Passionate Love* scale. (Their reactions fell midway between the heedless passion of the clingy, the measured passion of the clingy and the sour caution of the casual and uninterested.) In addition, the fickle were less likely than any other group to have ever managed an affectionate, companionate relationship. The more fickle they were, the lower they scored on the *Companionate Love* scale. They were less likely than any other group to have ever been involved in a loving, committed, intimate relationship. The more fickle people were, the less joy and the more anxiety, sadness, and anger they experienced in their relationships. Nothing seems to work out for the fickle.

The Casual

Casual affairs can often be fun. When they were in their twenties, two great Southern statesmen, James H. Hammond and Thomas J. Withers, penned antic and wanton letters to one another. This exchange, written on May 15, 1926, is typical:

> *Dear Jim:*
> *I got your Letter this morning about 8 o'clock, from the hands of the Bearer. . . . I was sick as the Devil, when the Gentleman entered the Room, and I have been so during most of the day. About 1 o'clock I swallowed a huge mass of Epsom Salts—and it will not be hard to imagine that I have been at dirty work since. I feel partially relieved—enough to write a hasty dull letter.*

I feel some inclination to learn whether you yet sleep in your Shirt-tail, and whether you yet have the extravagant delight of poking a punching a writhing Bedfellow with your long fleshen pole—the exquisite touches of which I have often had the honor of feeling? Let me say unto thee that unless thou changest former habits in this particular thou wilt be represented by every future Chum as a nuisance. And, I pronounce it, with good reason too. Sir, you roughen the downy Slumbers of your Bedfellow—by such hostile—furious lunges as you are in the habit of making at him—when he is least prepared for defence against the crushing force of a Battering Ram. Without reformation my imagination depicts some awful results for which you will be held accountable—and therefore it is, that I earnestly recommend it. Indeed it is encouraging an assault and battery propensity, which needs correction—& uncorrected threatens devastation, horror & bloodshed, etc. . . . (cited in Duberman, 1989, pp. 155–156)

When people are young, it is appropriate to be casual about love. In maturity, for example, both Hammond and Withers seemed secure in their ability to love. Both settled into committed, permanent relationships. They remained lifelong friends.

Of course, if people aren't in tune—if one is cavalier and the other is serious about, say, a marriage—things aren't likely to work out so well. In this excerpt from his book *Inside the Helmet*, Peter King (1993) discusses the failure of Jimmy Johnson's marriage (Johnson is the coach who led the Dallas Cowboys the two Super Bowl championships):

There are some key ingredients for NFL head coaches. No. 1: Jettison all influences and experiences that don't have to do with winning. Johnson divorced his wife, Linda Kay, after taking the Cowboys job because they'd grown apart and because he didn't want family stuff getting in the way of the biggest job of his life. . . . He doesn't remember birthdays, not even his two sons', and doesn't do Christmas. But he's stern about it. Don't tell me how to live my life, his glare tells you, and I won't tell you how to live yours. . . .

"I'm a selfish person, very selfish," he said once. "But I admit it. People know who I am. I have to do this to satisfy myself. I wouldn't be happy doing anything else, and I have to do it my way, all the way. Sometimes it hits me. I'll say to myself, 'Why am I like this? Why am I not doing a normal job and going home to the wife and kids every night for dinner at 6?' I don't know exactly why. I do know this: I have to do it. I'd be bad at living any other way."

He doesn't ask to be understood. . . . You cross him, you pose any threat to his winning, you attack his dream? "I'll crush you like a squirrel in the road. People don't realize what they are dealing with here. This is my life. A lot of people might say, 'This is s——, the life you're leading.' Hey, I'm not typical. This is what I am. Fortunately, my boys understand. If they didn't, I couldn't handle it. If they said: 'This is s——! Why don't we have a real father?' I couldn't handle it. But they understand nobody's going to throw a brick in my way, and if anybody tries, I'll kick their butt." (King, 1993, pp. 4–6)

In the study we described earlier, researchers (Singelis et al., 1995) found that the more casual college men and women were about relationships, the less likely they were to have experienced either passionate love or companionate love. Love, for them, was not a source of joy.

The Uninterested

In *The Stranger,* French novelist Albert Camus (1989) recounted this tepid encounter between Meursault, the hero, and Marie:

> That evening Marie came by to see me and asked me if I wanted to marry her. I said it didn't make any difference to me and that we could if she wanted to. Then she wanted to know if I loved her. I answered the same way I had the last time, that it didn't mean anything but that I probably didn't love her. "So why marry me, then?" she said. I explained to her that it didn't really matter and that if she wanted to, we could get married. Besides, she was the one who was doing all the asking and all I was saying was yes. Then she pointed out that marriage was a serious thing. I said "No." (p. 52–53)

A second, real-life example: In the late nineteenth century, Swedish playwright August Strindberg wrote to a friend, detailing his needs in a wife. He got right to the point:

> Help me . . . to obtain a young woman who has recently had a child; by a more or less unknown father who has skulked off. But a young woman with hip-muscles and breasts; an ex-maidservant would do as long as she has served in a superior household and has upper-class sympathies, so that she won't ally herself with the rustic farm-hands and skivvies against me, for I count myself upper-class and am happy to be thus connected. If she looks good, so much the better. Not above 25. Careful about her appearance and clean. She will be my housekeeper and I shall bring up her children in our home, and take care of the mother of course. I must have children because I can't work without the sound of children's voices. A whore would serve the same purpose but they are so unfaithful that she'd be false to me and wouldn't enjoy the loneliness. The best thing would be a fallen upper-class girl, but those bitches have all the instincts of lesbians and neglect their children. Above all I want a woman who loves children and wants to rise in the social scale and not sink. . . . By the beginning of October my novel will be ready. (Meyer, 1987, p. 178)

Not surprisingly, those who are uninterested in relationships are extremely unlikely to have experienced much passionate love or companionate love. The disinterested are simply uninterested in getting committed or even getting very involved in a very intimate relationship (Singelis et al., 1995). It is rather an odd question to ask how such love affairs "work out." The uninterested may be barely aware that they are involved in a relationship. Nonetheless, to the extent that the uninterested do pay attention, they may find every reason to stay uninterested. Their affairs bring them little joy and provoke a great deal of sadness and anger.

Conclusions: The Spread of Passion

Until recently, most cross-cultural theorists had assumed that passionate love was a Western phenomenon and that other societies were rarely infected with the "love bug." They assumed that it was only in the West would we find young men and women in love with love. Only in the West would young people often report being in love right at the moment, report having experienced intensely passionate love, or insist on marrying for love. The sparse data that we have unearthed, however, challenges such easy stereotypes. Tentatively, the existing research forces us to conclude that, throughout the modern world, people turn out to be surprisingly similar in the way they experience passionate love. So far, the Western or "modern" model of passionate love appears to be the best general model for understanding passionate love worldwide, and, in fact, it is the only model scientists currently possess. People throughout the modern world, for example, seem to be equally susceptible to love and to experience it with the same fervor. People's love schemas seem to affect men's and women's susceptibility to love in a variety of cultural and ethnic groups. When it comes to passionate love, personality appears to be at least as important as cultural identity. But the cross-cultural study of passionate love is in its infancy. We suspect that it will not be long until scientists from other, more "exotic" places begin to challenge these easy conclusions about love's universality. And more power to them! Once research begins to be conducted in the most traditional cultures—for example, those of China, Iran, Saudi Arabia and the other Arab countries, Pakistan, Bangladesh, and the nations of Africa—we are hopeful that we will begin to understand a great deal more about the dynamics of passionate love throughout the world. In this text, we have tried to highlight places where the existing research is primitive or nonexistent, in the hopes of inspiring young researchers to begin to provide some answers. No message can be clearer from this book than that fascinating and important work remains to be done, to tell us more of why and how peoples of different societies fall wildly in love.

Chapter 4

Sex: Then and There

"What is love?" . . . [I end by] confessing that, in the case of romantic love, I don't really know. If forced against a brick wall to face a firing squad who would shoot if not given the correct answer, I would whisper "It's about 90% sexual desire as yet not sated."

—Ellen Berscheid

Are passionate love and sexual desire the same thing? Thirty years ago, when Ellen Berscheid and we began our research together, we weren't certain. Some social commentators insisted that the two were one.

Others insisted that the two were very different. In the eighteenth century, the Marquis de Sade (1797/1968) violently opposed the equation of love and pleasure: "I do not want a woman to imagine that I owe her anything because I soil myself on top of her. . . . I have never believed that from the junction of two bodies could arise the junction of two hearts: I can see great reasons for scorn and disgust in this physical junction, but not a single reason for love." (p. 148)

In the Victorian era, romantic love was considered to be a delicate, spiritual feeling—the antithesis of crude, animal lust. Freudians, of course, mocked such pretensions. They irritated romantics by insisting that chaste love was simply a sublimated form of carnal love, which lay bubbling just below the surface.

What about today? In the West, most college students make a sharp distinction between "being in love" (which embodies sexual feelings) and "loving" someone (which is not necessarily associated with sexual desire). Ellen Berscheid and her colleagues (Meyers & Berscheid, 1995) found that most students assumed that although you could "love" someone platonically, you could only be "in love" with someone you were sexually attracted to and desired sexually. They concluded: "Thus, our findings suggest that although sexuality may not be a central feature of love, it is most definitely a central feature of the state of being in love" (p. 24). Most of us understand the distinction between passionate and companionate love. When

Ingrid Bergman told an ardent friend that although she loved him, she was not *in* love with him, he understood the difference. He committed suicide (Leamer, 1986). In a national survey, Andrew Greeley (1991) interviewed newly married couples who said they were still in the "falling in love" stage of marriage. He found that passionate love is a highly sexual state. He described the falling in love stage of marriage this way: "When one is in love, one is absorbed, preoccupied, tense and intense, and filled with a sexual longing which permeates the rest of existence, making it both glorious and exhausting. . . . Those who are falling in love seem truly to be by love possessed." (pp. 122–124)

In the end, we concluded that passionate love and sexual desire are "kissing cousins." Passionate love was defined as "a longing for union," whereas sexual desire was defined as "a longing for *sexual* union" (Hatfield & Rapson, 1987b). Today, this debate seems settled. As Susan and Clyde Hendrick (1987b) noted:

> *It is apparent to us that trying to separate love from sexuality is like trying to separate fraternal twins: they are certainly not identical, but, nevertheless, they are strongly bonded.*
> *. . . Love and sexuality are strongly linked to each other and to both the physical and spiritual aspects of the human condition. For romantic personal relationships, sexual love and loving sexuality may well represent intimacy at its best. (pp. 282 and 293)*

There is some experimental evidence in support of this contention (Regan, 1995; Regan & Berscheid, in press).

Although passionate love and sexual desire might be intimately linked in nature, in reality, culture surely has a powerful impact on how likely young couples are to link passionate love, sexual desire, and sexual *expression*.

In Chapter 3, for example, we read of Lester Frank Ward's courtship of the woman who would someday become his wife. Wooing and passionate love were intertwined through poetic exclamations of their closeness. But they courted in 1860, during the heyday of supposed Victorian prudery. Would their passionate words of love lead to sex? On that night wherein "his girl" proclaimed to Ward that "I love this mouth, I love those dear eyes, I love this head," it was getting very late. Carl Degler (1980), the historian who excavated the Ward diaries, went on:

> *At around 3:00 A.M., when they became sleepy, they arranged the chairs in such a way that they could lie lengthwise facing each other and he opened his shirt, placing her hand on his bare chest. She said she thought she might be doing something wrong, but significantly, she did not stop. "As we lay in this position," he noted, "the cocks crowed." (pp. 21–22)*

Things continued in this vein for several months. By early 1861, "their physical attraction to one another had become so strong that it began to worry them."

> *"I had a very affectionate time with the girl, kissing her almost all over and loving her very deeply and she does me." Two weeks later Ward referred to a "very secret time" with her. "I kissed her on her soft breasts, and took too many liberties with her sweet person, and we are going to stop. It is a very fascinating practice and fills us with very sweet, tender, and familiar sentiments, and consequently makes us happy." They talked about their fear that "we might become so addicted in that direction that we might go too deep and possibly confound ourselves by the standards of virtue." Even when he was not with her, he dreamed about her and during the day fantasized about "kissing her sweet breasts and sleeping in her arms." A week later he characteristically, if enigmatically wrote, "I slept in her arms; yes, I lay with her, but did nothing wrong." (p. 22)*

Despite these powerful feelings, their relationship was not settled. She continued to see other young men, which drove him into intense jealousy. Eventually they returned fully to their love affair. One night after that happened:

> *". . . closely held in loving arms we lay, embraced, and kissed all night (not going to bed until five in the morning). We have never acted in such a way before. All that we did I shall not tell here, but it was all very sweet and loving and nothing infamous," he assured himself. By the end of that year of rather steady courtship little restraint was left on their emotions. "When I arrived at the house of sweetness, she received me in her loving arms and pressed me to her honey-form, and our lips touched and we entered Paradise together. . . . That evening and night we tasted the joys of love and happiness which only belong to a married life." Early the next year, in 1862, they were married. (pp. 22–23)*

By the standards of nineteenth-century America, these excerpts from Ward's diaries are unusually explicit when it comes to the physical and sexual side of love. Yet by our standards, though they are wonderfully sweet, they seem modest, even decorous, and somewhat quaint. This reminds us of how difficult it was not so long ago for people to talk about sex, even privately. This point is capped by the fact that Ward felt constrained to write his diary in French! This probably accounts, Degler thought, "for [Ward's] uncommon explicitness of language." Nonetheless, Degler went on to state that "there is no reason to believe that the behavior he described was rare or exceptional" (p. 23).

Ward had no trouble describing passionate love, but brave as he was, writing about sex did not flow easily. Sex is not a topic about which most people in most ages have been relaxed; it is a subject of complexity that engenders tension, intensity, fascination, and tremendous controversy.

Of course, in some cultures, there would be no chance for such sexual feelings to be translated into sexual behavior. Young men and women may be strictly chaperoned and married to whomever their parents and kin prefer. So, although passionate love, sexual desire, and sexual activity tend to be so intertwined, that linkage is not inevitable. It is a very long and winding road from the troubadour to Lester

Frank Ward to Madonna II. Evolutionary psychologists, historians, and cross-cultural theorists have speculated about the impact of culture, ethnicity, and gender on sexual attitudes, feelings, and behavior. We now consider some of this research.

Evolutionary Perspectives

> *Why does a woman have to be beautiful rather than intelligent? Because men can see better than they can think.*
>
> —*Eva Heller*

In Chapters 1 and 2, we reviewed evolutionary psychologists' speculations that men and women are programmed to desire somewhat different things in brief affairs and in long-lasting sexual relationships. According to David Buss and Schmitt (1993), men and women are genetically programmed to exhibit the following differences: Men should have more and more creative and varied sexual fantasies than do women (Ellis & Symons, 1990). They should find erotica (pornography) more appealing than do women (Ehrlichman & Eichenstein, 1992). In *casual sexual encounters*, men should be eager to engage in sexual relations with a wide variety of women,

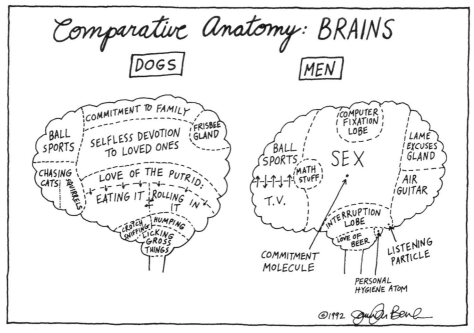

Comparative Anatomy

Jennifer Berman, 1992.

in a wide array of circumstances. Women should be far more cautious. Women should be willing to risk a sexual encounter only when it is profitable (if they choose to pursue a short-term strategy) or if it seems likely to lead to a serious long-term relationship (if they take the longer view) (Buss & Schmitt, 1993). *In serious, monogamous, relationships,* however, men's and women's sexual desires and behavior should be similar.

General Critiques

Many historians, anthropologists, sociologists, and psychologists have sharply criticized the evolutionary approach. Sociobiologists themselves acknowledge that probably the main way in which *Homo sapiens* differ from their rivals is in their unrivaled ability to adapt—to change themselves and their worlds. In different times and places, men and women have been forced to adapt to very different social realities. Cultural gender roles provide a clear guide for how men and women are supposed to think, feel, and behave; generally, men and women conform, behaving as they are "supposed" to. Men and women have different attitudes toward casual sex, these critics continue, not because they are propelled by ancient genetic codes, but because they are responding to different sociocultural realities. For most of human history, men and women who indulged in casual sex were likely to face very different consequences.

In this excerpt from a short story of a young Mexican girl, Sandra Cisneros (1992) searingly depicts how much women have traditionally had to lose from a single casual sexual encounter. A young Mexican woman meets Chaq, a drifter who claims to be Chaq Uxmal Paloquín, descended from an ancient line of Mayan kings. He makes love to her. At first, she takes it lightly. Then she discovers it is she who is to pay.

> The truth is, it wasn't a big deal. It wasn't any deal at all. I put my bloody panties inside my T-shirt and ran home hugging myself. . . . I know I was supposed to feel ashamed, but I wasn't ashamed. . . . Bit by bit the truth started to seep out like a dangerous gasoline. . . . When Abuelita found out I was going to *das a luz,* she cried until her eyes were little, and blamed Uncle Lalo, and Uncle Lalo blamed this country . . . Abuelita took me out of school when my uniform got tight around the belly and said it was a shame I wouldn't be able to graduate with the other eighth graders. . . . I could hear Abuelita and Uncle Lalo talking in low voices in the kitchen as if they were praying the rosary, how they were going to send me to Mexico to San Dionisio de Tlaltepango, where I have cousins. (pp. 112–117)

In societies around the world, girls and women are often severely punished for sexual dalliance. Those who dare to show their faces or to look at or talk to men may be beaten. Those who risk premarital sex may be killed (Abu-Lughod, 1986; Counts, 1991; Lateef, 1990; Lewin, 1994). Adulterous wives are often beaten or killed. Barbara Smuts (1991) observes:

In a variety of cultures, women have had their genitals cut out or sewn together to discourage sexual activity; their movements curtailed by mutilation of the feet, the threat of rape, and confinement to guarded harems; their noses bitten off in cultur-ally sanctioned responses to adultery; and their bodies beaten and mutilated during gang rapes considered a normal part of adolescent male sexuality. . . . Assertive female sexuality leads to abandonment of wives among the Yanomamos and to gang rape among the Mundurucus. . . . In some cultures, force is considered an integral part of normal marital sex; the man's struggle to overcome a frightened and resistant woman heightens his sexual satisfaction. . . . Because of these and other similar practices, women associate sex with danger. (p. 29)

In such tyrannical cultures, she points out, women are forced to respond to men's sexual needs and desires, not their own. Women's sexual feelings are so influenced by repression and the fear of violent coercion that, in most societies, it is impossible to identify the "intrinsic" nature of female sexuality. Thus, "it seems premature, for example, to attribute the relative lack of female interest in sexual variety to women's biological nature alone in the face of overwhelming evidence that women are consistently beaten for promiscuity and adultery" (p. 29). Smuts points out that evidence from nonhuman primates and from women in societies with relatively few coercive constraints on female sexual behavior, such as the !Kung San or modern Scandinavia, makes it clear that under permissive conditions women are far more active and assertive sexually and far more excited by sexual variety (see also Hrdy, 1981; Shostak, 1981).

As cultural historians, living through the 1950s, 1960s, and so forth, we have witnessed breathtaking changes in men's and women's romantic and sexual behav-ior (more about this in Chapter 5). In the 1950s, Elaine Hatfield recalls her mother casually referring to the four-year-old "retarded boy" down the street. Why re-tarded? In hushed whispers: "Gertie said he pulled down his pants." Elaine recalls her father (a policeman) telling her mother that Sophie, a little girl on his beat, had been "ruined." Why? She had been molested by an uncle. By the 1960s, the Sexual Revolution had changed all this, or at least people pretended it had. By the late 1960s, Dick Rapson was invited by one of his students to participate in a sexual triad with her and her boyfriend. When he thanked her but politely declined, she deliv-ered a withering lecture: "I'm so disappointed in you. I thought you were someone who cared about students; someone who was creative and ready to challenge con-vention. But no, you turn out to be just like all the rest."

By the 1990s, this has changed yet again. Only the most foolhardy of professors would even *think* about dating a student, much less participating in group sex with two of them. Only the most politically incorrect of students would even think of asking. Times are very different. Today, Antioch College has passed legislation decreeing that men and women must secure willing verbal consent for each sexual act. In a Freshman orientation class, Karen Hall hammered the point home. "Each step of the way you have to ask . . . . If you want to take her blouse off, you have to ask. If you want to touch her breast, you have to ask. If you want to move your hand down to her genitals, you have to ask. If you want to put your finger inside her, you have to ask" (Gross, 1993, p. A1 and Y7).

One student reassured his fellow students that the new policy was less daunting than it seemed. "You don't have to say, 'Is it O.K. to touch you here?'" . . . "You can say, 'Is this cool? Does this feel good?' You can make it more of an erotic thing" (Gross, 1993, p. Y7).

No one living from the conforming 1950s, through the 1960s "Age of Aquarius," and on to today could fail to notice that as social norms change so do young men and women's preferences, desires, and behavior. So it is not surprising that, since throughout most of history it is women who have been forced to pay the price for sexual dalliance, women that tend to approach casual romantic encounters warily (Prather, 1990).

As therapists in a multicultural community, we have often thought that if sociobiologists were to listen to many of our sessions, their conviction that men and women are very, very different would be shattered. In one session, a deeply religious Mormon woman, every inch the impeccable businesswoman, casually mentions that the first time she was allowed to leave home, she "went wild," carousing with dozens of boys. "Of course, I can't afford to do that any more, but still . . ." she recounts wistfully. Sociobiologists would see that in numerous marriages, it is the woman who pleads with her husband to stir up a little more interest in sex; it is the man who sits entombed like King Tut in his bedroom, watching a flickering television screen.

Sociobiological Critiques

Some evolutionary psychologists have criticized the sociobiological theories of Buss and his colleagues as being "male centered." They point out that throughout history, social commentators (generally male) have pontificated about what men and women are "really" like. Alas, their visions have been remarkably inconsistent. In Victorian England, for example, "pure" women were supposed to be angelically chaste, passive, and sexually innocent. Dr. William Acton (1865), a man very much of his times, observed: "The majority of women (happily for them) are not very much troubled with sexual feelings of any kind. What men are habitually, women are only exceptionally" (p. 133). (Some sociobiological theories are based on this view of women: passive, nurturant, and sexually apathetic.)

In the Renaissance, Pope Innocent VIII put his imprimatur on the *Malleus Maleficarum*, which presented a very different view of women's sexuality:

> *A woman is beautiful to look upon, contaminating to the touch, and deadly to keep . . . a foe to friendships . . . a necessary evil, a natural temptation . . . a domestic danger . . . an evil of nature, painted with fair colors . . . a liar by nature . . . [She] seethes with anger and impatience in her whole soul. . . . There is no wrath above the wrath of a woman. . . . Since [women] are feebler both in mind and body, it is not surprising that they should come under the spell of witchcraft [more than men].*

> *. . . A woman is more carnal than a man. . . . All witchcraft come from carnal lust,*
> *which is in women insatiable. (cited in Hunt, 1959, p. 177)*

A few sociobiologists' visions smack more of *this* hostile view of women.

Recently, scientists have begun to view both men and women as being far more similar than different and both as sexual beings. Some of the newer sociobiological theories reflect this reality. Sarah Hrdy (1981), for example, argued that in the course of evolution, both men and women should have been programmed to be intelligent, competitive, sexually assertive, and desirous of sexual variety. The argument as to why men should be programmed to desire sexual variety has been spelled out. But why should women desire such variety? Hrdy argued that to be "successful" at producing as many superior, surviving children as possible, women face a duo of tasks: They must somehow can manage to have sexual relations with a dominant, genetically superior man (regardless of whether or not he is their husband) so they can pass those genes on to their offspring. They must find a way to protect those offspring. Men may have a vested interest in protecting and caring for children that they think might be their own; they have an equal interest in wiping out their rivals' progeny. Hrdy points out: "A female's success at tapping the services of males or forestalling males from harming her offspring will often depend on her capacity to forge sexual relationships with these males, and thereby confuse the issue of paternity" (p. 158).

If women have sexual relations with a number of men, each of those men may be motivated to protect and provide for the children that could, after all, be their own. At the very least, they might hesitate before brutalizing or killing them. Thus, Hrdy concluded, in the course of evolution, women, like men, should have been programmed to be intelligent, passionate, sexually assertive, and adventuresome, as well as nurturant in some situations and competitive in others. (For other sociobiological perspectives on these issues, see Fausto-Sterling, 1986.)

While evolutionary theorists have been interested in cultural universals, historians and cross-cultural researchers have looked at how people actually behave and have focused on human variability. They remind us that in different times and places, people have had very different sexual values and experiences. Today, of course, the gentle winds of change are wafting throughout the world.

Historical Perspectives

Historians make it clear that sexual attitudes have varied greatly from culture to culture and from one era to another. The sage Vatsyayana advised men and women to marry for love; the Medieval church condemned such sinful indulgence. The early Egyptians practiced birth control and some Polynesians practiced infanticide; the classical Greeks rewarded couples who were willing to conceive. The Eskimos considered it hospitable to share their wives with visitors; the Muslims jealously locked their wives and concubines away in harems. Sumerian and Babylonian temples were staffed by priests, priestesses, and sacred prostitutes; the ancient Hebrews stoned "godless" prostitutes. Hellenes idealized the pure, sexual love between older men and young boys; the Aztecs punished homosexuality by tying men to logs, disemboweling them, covering them with ash, and incinerating them (Tannahill, 1980). Cultural values and practices can and have varied enormously. To explore just how they have been transformed over time, let us take a leisurely look at two of these very different cultures—Chinese and Anglo American. In so doing, we may be better able to illustrate the impact of culture on the very physical, emotional, and chemical universe of sex.

The East: China

China is an ancient culture. The Peking Man, a forerunner of early humans, lived approximately 578,000 years ago. China's archeological cultural record begins 5,000 years ago in the Hongshan (Red Mountain) dynasty. Its historical record begins 4,000 years ago in the Xia (or First Dynasty). The oldest Chinese medical texts on sexuality go back two thousand years.

Historians divide traditional Chinese history into three periods: the Formative Age (Prehistory to 206 B.C.), the Early Empire (206 B.C. to A.D. 960), and the Later Empire (960 to 1911). The Chinese historian Fang Fu Ruan (1991), on whose work we will focus in this section, has written that Chinese attitudes toward sex were generally positive for the first 4,000 years of their history. In the Late Empire (1,000 years ago), however, Chinese attitudes began to change, gradually becoming more and more negative and repressive.

Classical Sex
The earliest Chinese sexual attitudes were shaped by folk religions, Confucianism, Taoism, and Buddhism. In all traditions, Ruan (1991) explained, the concept of Yin-Yang was critically important:

> *According to Yin-Yang philosophy, all objects and events are the products of two elements, forces, or principles: Yin [the female force], which is negative, passive, weak, and destructive, and Yang [the male force], which is positive, active, strong, and constructive.*
>
> *. . . The Chinese have used the words Yin and Yang to refer to sexual organs and sexual behavior for several thousand years. Thus "Yin Fu" ("the door of Yin") means vulva, "Yin Dao" ("the passageway of Yin") means vagina, and "Yang Ju" ("the organ of Yang") means penis. The combination of these words into the phrases "Huo Yin Yang" or "Yin Yang Huo He," or "the union or combination of Yin and Yang," describes the act of sexual intercourse.*
>
> *. . . In general, the Yin-Yang doctrine supported men's higher social status, since not only masculinity but also light, good fortune and all that is desirable were associated with Yang, while darkness, evil, and femininity were associated with Yin. (pp. 11–12)*

Archaeologists have unearthed medical texts on sexuality dating back to 168 B.C. These texts, *Ten Questions and Answers, Methods of Intercourse between Yin and Yang*, and *Lectures on the Super Tao in the World: Seven Injuries and Eight Advantages*, make it clear that the ancients assumed that sexual pleasure was one of the great joys of life. Classical scholars also possessed a great deal of scientific information about sexual response. For example, the fourth-century classic, *Secret Instructions Concerning the Jade Chamber*, provided information concerning the selection of sexual partners, foreplay, and positions for intercourse. They taught men and women how to identify the stage their partner had reached in the sexual response cycle:

> [The Yellow Emperor asked:] "How can I become aware of the joyfulness of the women?
>
> Replied the Immaculate Girl: There are five signs, five desires, and ten movements. By looking at these changes you will become aware of what is happening in her body. The first of the five signs is called "reddened face"; if you see this you slowly unite with her. The second is called "breasts hard and nose perspiring"; then slowly insert the jade stalk [penis]. The third is called "throat dry and saliva blocked"; then slowly agitate her. The fourth is called "slippery vagina"; then slowly go in more deeply. The fifth is called "the genitals transmit fluid" [female ejaculation]; then slowly withdraw from her.
>
> . . . The Immaculate Girl said: "Through the five desires, one is made aware of the woman's response, or what she wants you to do to her. First, if she catches her breath, it means that she wants to make love with you. Second, if her nose and mouth are dilated, it means that she wants you to insert your penis. Third, if she embraces you tightly, it means that she is very stimulated and excited. Fourth, if her perspiration flows and dampens her dress, it means that she wants to have her orgasm soon. Fifth, if her body straightens and her eyes close, it means she has already been satisfied. (Ruan, 1991, p. 43–44)

These early physicians obviously were careful observers. Their descriptions of the stages of sexual response sound much like those of Alfred Kinsey and his associates (1948 and 1953) and of William Masters and Virginia Johnson (1966).

In ancient China, courtly love and sexual activity—homosexual and heterosexual—were considered virtuous, among both rulers and their subjects (Hinsch, 1990). Vincent Gil (1992) observed:

> The surviving literature of the Spring-Autumn Period (770–745 B.C.), the Warring States Period (475–221 B.C.), and of the Chou and Han dynasties (206 B.C.–A.D. 220) indicates that homosexuality was accepted by the royal courts and its custom widespread among the nobility. . . . The dynastic record is one, then, of general tolerance for the male homosexual, and an amoral if not moral construction of the lifestyle itself. (p. 570)

In early China, lesbianism, which was sometimes called *mojingzi* (mirror grinding), was celebrated in literature and art. In households where there were many wives, concubines, slaves and servants, it was taken for granted. Fang Ruan and Vern Bullough (1992) observed:

> *Several of the ancient Chinese sexual handbooks include positions involving two women and one man in which lesbian acts comprise part of the sexual activity. Some of the illustrations show lesbian activity. . . .*
>
> *Lesbian relationships are also celebrated in Chinese literature and art. Perhaps the best known example of lesbian love is in the play,* Lien-hsiang-pan [Loving the Fragrant Companion] *written by the Ming author Li Yu (1611–1680). This describes the love of a young married woman for a younger unmarried woman whom she met while visiting a temple. The married woman, Shih, falls in love with the beautiful and talented Yun-hua, and promises the girl that she shall try to have her made a concubine of her husband so that they will always be together. Her scheme ultimately succeeds to the delight of not only Yen-hua and Shih but also Shih's husband. (p. 218)*

In the same century that Christian theologians were preaching abstinence as the key to salvation, Chinese philosophers and physicians were advocating sexual gratification as the way to health and longevity. Taoist classics, for example, assured men they could increase sexual pleasure, improve health, and live thousands of years (if not forever) if they had sexual relations with young, virginal boys and girls or with multiple partners—provided they precisely followed recommended ritual practices. In *Secret Instructions Concerning the Jade Chamber,* for example, Tao sexologists recommended:

> *Now men who wish to obtain great benefits do well in obtaining women who don't know the Way. They also should initiate virgins (into sex), and their facial color will come to be like (the facial color of) virgins. However, (man) is only distressed by (a woman) who is not young. If he gets one above 14 or 15 but below 18 or 19, it is most beneficial. However, the highest (number of years) must not exceed 30. Those who, though not yet 30, have already given birth, cannot be beneficial (to the man). The masters preceding me, who transmitted the Way to each other, lived to be 3,000 years old. Those who combine this (method) with (use of) medicines can become immortal. (Ruan, 1991, p. 57)*

In Taoist sex manuals, sexual intercourse was often described as a battle. Men should try to defeat their enemies (women) by keeping themselves under strict control. They should be careful not to "squander" their *yang* essence in ejaculation. They should try to excite their partner so that she will "surrender" her *yin* essence in orgasm. Men could then absorb this source of power. Tao Hongjing (A.D. 452–536), in *Achieving Longevity and Immorality by Regaining the Vitality of Youth* suggested the following sexual regimen:

> *Changing of partners can lead to longevity and immortality. If a man unites with one woman only, the Yin chi [vital energy] is feeble and the benefit small. For the*

Tao of the Yang is modeled on Fire, that of the Yin on Water, and Water can subdue Fire, the Yin can disperse the Yang, and use it unceasingly . . . so that the latter becomes depleted, and instead of assistance to the repair and regeneration (of the Body) this is loss. But if a man can couple with twenty women and yet have no emission, he will be fit and of perfect complexion when in old age. . . . When the store of ching [reproductive essence] sinks low, illnesses come, and when it is altogether used up, death follows. (Ruan, 1991, p. 38)

In *Prescriptions Worth a Thousand Pieces of Gold for Emergencies*, the ancient Taoists promised: "If one can copulate with twelve women without once emitting semen, one will remain young and handsome forever. If a man can copulate with 93 women and still control himself, he will attain immortality" (Ruan, 1991, p. 58).

Unfortunately, these techniques for insuring immortality seemed not to have worked very well. Mythology may claim that the ancient Chinese lived exceptionally long lives, but the anthropological evidence indicates that, until recently, most people generally lived only into their early thirties (Chang, 1977).

Turning Points

About one thousand years ago, during the Sung dynasty, Chinese attitudes toward sexuality began to change (Ruan, 1991). The Neo-Confucianists gained political and religious power. Men were considered to be far superior to women. Displays of love outside of marriage were forbidden, erotic art and literature were burned.

Making Love Is Insanity

When the People's Republic of China was established in 1949, Communist officials tried to impose even tighter controls on "inappropriate" sexual activity. On a visit to Beijing, John Money (1977) reported: "I came across a slogan: 'Making love is a mental disease that wastes time and energy'" (p. 544). Gil (1992) noted:

A puritanical, if not heavy-handed, sexual "primness" became firmly established. . . . This included a denial of romantic love, the affirmation of the absolute role of the collective over the individual as a basic tenet toward which one should direct any affections. The Great Leap Forward demanded, in communist parlance, the "renunciation of the heart." Party policy deliberately constructed an altruism which sought (for every man and woman) hard work during the day, without being "deflected or confused" by love, sexual desire, or any strivings for private happiness. (p. 571)

M. L. Ng and M. P. Lau (1990) have noted that many modern-day Chinese sexual superstitions can be traced to the early Yin-Yang doctrine—that is, the beliefs that men should try to retain semen; that nocturnal emission, masturbation, and homosexuality are unhealthy practices; and that it is unwise to have intercourse at certain times or in certain environments.

Chinese Whispers: Misunderstandings in Passion

In China today, there is almost no sex education. Most couples are ignorant about the basic mechanics of sex. In 1988, China's top leader, Deng Xiaoping, suggested that those who published pornography deserved the death penalty (Ruan, 1991, p. 103). Currently, it is illegal to disseminate sexually explicit material. Publishers of such material can be sentenced to life imprisonment.

Fox Butterfield (1982) reported this conversation with Hua, a member of the Sports Commission:

> When I asked if she had ever experienced an orgasm, Hua's face furrowed into a frown. . . . "What is that?" she asked in reply. She had never had any such sensation. Intercourse, as she knew it, consumed three or four minutes and ended when her husband withdrew. The only position they had tried, she said, was for her to lie flat on her back and her husband to climb on top of her.
>
> Had she ever tried oral sex then? I asked. "What is that, kissing?" she responded. (p. 139)

Sadly, when Butterfield's observations were published in the *New York Times Magazine*, the news somehow made its way to China, and Hua was arrested and sent to a labor reform camp for talking about her sex life. Talking about sex in China, it turned out, was a crime. In Box 4.1 on page 102, Pico Iyer (1988) reported on this interview with Joe, from Guangzhou, China, an advocate of a modern, "New China."

Such ignorance is not uncommon. Nor is sexual conservatism. Recent surveys of Chinese sexual behavior find that most Chinese are extremely prudish:

> Free-wheeling in a Chinese context may mean little more than removing one's clothes. . . . Foreplay is often rudimentary or nonexistent, the survey found, perhaps because many couples keep as much clothing on as possible. Among peasants, 34 percent engaged in less than one minute of foreplay. . . . Partly because of the hasty and purposeful manner with which sex is apparently conducted, more than a third of women reported pain during intercourse. The survey did not ask about female orgasm, for fear that many respondents would not understand the concept, but only a third of urban women and a quarter of rural women said they "very often" felt pleasure during intercourse. (Kristof, 1991, p. A1 and A7)

Men reported they got more satisfaction from sex than did women, especially in rural areas. Liu Dalin found that only 17 percent of couples living in the city, but a full 34 percent of the couples living in the countryside, said they engaged in either no foreplay at all or in less than a minute of foreplay. Partly as a result of this, 37 percent of the rural wives reported having pain during intercourse. Pan (cited in Burton, 1990) found that while men reached orgasm about 70 percent of the time, women did so only 40 percent of the time. Urban couples appear to be a bit more knowledgeable but not much more fulfilled. Not surprisingly, more than 70 percent of couples reported that they were unhappy with their sex lives (Ruan, 1991, p. 171).

BOX 4.1   A Conversation with a Chinese Friend

As we walked past the hotel gift shop, Joe let out a cry, and pointed to a picture of Deng Xiaoping on the cover of a glossy magazine: we went in to take a closer look, and there, to my companions' delight and my amazement, was a *Time* cover story on China that I had written before leaving New York three months earlier. Impressed by this, my friends led me up to a lobby filled with huge armchairs, and as we munched on a selection of French pastries, they asked me to describe my impressions of a homeland that was still a little strange to them. In response, I rhapsodized at length about the sunlit lamaseries of Tibet, talked a little about the capitol and then, by way of amusing parenthesis, mentioned some of the quirks of the fabled Black Coffee. At that instant, I happened to look across at Joe, my all-knowing guide to every deal in China. He was looking absolutely stunned. I stopped what I was saying. For many moments, he could not speak. Finally, he went on shakily: You mean that there were prostitutes there? I think so, I said; indeed, a colleague of mine had once been approached by a male prostitute on the streets of Shanghai. That left Joe quite devastated.

But prostitutes, he said after a very long while, existed only in the West. And even that he found hard to understand. In *Kramer vs. Kramer,* he had seen Dustin Hoffman meet a girl at a party and invite her home. Did that really happen? And if it was so easy to meet girls, why would any Westerner look for a prostitute? And was it true, Wu piped up, about the American man who had slept with 1,000 women in three years? Or the nymphomaniac who had slept with 500 men before realizing that her thirst would go forever unslaked and had therefore become a prostitute? And was there also much wife swapping in the United States? Wu had read about a Chinese couple visiting America who had been invited to a party only to find, to their horror, that they were expected to trade partners for the evening. Was that very common?

The Chinese, I had always heard, regarded sex less as something to do than as something to have done, and so be done with. And indeed,

my friends delivered these questions with none of the smirking or swagger one might expect from young males elsewhere in the world, but rather with a great and somber earnestness. They seemed, in fact, to be delving into the subject in as fearful a way as I might ask about kidnappings in Beirut or the atrocities of the Khmer Rouge. Joe had clearly been much heartened by the American he had once met who had been traveling through China for thirty days with a Swedish girl. "He never kissed her, never once," reported Joe. "I said, 'That's incredible.' He said, 'We've both had enough of that kind of thing.'"

In China, Joe went on, it was difficult even to contemplate the subject. "We can say the words in English, but in Chinese we are embarrassed. We were worried when the lady in *Daughter of a Miner* was undressing. When I was at school, I got a sex education manual. I said it was for learning English. At first, when I read the book, I got excited. In college, we talked about intercourse position. But that's all. We are polite in China."

Even marriage, Wu volunteered, was not so easy in China. It was possible for a man to visit a marriage agency and find a partner for 2 yuan (quite a bargain, I thought, next to a bowl of tiger's urine), "but it is harder to find a flat than a fiancée." A typical couple could get an apartment, if they were lucky, of six square meters. Then too, he went on, there was an entire phantom generation of people now in their late twenties or thirties who had lost their best years to the Cultural Revolution. "They are very talented. If they just had a little education, they could do marvelous things. It's sad." Sadder still, perhaps, these "young old people" had never learned to be at ease with the opposite sex. And the longer they lived without contact, the less chance of contact they had. Many women in particular were turning bitter as they found themselves spinsters. But if they tried to find a husband, the man would dismiss them curtly: "Marriage is not only a product of love." (pp. 141–143)

Since couples are expected to sacrifice their private feelings to the good of the state, married couples have no recourse if the government assigns them to work in different provinces. Some are granted only fourteen days a year to meet. Such enforced separations may go on from one to ten or more years. Couples who have more than two children are punished.

Premarital sexual relations, homosexuality, and extramarital sex are taboo. The Revolution of 1949 declared that homosexuality, "a bourgeois and decadent practice," would be swept away. While China lacked explicit laws against homosexuality, homosexuals were considered to be "hooligans," engaging in "lewd conduct," and "perverse and immoral acts." They were often sentenced to labor reform camps, prison, or given electric shock treatments (Gil, 1992).

A survey of young people (eighteen to twenty-seven years of age) in Hong Kong found that most of them disapproved of homosexual behavior. They were asked whether or not they agreed with two statements: "Male homosexual behavior is acceptable" and "Lesbianism is acceptable." Only 15 percent of men and 6 percent of the women agreed that such activities were acceptable. Both men and women were less tolerant of gay relations than lesbian relationships. About a third were neutral in their feelings. A full 62 percent of men and 70 percent of women disapproved of such activities (The Family Planning Association of Hong Kong, 1987).

Even sex educators and researchers had startlingly negative attitudes toward homosexuality. In his "modern" treatise on human sexuality, Ching-sheng Chang (1928/1968) said:

> We understand from the statements made by many men and found in various books that the preference of some men for pederasty is because the anus is tighter than the vagina. Considering this fact, one can say that the laxness of the vagina indirectly promotes the fondness for pederasty. However the anus is the fecal gate and is dirty. . . . Therefore I should like to urge all of my gentlemen readers to note that through giving full consideration and research to the vagina not only can one bring about a perfection and completeness of intercourse between the sexes but one can also exterminate the evil habit of pederasty, a habit which is abnormal, dirty, meaningless, inhuman, and not even indulged in by the birds and the beasts. (pp. 90–91)

This harsh view of homosexuality was considered so liberal that the treatise was suppressed and banned.

Homosexual behavior is also rigidly suppressed. Lenore Norrgard (1990) reported on her experiences in China:

> In nearly ten years of visiting, studying, working, and living in China and Hong Kong, I had never managed to meet any women who identified as lesbians. It wasn't because I didn't look: Whenever I got on a conversational basis with someone who seemed relatively open or enlightened, I would ask about homosexuality.
>
> In China the response usually revealed an incredible degree of innocence and naiveté. It was refreshing not to be with homophobia, but the widespread ignorance was baffling. It was considered slightly scandalous even for a man and woman to hold hands in public, even if they were married, and sexual knowledge was scarce.

Later, when I was studying in Beijing, I asked a young friend about lesbians, and she got that by-then-familiar blank look on her face. In a few minutes, though, she recalled a story she'd heard about two young women who went to the Marriage Bureau to register their bond. They were promptly arrested for their naiveté. Homosexuality is illegal in China, yet ignorance about it is so vast that the two apparently were not even aware of the taboo. (p. 222)

In the last four or five years Chinese sexologists have begun to collect more information about homosexual activity (Hinsch, 1990; Ruan & Bullough, 1992; Samshasta, 1989). Two studies have been conducted in nearby capitalist Taiwan. In the first survey, J. K. Wen (1973, 1978) asked men and women if they had ever had homosexual "inclinations" or engaged in homosexual practices. Only 1 percent of them admitted having such feelings or engaging in homosexual activities. In a second study, conducted five years later, Wen sought to determine how many women had, at least on some occasions, felt lesbian "inclinations" or engaged in pleasurable lesbian practices. Now, 21 percent of the women said they had lesbian inclinations at some time; 1 percent reported having engaged in pleasurable lesbian practices.

Leaping the Fence

Taiwan is not China. Nonetheless, in China as everywhere else, the breath of change is in the air. During the 1986–87 nationwide demonstrations by university students, posters advocating sexual freedom were prominently displayed. In Beijing, popular newspapers such as *Southern Weekend* and magazines have begun to give men and women sex advice—telling them how to produce "high tide" (orgasm) (Tyler, 1994). In Kuwait, popular radio host Talal al-Yagout broadcasts a weekly talk show "The Love Line," which answers callers' questions about love and sex (Hedges, 1994). Western ideas are coming in via telephone and fax.

In 1989 and 1990, Liu and 500 volunteer social workers (Liu, Ng, & Chou, 1992) asked 23,000 men and women in fifteen Chinese provinces to complete a 240-question survey, in itself a sign of change. Eighty-six percent of the respondents said they approved of premarital sex. Liu estimated that 30 percent of Chinese youth have probably engaged in such relations (Burton, 1990).

At one time, the state weighed down adulterers and adulteresses with stones and drowned them. Today, a surprising 69 percent of the respondents in Liu's (1991) study said they saw nothing wrong with extramarital affairs. In a second survey conducted by Professor Pan at Chinese People's University in Beijing, 10 percent of the 600 couples interviewed reported that they had had such extramarital relations (Ruan, 1991, p. 170).

In the largest cities some gay dance clubs have begun to appear. Homosexuals in Shanghai are generally left alone so long as their activities involve consenting adults. Beijing, Shanghai, and Canton have a few public areas and bars where homosexuals can meet.

As modernization and industrialization spread in China, the desire (among women as well as men) for love, happiness, personal freedom, and sexual experience is likely to further alter current norms among one-fifth of the world's population. (Other historians who have studied the history of Chinese sexuality are Chang, 1928/1968; Jankowiak, 1993; Ng & Lau, 1990.)

The West: America and England

Western attitudes about sexual desire and behavior have also changed enormously over time. Once Westerners viewed sex as sin; now the majority exalt sex as an expression of love and friendship and a source of excitement. An entire generation of historians has turned its attention from the study of political leaders and wars to an examination of the everyday lives of men and women. To find out about people's sexual attitudes and behavior during the last five centuries of social upheaval, these scholarly detectives have sorted through a staggering array of documents and artifacts. They have poured over theological tracts, legal treatises, medical handbooks, and demographic statistics. They have studied letters, diaries, and autobiographies. They have analyzed poems, books, and plays. They have looked freshly at cartoons and at romantic and pornographic art. They have examined architectural plans and remains and, in general, excavated the world of the inarticulate. Even though much guesswork remains, they have labored to remarkable effect.

In the Medieval world, before the coming of the Renaissance, a number of factors conspired to make sexual activity relatively unappealing. Religious, medical, and scientific authorities almost uniformly condemned passion. The early Catholic Church decreed that *all* passionate love and sexual pleasure were sinful whether or not couples were married. The church urged Christians to be celibate. As Reay Tannahill (1980) observed:

> *It was Augustine who epitomized a general feeling among the Church Fathers that the act of intercourse was fundamentally disgusting. Arnobius called it filthy and degrading, Methodius unseemly, Jerome unclean, Tertullian shameful, Ambrose a defilement. In fact there was an unstated consensus that God ought to have invented a better way of dealing with the problem of procreation. (p. 141)*

The only conceivable excuse married couples had for engaging in nonpassionate, tepid, duty-bound sexual activity was the desire to produce children. So, for married couples, sex was grudgingly permitted. Added Tannahill (1980):

> *Though not very often. Some rigid theologians recommended abstention on Thursdays, in memory of Christ's arrest; Fridays, in memory of his death; Saturdays, in honor of the Virgin Mary; Sundays, in honor of the Resurrection; and Mondays, in commemoration of the departed. Tuesdays and Wednesdays were largely accounted for by the ban on intercourse during fasts and festivals—the forty days before Easter, Pentecost, and Christmas; the seven, five, or three days before Communion; and so on. (p. 146)*

The thirteenth-century theologian St. Thomas Aquinas argued that sexual pleasure was always a sin. The Creator had designed the sexual organs for reproduction, and they could be used only for that purpose. Thus, the only acceptable position for sexual intercourse was with the man in the superior position (since that presumably guaranteed that there would be as little pleasure as possible). Oral and anal intercourse were deemed odious. Contraception was prohibited and homosexuality taboo. In the eighth century, Pope Gregory III claimed that sodomy was "a vice so abominable in the sight of God that the cities in which its practitioners dwelt were appointed for destruction by fire and brimstone" (Bailey, 1955, p. 106).

Secular authorities added to the fear-mongering about sex. Until the eighteenth century, physicians generally assumed that masturbation was unhealthy. Even into the revolutionary Enlightenment of the eighteenth century, Swiss physician Samuel Tissot (1766/1985) claimed that masturbation drained away men's and women's strength and left them vulnerable to almost every ailment known to humankind, including pimples, blisters, constipation, tuberculosis, blindness, insomnia, headaches, genital cancer, insanity, feeblemindedness, weakness, jaundice, nose pain, intestinal disorders, confusion, insanity, and a host of other grotesque maladies. He left out dandruff.

A pamphlet by Daniel Defoe (1727) warned about the pitfalls of any kind of sexual excess: "Whence come Palsies and Epilepsies, Falling-Sickness, trembling of the Joints, pale dejected Aspects, Leanness, and at last Rottenness, and other filthy and loathsome Distempers, but from the criminal Excesses of their younger times?" (p. 91).

Until the changes that were launched between 1500 and 1800, men wielded virtually all the power. As with the Chinese during Mao's Cultural Revolution, sexual intercourse generally lasted only a few minutes. Most couples had never even heard of foreplay. Men simply climbed on top, thrust for a few minutes, and ejaculated. Women rarely enjoyed sex or experienced orgasm. Women's pleasure in sex was naturally tempered by their fear of getting pregnant and perhaps dying in childbirth. At the beginning of the Early Modern period, the double standard held sway. Men's extramarital affairs were ignored. Women's were not. Women were regarded as the sexual property of men. Their value was diminished if they were "loaned" out to anyone other than their legal owner. In 1700, De la Rivière Manley, observed of a "fallen" woman: "*If she had been a man, she had been without Fault:* But the Charter of that Sex being much more confin'd than ours, what is not a Crime in Men is scandalous and unpardonable in Woman" (cited in Needham, 1951, p. 272). As late as 1825, Sir John Nicholls declared that "forgiveness on the part of a wife . . . is meritorious, while a similar forgiveness on the part of a husband would be degrading and dishonorable" (cited in Thomas, 1959, p. 202).

Perhaps there wasn't as much temptation to have sex in this era as today. At the beginning of the Early Modern period, Lawrence Stone (1977) pointed out that young men and women rarely encountered anyone who was very sexually appealing or who had enough energy to be interested in sex. People's hair was filled with lice. They had bad breath and rotting teeth. They rarely washed. Their skin crawled with eczema, scabs, running sores, oozing ulcers, and other disfiguring skin diseases.

Women suffered from gynecological problems—vaginal infections, ulcers, tumors, and bleeding, which made sexual intercourse uncomfortable, painful, or impossible. Men and women who engaged in sexual relations were likely to catch any number of venereal diseases. (For example, James Boswell, the eighteenth-century biographer, contracted gonorrhea at least seventeen times.)

People generally had little energy to "squander" on sex. Robert Darnton (1984) described French peasant life in the sixteenth and seventeenth centuries this way:

> *Men labored from dawn to dusk, scratching the soil on scattered strips of land with plows like those of the Romans and hacking at their grain with primitive sickles, in order to leave enough stubble for communal grazing. Women married late—at age twenty-five to twenty-seven—and gave birth to only five or six children, of whom only two or three survived to adulthood. Great masses of people lived in a state of chronic malnutrition, subsisting mainly on porridge made of bread and water with some occasional, home grown vegetables thrown in. They ate meat only a few times a year, on feast days or after autumn slaughtering if they did not have enough silage to feed the livestock over the winter. They often failed to get the two pounds of bread (2,000 calories) a day that they needed to keep up their health, and so they had little protection against the combined effects of grain shortage and disease. . . . (p. 24)*
>
> *Whole families crowded into one or two beds and surrounded themselves with livestock in order to keep warm. So children became participant observers of their parents' sexual activities. No one thought of them as innocent creatures of or childhood itself as a distinct phase of life. . . .*
>
> *The peasants of early modern France inhabited a world of stepmothers and orphans, of inexorable, unending toil, and of brutal emotions, both raw and repressed. The human condition has changed so much since then that we can hardly imagine the way it appeared to people whose lives really were nasty, brutish, and short. (p. 29)*

In the 300 years from 1500 to 1800, England and America showed important change in *mentalité*. The West began to question the patriarchal and repressive attitudes we have just described and began to evolve slowly in the direction of the more individualistic, egalitarian, and permissive attitudes toward sexuality that are common today. Stone (1977) wrote:

> *The four key features of the modern family—intensified affective bonding of the nuclear core at the expense of neighbors and kin; a strong sense of individual autonomy and the right to personal freedom in the pursuit of happiness; a weakening of the association of sexual pleasure with sin and guilt; and a growing desire for physical privacy—were all well established by 1750 in the key middle and upper sectors of English society. (p. 22)*

By the 1800s, people had adopted a more individualistic orientation; they were less concerned with kin and community than before. Couples felt bound together more by affection, sexual attraction, and habit than by ties of political, familial, or economic interest. Couples were becoming more sexually liberated. They began to rely on birth control to limit pregnancy.

Of course, history rarely proceeds in a straight line. (The only history that appears to move in a fairly consistent linear way is the history of technology.) At any given time, different segments of English society in varying regions held very different convictions about what was appropriate sexually. Experimental periods were often followed by more traditional epochs. Witness the Victorian era following the more "liberated" eighteenth-century "Age of Reason":

> *Early Modern English society was composed of a number of very distinct status groups and classes: the court aristocracy, the country gentry, the parish gentry, the mercantile and professional elite, the small property owners in town and country, the respectable and struggling wage-earners, and the totally destitute who lived on charity and their wits. These constituted more or less self-contained cultural units, with their own communication networks, their own systems of value and their own patterns of acceptable behavior. (Stone, 1977, p. 22–23)*

Different social groups found different aspects of affective individualism to be appealing. The higher aristocracy, who had property to worry about, were still arranging marriages long after other groups had begun to marry for love. They quickly caught hold of the idea that sex should be one of the pleasures of life. The professional and bourgeois classes were the first to promote the ideal of married love. They were the last to be convinced that marriage should involve frank sexual passion.

When social change did occur, it was often followed by a backlash. That backlash, in turn, generated a counterreaction. Stone (1977) observed:

> *In the terms of the sexual attitudes of the upper classes, who more or less successfully imposed their values on their social inferiors, English society thus passed through several phases: a phase of moderate toleration lasting until towards the end of the sixteenth century; a phase of repression that ran from about 1570 to 1670; and a phase of permissiveness, even license, that ran for over a century from 1670 until 1810. This was followed by a new wave of repression that began in 1770, was spreading fast by 1810, and reached its apogee in the mid-Victorian period. After about 1870 this wave in turn receded, to be followed by a new period of permissiveness that has perhaps reached it apogee in the 1970s. . . . Both sexual repression and sexual permissiveness eventually generate extremist features, which in turn set in motion counterforces which by a process of 'social reversion' slowly turn the pendulum back in the other direction. The duration of each of these swings of religio-ethical attitudes toward sexuality seems to have been about a hundred years. (p. 339)*

In the early 1900s, fueled by rapidly changing ideas about the value of individualism, personal freedom, and personal happiness and by advances in birth control, the sexual revolution again picked up speed. In the 1960s, the women's movement sparked an explosion of change. There is no question that today, in the twentieth century of the West, a startling change in the way men and women view sensuality and sexuality has occurred. There is no guarantee that the current attitudes toward sexual freedom will continue forever. The AIDS epidemic has already slowed the pace of change. America may be poised on the threshold of another pendulum swing. But the best bet is that there will never be a return to the kind of sexual "repression" or "restraint" (the term depends on your value system) that existed before 1500. The West, and increasingly the rest of the world, are likely to continue to view sexual desire and expression positively. The debate over how much affective individualism and how much communitarianism or how much sexual freedom and how much sexual restraint is ideal is taking place over a narrower range and around a more tolerant base. (For other histories of Western sexuality, see Bullough, 1990; D'Emilio & Freedman, 1988; and Tannahill, 1980.)

Cross-Cultural Perspectives

> *There is no such thing as* human *sexuality.*
> —*William Davenport*

A half century ago, Margaret Mead (1935/1969) in *Sex and Temperament in Three Primitive Societies* discussed three cultures of Papua New Guinea and their gender role standards. She described the gentle Arapesh, a culture in which both men and women had "feminine" traits; the fierce Mundugamur, in which both genders were "masculine"; and the Tchambuli, in which the men were "feminine" and the women were "masculine."

Other anthropologists have documented the great plasticity of human sexual behavior. Traditionally, for instance, the Batak boys and girls of Lake Toba in northern Sumatra moved into segregated huts at puberty. Young boys were introduced to sex by an older man—they masturbated together. When men reached adulthood, they were expected to marry. But even after marriage, they spent most of their free time in the men's hut, sharing sexual gossip with their friends. In the women's huts, girls were not given the same kind of explicit sexual instruction that the boys received. A girl could gossip about love and sex, but talk was all she could do. It was considered critically important for a girl to be a virgin when she married. Girls who were discovered having premarital sex often committed suicide. After marriage, neither men nor women were supposed to have extramarital affairs. Marriage was expected to be exclusive and permanent. That is how "real" men and women were expected to behave (Geertz, 1960).

Among the Marind Anim, a headhunting people of southern New Guinea, men and women lived separately all their lives—women in the women's huts, men in the men's. Couples met briefly only when they planned a sexual excursion or had business together, and this did not happen very often. From infancy to four or five, both boys and girls stayed with their mothers. Around age five, boys moved in with their fathers and learned to hunt, fish, and garden. Girls always remained with their mothers and learned about housekeeping and gardening. Children's sexual experiences began early. When older people played with young boys and girls, they often soothed them by petting their genitals. Young boys had numerous homosexual encounters; girls did not. As soon as boys and girls reached puberty, they were expected to marry. The marriage ceremony was a lengthy one. First, the girl was escorted to a special spot where she was required to have sexual intercourse with all the men in her husband's clan. This was thought to increase her fertility. Only then could she embark on sexual relations with her new husband. Throughout her marriage she was expected to continue to participate in this kind of sequential group sex at regular intervals. Women regarded such group sex as a duty—unpleasant, but necessary to ensure their fertility.

Among the Pelaga Indians in Argentina, boys' and girls' sexual experiences began early. Until age four or five, boys and girls openly masturbated with their friends. At about five years of age, boys and girls began playing at coitus. From then on, most of their sexual activities were with partners of the opposite sex. When boys and girls reached puberty, they experimented with a variety of sexual partners before settling down to one.

These examples and others (Ford & Beach, 1951; Suggs & Miracle, 1993) document how greatly sexual attitudes and behavior have varied from culture to culture.

Conclusions

Evolutionary psychologists have cautioned that to some extent "genes and gender are destiny." They point out that men and women in a variety of cultures experience many of the same sorts of sexual desires and preferences.

Other scientists, however, are equally insistent that it is culture, more than gender or genes that is destiny, and they provide compelling evidence for that contention. During our brief excursions into the Chinese and Anglo American pasts, we saw how dramatically beliefs and behaviors, once thought to be eternal, have metamorphosed over time. Cross-cultural researchers, too, document how much sexual attitudes and behavior vary from culture to culture. These disciplines teach us skepticism in the face of claims to the universality and rightness of sexual "norms," whether they derive from some church or tribe or from more modern, scientifically framed "biological imperatives." The case for human adaptability in sex, as in many other arenas, seems a strong one.

In this chapter, we have become acquainted with "Sex: Then and There" and with the reigning evolutionary, historical, and cross-cultural perspectives on sexual attitudes, desires, and behaviors. Next, we turn to the here and now and learn what has been discovered about culture and sexual attitudes and behavior in the twentieth century.

Chapter 5

Sex: Here and Now

Political, religious, and legal experts sometimes take it for granted that wise people can easily agree about the kinds of sexual attitudes and behaviors that are "right." Sociobiologists sometimes write as though, throughout the ages, men and women have been marching to the ancient rhythms of biologically encoded sexual imperatives. Yet, the history of sex is a story of change. In Chapters 4 and 5, we engage in a bit of time-travel. In Chapter 4, we looked at the Then and There, at the historical documentation of men's and women's remarkable adaptability through the ages. In this chapter, we focus on where people in different corners of the world stand, right at this moment, with regard to sex.

Finally, we attempt to catch a fleeting glimpse of the future. For although nothing is certain, much less the future, the historical record also suggests a direction to that current of historical change. When we consider the impact of culture and time on sexual attitudes and behavior, we are struck by a number of facts. Although cultures still vary wildly in their attitudes, most do seem to be groping, differentially, toward a more individualistic, egalitarian, and permissive view of sexuality. Several kinds of changes seem especially common.

1. In most societies, young people are beginning to insist on marrying for love rather than agreeing to settle into arranged marriages. (We discussed data in support of this contention in Chapter 2.)
2. People of all ages are beginning to adopt more favorable views of passionate love and sexuality.
3. Even in the most traditional societies of the world, the two sexes seem to be becoming more similar in their sexual attitudes and behaviors.
4. People are beginning to engage in more sexual activity and experimentation.

We must qualify these conclusions by pointing out that in most places of the world, a stark double standard continues to prevail, gender equality is a long way off, throughout the world there are still powerful voices passionately opposed to equality and permissive sex, and in history nothing is guaranteed.

Caveats aside, let us survey a sampling of findings from articles on sexual attitudes and behavior that have been published since 1980. We should point out that scientists' achievement in collecting data in very traditional societies should not be taken for granted; their pioneering work merits great praise. Any traditional society that wants to prevent people from even *thinking* about sex is not likely to view attempts to collect information on sexual attitudes and behavior with equanimity. When we think of how difficult it is to conduct national surveys on sexuality in the United States, a society that many say is obsessed with sex, we get some idea of the difficulties that researchers in Turkey, China, Iran, Cuba, and the like encounter. Sexuality researchers have been harassed, fired, sent to thought reform camps, tortured, and killed for asking too many questions. Cross-cultural sex research has just begun, past researchers have done some heroic work, and the prospects for future exploration in this area are almost limitless.

The Meaning of Sex

In different eras and in diverse societies, the words *love* and *sex* have evoked an array of separate and contradictory images and feelings (Bullough, 1990; Degler, 1980; D'Emilio & Freedman, 1988; Gay, 1986; Gillis, 1985; Mintz & Kellogg, 1988; Phillips, 1988; Stone, 1977, 1990). Throughout history people have endowed sexual desire with a wide range of meanings (D'Emilio & Freedman, 1988). Sex has been equated with spiritual transcendence, sin, power, weakness, the procreation of children, romantic intimacy, erotic pleasure, and recreation or sport.

As Ruth Bleier (1984), a biologist, argued:

> *Our individual sexualities, like our natures, are socially constructed from our individual histories of interactions with people and society, and they continually change. . . . A person's sexuality may express a desire or need to be vulnerable to another person or, alternatively, a determination never to be vulnerable to another person. It can express a general need to experience commitment to, dependence on, submission to, transcendence with, or physical-psychic unity with another person. It can express a need to always be in control of oneself, of another person, of all situations, or of all people one develops any relationship with. On the other hand, it can express the need to be, for once, not in control, but to surrender control to another. Sexuality can be seen also as a survival mechanism; a trading of needs and desires, a desire to be liked, needed, wanted, indispensable, the highest priority in someone else's life. Sexuality can be perceived as a measure of one's attractiveness to other people, as a route to intimacy, as the way to be entrusted with another's vulnerability. Perhaps too obvious to mention is the possibility that sexuality may also have something to do with love . . . and with (uncomplicated?) physical pleasure. And, of course, our sexuality can express many of these needs at different times and even simultaneously. (p. 166)*

In classical Athens, sex was a demonstration of power. Sexual partners came in two kinds of "packages"—not male and female, but dominant and submissive, active and passive. The "proper" target of a powerful man's desire were the powerless—women, boys, foreigners, and slaves (Halperin, 1990).

Today, in the West, three views of sex are most common. Some deeply religious people still view sex as self-indulgent and sinful. For them, sex is justified only if it is linked to reproduction. Other people assume that "all you need is love." For them, love and sex are intimately linked. Sexual intercourse is a way of expressing love and affection. Still others feel that the purpose of sex is recreational. Sex is merely another source of fun and pleasure (Sprecher & McKinney, 1993).

In Western society, men often separate love and sex. Women tend to be taught to equate love, commitment, intimacy, and sex (Glass & Wright, 1985; Regan, 1995; Regan & Berscheid, in press; Whitley, 1988). This is true of Americans regardless of their ethnic background (African American, Asian American, European American, and Hispanic American) or their sexual orientation (heterosexual, bisexual, or homosexual) (Leigh, 1989). Such gender differences have been found in a variety of countries as well, including Africa (Gay, 1986), the United States (Foa et al., 1987), Hong Kong (Family Planning Association of Hong Kong, 1987), and Sweden (Foa et al., 1987). Historians have suggested that future researchers would do well to explore the extent to which, in the past, men had more power than women to "socially construct," or to define, the purposes of sexual behavior.

There is also some evidence that in different cultures people view sexuality in very different ways. Swedish men and women, for example, tend to equate love and sex to a greater extent than do most Americans (Foa et al., 1987).

The Developmental Sequence

Most individuals in Western cultures now begin their sexual experimentation in early adolescence. Most start out timidly. A boy may awkwardly drape his arm over the back of the chair of the girl sitting next to him. (Increasingly, girls will initiate the clumsy ballet, though often less directly.) Both their hearts pound, partly in excitement but mainly in terror. He hopes she will think his arm just happens to be resting there. She doesn't know whether to pull away, let things happen, or give him a bit of encouragement. If she draws away, he can mumble an embarrassed "sorry" and remove his arm. If she snuggles into his arm, he may more boldly hug her. Probably not. They are thrilled with very little. With time and practice, couples move on to more daring behavior—kissing. They learn how to kiss with their glasses or braces on, what to do with their noses, and how to keep breathing while their mouths are otherwise engaged.

In the 1970s, in a now classic study, John DeLamater and Patricia MacCorquodale (1979) interviewed more than 2,000 young men and women. They found that their sexual histories were remarkably similar. Men and women began to kiss, fondle, and have sexual relations at almost the same ages. In general, boys were a little more adventuresome than were girls. Boys began "necking" at 14, while most girls waited until they were almost 15. Boys began "petting" when they were almost 16, girls at about 16½. Boys first had intercourse at 17½, girls hesitated until they were almost 18. Men and women also progressed from holding hands, to kissing, to fondling various body parts, to intercourse at about the same pace. This progression usually occurred over a four-year period.

Studies indicate that young people in a variety of countries usually progress through much the same sequence. Yoshiro Hatano (1991) interviewed 30,000 Japanese men and women, ranging in age from 12 to 23 years of age. They came from small towns and from large metropolises. Men and women began by kissing, were emboldened to engage in petting, and ended with sexual intercourse. The Japanese men and women began sexual experimentation far later than did men and women in the West (at 20 years of age rather than at 14 or 15), but they made up for lost time by progressing faster from the first timid experimentation with kissing to intercourse than did their Western counterparts. Japanese men typically kissed for the first time at 20 and had sexual relations at 21; women first kissed at 20 and had intercourse at 22.

Researchers have found that in a variety of countries—Hong Kong (Family Planning Association of Hong Kong, 1987) and the United Kingdom (Breakwell & Fife-Schaw, 1992), for example—young people progress through a similar developmental sequence.

Sexual Orientation

What percentage of the population is heterosexual? bisexual? gay? lesbian? uninterested in sex? That is hard to say. There are several reasons why it is almost impossible to pigeonhole people. First, people's answers vary depending on the questions you ask. Second, politicians, moralists, and the general public have vested interests in the answer and their agendas sometimes shape the way data are interpreted. Finally, it is often difficult to collect the data that would allow us to answer the question. (See Bolton, 1994, for a detailed discussion of these problems.)

What do we mean, for example, when we say someone is heterosexual, bisexual, or homosexual? Perhaps we should accept *self-definitions*. If we do, we sometimes come up with some surprising answers. When Elaine Hatfield spent a summer at the Kinsey Institute in Bloomington, Indiana, she had a chance to sort through some of the Kinsey protocols. One man, for example, identified himself as "heterosexual, all the way." Yet, he had never had an affair with a woman, while he had had thousands with men. He was a male prostitute and insisted he "only did it for the money."

Perhaps we should look at sexual *desires*. If so, how would we classify one Greek American in the Kinsey sample? He planned to marry as soon as he could. Until then, he and his male friends "found release" with one another. For him, what was important was whether you were a "man" (who presumably took the active role in homosexual encounters) or "a nothing," who took the passive role. He spoke of passive men with disgust.

Perhaps, then, we should look at *behavior.* How then should we classify one man who was married and had two children? He was a devout Mormon. He had always been wildly attracted to men but had chosen to marry to fulfill his duty to the church. He considered it to be a chore to make love to his wife. Even if researchers do choose to focus on behavior, they still confront problems. In classifying someone, does youthful experimentation "count"? What about behavior that occurs when men or women aren't available, say, when someone is in the armed forces or prison? What percentage of male and female partners does one have to have before one should be classified as heterosexual, bisexual, or homosexual? Is someone who has two partners of the same sex and twenty of the opposite sex heterosexual? bisexual? homosexual? (See Duberman, Vicinus, & Chauncey, 1989, and Laumann, Gagnon, Michael, & Michaels, 1994, for a complete discussion of this problem.)

Different researchers have answered these questions in different ways. In Table 5.1 on page 116 we have listed the percentage of people that have been classified as heterosexual, bisexual, or homosexual in studies conducted in a variety of countries. We have also included the questions people were asked. Although standardization is, of course, the ideal, researchers have never been allowed to interview a random sample of people throughout the world about their sexual behavior. These are the only data available. And they are a start.

Overall, in the West, how do people classify themselves? Recently the National Opinion Research Center surveyed a random sample of Americans about their sexual preferences. They concluded that approximately 91 percent of Americans consider themselves to be heterosexual, 6 percent consider themselves to be bisexual, and 1 percent consider themselves to be homosexual (Smith, 1991).

Even more recently, in a landmark study, Edward Laumann and his colleagues (Laumann et al., 1994) collaborated with the National Opinion Research Center at the University of Chicago. They conducted 90-minute interviews with 3,432 men and women between the ages of 18 and 59. The subjects were randomly chosen from a cross-section of American households. The authors asked subjects several kinds of questions about their sexual interests: To whom were they sexually attracted—men or women? How did they think of themselves—as heterosexual, homosexual, bisexual, or something else? Had they sex with someone of the same sex in the past year? the past five years? ever? As you might expect, the authors found that the number of people classified in one way or another depended on the questions asked: only 2.8 percent of men and 1.4 percent of women identified themselves as homosexual or bisexual. More, 5.3 percent of men and 3.5 percent of women had had sex with someone of their own sex at least once since puberty. Even more, 7.7 percent of men and 7.5 percent of women reported they had felt sexual desire for a person of the same sex. And a full 10.1 percent of men and 8.6 percent of women said that they had had some same-sex desires or experiences.

Milton Diamond (1993) surveyed all existing survey research and concluded that today, from 5 to 6 percent of men and from 2 to 3 percent of women consider themselves exclusively homosexual.

TABLE 5.1 **Percentage of Men and Women Engaging in Homosexual or Bisexual Activity**

Culture	Men	Women
United States		
Q. Any same-sex partners during the last year?	3.8	2.8
during the last five years?[1]	4.4	3.6
Q. How many opposite-sex and same-sex partners have you had?[2]		
Last year		
Homosexual *or* bisexual	1.6	1.6
Ever		
Bisexual	5.6	5.6
Homosexual	0.7	0.7
Q. Any sex with another man 1978–1989?[3]	7.3	—
China[4]		
Q. Have you ever had homosexual experiences or attractions?		
College students	7.6	—
Peasants	2.3	—
City dwellers	0.5	
Denmark[5]		
Q. Any same sex experience during adulthood?	—	0.0
Finland[6]		
Q. Homosexual experience ever?	4.0	3.8
France[7]		
Q. Homosexual experience in the past 12 months?	1.1	0.3
Homosexual experience ever?	4.1	2.6
Japan		
Q. Any homosexual contact such as kissing, petting, or mutual masturbation?[8]	7.1	4.0
Q. Ever any homosexual body contact?[9]	3.7	3.1
Netherlands[10]		
Q. Had heterosexual/bisexual/homosexual experience in last 12 months?		
Heterosexual	81.7	88.4
Bisexual	1.9	0.5
Homosexual	3.6	0.3
Abstinent	12.8	10.7
Ever had same-sex sex?	12.0	4.0
Lima, Peru[11]		
Q. Have you ever had sex with men/women?	10.5	0.0
Philippines[12]		
Have men and women engaged in homosexual activity? (Anthropological field world: total population)	1.6	0.0
Republic of Palau[13]		
What types of sex experience in the last 12 months?		
Homosexual	1.9	2.8
Bisexual	2.8	0.7

TABLE 5.1 *Continued*

Culture	Men	Women
Thailand[14]		
Q. Any same-sex experience during adulthood?	3.4	1.2
United Kingdom[15]		
Q. Any same-sex experience?	9.0	4.0

[1]Harris Poll (1988).
[2]Smith (1991).
[3]Dixon, Streiff, & Brunwasser (1991).
[4]Liu, cited in Chenault (1992).
[5]Schover & Jensen (1988).
[6]Kontula (1993).
[7]Aldhous (1992).
[8]Asayama (1976).
[9]Japanese Association of Sex Education (1987, reported in Diamond, 1993).
[10]Zessen & Sandfort (1991).
[11]Holmes (1993).
[12]Hart (1968).
[13]Morens & Polloi (in preparation).
[14]Sittitrai, Brown, & Virulrak (1992).
[15]Wellings et al. (1990).

Some people, of course, have no sexual interest in anyone, male or female. Kinsey and his colleagues (1948, 1953) observed that a few men and women preferred to abstain from sex or engaged in it only reluctantly. Abstinence is fairly common even today. People may, of course, choose to abstain from sex for a variety of reasons. They may find the idea of sex unappealing. They may be single and abstinent for romantic, ethical, or practical reasons. They may be unable to find a lover. They may be worried about AIDS. Or, they may be too old or ill to engage in sexual activity. In any case, in a recent national survey, the National Opinion Research Council found that about 22 percent of adult Americans—14 percent of men and 28 percent of women—had not engaged in sexual relations with anyone during the preceding year. Not surprisingly, perhaps, many of those who abstained were single. About 25 percent of single men and women reported that they had not engaged in sexual activity during the previous twelve months. About 9 percent of married couples had not had sexual relations during the previous year. A full 86 percent of widowed men and women did not engage in such activity (Smith, 1991).

Homosexuality

Italian novelist Pier Tondelli (1989), in *Separate Rooms,* evoked Leo's passionate and consuming love for Thomas:

Now love is a lean and long-legged body, its limbs still those of a teenager, soft and sinuous, and princely. Love is a long face with a strong, square jaw. Love is two bright, dark eyes, with a lock of dark honey-coloured hair falling across them every so often. Love is a special way of moving the hands or letting them hang down by the legs. Last but not least, love is a voice, the pitch of a stifled kiss, the feelings of a bright, open burst of laughter. Love is the simplicity of a person's ways, the essence and gracefulness of a being who, as this dream currently stands, answers to the name of Thomas. (p. 22)

Attitudes toward Homosexuality

Cultures differ greatly in their attitudes toward homosexuality. Most tribal societies (64 percent) assume that homosexual activities of one sort or another are socially acceptable for some members of the community, at least some of the time (Ford & Beach, 1951). Among the Siwans of Africa, for example, all men and boys engage in anal intercourse. Prominent Siwan men lend their sons to one another, and they talk about their masculine love affairs as openly as they discuss their love of women. Both married and unmarried men are expected to have both homosexual and heterosexual affairs. Men are considered to be peculiar if they do not indulge in such activities (Ford & Beach, 1951). In the Azande, Dahomey, !Kung, and other societies in Africa, adolescent girls commonly get involved in homosexual love affairs (Blackwood, 1986; Gay, 1986). Some cultures assume that normal young people ought to begin their sexual experimentation with a lover of the same sex. Some societies don't care much one way or another. Still others strongly disapprove of such relations.

Americans and Europeans, since the heyday of Greece and Rome, have generally disapproved of homosexual activity. In 1991, the National Opinion Research Center (NORC) interviewed a random sample of 986 Americans about their sexual attitudes (Davis & Smith, 1991). They asked: "What about sexual relations between two adults of the same sex—do you think it is always wrong, almost always wrong, wrong only sometimes, or not wrong at all?" (p. 257). About 75 percent of Americans thought homosexual relations were always or almost always wrong; 4 percent thought they were sometimes wrong; 15 percent thought they were not wrong at all; and 6 percent just weren't sure.

Researchers have developed several scales to measure homophobia (the fear of homosexuals and homosexuality) (see Herek, 1984; Hudson & Ricketts, 1980; Kite & Deaux, 1986). Mary Kite and Kay Deaux (1986) developed the *Kite Homosexuality Attitude Scale*. It included questions such as these:

1. I would not mind having homosexual friends.*
2. I would look for a new place to live if I found out my roommate was gay.
3. I would not be afraid for my child to have a homosexual teacher.*
4. I see the gay movement as a positive thing.*

Possible answers ranged from 1 (strongly agree) to 5 (strongly disagree). The higher the score, the more homophobic respondents were said to be. (Items followed by an asterisk assess sexual tolerance and thus are scored in the reverse direction.)

Surveys indicate that the most homophobic people are generally those who hold traditional views, are older, have conservative religious beliefs, hold stereotyped views of the roles of men and women, are relatively uneducated, and hail from rural areas (Britton, 1990; Kite & Deaux, 1986; Seltzer, 1992). Most people seem to feel much the same way about gays and lesbians (Kite & Deaux, 1986). In the West, however, people seem to be becoming more comfortable with diversity (Ariès, 1985; Specter, 1995).

What about attitudes in modern societies outside America? Maria Werebe and Max Reinert (1983) asked French adolescents what they thought about homosexuality. Their conclusion: most students weren't quite sure what they thought. They gave such answers as "I don't know," "Neither for nor against," and "I have no experience" to the question. When they did have an opinion, it was most likely to be an accepting one. The researchers wrote:

> *Moral "condemnations" have practically disappeared from the judgments made by the subjects. These seem to have been replaced by a "medical condemnation" ("it's abnormal," "it's a sickness") for 23% of the subjects. . . . Others (17%) considered homosexuality as absolutely normal; some (7%) even said that it is the "same as heterosexuality," that it represents "a sexual tendency like any other." A small number of subjects (3.4%) mentioned the bisexual tendencies "present in all individuals." (p. 151)*

Probably French society has always been more tolerant of sexual diversity than is the United States with its Puritan heritage and high degree of anxiety about sexuality (Samson et al., 1991).

Douglas and Susan Davis (1994) report that in Morocco people are not so homophobic as in America. Their attitudes toward homosexuality are mixed. In Zawiya, for example, boys in their early teens engage in all sorts of homoerotic play, including nude swimming and group masturbation. Older boys sometimes engage in homosexual acts. Young men who engage in such sexual activities do not think of themselves as homosexual, but assume they are going through a phase. Separate terms are used for the man who plays the active role and the one who has the passive role in intercourse. The term for the passive participant (*zamel*) is an insult. It is frequently seen in graffiti on walls in Moroccan schoolyards. Among adult men, homosexual activity is fairly rare and is considered somewhat shameful. Things are completely different for young women. Their sexual lives are far more rigidly controlled. Most had not even considered the possibility of lesbian relationships; both men and women insisted that lesbian relationships were very rare.

In any case, there is considerable evidence that around the world, people's attitudes toward homosexuality are becoming more accepting, including in French Canada (Samson et al., 1991) and Hong Kong (Family Planning Association of Hong Kong, 1987).

Homosexual Activity

Earlier, when discussing sexual orientation, we reported that in the United States, about 5.3 percent of men and 3.5 percent of women have engaged in homosexual activities at some time in their lives (Laumann et al., 1994). In other areas of the world, homosexuality has been and is more common. Leigh Minturn and her colleagues (1969) sampled 135 of the societies listed in the *Human Relations Area Files (HRAE)*, which contains detailed information on 120 cultures from sixty distinct regions. Anthropologists had provided information on men's sexual preferences in only fifty-two of the societies listed in the *HRAF.* Unfortunately, they almost never mentioned women's preferences. They found that male homosexuality was strongly condemned or mocked and ridiculed in 48 percent of societies. Its existence was ignored or not understood in 8 percent of societies; it was considered an acceptable form of sexual behavior in 27 percent of societies; and it was a traditional, well-accepted practice in 17 percent of societies. In 83 percent of the societies, fewer than 20 percent of men engaged in such activities. In 15 percent of the societies, from 20 to 50 percent of men engaged in homosexual activity, and in only 3 percent of the societies did at least 50 percent of men engage in homosexual activity. You can see, then, that there are enormous cultural differences in whether men have been encouraged or forbidden to engage in homosexual sex.

In the Arab countries, where women are often kept in strict seclusion, boys and men are likely to have their first sexual experiences with either prostitutes or other young boys. Some researchers have found that 40 percent of young men's first sexual encounters are with other boys (Melikian & Prothro, 1954, 1967).

In the last four or five years Chinese sexologists have begun to collect more information about homosexual activity (Hinsch, 1990; Ruan & Bullough, 1992; Samshasha, 1989.) When J. K. Wen (1973, 1978) asked men and women if they had ever had homosexual "inclinations" or had engaged in pleasurable homosexual activities, he found that in 1973, only 1 percent of them admitted to having such feelings or having acting on them. In a second study, conducted five years later (when he interviewed only women) he found that 21 percent of the women had, at least on some occasions, felt lesbian "inclinations" or had engaged in pleasurable lesbian practices. Such surveys indicate that even in the most repressed societies, male homosexuality and lesbianism still exist.

For a sampling of information on a variety of cultures, see Table 5.1. A note: In Table 5.1 (and later in Tables 5.2 to 5.6), we present statistics from a number of societies. Because in the various countries researchers chose to sample different populations (e.g., grade school, high school, or college students; the entire population), who varied greatly in age, and because researchers often asked slightly different questions, it is not really appropriate to compare countries, one to another. What students can do is: (1) Get a rough sense of how common various kinds of activities may be in different countries, and (2) find a source for information about countries which are of particular interest to them. (In Table 5.1, we provide the exact question the interviewers asked, since different questions may well elicit very different answers.)

How often do gay and lesbian couples have sexual relations compared to heterosexual couples? Philip Blumstein and Pepper Schwartz (1983) interviewed 950 gay, 768 lesbian, and 3,603 married couples about their sexual habits. When we look at couples who have been together two years or less, we find that gay men had the most active sexual lives—67 percent had sex at least three times a week. Only 45 percent of newly married couples had sex this often. Lesbians engaged in far more cuddling, touching, and hugging than did other couples, but they had less genital sex—only 33 percent of the women engaged in oral sex or clitoral stimulation at least three times a week. These differences make some sense. If women in general often prefer more hugging, cuddling, and touching than they are getting, while men are usually more concerned with having an orgasm, homosexual couples can spend their time doing just as they both please in a sexual encounter. Women can cuddle and men can go for the climax. Married couples, forced to compromise, do a little more and a little less of both than they would like.

For all couples, the frequency of sex declined over time. By the time they had been together for ten years, only 18 percent of married couples were still having intercourse at least three times a week. (Only rarely were they having sex outside of their marriages. See Extramarital Sex later in this chapter.) Only 11 percent of gay couples reported having sex this often. The gay men were still very interested in sex, but now their sexual liaisons were generally occurring outside the committed relationships. Only 1 percent of lesbians were still having genital sex at least three times a week, nor did they engage in much outside sexual activity.

When they do make love, what types of activities do homosexual and heterosexual couples prefer? Homosexual couples, particularly lesbian couples, spend more time in foreplay than do heterosexual couples. Masters and Johnson (1979) found that lesbian couples spent more time kissing, holding, caressing, and in breast stimulation than did heterosexual couples. Gay couples were also found to engage in more body contact, including nipple stimulation, than heterosexual couples.

Homosexual and heterosexual couples also differed in how often they reached orgasm, particularly when we compare the sexual responsiveness of homosexual and heterosexual women. Lauren Bressler and Abraham Lavender (1986) interviewed twenty-three heterosexual, twenty-two bisexual, and twenty-five homosexual women who had been involved for six months or more. Heterosexual women had fewer orgasms per week (4.7) than did either bisexual (8.8) or homosexual women (6.2). Heterosexual women were also less likely to describe their orgasms as "strong" than were other women. Only 48 percent of heterosexual women described their orgasms that way, whereas 86 percent of bisexual and 80 percent of homosexual women described them that way (Bressler & Lavender, 1986). Similar results were reported by Coleman, Hoon, & Hoon, 1983. Researchers have speculated that there are probably three reasons why women are so much more responsive with women than with men:

- Most women prefer more kissing, hugging, cuddling, touching, and oral-genital sex than they get in their marital relations. In love affairs with other women, they are likely to get all the kissing, petting, and oral-genital sex that they want—the kinds of loving foreplay that excites most women.

- Women may be more sensitive to other women's preferences or find it easier to guess what would be arousing for another woman.
- Women may find it easier to communicate with one another about their sexual preferences. (Bressler & Lavender, 1986; Coleman, Hoon, & Hoon, 1983; Peplau, 1981).

Premarital Sex

Researchers have also been interested in people's attitudes toward premarital sex, worldwide.

Attitudes toward Premarital Sex

In the 1960s, Ira Reiss (1967, 1989) began to assess American college students' attitudes toward premarital sexual activity. The first problem he faced was to settle on a definition of premarital sex. Does oral sex "count"? anal sex? What about "secondary virginity" (people who have had sexual relations at least once but who have since decided to abstain)? What about people who were raped? Does that count? Reiss settled on a simple definition: by premarital sex he meant the decision voluntarily to participate in sexual intercourse.

Students were asked to complete the *Premarital Sexual Permissiveness Scale,* which asks how acceptable it is for men and women to engage in premarital sex in various kinds of relationships: if they are engaged, in love, feel strong affection for the other, or do not have any particular feelings for the other. Reiss found that in the 1960s, most students believed in either abstinence or a double standard. They either believed that both men and women should abstain from premarital sexual intercourse or that premarital sex was acceptable for men but not for women. (Other early studies secured similar results: see Darling, Kallen, & Van Dusen, 1984; Sprecher & McKinney, 1993.)

Over the decades, sociologists have continued to ask American college students about their sexual codes of behavior. Researchers agree that in the United States a sexual revolution has occurred. First, the double standard, if not already dead, is rapidly wasting away. Second, since the 1960s, young people's sexual codes have become increasingly permissive. The advent of AIDS, sociologists admit, may be slowing this trend toward increased permissiveness (Oliver & Hyde, 1993).

In the West, the Double Standard Is Eroding

Today, American researchers find that only the last remnants of a double standard still exist. When men and women are asked whether it is appropriate for men and women who are in love, steadily dating, or engaged to have sex, researchers find that most people think exactly the same rules apply to men and women. Most people consider such activities to be equally acceptable for both (Sprecher et al., 1988;

Sprecher, 1989; Sprecher & Hatfield, 1995). It is only when men and women are asked whether it is appropriate for men and women to engage in casual sex, one night stands, group sex, or sex under strange and wondrous circumstances that the old double standard still rears its head. People are generally more tolerant of men who engage in such adventures than of women who do so.

Susan Sprecher and Elaine Hatfield (1995), for example, interviewed 389 men and 654 women from five different colleges: Illinois State University, Southern Methodist University (in Texas), the University of Hawaii, Bradley University (in Illinois), and Millikin College (in Illinois). They asked students whether or not they thought it was appropriate for men and women to have sexual relations on a first date, when they were casually dating, seriously dating, talking about getting married, or engaged. Whether or not a double standard was found to exist depended on who was asked (men or women) and what was asked. Sprecher and Hatfield found that today, although some American men are still clinging to the old double standard, American women are no longer willing to accept such biased treatment.[1] When men were asked whether or not they approved of men and women engaging in sex on a first date or in a casual relationship, they spoke up in favor of the traditional double standard: they thought it was fine for them but not for women to have such casual sexual encounters. Not surprisingly, women did not agree. When men and women were asked about more serious dating relationships— whether they approved of couples who were "engaged to be engaged" or actually engaged having sexual relations—there was no evidence of a double standard. Both men and women advocated a single, relatively permissive standard. Men tended to be a bit more permissive than were women. Apparently, once relationships were sanctified by love and impending marriage, both sexes considered it appropriate for both men and women to enjoy premarital sex.

Recently Mary Beth Oliver and Janet Shibley Hyde (1993) conducted a "meta-analysis" of 239 interviews conducted with 128,363 men and women in the United States and Canada from 1966 to 1990. Meta-analysis is a statistical technique that allows researchers to sum up the data from numerous studies. The scientists found that, in general, men are more tolerant of all sorts of sexual behavior than are women. They are more accepting of premarital intercourse than are women, especially of casual sexual activity. The authors found that these gender differences, however, are rapidly disappearing. When they compared studies conducted from the 1960s to the 1990s, they found that gender differences had become smaller over the years. By the 1990s, they have almost disappeared.

Men, however, still seem more willing to engage in sexual activity at unusual times and places and to engage in more "taboo" kinds of activity than are women (Clark & Hatfield, 1989; Hatfield et al., 1988; Muehlenhard & Quackenbush, 1988).

John DeLamater (1987) pointed out that, in the United States, a second kind of double standard may still exist. Men and women may choose to engage in sexual relations for somewhat different reasons. To some extent, men and women are still handed somewhat different sexual scripts in life. Women are taught to take a "person-centered" orientation to sexuality. They learn that love, sex, and commitment are inextricably entwined. Men are taught to take a recreational, or "body-centered," approach toward sex. For them the goal of sex is physical gratification (Whitley,

1988). This difference in perspective has been found to exist in a variety of ethnic groups—African Americans, Asian Americans, European Americans, and Mexican Americans—and among people of all sexual orientations (heterosexual, bisexual, and homosexual) (Leigh, 1989).

Culture and the Double Standard

Evolutionary psychologists contend that the double standard is genetically based and thus likely to be a cultural universal. Men, who can never be sure of a child's paternity, must be far more concerned about their mate's fidelity than are women, who are, of course, always certain that they are the mother. In a study described earlier, David Buss (1989) attempted to test the hypothesis that, worldwide, men would be more concerned with the chastity of their mates than would women. Buss asked men and women in thirty-three countries how critical chastity was in a mate. He found that, around the world, men *were* more concerned with the virginity of potential mates than were women. Men thought chastity was more important than did women in 62 percent of the societies, including the United States. Men and women agreed about the importance, or unimportance, of chastity in 38 percent of the societies. Figure 5.1 illustrates the importance of chastity to men and women in various geographical regions.

Buss was interested in ferreting out cultural universals. Nonetheless, he could not help but be struck by the powerful impact that culture had on whether or not people endorsed the double standard. There was nothing people in different cultures disagreed about more than the importance of chastity. Culture accounted for a full 37 percent of the variance on this trait.

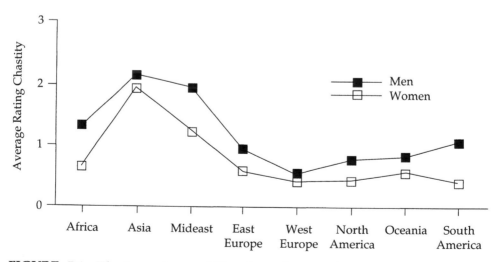

FIGURE 5.1   The Importance of Chastity to Men and Women in Various Geographical Regions

Wallen (1989), p. 38. Based on Buss (1989).

Other researchers have observed the same cultural variability. In one Hong Kong study, for example (Family Planning Association of Hong Kong, 1987), researchers asked men and women (from 18 to 27 years of age) whether they agreed with the statement that "men and women are equal in sexual rights: A woman is free to engage in any sexual relation in which a man is permitted." Although 54 percent of men and 67 percent of women agreed with those egalitarian sentiments, about a fourth were neutral, and 11 percent of men and 12 percent of women thought that the two sexes should *not* possess equal sexual rights.

In different cultures—which possess different traditions, political and economic systems, religions, family structures, and values—men and women differ greatly in how much political and economic power they possess and thus in their sexual rights. Cross-cultural researchers (Shapurian & Hojat, 1985), have argued that in a society, the more power men possess relative to women, the more likely men will be to enforce a double standard to serve their interests. As cultural power balances shift and men and women begin to share power, women begin to insist on their sexual rights, and the double standard begins to disappear. There is at least some anecdotal evidence in support of this contention. Anthropologists, sociologists, and cross-cultural researchers have reported that the double standard is beginning to decrease or entirely disappear in China (Chan, 1990), Finland (Kontula, 1993; Kontula & Haavio-Mannila, 1995), Iran (Shapurian & Hojat, 1985), Morocco (Davis & Davis, 1994), Russia (Kon, 1993), Sweden (Popenoe, 1987), and Thailand (Bumroongsook, 1992).

In the West, a More Permissive View of Premarital Sexual Activity
Every few years, the National Opinion Research Center (NORC) interviews a random sample of Americans concerning their attitudes toward premarital sexual activity. An examination of the surveys conducted from 1972 to 1991 makes it clear that Americans have become increasingly tolerant of premarital sex over the decades (Reiss & Lee, 1988).

In the latest 1991 survey (Davis & Smith, 1991), interviewers asked 1,021 Americans: "There's been a lot of discussion about the way morals and attitudes about sex are changing in this country. If a man and woman have sex relations before marriage, do you think it is always wrong, almost always wrong, wrong only sometimes, or not wrong at all?" (p. 256). By 1991, only 36 percent of Americans thought premarital sex was always or almost always wrong; 18 percent thought it was wrong only sometimes; 43 percent thought it was not wrong at all; and 3 percent just didn't know.

The most recent surveys suggest that today most young men and women possess a single, liberal standard concerning premarital sexual activity. Many believe that young couples should engage in sexual relations only if they both feel at least some affection for their partners (Clayton & Bokemeier, 1980; Greeley, 1991). Most are willing to grant their friends more leeway, however; they think that it is all right for *them* to have sexual relations with casual acquaintances (Sprecher & McKinney, 1993).

Generally, researchers also find that in America, the various ethnic groups differ somewhat in their sexual standards. African Americans hold to more permissive premarital sexual standards than do European Americans (Harrison, Bennett, Globetti, & Alsikafi 1974; Staples, 1978; Weinberg & Williams, 1988). Gail Wyatt (1989 and Wyatt et al., 1993) points out that if researchers control for differences in family income and family structure (single-parent homes versus two-parent families), however, these ethnic differences disappear. European American and Chinese American students, in turn, have more permissive premarital sexual standards than do Hispanic American college students (Hendrick & Hendrick, 1987a; Huang & Uba, 1992; Padilla & O'Grady, 1987).

Culture and Sexual Permissiveness
Cultures differ enormously in how they view premarital sexual activity. In the Buss study, which we described earlier, for example, Buss (1989) found that cultures disagreed more on the value of premarital sexual experience (or inexperience) than on any other issue. In China, India, Indonesia, Iran, Israel (the Palestinian Arabs), and Taiwan, young people were insistent that chastity was "indispensable" in a partner. In contrast, men and women from Finland, France, Norway, the Netherlands, Sweden, and West Germany were equally likely to insist that chastity was relatively unimportant. Some even felt that it was a disadvantage.

Other studies have secured similar results. Young people in Asia, Mexico, the Middle East, and South America generally strongly disapprove of premarital sexual activity. Young adults in the United States, Belgium, France, and the Scandinavian countries hold relatively permissive sexual standards. They tend to accept the "permissiveness with affection" principle (Alzate, 1984; Christensen, 1973; Iwawaki & Eysenck, 1978; Kontula & Haavio-Mannila, 1995; LaBeff & Dodder, 1982; Shapurian & Hojat 1985; Werebe & Reinert, 1983).

Susan Sprecher and Elaine Hatfield (1995), for example, questioned 1,667 men and women, all college students, in the United States, Russia, and Japan. They were asked to what extent they agreed with five statements:

1. I believe that sexual intercourse is acceptable for me on a first date.
2. I believe that sexual intercourse is acceptable for me when I'm casually dating my partner (dating less than one month).
3. I believe that sexual intercourse is acceptable for me when I'm seriously dating my partner (dating almost one year).
4. I believe that sexual intercourse is acceptable for me when I'm pre-engaged to my partner (we have seriously discussed the possibility of getting married).
5. I believe that sexual intercourse is acceptable for me when I'm engaged to be married.

Possible answers ranged from (1) strongly agree to (6) strongly disagree.

Do young people from these three very different cultures differ in their sexual mores? In this part of the study the authors focused on how tolerant subjects were of their own sexual behavior (permissiveness for self, or "me") in a variety of casual to serious relationships. They found that young Americans were far more tolerant of premarital sexual activity than were students from Russia or Japan. In all three cultures, people tended to disapprove of casual sex. There were significant cultural differences in how early in a love affair people thought it was appropriate to have sexual relations. The Russians were a bit more approving of sex on a first date than were the others. Americans were slightly more tolerant of sex in serious dating relationships than were others. They were somewhat more tolerant than others once couples were pre-engaged, and they were considerably more tolerant than others once couples were formally engaged. For Americans, the touchstones seemed to be love and commitment; they were the prerequisites for sex. For the Russians and the Japanese, the real dividing line seemed to be marriage.

Observers comment that in China (Butterfield, 1982), Finland (Kontula, 1993; Kontula & Haavio-Mannila, 1995), French-Canada (Samson et al., 1991), Russia (Kon, 1993) and in the United States (Frayser, 1985) premarital sex is beginning to be viewed more tolerantly.

Premarital Sexual Activity

Anthropologist Suzanne Frayser selected sixty-two hunting, foraging, and agricultural societies from the *Standard Cross-Cultural Sample*. She found that most of these preindustrial societies (64 percent) allowed men and/or women to have premarital sexual liaisons. Generally societies had a single standard of behavior; in 82 percent of societies either both boys and girls were permitted to engage in sexual relations or both were forbidden to do so. In a minority of societies (18 percent), however, there was a double standard—boys were encouraged or at least allowed to have premarital sex, but girls were not (Frayser, 1985). A comparison of two societies, the Silwa in Aswan, Egypt, and the Marquesans in Polynesia, illustrates two starkly contrasting views.

The Silwa disapproved of even talking about sex, much less engaging in it. Young girls' clitorises were removed when they were 7 or 8 years old. Excision was designed to eliminate women's sexual feelings and thus aid them in avoiding temptation. At adolescence, young women were required to hide their faces behind a veil and to disguise their figures in billowy clothing. Young people found the idea of premarital sexual experimentation so shameful and terrifying that no one is known ever to have violated the taboo (Ammar, 1954).

The Marquesan girl's skin was rubbed with coconut oil and scented with sandalwood. Older men and women initiated young people into sex. Girls usually had intercourse for the first time when they were 8 to 10 years old, boys when they were 7 to 12. Adolescents continued to experiment sexually with both boys and girls (Handy, 1923; Suggs, 1966). Frayser (1985) observed: "The image that best conveys a sense of Marquesan adolescence is that of a group of youths, fragrant with the scent of saffron and other herbs, who band together in the pursuit of the exciting pleasures that await them" (p. 202).

John DeLamater and Patricia MacCorquodale (1979) found that American men and women first experienced sexual relations at roughly the same age. Men had sexual relations for the first time at 17.5 years of age; women at 17.9 years of age. In their meta-analysis of all the studies that have explored gender differences, Oliver and Hyde (1993) found that from 1966 to 1990, men still were more sexual than were women. Men and women of various ages were equally likely to have kissed or petted. However, as things began to get more serious, gender differences began to appear. Men at any given age were more likely to have had intercourse than were women. Men had sex at a younger age than did women. They had sex more often and with more partners than did women. They also felt less guilt and anxiety about their sexual experimentation than did women. Here, too, however, things were changing. When the authors compared the results of studies conducted in the 1960s through the 1990s, they found that men's and women's sexual behavior had become increasingly similar over the decades.

Recently, the National Opinion Research Center asked a random sample of Americans how many sexual partners they had since they were 18. Men reported an average of 12.3 partners and women an average of 3.3 (Smith, 1991). Obviously men must exaggerate their number of conquests, whereas women conveniently forget some of theirs.

Cross-cultural researchers have also asked men and women in various cultures about their sexual experiences. Table 5.2 lists the percentages of young men and women in a variety of countries who report that they have engaged in sexual intercourse at least once.

TABLE 5.2   Percentage of Men and Women Who Have Engaged in Premarital Sexual Relations

Culture	Age of Respondents (Average Age or Age Range)	Men (percent)	Women (percent)
United States[1]	21	—	87
United States[2]	20	84	61
Asian American[3]	20	80	80
African American[4]	20	95	90
African American[5,6]	15–19	81	61
Chinese American[7]	20	37	46
European American[4]	20	80	80
European American[5,6]	15–19	57	52
Hispanic[5,6]	15–19	60	48
Hispanic[8]	15–24	80	60
Mexican American[8]	15–24	81	58
Puerto Rican American[8]	15–24	77	68
Africa			
Liberia[9]	18–21	93	82
Nigeria[9]	19	86	63
Australia[10]	By age 20	58	47

TABLE 5.2 *Continued*

Culture	Age of Respondents (Average Age or Age Range)	Men (percent)	Women (percent)
Brazil[11]	15–19	73	28
	20–24	94	60
Chile[11]	15–19	48	19
	20–24	86	57
Colombia[11]	20	89	65
Federal Republic of Germany[10]	By age 16	35	30
Hong Kong[12]	13–18	6	4
	13–27	27	19
	By 27	38	24
India[13]	20	75	60
Nigeria[10]	14–19	68	43
Northern Ireland[14]	20	50	44
Israel[10]	14–19	42	11
Japan[15]	21	27	10
Japan[11]	16–21	15	7
Kenya[10]	By age 19	80	—
Republic of Korea[10]	12–21	17	4
Mexico[11]	15–19	44	13
	20–24	86	39
Norway[16]	20[a]	78	86
United Kingdom[17]	19–20	84	85
West Germany[18]	20	78	83

[1]DeBuono et al. (1990).
[2]Darling & Davidson (1986).
[3]Sue (1982).
[4]Belcastro (1985).
[5]Forrest & Singh (1990).
[6]Sonenstein et al. (1989).
[7]Huang & Uba (1992).
[8]Ford & Norris (1993).
[9]Liskin (1992).
[10]Hofman (1984).
[11]Robey et al. (1992).
[12]Family Planning Association of Hong Kong (1987).
[13]Bhatia (1986).
[14]Sneddon & Kremer (1992).
[15]Asayama (1975), actually 1960.
[16]Sundet et al. (1992).
[17]Breakwell & Fife-Schaw (1992).
[18]Clement et al. (1984).
[a]Respondents are 18 to 60 years of age. They are recalling behavior at age 20.

Gail Wyatt (1993) pointed out that in many parts of the world, boys and girls do not have a choice about whether or not to engage in sexual relations. In some places, children are sold into prostitution. Sometimes children are raped. Others are married at very young ages to mates not of their own choosing.

In her autobiography, Princess Sultana of Saudi Arabia (Sasson, 1992), recounted a searing story. As soon as she reached puberty, tradition required Sultana to wear a thick black veil and *abaaya*. Men were not allowed to look upon her face. But Sultana and her teenage friends were rebels. They believed in women's liberation. Secretly, they flirted and petted with young men they met clandestinely. When their fathers discovered what they were up to, Nadia's father covered her head with a dark hood, bound her in chains, and drowned her in a swimming pool. Wafa was hastily forced to marry a 53-year-old villager to remove her from temptation. Thus, it came as a shock to Sultana when, on a holiday to Cairo, she and her friends walked in on her brother Ali and his sanctimonious friend Hadi raping a terrified Egyptian girl, no more than 8 years old. It was then that Sultana learned that her father, her brother, and his friends routinely patronized this service.

In light of such practices, Gail Wyatt (1993) argued that in cross-cultural research, it is misleading to ask, "When did you first have intercourse?" What researchers should really ask is, "When did you first *choose* to have intercourse?" This argument makes sense, but not surprisingly previous researchers have not delved into the murky waters of intent. They have merely asked men and women when they first had intercourse, whether or not they had wished to do so. In Table 5.3 we present the age at which men and women first experience sexual intercourse.

Why Men and Women Have Sexual Relations

When young people are asked why they have sex, women typically begin to talk about love and intimacy, while men say they were motivated by "lust" or a desire for "physical release." B. E. Whitley (1988) asked men and women, "What was your most important reason for having sexual intercourse on the most recent occasion"? He found that 51 percent of women but only 24 percent of men gave love or emotion reasons, while 51 percent of men but only 9 percent of women gave lust or pleasure reasons. Barbara Leigh (1989) asked men and women from African American, Asian American, European American, and Hispanic American groups and with heterosexual, bisexual, or homosexual orientations to rate the importance of seven possible reasons for having sexual relations. In general, men attached more importance to sexual pleasure, conquest, and the relief of sexual tension than did women. Men also approved of casual sex (sex without love) and sex just "for fun" more than women did. Women attached more importance to emotional closeness than did men. Men's and women's motivations for sex were different, no matter what the sex of their partners. Such gender differences have been found in the United States (Foa et al., 1987), Hong Kong (Family Planning Association of Hong Kong, 1987), Finland (Kontula & Haavio-Mannila, 1995), and Sweden (Foa et al., 1987).

The Consequences of Premarital Sex

In the West, young men and women generally react very differently to their first sexual experiences. Young men often think of a sex as a "rite of passage" into

**TABLE 5.3   Age at First Intercourse
(For Those Who Are Sexually Experienced)**

Culture	Men	Women
United States		
African American[1]	—	16.7
African American[2]	13.6	16.2
Chinese American[3]	18.5	18.8
European American[3]	16.9	17.7
Africa		
Nigeria[4]	16	17
Brazil[5]	15	17
Chile[5]	16	18
Japan[6]	21	22
Mexico[5]	16	17
Norway[7]	18.3	17.2
Lima, Peru[8]	16.2	19.2
Russia[9]	19.3[a]	19.3[a]

[1]Wyatt (1989).
[2]Belcastro (1985).
[3]Huang & Uba (1992).
[4]Liskin (1985).
[5]Robey et al. (1992).
[6]Hatano (1991).
[7]Sundet et al. (1992).
[8]Holmes (1993).
[9]Golod (1993).
[a]Separate statistics not reported for men and women.

manhood (Carns, 1973). Most men said they felt "excited," "happy," "satisfied," and "thrilled" the first time they had sexual intercourse. For women, however, it was more risky to experiment with sex. They felt it was only "legitimate" if they were involved in a serious, meaningful relationship (Carns, 1973). Women often felt guilty, sad, disappointed, and afraid after their first sexual encounter (DeLamater, 1987; Sprecher, Barbee, & Schwartz, 1995). Interestingly, men were usually unaware of their partners' negative reactions (Sorensen, 1973).

Men were likely to boast to their family and friends about their sexual escapades, and their family and friends were likely to approve of their behavior. Women were less likely to confide in others. It is easy to see why. Unless the couple's relationship was a deeply committed one, her family—brought up, as they were, on different and more conservative sexual mores—and even her friends generally disapproved of her behavior (Carns, 1973; DeLamater, 1987).

In traditional double standard cultures, men and women who engage in sexual relations are generally treated very differently. In the next few pages, we will depart from our usual format. Instead of selecting a brief literary example to illustrate a scientific finding, we present two extended literary passages to drive home a single point: in traditional societies, men and women who choose to engage in premarital sexual activity can expect to suffer very different fates.

First, let us consider the fate of a young man who hurled himself into sexual activity. Zulfikar Ghose (1984) described the reaction of 14-year-old Gregório Peixoto da Silva Xavier, a volunteer in the Brazilian army, to his first sexual encounter with a very young Indian prostitute:

> *The girl who sat on the bed was thin and small. . . . She was so underdeveloped that her ribs were more in evidence than her breasts. . . . She sat on the edge of the bed, her hands tightly clutched in front of her thighs, and it was obvious that she was not a little frightened. She watched me with apparent fear and hatred. . . . The prospect was not altogether promising. I decided that I had best undress myself. . . . Presently I was completely dispossessed of my clothes and for a moment I stood there on the floor wondering how I should proceed.*
>
> *. . . I was just about to take a step towards her when she sprang out of the bed, rushed at me and, grabbing hold of my penis in no uncertain manner, gave it a sudden and desperate pull, and retreated back, all in a second. It hurt, it really hurt badly, and I could not help uttering a sharp little scream. In retrospect, I am thankful to her for the pain she caused me, for it stopped my mind from wondering how to proceed. Instead, I made an instinctive rush at her, almost diving through the air and, catching her at her hips, flung her back and pressed down upon her. But she was agile, slippery, and extricated herself in an instant. It struck me that we were more like two boys playing on the bank of a river than lovers in a bedroom. Before I could turn round and raise myself, I felt her fall with a thud upon me and dig her teeth into my shoulder. I gave another little scream and pushed her aside. She fell back to the floor and I found myself falling on her; but before I could actually fall on her, she slipped out of the way and jumped back on to the bed and sat right in the middle of it while I went crashing against the floor. I could hear her soft, girlish laughter. Rising, I stood beside the bed, just out of reach. She fell back, her short black hair bouncing on her head, and giggled, her bright black eyes fixed on me. . . . While I still stood, she shuffled in the bed as if she wished to make room for me, and indeed that seemed to be her suggestion for she patted the bed as if to indicate that I should come and lie there. I approached the bed gingerly and sat on its edge. She leaned up and put a hand gently to my arm and stroked it and then again patted the bed. Well, I thought, this is as clear an invitation as I am likely to receive and so, lifting up my legs, lay back on the bed. She began to take little bites around my chest which I did not feel unpleasant and thought that this must be a form of love-making which some instinct had suggested to her. So, I raised my head and gave her shoulder a little nibble, too. She giggled and, drawing back, sat up on my thighs and gradually began to wiggle her way up my body. The sensation, though a trifle harsh, was quite pleasant, and as her soft little behind moved slowly over my groin, the sudden heat from her body sent a wave of pure lust through my body. But she was still moving up and presently the little triangle of tiny black hairs, more a delicate brushmark than an actual growth, was within an inch of my chin. From that area emanated a smell which was both awfully repugnant and desperately*

attractive. I was just beginning to think that for a frightened little Indian virgin, the girl knew quite a few tricks of a trade at which she was not even an apprentice as yet when she suddenly lifted herself and, raising herself so that her buttocks were now directly above my face as if she wished my nose to play at the cleavage there, farted, and jumped off the bed. Her soft laughter again filled the room.

'You bitch!' I called, jumping after her. But she had become coy and holding me rubbed her nose against my chest in an endearing fashion. I held her, watching her head just below my chin, her hair swirling as she continued to rub her nose on me. I lifted her up and placed her on the bed. She seemed to have become docile and not wishing to give her another opportunity to play the fool, I lay upon her. After all her childish tricks, she now surprised me, behaving as though she had long waited for this moment of ecstasy. She guided me in and, the penetration accomplished with some difficulty, she sighed and held me more tightly. I felt separated from what was happening to me, for my mind seemed more concerned with observing the behaviour of the girl than anything that my body experienced. I saw myself going through an action which was nearly devoid of all sensation as if it were an experiment I observed. I am not sure whether I did have any real sensation though I do remember that the climactic moment had a certain breathlessness about it. (pp. 47–50)

Gregório's first sexual encounter may have gone less than smoothly, but it did generate some side benefits. When his young comrades-in-arms discovered that Gregório had completed his "long delayed" rite of passage into sexuality, they accepted him into their ranks for the first time:

From now on, I was one of the men, initiating the kind of hilarity that goes on among comrades who think they are in a peculiarly masculine situation, and no longer the shy boy who witnessed the mirth of others with a mixture of awe and incomprehension. It was satisfying to realize that the adult world offered a greater variety of games than one's boyhood and that, far from being a hardship, losing one's youth was a definite gain. (pp. 51–52)

Now let us consider the fate of one woman in a traditional culture who dared to experiment sexually. If Rifi Berber women in tribal Morocco lose their honor, they may be killed by their husbands or brothers (Hart, 1976). Bouthaina Shaaban (1991) remembered her own experiences as a young girl in another Arab land, Syria:

It was a bright morning early in 1968. The pupils were streaming from my village in groups of twos and threes towards the only secondary school in the area. . . . I had just reached the police station, heading towards the school, when I saw my class-mate Aziz joyfully descending a hill in the centre of the village, waving a dagger dripping with blood and chanting, "I've killed her and saved the family's honour!" He ran up to two policemen who were standing outside the station, handed them the dagger and said in a voice loud enough for everyone around to hear, "I have killed my sister and have come to hand myself over for justice." The three of them strolled slowly into the police station, chatting amicably.

With that scene etched upon my mind, I got to school. The first lesson that morning was taught by a young teacher who happened to be a Christian. When he came into the class he looked deathly pale, his hands were trembling and he avoided the pupils' eyes, until he lighted on two sisters sitting just in front of me, Sahar and Samar, and began to question them: "How did he kill her? Where was your father? Did she cry out?" Reluctantly the two girls described how they had been sleeping in the same bed as Yemen, the sister of Aziz, and had woken up to find her murdered, in a pool of blood.

Yemen was sixteen years old. At that time a trade in women servants flourished between our village and some of the wealthy families of Beirut. . . . The fathers would go once a year to collect their wages and see them. . . . When girls came of age, however, they would be brought back to wait for their prospective husbands. . . . Only a few months after Yemen's arrival, underground gossip erupted with the news that she was pregnant.

On the same day, Yemen's aunt and mother put her on a hired motorcycle and took her to the neighbouring town, Salamia, where the doctor confirmed the pregnancy. Her mother didn't dare bring her back home, fearful that her brothers might kill her. So she took her to the house of Al Mokhar (village master or chief) in the next village and asked him to protect her from her brothers. According to our Arabic traditions, anyone who enters one's home and asks for protection should be protected. Traditionally, the host would sacrifice his life rather than let Al Dakhiel (the one who has asked to be protected) be assaulted in his home. Al Mokhtar put her with his two young daughters and, by all accounts, was looking after her well until, on a moonlit night, Aziz climbed walls and roofs and managed to reach the room where the three girls were sleeping. With a sharpened dagger he cut Yemen's throat. Unlike most criminals who try their best to leave no trace of themselves, he dipped his hands in the warm, innocent blood and went out triumphantly to celebrate publicly the cleansing of his honour.

Burial ceremonies are usually not allowed for the victims of such "crimes of honour"; any respect shown towards the dead body would be construed as condoning the victim's ignoble act. Thus, Al Mokhtar had no choice but to invite young children in and ask them to pull the body to the graveyard at the other end of the village. Children were pulling her by the hair, throwing big stones at her misshapen, pregnant abdomen and spitting at her. On our way back from school we saw the naked body still lying in the graveyard like a dead sheep. None of us dared show the slightest sign of pity, but most of the girls didn't go to school the next morning to avoid the appallingly sad scene. Two days later the news reached us that the body had been removed, either by wild beasts or by someone who had taken pity on her and buried her at a time when he or she would not be seen.

Aziz was imprisoned for only six months. (pp. 3–5)

Shabban (1991) found such differences to exist in most of the Arab countries—Algeria, Lebanon, Palestine, and Syria. In the earlier Saudi Arabian example, you will recall, Nadia and Wafa were banished and killed when they were caught petting. Her brother and his friends, Ali and Hadi, on the other hand, were encouraged to force young Egyptian girls to have sex with them. The boys blamed the little girls for the rapes.

Marital Sex

> *All societies attempt to control individuals' sexuality.*
> —David Suggs and Andrew Miracle

Attitudes toward Marital Sex

In the United States, about 80 to 90 percent of people marry (Gagnon, 1977). Western psychologists, probably assuming that everyone approves of sex in marriage, have rarely conducted research on attitudes toward conjugal sex. The moment we try to take a broader historical and cross-cultural perspective, however, we begin to wish we knew a bit more about attitudes toward marital sex in the West and elsewhere. Throughout history, people have had a wide array of attitudes toward marital sex. In medieval times, for example, the Catholic church was not altogether approving of sex, even within marriage. Today, worldwide, attitudes toward marital sex vary. Many Chinese physicians, for example, believe that a harmonious balance between the *yin* (female) and the *yang* (male) elements is essential to good health. Semen loss (through masturbation, homosexual activity, and to some extent even spousal sex) presumably disrupts this balance and makes men susceptible to disease. Many of these same physicians assume that since women do not lose *yang* from sexual relations, such activities are not dangerous for them (Yap, 1965; Ruan, 1991). In the 1920s, for example, Ching-sheng Chang (1928/1968) wrote a treatise on sex that was considered so revolutionary that it was suppressed throughout China. But his views are clearly those of another, distant time. Consider his views on masturbation:

> *According to a famous Peking physician, some of the young persons whom he treated may have died because of a suicidal cruelty toward their reproductive organs.*
> *Flower-like maidens suddenly lose their fragrance; intelligent youths contract tuberculosis. It is truly regrettable when we think of young lives being buried among the five fingers. The basis for this kind of criminal evil arises from an ignorance of sexology. Both sexes reduce their bodily vigor through giving vent heedlessly to their lusts. (p. 17)*

In India, the Ayrvedic medical system teaches that it takes forty days and forty drops of blood to make one drop of semen. Celibacy is the first requirement of true fitness, because semen is lost in every orgasm. Men who lose too much semen presumably experience malaise, bodily weakness, and wasting away (Carstairs, 1956; Dewaraja & Sasaki, 1991).

When people in various cultures experience a panic attack or feel anxious or just tired and miserable, they can attribute their problems to any number of causes. The hardworking Japanese, for example, often attribute their mental and physical problems to stress and overwork. In India, men often complain of *jiryan* or *viriya nasta* (semen loss). One Deoli physician, for example, reported that in his village, men often complained that their bodily store of semen had curdled and gone bad. Any infection or weakness was assumed to be due to spoiled semen. *Jiryan* was the third most common medical complaint (Carstairs, 1956). In Malaysia, Southeast Asia, southern China, and the Sudan, men sometimes fall victim to *koro*. In this syndrome, men experience anxiety, have panic attacks, and fear impending death. A main feature of *koro* is the delusion that the penis is shrinking and is just about to disappear into the body for good. The "cause" of this ailment, men believe, is the semen loss that occurs in nocturnal emissions, masturbation, and "excessive" marital sex (Dewaraja & Sasaki, 1991; Yap, 1965).

Recently, Ratnin Dewaraja and Yuji Sasaki (1991) decided to study the prevalence of the belief in Sri Lanka and Japan that semen loss causes disease. They interviewed 254 undergraduates in Sri Lanka, 516 undergraduates in Japan, and 35 patients at the General Hospital of Colombo (Sri Lanka) who complained that they were suffering from semen loss syndrome. Sri Lankan students tended to attribute their ailments to semen loss; Japanese students did not. Most of the Sri Lankan patients were young, single men with limited sexual experience. These men worried about their ability to perform on their wedding night. They were concerned about the size of their penis and their ability to get and keep an erection. They felt weak and lethargic and complained of numerous aches and pains. They worried that their body was getting thin and wasting away. These young men attributed their problems to too many nocturnal emissions, too much masturbation, and too much sexual experimentation. Married men had the same worries. In the West we might attribute their problems to too much sexual guilt and too little sexual confidence and experience.

Researchers have become interested in changes in the way marital sexuality, especially that of wives, is viewed. Couples in the West have begun to pay greater attention to women's (rather than simply men's) sexual satisfaction. They have also become more sexually sophisticated: more willing to engage in foreplay, to try various sexual positions, and to experiment generally.

One way researchers have tried to chart changing attitudes about sexuality in marriage is to analyze the content of marriage manuals. Martin Weinberg, Rochelle Swensson, and Sue Hammersmith (1983), for example, carefully analyzed forty-nine sex manuals published in the United States between 1950 and 1980. During that period, the view of female sexuality changed markedly. In the early manuals (published from 1950 to 1973), writers took it for granted that men and women were *different and unequal*. Though these early writers rejected the still earlier notion that sex was a woman's distasteful duty and urged women to shed their traditional passivity and enjoy sex, today these manuals seem dated. They still portrayed men and women as fundamentally different in the sexual realm. Men were considered far more passionate and more sexually skilled than were women. Thus, the man was cast as the sexual teacher. In this "sleeping beauty" model, it was the husband's job to awaken his wife's dormant sex drive. By 1975, however, the authors' views had changed markedly. Here, the ideal was of male and female *sexual autonomy*. Both men and women were portrayed as sexual, independent agents, self-sufficient, and in control of their own sexuality. These manuals provided step-by-step procedures to help women achieve orgasm.

Marital Sexual Activity

Researchers interested in marital sexuality have been interested in such questions as what sorts of foreplay couples do, how much foreplay they engage in, how often they have sexual relations, what kinds of sexual activities they wish they could perform or actually do engage in, and how satisfactory are their sexual relations.

Foreplay

In different cultures, couples differ in how much kissing, hugging, and petting they engage in. When the Thonga (in Mozambique, Africa) first saw Europeans kissing, they thought it was hilarious. They chortled: "Look at them—they eat each other's saliva and dirt" (Ford & Beach, 1972, p. 49). The Lepcha (a tribe in the southeastern Himalayas) rarely engaged in any preliminaries before proceeding to intercourse. The Trobriand Islanders of Melanesia, on the other hand, usually devoted hours to foreplay (Ford & Beach, 1951). In the West, couples typically begin lovemaking by kissing and hugging and engaging in at least some foreplay before proceeding to intercourse or oral-genital sex.

When Kinsey and his colleagues conducted their research in the late 1930s and 1940s, couples in the United States were investing only about ten minutes in foreplay before proceeding to sexual intercourse. In the 1990s, young American couples move more slowly. A variety of studies document that men and women now spend a bit more time on foreplay. In one study, men and women reported spending an average of 17.5 minutes in foreplay (Darling, Davidson, & Cox, 1991). In another, African American and European American women reported that they and their partners typically spent 12.2 and 13.48 minutes on foreplay, respectively (Fisher, 1980). Men may be satisfied with this amount of foreplay, but most women are not. On the average, women say they would prefer at least 17.5 minutes of foreplay prior to penetration (Darling et al., 1991).

Since Kinsey's day, men and women have begun to engage in a larger repertoire of activities (kissing, hugging, oral-genital sex, and so forth) during foreplay. One of the most dramatic changes in the past twenty-five years is the acceptance of oral sex as a regular part of lovemaking. In the 1940s and 1950s, only 11 to 12 percent of couples dared to practice *fellatio* (the woman's mouth encloses the man's penis) and *cunnilingus* (the man's tongue caresses the woman's clitoris). By the 1980s, 90 to 93 percent of married couples had experimented with both fellatio and cunnilingus (Blumstein & Schwartz, 1983; Gagnon & Simon, 1987; Griffitt & Hatfield, 1985).

Japanese researchers found that about 65 percent of married couples always engage in some sort of foreplay—kissing, touching, and so forth. Generally, they spend only 10 to 15 minutes during each act of intercourse (Asayama, 1975).

Frequency of Sexual Relations

Throughout the world, there has been and is still a great deal of variability in how often couples have intercourse. The Keraki (in southwestern Papua, New Guinea) generally had intercourse only once a week. In most tribal societies, couples had intercourse once a night. The Aranda of Australia had intercourse as often as three to five times a night, pausing only to sleep for a while between each sex act. Among the Thonga of Africa, it was not unusual for men to have intercourse with three or four of their wives in a single night. For Chagga couples, it was reported that intercourse ten times in a single night was not unusual (Ford & Beach, 1972).

Philip Blumstein and Pepper Schwartz (1983) asked a national sample of 4,314 couples who were living together or married: "About how often during the last year have you and your partner had sexual relations"? Possible answers ranged from 1, daily or almost every day, to 7, a few times. They found, as other survey researchers have, that on the average, young married couples in the United States usually had sex two or three times a week (see Table 5.4). They, like other sex researchers, were surprised by the wide variation in marital sexual appetites. Some couples were extremely sexual; they liked to have sexual relations (and often did) several times

TABLE 5.4 Married Couples' Frequency of Sexual Intercourse

Culture	Average Age of Sample	No. of Times per Week
United States		
African American[1]	29	4.65
European American[1]	29	3.79
Finland[2]	18–54	1–2
French-Canada[3]	25–34	2.3
	35–44	1.8
	45–54	1.6
	55–64	0.8
	65+	1.0
Japan[4]	20s	2.0
	30s	2.0
	40s	1.0
	50s	0.25
Norway[5]	15–54	2.0

[1]Fisher (1980).
[2]Kontula (1993).
[3]Samson et al. (1991).
[4]Asayama (1975).
[5]Lidegaard & Helm (1990).

a day. Others just weren't interested, ever! Similar results were secured by Donnelly (1993), Greenblat (1983), Hyde (1990), and Laumann et al. (1994).

As couples age, they copulate less and less frequently. As one American sex researcher stated: "It has been observed since ancient times that frequency of intercourse declines with age in human beings" (Udry, 1980, p. 320). Geoffrey Gorer (1938) wrote of the Lepcha, who live in the southeastern Himalayas:

> *In their youth and young manhood . . . Lepcha men would appear to be remarkably potent; trustworthy people said that when they were first married they would copulate with their wives five or six, and even eight or nine times in the course of the night, though they would then be tired the next day. . . . This potency diminishes around the age of thirty, but copulation once nightly is still the general rule for married couples. Tafoor claimed that in his youth he was almost indefatigable, but says that now he only sleeps with his wife once every three or four nights. (pp. 329–330)*

Lillian Rubin (1990) also addressed the question of what happens to sex in marriage over time in her recent interview study of almost 1,000 people from all over the United States. She concluded:

> *On the most mundane level, the constant negotiation about everyday tasks leaves people harassed, weary, irritated and feeling more like traffic cops than lovers. Who's going to do the shopping, pay the bills, take care of the laundry, wash the dishes, take out the garbage, clean the bathroom, get the washing machine fixed, decide what to eat for dinner, return the phone calls from friends and parents? When there are children, the demands, complications and exhaustion increase exponentially. And hovering above it all are the financial concerns that beset most families in the nation today. . . .*
>
> *Even when relative harmony reigns, the almost endless series of tasks, demands, and needs unfilled do nothing to foster the kind of romantic feelings that tend to stimulate sexual desire. "Christ, by the time we get through dealing with all the shit of living, who cares about sex? I sometimes think it's a miracle that we still want to do it at all," said 28-year-old Brian, a Detroit factory worker, married nine years, the father of two small children. (p. 165)*

Recently, Vaughn Call, Susan Sprecher, and Pepper Schwartz (in press) analyzed data from a national representative sample of more than 7,000 adults in the United States. They found that as the age of couples increased and the longer they were married, the less often they had sexual relations. During the first month of their marriage, newlyweds had sexual intercourse slightly more than four times a week on average. After the first year of marriage, they averaged having intercourse only twice a week. After twenty years of marriage, they were making love only once a week (James, 1981). Later in life, couples generally continued to have sexual relations until they were overtaken by ill health (Weiler, 1981). Similar results were secured by Laumann et al., 1994 and Smith, 1991.

Positions Used

Since ancient times, sculptures, paintings, and love manuals such as *The Kama Sutra of Vatsyayana* (1st–4th century A.D./1963) have illustrated a variety of positions for intercourse. In Kinsey's day, the "missionary position" (man on top) was used by almost all married couples in the United States; 70 percent of his respondents used this position almost exclusively. Today, most American couples are far more comfortable with gender equality and are more liberal sexually (Blumstein & Schwartz, 1983). They use a variety of different sexual positions. During intercourse, the man may be on top, the woman may be on top, the man may enter the woman from the rear, or couples may have relations side-to-side (Darling et al., 1991; Griffitt & Hatfield, 1985).

Shin'ichi Asayama (1975) asked Japanese couples to estimate how often they used various sexual positions. Young couples (in their twenties) reported that generally the husband was on top during intercourse (55 percent of the time); the wife was on top only rarely (11 percent of the time). The rest of the time they experimented with sideways (11 percent), rear (11 percent), or sitting positions (11 percent of the time). None of the couples had tried the standing position.

Interest in Sexual Diversity

There is some evidence that men may be slightly more venturesome in their sexual relationships than are women. Hatfield and her students (1988) interviewed casually dating, steadily dating, and married couples about their sexual preferences. They asked: During sex, do you wish for more (or less) of a series of activities? Do you wish your partners were more loving? Do you desire more loving talk, more warmth, more involvement? How eager are you to try a variety of experiences? Do you wish your partner would surprise you by initiating sex, being more unpredictable and experimental as to when, where, and how they had sex; talk "dirty," be wilder, and sexier? Men and women were similar in their mutual desire for more loving, warmer, and closer sexual relationships. They were very different, however, in their preference for raw excitement and diversity. Men wanted their partners to take the initiative and be more dominant. They longed for rougher treatment, dirtier talk, and wilder sex (Table 5.5 on page 142). Similar lists of desired changes were secured by Darling et al., 1991.

One troubling finding: couples seemed to have a communication problem. Both men and women wished their partners would be braver and tell them exactly what they wanted sexually. These same men and women, however, were reluctant to tell their partners what they wanted. They kept hoping their mates would somehow be able to read their minds.

Frequency of Orgasm

Margaret Mead (1968) pointed out that there are enormous cultural differences in how sexually responsive men and particularly women are. The Arapesh language does not even possess the words to allow women to talk about a "sexual climax." Yet, a few Arapesh women report they do have orgasms. The vast majority cannot even understand what the anthropologist is talking about. Among the fierce Mun-

HEY, GALS! BAFFLED BY YOUR BEAU?
YOU'RE NOT STILL TAKING HIM LITERALLY, ARE YOU?
BERLITZ PROUDLY PRESENTS *OH, NO!*
SAY IT IN GUY!

BEFORE RELATIONSHIP		DURING RELATIONSHIP		AFTER RELATIONSHIP	
GUY	ENGLISH	GUY	ENGLISH	GUY	ENGLISH
YOU'RE THE MOST FASCINATING WOMAN I'VE EVER MET	I THINK I'D LIKE TO GET INTO YOUR PANTS	I LOVE YOU MORE THAN ANY HUMAN HAS LOVED ANY OTHER HUMAN	I LOVE GETTING INTO YOUR PANTS ON A REGULAR BASIS	I NEVER REALLY LOVED YOU	THANK-YOU FOR LETTING ME INTO YOUR PANTS
YOU'RE THE MOST BEAUTIFUL WOMAN I'VE EVER MET	MAY I PLEASE GET INTO YOUR PANTS NOW?	I LOVE YOU MORE THAN THE WORLD SERIES	I AM A PATHOLOGICAL LIAR	LET'S JUST BE FRIENDS	I HAVE GOTTEN INTO SOMEONE ELSE'S PANTS
YOU ARE MY SPIRITUAL TWIN	HOW ABOUT NOW?	I'LL CALL YOU SOON	I'LL CALL YOU WHEN I NEED SOMETHING	OUR FRIENDSHIP IS VERY IMPORTANT TO ME	PLEASE INTRODUCE ME TO YOUR GIRLFRIENDS

REMEMBER, SPEAKING TWO DIFFERENT LANGUAGES CAN ONLY SPELL DISASTER. LEARN GUY. TODAY. ©1992 *Jennifer Berman*

Say It In Guy

Jennifer Berman (1992).

dugumor, on the other hand, women take it for granted that they are entitled to the same kind of sexual pleasure that men are. Mundugumor women almost always experience a sexual climax.

How often do American men and women have orgasms? Men are far more likely to reach orgasm during their sexual encounters than are women (Masters & Johnson, 1966). Men reach orgasm during almost every sexual encounter. Women

TABLE 5.5   What Men and Women Wish They Had More of in Their Sexual Relationships

Dating Couples	
Men	Women
Wish their partners would:	
Be more experimental	Talk more lovingly
Initiate sex more often	Be more seductive
Try more oral-genital sex	Be warmer and more involved
Give more instructions	Give more instructions
Be warmer and more involved	Be more complimentary

Married Couples	
Men	Women
Wish their partners would:	
Be more seductive	Talk more lovingly
Initiate sex more	Be more seductive
Be more experimental	Be more complimentary
Be wilder and sexier	Be more experimental
Give more instructions	Give more instructions
	Be warmer and more involved

Based on Hatfield & Rapson (1993b), p. 92.

experience orgasm less often. In recent studies, only 89 percent of married women had ever enjoyed an orgasm during intercourse (Darling et al., 1991). Fewer men than women, on the other hand, are capable of multiple orgasms (Masters & Johnson, 1966). These statistics are consistent with those of Kinsey et al., 1953 and Kaplan, 1987.

Men occasionally fake orgasm; women do so far more often. Many women feel guilty if they do not experience orgasm and thus they choose to pretend to have one. In one study, 27.5 percent of women reported that they sometimes or always faked it. The reason they gave for this pretense was to please their partner and to avoid disappointing or hurting him (Darling, Davidson, & Cox, 1991).

Many have speculated that part of the problem women have in reaching climax is that couples' sexual activities are generally designed to be more appealing to husbands than to wives. When women were asked what were the biggest "turn offs" preventing them from reaching orgasm, they complained most about lack of foreplay, fatigue, and preoccupation with nonsexual thoughts (Darling, Davidson, & Cox, 1991).

Cross-cultural sex researchers echo these conclusions. Japanese researchers, for example, found that after a year of marriage, only 60 to 67 percent of Japanese wives had experienced orgasm. About 20 percent of Japanese wives never experience orgasm (Asayama, 1975).

Extramarital Sex

> *A man, like a bull, cannot be confined to a krall.*
> —*Kgatla (African) proverb*

Researchers have had a hard time finding just the right term to describe a committed couple's extradyadic involvements. The terms scientists select seem to depend in part on whether they are talking about gay or straight, dating, cohabiting, or married couples' affairs; on whether they are focusing on emotional involvements, sexual involvements (these may range from flirtations to long-term relationships), or both; and on whether the scientists themselves or their subjects approve, are indifferent to, or disapprove of such affairs (in the latter case they tend to talk about "infidelity" or "cheating").

Regardless of what you call it, it is not surprising that lovers and husbands and wives are often tempted to engage in extradyadic sexual relations. Playwright Girish Karnad (1975) recounted an ancient Indian myth of tangled erotic passion. Two young men, Devadatta and Kapila, were the best of friends. Devadatta was intelligent, sensitive, and very rich. Kapila was passionate, reckless, and the possessor of a powerful physique. Padmini, who was desired by both men, chose to marry the scholarly Devadatta. At first, Padmini was happy with her decision. But soon she began to feel a powerful attraction to what she didn't have—Kapila. On a picnic she observed:

> *How he climbs—like an ape. Before I could even say "yes" [to bring her a Fortunate Lady's flower], he had taken off his shirt, pulled his dhoti up and swung up the branch. And what an ethereal shape! Such a broad back—like an ocean with muscles rippling across it—and then that small, feminine waist which looks so helpless. . . . He is like a Celestial Being reborn as a hunter. . . . How his body sways, his limbs curve—it's a dance almost. (pp. 25–26)*

In classical Indian myth, some things are easily solved. Devadatta and Kapila, determined to ease the other's suffering, severed their own heads. Then the goddess Mother Kali conveniently intervened to set things right. She fixed Devadatta's clever head to Kapila's powerful body and Kapila's oxlike head to Devadatta's puny torso. Padmini got her choice—which did she want? Devadatta/Kapila or Kapila/Devadatta? The answer seemed obvious; she chose the ideal combination of mind and body—Devadatta/Kapila. The loser, Kapila/Devadatta went off into the forest to brood.

Alas, the best of times were short-lived. Padmini started to long for the absent Kapila/Devadatta. She tracked Kapila/Devadatta down and they began a passionate, consuming affair. Alas, Devadatta/Kapila soon discovered the hapless couple. The trio considered living together but realized that was (in their world) impossible. There was only one solution to the problem. All of them must die. Kapila/Devadatta and Devatta/Kapila cut off their heads once more. Padmini prepared a large funeral pyre and threw herself upon it. (Traditionally, Indian women were supposed to die with their husband[s]). And so they died happily ever after, having solved, Indian-style, the problem of fickle couples: always wanting what you can't have.

Attitudes toward Extramarital Sex

Some societies encourage or at least allow extramarital relations under "appropriate" conditions. The Toda of India, for example, was a polyandrous society. Women often possessed several husbands and lovers. The Toda language, interestingly enough, did not even have a word for *adultery* (Ford & Beach, 1951). Some societies allow adultery on special occasions. When a Fijian war party, for example, arrived home victorious, with the dead bodies of men and women lashed to the prows of their canoes, the women rushed down to the beach to meet them. During the joyous celebration that followed, conventional restraints were set aside and extramarital sex was permitted (Thomson, 1908). Most tribal societies (74 percent), however, forbid men and women to engage in sexual liaisons. In a few societies (26 percent), a double standard existed. Husbands, but not wives, were permitted to have extramarital affairs.

How severely men and women are punished for extramarital dalliances also varies. In a few societies (15 percent), men and women who were caught engaging in such relations received mild punishment, such as a stern warning or a small fine. In most (85 percent), they received moderate to severe punishment; they may have been fined, beaten, or imprisoned. In a few, they may have been mutilated or killed (Frayser, 1985). If a Comanche couple was caught in an extramarital affair, both might suffer. The man might be required to pay damages, for example, providing bridles, saddles, horses, and war costumes or be publicly whipped. The woman generally suffered a far worse fate. A husband often cut off his adulterous wife's nose, slashed the soles of her feet, and whipped her. Sometimes he killed her (Hoebel, 1940).

In the West, people differ in their attitudes toward the acceptability of extramarital sex. Blumstein and Schwartz (1983), for example, found that one married couple, Diane and Bruce, had very different attitudes toward extramarital sex without even realizing it:

> *When we reread our interviews with another couple, Diane and Bruce, it struck us that when it came to a shared understanding about extramarital sex, they seemed not to be in the same marriage. Diane is a homemaker of twenty-four, and Bruce an electrician of twenty-six. They have been married for five years.*
>
> Bruce's view: *"Sure we have an understanding. It's: 'You do what you want. Never go back to the same one.'" See, that's where it's going to screw your mind up, to go back the second time to the same person."*

Diane's: *"We've never spoken about cheating, but neither of us believe in it. I don't think I'd ever forgive him. I don't think I'd be able to. I don't know. I haven't met up with that situation." (pp. 286–287)*

This couple may be in for trouble.

Researchers have developed a number of scales to assess couples' attitudes toward extramarital sex. Ira Reiss (Reiss & Lee, 1988), for example, created the *Extramarital Sexual Permissiveness Scale*, which asks people whether or not they would approve of a man or woman who embarked on an extramarital affair under various conditions. Suppose a husband or a wife in a happy marriage had an affair. How would they feel about that? What if the marriage were unhappy? What if it were a love affair? Merely a sensual experience? What if the mate approved (disapproved) of such activity? In such situations, the test asks, is extramarital coitus acceptable or not?

The evidence suggests that in the West, most people disapprove of extramarital sex under any and all conditions (Lawson & Sampson, 1988; Reiss, Anderson, & Sponaugle; 1980; Sprecher & McKinney, 1993). In 1991, for example, the National Opinion Research Center (NORC) (Davis & Smith, 1991) asked a random sample of 987 Americans: "What is your opinion about a married person having sexual relations with someone other than the marriage partner—is it always wrong, almost always wrong, wrong only sometimes, or not wrong at all?" (p. 257). They found that 88 percent of people thought extramarital sex was always or almost always wrong; 6 percent thought such affairs were wrong only sometimes; 3 percent thought they were not wrong at all; and 2 percent just didn't know.

Andrew Greeley (1991), in a national survey of American's attitudes, found that 86 percent of men and women thought that marital infidelity was always wrong or almost always wrong. Men were more tolerant of extramarital sex, especially when they were engaging in it, than were women. Similar results were secured by Margolin, 1989 and Oliver & Hyde, 1993.

American college students, from a variety of ethnic groups (African American and European American), religions (Catholic, Mennonite, and Mormon), and regions (the Midwest, South, and Mountain states) were also sampled. These groups varied greatly in their attitudes. African American students from the South and European American students from the Midwest were most permissive: about 31 percent and 39 percent of the students thought extramarital affairs were always wrong, respectively. Not surprisingly, students in religious colleges were most conservative: a full 65 percent of Catholic men, 69 percent of Mormons, and 90 percent of Mennonites thought such relations were always wrong (Christensen, 1973).

Shirley Glass and Thomas Wright (1992) pointed out that married men and women may differ in the kinds of things they think justify an extramarital affair. Couples may embark on affairs for a variety of reasons: their self-esteem may be at an all-time low and they find others' attention irresistible; they may be in love or longing for a little attention and understanding; they may be frustrated by an emotionally or sexually "stingy" spouse; they may be curious as to what a new body would be like; or simply take it for granted that it is the thing to do. Glass and Wright asked married persons whether they would feel justified in having an extramarital affair under various conditions. Married men and women differed in kinds of things they thought justified infidelity. Men tended to separate love and sex and women to combine them. Thus, men generally thought that they might be tempted to have an affair strictly for sexual pleasure. Women, on the other hand, felt that they would be willing to risk an affair only if they were in love and involved in an emotionally intimate relationship.

Similar results were reported by Annette Lawson (1988) on the basis of surveys, group discussions, and in-depth interviews with 679 married men and women in England, Scotland, and Wales. She concluded that traditional men were most likely to get involved in "casual extra-marital affairs," "brief encounters," or "one-night stands." A traditional woman, on the other hand, "commits adultery generally only when her feelings are deeply involved or likely to become so—the risks are too great for her to play as he can—while he is entitled to his 'bit on the side'" (p. 39).

Cultural and Ethnic Group Differences in Attitudes toward Extramarital Sex
There are vast cultural and ethnic group differences in the acceptance of extramarital sex. Ancient Indian epics such as the *Mahabharata* warned of adultery as one of the five great sins for which there was no atonement. They warned against the frightful consequences of sexual betrayal:

> *In all castes a man must never approach the wife of another. For there is naught in the world which so shortens life as that the man on earth should visit the wife of another. As many pores as are on women's bodies, so many years will he sit in hell. . . . He that touches another man's wife is born as a wolf, as a dog, as a jackal, then born as a vulture, a snake, a heron, as also a crane. (Meyer, 1930, pp. 246–247)*

Harold Christensen (1973) asked college students from nine different cultures whether or not they thought sexual fidelity was always wrong. (What if the couple had fallen in love? What if their mates had been away for a long time?). They found that college students in Denmark, Sweden, and Belgium were generally fairly tolerant of extramarital sex. Only about 7 percent of students in Denmark, 31 percent in Sweden, and 56 percent in Belgium thought that extramarital sexual infidelity was always wrong. Taiwanese students were more conservative. A full 71 percent of them insisted that infidelity was always wrong.

When Christiansen (1973) compared studies conducted in the 1960s and 1970s, he found that the old double standard, which said that men could be "forgiven" for adultery more easily than could women, had more or less disappeared by the 1970s. Only about 2 to 10 percent of students still endorsed a double standard. In all cultures, men seemed to be the die-hards. Twice as many men as women endorsed a double standard of extramarital sex. This is probably not surprising, since it favored men. Secondly, in the 1970s, students seemed slightly more tolerant of extramarital sex under "mitigating" circumstances than they had been in the 1960s.

Bram Buunk (1980) interviewed Dutch couples who were married or living together. He concluded that couples in the United States and the Netherlands differed markedly in their attitudes toward extramarital liaisons. In Holland, men and women had a more positive attitude toward extramarital sex than did their U.S. counterparts. They were more likely to feel that they could discuss their affairs with their mates without precipitating a crisis. Many of these Dutch couples possessed a strong need for deep personal relations with others, rejected traditional views about men's and women's roles, and were quite independent. They were likely to have friends who accepted extramarital sex and engaged in extramarital affairs with some regularity.

Extramarital Sexual Activity

Americans generally believe that extramarital relations are wrong. How do they behave? Recently, the National Opinion Research Center (Smith, 1991) asked a sampling of Americans whether or not they had engaged in sexual relations with someone other than their mate during the past year. They found that Americans generally were faithful to their mates. Just 1.5 percent of married people (2.1 percent of married men and 0.8 percent of married women) reported having had an affair during the previous year. Men and women did not differ in how often they were unfaithful. African American respondents were most likely to have had an affair during the previous year (5.3 percent); European Americans were intermediate (1.3 percent), and those from other ethnic groups were least likely to have had an affair (0.0 percent).

In 1991, the National Opinion Research Center (NORC) (Davis & Smith, 1991) interviewed a random sample of 999 Americans: "Have you *ever* had sex with someone other than your husband or wife while you were married?" (p. 256). About 15 percent of Americans said they had had an affair sometime during the course of their marriage; 85 percent said they had not. In their recent large scale survey, Laumann and his colleagues (1994) found that more than 75 percent of married men and 90 percent of married women claimed they had never had extramarital sex. In many studies, men have been found to engage in extramarital sex earlier in their marriages, to have extramarital relations more often than women, to have more extramarital sexual partners, and to feel less guilty about infidelity than do women (Glass & Wright, 1985; Lawson, 1988; Spanier & Margolis, 1983). Such gender differences have been found in Australia (Thompson, 1984), England, and the Netherlands (Buunk, 1980).

Some researchers disagree with the preceding conservative estimates, however. Some have reported that 37 percent of men and 29 percent of women have engaged in extramarital sexual relations at some time in the course of their marriages (Reinisch et al., 1988). Others insist that as many as 50 percent of men and women have had affairs (Blumstein & Schwartz, 1983; Thompson, 1983). At the moment, it is difficult to say exactly how common is extramarital sex.

Researchers do agree that, in the West, two changes are evident: (1) Once again, a double standard of sexual behavior seems to be eroding. Men and women are becoming increasingly similar in their willingness to experiment with extramarital sex. (2) Men and women are beginning to experiment with extramarital relations earlier, more often, and with more partners than in the past.

Culture and Extramarital Sexual Behavior

In *Raise the Red Lantern*, Su Tong (1993) recounts the story of the 19-year-old Lotus, who was the Fourth Mistress of the elderly Old Master Chen Zuoqian. At first, Chen lavishes attention on Lotus. Then he loses interest. The lonely Lotus finds her interest growing in Feipu, Chen's oldest son:

> *The two of them sat there, vacantly sipping their wine. Lotus turned the wine cup around playfully on her palm and looked at Feipu sitting directly opposite her. His head was lowered, his youthful crop of hair was thick and black, his neck stuck straight out, strong and proud, and a few fine blue veins twitched slightly in his eyes. Lotus felt a liquid warmth in her heart. An unfamiliar desire swept like a spring breeze throughout her body; she felt out of breath, and the image of Coral and the doctor's legs intertwined beneath the mahjong table once again occupied her mind. She looked at her own long, lovely legs, resembling finely turned rolls of thin gauze, as they slid warmly and passionately toward their goal—Feipu's feet, knees, and legs; now she was powerfully aware of his physical presence. Her expression grew misty as her lips parted weakly and trembled slightly. She heard the sound of something being torn apart in the air, or perhaps the sound was only coming from somewhere deep inside her body.*
>
> *Feipu raised his head; a look of passion poured forth from his eyes as he stared at Lotus. His body, especially his legs, remained stiffly poised in his original posture. He did not move a muscle. Lotus closed her eyes; she listened to her irregular heart beat—one fast, one slow—as she leaned her legs fully against Feipu's and waited for something to happen.*
>
> *It seemed as though several years went by in an instant. Then Feipu pulled his knees back, crouched sideways against the back of his chair like someone who'd been beaten up, and said in a hoarse voice, "This is no good."*
>
> *Lotus mumbled like one just waking from a dream, "What's no good?"*
>
> *Feipu raised his arms slowly and bowed slightly. "It's no good. I'm still afraid."*
> *His face twisted in pain as he spoke. "I'm still afraid of women. Women are too frightening." (p. 89)*

In many, perhaps most, of the world's cultures, the double standard is very much alive. Men's sexual dalliance is winked at, while women are punished, severely beaten, or even killed for such behavior (Campbell, 1964; Lateef, 1990; Peristiany, 1966; Smuts, 1991).

In *The Woman Warrior*, Maxine Hong Kingston (1975) told of the plight of her aunt, who became pregnant in her husband's absence. In the silence, Kingston tries to piece together what must have happened, sorting out legends, dreams, and fact. Eventually, she recognizes that she is hearing a heart-rending story of traditional male power. Her aunt was innocent. She had been raped. No one would come to her aid. Yet, when she became pregnant, it was she who was held responsible. She who must pay.

"You must not tell anyone," my mother said, "what I am about to tell you. In China your father had a sister who killed herself. She jumped into the family well. We say that your father has all brothers because it is as if she had never been born."
. . . My aunt could not have been the lone romantic who gave up everything for sex. Women in the old China did not choose. . . .
When the family found a young man in the next village to be her husband, she stood tractable beside the best rooster, his proxy, and promised before they met that she would be his forever. . . .
The other man was not, after all, very much different from her husband. They both gave orders: she followed. "If you tell your family, I'll beat you. I'll kill you. Be here again next week." No one talked sex ever. . . . The fear did not stop but permeated everywhere. (p. 3, 7–8)

Regardless of what happened, the community reaction was swift and fierce. Her mother continued:

"In 1924 . . . I remember looking at your aunt one day when she and I were dressing; I had not noticed before that she had such a protruding melon of a stomach. But I did not think, 'She's pregnant,' until she began to look like other pregnant women, her shirt pulling and the white tops of her black pants showing. She could not have been pregnant, you see, because her husband had been gone for years. No one said anything. We did not discuss it. In early summer she was ready to have the child, long after the time when it could have been possible.
"The village had also been counting. On the night the baby was to be born the villagers raided our house. Some were crying. Like a great saw, teeth strung with lights, files of people walked zigzag across our land, tearing the rice. Their lanterns doubled in the disturbed black water, which drained away through the broken bunds. As the villagers closed in, we could see that some of them, probably men and women we knew well, wore white masks. The people with long hair hung it over their faces. Women with short hair made it stand up on end. Some had tied white bands around their foreheads, arms, and legs.
"At first they threw mud and rocks at the house. Then they threw eggs and began slaughtering our stock. We could hear the animals scream their deaths—the roosters, the pigs, a last great roar from the ox. Familiar wild heads flared in our night windows; the villagers encircled us. Some of the faces stopped to peer at us, their eyes rushing like searchlights. The hands flattened against the panes, framed heads, and left red prints.

"The villagers broke in the front and the back doors at the same time, even though we had not locked the doors against them. Their knives dripped with the blood of our animals. They smeared blood on the doors and walls. One woman swung a chicken, whose throat she had slit, splattering blood in red arcs about her. We stood together in the middle of our house, in the family hall with the pictures and tables of the ancestors around us, and looked straight ahead.

"At that time the house had only two wings. When the men came back, we would build two more to enclose our courtyard and a third one to begin a second courtyard. The villagers pushed through both wings, even your grandparents' rooms, to find your aunt's, which was also mine until the men returned. From this room a new wing for one of the younger families would grow. They ripped up her clothes and shoes and broke her combs, grinding them underfoot. They tore her work from the loom. They scattered the cooking fire and rolled the new weaving in it. We could hear them in the kitchen breaking our bowls and banging the pots. They overturned the great waist-high earthenware jugs; duck eggs, pickled fruits, vegetables burst out and mixed in acrid torrents. The old woman from the next field swept a broom through the air and loosed the spirits-of-the-broom over our heads. 'Pig.' 'Ghost.' 'Pig,' they sobbed and scolded while they ruined our house.

"When they left, they took sugar and oranges to bless themselves. They cut pieces from the dead animals. Some of them took bowls that were not broken and clothes that were not torn. Afterward we swept up the rice and sewed it back up into sacks. But the smells from the spilled preserves lasted. Your aunt gave birth in the pigsty that night. The next morning when I went for the water, I found her and the baby plugging up the family well.

"Don't let your father know that I told you. He denies her. Now that you have started to menstruate, what happened to her could happen to you. Don't humiliate us. You wouldn't like to be forgotten as if you had never been born. The villagers are watchful." (pp. 3–5)

This terrible story is echoed in many other places. In many African, Far Eastern, and Middle Eastern societies, it is considered so important to mute women's sexual responsiveness, that from 80 to 100 million girls have been forced to endure clitorectomies and even more drastic sexual mutilations in pubertal initiation rites. (Girls' clitorises are removed, so that they will no longer be able to feel sexual pleasure [Gregersen, 1982; Rosenthal, 1993].) In India, widows were once required to commit *suttee* (to immolate themselves on their husbands' funeral pyre) to ensure that they would remain faithful to their husbands after death (Upreti & Upreti, 1991). Many have asked how culturally tolerant do we wish to be in the face of practices such as these.

Passion out of Bounds
In Table 5.6 we present the percentage of men and women who have reported engaging in extramarital sexual relations in various societies. Researchers in a variety of countries find that women are more likely to fall in love with someone else than are men; men are more likely to engage in a loveless sexual encounter. This has

TABLE 5.6   Percentage of Men and Women Who Have Ever Engaged in Extramarital Sexual Affairs

Culture	Men	Women
United States[1]	—	32
United States		
Married Couples[2]	26	31
Cohabitors[2]	33	30
Gays/lesbians[2]	82	28
African Americans[3,a]	76	29
European Americans[3,a]	40	8
Africa: Zimbabwe[4]	67	3
Australia[5,b]		
"In love" and emotional: ever	13	21
Sexual intercourse: ever	31	16
Both	21	18
England, Scotland, Wales[6]	45	42
Finland[7]	44	19
Japan[1]		27
Japan[8]	75–90	3–5
Netherlands[9]		
"In love" during past year[b]	31	29
Sexual relationship during past year[b]	28	18

[1]Maykovich (1976).
[2]Blumstein & Schwartz (1983).
[3]Gebhard & Johnson (1979); Weinberg & Williams (1988).
[4]Mhloyi (1990).
[5]Thompson (1984).
[6]Lawson (1988).
[7]Kontula (1993).
[8]Asayama (1975).
[9]Buunk (1980).
[a]The question was asked about "petting or coitus" not just intercourse.
[b]Cohabiting and married couples.

been found to be true in Australia (Thompson, 1984) and in England, Scotland, and Wales (Lawson, 1988).

Conclusions

Recent evidence makes it clear that a sexual revolution is taking place, both in the West and throughout much of the rest of the world. Of course, that revolution is far from being consummated. In the West, especially, men and women appear to be moving slowly toward social equality in their sexual preferences, feelings, and experiences. Most modern societies are also moving in the direction of allowing greater sexual freedom for all individuals.

These same developments appear to be going on, differentially, in Asia, Latin America, Eastern Europe, and parts of Africa. It is hard to imagine that non-Western cultures can long hold off the deeper advancing currents of individualism or that they can restrain the spirit of sexual equality and experimentation. As existential theory suggests, the ways in which people experience sex and their own sexuality is in no small part a function of their belief systems and perceptions. As those belief systems become more universally Westernized or modernized, we can anticipate the slow, uneven, contested spread throughout the world of Western modes of sexual conduct.

What should we make of all this? Anyone who dares to comment on the future of sex must anticipate unleashing a floodtide of passionate feeling. In the West itself, for example, there is continuing disagreement about the wisdom of the "sexual revolution." Traditionalists often view existing social changes with alarm. They worry that the erosion of sexual restraint will encourage selfishness at the expense of communal concern, pleasure at the expense of responsibility, and sensualism at the expense of tradition, religion, and sobriety. Traditional voices still ring out loud, clear, and passionately.

Social reformers are divided as to what they think about the social revolution. Some feminists, for instance, remind us that for many women the sexual revolution simply means more of the same: oppression. For many, the sexual revolution has brought the "freedom" to be thought of as a sex object, the obligation to be beautiful, thin, sexy, and without restraint, the "freedom" to risk socially transmitted diseases and AIDS, the "freedom" to have not love *and* lust, but casual, meaningless, recreational sex (like it or not). Men, they contend, have simply used the concept of sexual freedom to increase their power over women. Other women's rights leaders insist that the issue that counts is *choice* for women, in sex as well as in everything else. The debate rages furiously as we write these words.

Sexual doubts have always resided close to the center of the great ethical and political conflicts, within all cultures and throughout history. Today's sexual revolution will hardly put these debates to rest. Issues of conscience and social policy are sure to be argued more intensely than ever as the revolution continues along its bumpy but perhaps inexorable course, not only in the West, but, in its shattering ways, beyond the shores of Europe and America. The implications of this sexual struggle, we believe, will transcend in importance those political events that tend to dominate the headlines and the evening news programs throughout the world.

From our own point of view, it seems odd that sex should arouse such cultural fervor. Cultures have, we think, been a little crazy when it comes to sex. After all, at the core of the sexual revolution reside some fairly harmless and reasonable notions: Sexual expression is not incompatible with civilization. Sexual feelings are natural and can be safely expressed without causing the collapse of empires, nations, and families. Relationships can risk sex without risking an abuse of power. We like to think that societies, when it comes to sex, could allow some room for calm and common sense. But we wouldn't bet on that happening.

Endnote

1. Studies conducted in the 1960s and 1970s generally found that women were stronger advocates of the traditional double standard than were men (Oliver & Hyde, 1993). The fact that women were more accepting of traditional standards, in general, probably accounts for that perplexing finding. That is no longer so.

Chapter *6*

Passion—For Better
or Worse

*Americans are firmly of two minds about it all, simultaneously hardheaded and
idealistic, uncouth and tender, libidinous and puritanical; they believe
implicitly in every tenet of romantic love, and yet they know perfectly well that
things don't really work that way.*

—Morton Hunt

Passionate love rarely fails to evoke a response. The Beatles shouted out (to besotted audiences) that "all you need is love." Cooler voices cautioned, however, that "falling in love with love is falling for make-believe." In the West, passionate love is seen as a magic elixir for finding fulfillment in life, as heady a brew as power, money, or freedom. Like many domestic wines, however, love is reputed not to travel well. Outside of the West, the sparkling wine of love is said to fall flat. Life choices made under the influence of ardent spirits are seen as a weak foundation for marriage, let alone life. Sober words such as "duty" or "respect" or the avoidance of "shame" often carry more weight.

Peter Carey (1988), in *Oscar & Lucinda,* told the love story of an unlikely nineteenth-century Australian couple who decided to open a glassworks. In Carey's commentary on Prince Rupert's drops, he metaphorically described the delight, strength, and resilience of passionate love as well as its stunning fragility. His metaphor takes us well into the complexities of passion.

I have . . . right here beside me as I write . . . a Prince Rupert drop—a solid teardrop of glass no more than two inches from head to tail. And do not worry that this oddity, this rarity, was the basis for de la Bastie's technique for toughening glass, or that it led to the invention of safety glass—these are practical matters and shed no light on the incredible attractiveness of the drop itself which you will understand

155

faster if you take a fourteen-pound sledgehammer and try to smash it on a forge. You cannot. This is glass of the most phenomenal strength and would seem, for a moment, to be the fabled unbreakable glass described by the alchemical author of Mappae Clavicula. *And yet if you put down your hammer and take down your pliers instead—I say "if," I am not recommending it—you will soon see that this is not the fabled glass stone of the alchemists but something almost as magical. For although it is strong enough to withstand the sledgehammer, the tail can be nipped with a pair of blunt-nosed pliers. It takes a little effort. And once it is done it is as if you have taken out the keystone, removed the linchpin, kicked out the foundations. The whole thing explodes. And where, a moment before, you had unbreakable glass, now you have grains of glass in every corner of the workshop—in your eyes if you are not careful—and what is left in your hand you can crumble—it feels like sugar—without danger.*

　. . . The glass was by way of being a symbol of weakness and strength; it was a cipher for someone else's heart. It was a confession, an accusation, a cry of pain. . . . Fireworks made of glass. An explosion of dew. Crescendo. Diminuendo. Silence. . . . In short, a joyous and paradoxical thing, as good a material as any to build a life from. (pp. 10–11)

The complexity of the Prince Rupert drop reflects love's paradoxes—its raptures and its abject miseries; its power and its fragility.

Let us begin by looking at the "up" side of passionate love: that rush of exultation, that yearning, the erotic passion that is the dizzying ecstasy of passionate love. What are, to begin with, some of the reasons people fall in love with love?

The Ecstasy of Passionate Love

In Chapter 1, we defined passionate love as "a state of intense longing for union with another. Reciprocated love (union with the other) is associated with fulfillment and ecstasy. . . ." (Hatfield & Rapson, 1993b, p. 5). Poets, playwrights, and novelists have had something to say about the enchantments of love (but not so much as one might expect). As the poet W. H. Auden (1980) noted:

Of the many (far too many) love poems written in the first person which I have read, the most convincing were, either the fa-la-la's of a good-natured sensuality which made no pretense at serious love, or howls of grief because the beloved had died and was no longer capable of love, or roars of disapproval because she loved another or nobody but herself; the least convincing were those in which the poet claimed to be earnest, yet had no complaints to make. (p. 529)

Perhaps, not surprisingly, there has been little research on the joys of love and sex. Nonetheless, we would be remiss if we did not remind readers that people look for love for a reason—its rare delights.

Moments of Exultation

When love is realized, lovers may experience moments of passionate bliss, moments that are epiphanies. In Italian author Pier Tondelli's (1989) novel of a love affair between Leo and Thomas, he described their giddy encounter when meeting after a long absence.

> *They were like two drunks in the latter stages of getting sozzled: lurching about, unsteady on their legs, full of mirth and all over the place. They laughed for no reason. They pinched and nipped each other or slapped each other on the back, pretended to put on a trial of strength, tumbled on the ground with their legs in the same pair of jeans. Leo said he felt like a happy fool; he said it was like a moment of enlightenment, and he was approaching the state of consciousness of an eastern sage. Thomas agreed that at that hour, after everything that had happened, they were both truly weird.*
>
> *They went on joking in the car and the situation between them was quite the opposite to what it had been a few hours earlier. If no words happened to pass between them, their silence was full of tenderness. It was a gentle, affectionate silence—the silence of a nestful of sleeping cubs. They reached the café and Thomas started voraciously eating the toy-like Turkish sweets, apple fritters and brioches. Leo drank very strong tea and ate out of Thomas's plate. (p. 157)*

Beverley Fehr (1993) asked college men and women in Australia and the United States to list the characteristics they associated with love. When people thought of love, they almost always thought of the promises and fulfillments of love. They usually listed such positive emotions as euphoria, excitement, laughing, and contentment. Similar results were secured by Davis & Todd, 1982; Fitness & Fletcher, 1993; and Marston, Hecht, & Robers, 1987.

A Sense of Union

> *The lane of love is narrow / There is room only for one.*
> —The Indian poet Kabir

In many ancient cultures, creation myths assumed that from the beginning lovers were one. In the fifth century B.C., in his *Symposium*, the great Greek philosopher Plato recounted the following tale: Once upon a time there were three kinds of people: men-men, women-women, and the androgynous—a union of the two. These early beings consisted essentially of two people, folded together in a spherical ball. They could walk upright or roll about, turning nimbly on their four hands and four feet like tumblers. Eventually, these arrogant beings managed to enrage the gods. To punish them, Zeus cut them in half, "like a Sorb-apple which is halved for pickling." From then on, each desolate half was left to wander the earth, searching for its other half. If men and women ever did meet their "better half," they were determined not to be separated ever again. They clung to one another. They did not want to do anything apart. They were willing to die rather than risk separation.

Other cultures possess similar creation myths. In India, the delicate figure of Siva (half man and half woman) graphically symbolizes the belief that men and women were once united. In the ancient Persian creation myth, Mashya and Mashyoi were sketched intertwined in the flowing forms of a single tree. It was impossible to tell which features belonged to one and which to the other (Kakar & Ross, 1986). Through the ages, such myths spoke to the deepest longings of men and women, lovers and beloved, to be lost in one another. Of course, in real love relationships, couples have to forge a balance—spending some time together but some time alone or with family, friends, and colleagues. Most young couples find that too much togetherness is boring and makes them feel imprisoned.

Feeling Secure and Safe: Commitment

> *Never give in, never give in, never never, never, never; in nothing great or small, large or petty, never give in.*
>
> —*Winston Churchill*

When people are passionately in love, they usually wish that love could last forever. Sometimes, it does. More commonly, people's turbulent emotions cool or darken. Social psychologists have discovered some of the things that increase commitment and the chances that brief infatuations will be translated into a lifetime of companionate love. George Levinger (1979) proposed that three kinds of forces influence commitment: (1) the appeal of the relationship, (2) the lure of rival attractions, and (3) the seriousness of the barriers against leaving the relationship. The same three factors have been found to effect the commitment of gay and lesbian couples as well as heterosexual couples (Kurdek, 1991).

Paul Rosenblatt and David Unangst (1979) noted that those cultures that have a vested interest in "trapping" young people into making a lifetime commitment usually rely on some of the "tricks" Levinger discussed to facilitate commitment. A society, for example, may encourage the engaged couple, their parents, and kin to invest so much in elaborate wedding ceremonies that it is difficult if not impossible for a couple to decide to end things later on. To test this notion, the anthropologists selected a random sample of fifty representative societies. They classified societies into two groups on the basis of a single question: did the marriage have important financial implications for the families involved (substantial bridewealth, dowry, rights to substantial land or livestock, or gift exchange) or did the marriage have few financial implications for the families (minimal or no wealth transfer)? They proposed that the more the families had to gain, the more tactics they would employ to commit the young couple to the marriage. For example, they should publicize the engagement. (It is one thing to back down on a private commitment, quite another to go back on your word publicly.) Preparations should be tedious or difficult. A great deal of money should be invested in musicians, feasting, and gifts.

TABLE 6.1   Marriage Ceremonies and Magnitude of Wealth Transferred

Marriage Ceremonies			
Absent	Minimal	Present	Substantial

Societies Having Substantial Bridewealth, Dowry or Gift Exchange

		Present	Substantial
		Ashanti	Burmese
		Bamileke	Egyptians of Silwa
		Barabra	Fang
		Cambodians	Fulani
		Lau Fijians	Ganda
		Lesu	Herero
		Maori	Khalka
		Otoro	Maria Gond
		Riffians	Turks
		Rural Irish	

Minimal or No Wealth Transfer

Absent	Minimal	Present	Substantial
Bohogue	Creek	Ancient Babalon	Javanese
Shoshoni	Huichol	Cagaba	Koreans
Chippewa	Nicobarese	Haitians	Spaniards
Kaska	Seneca Iroquois	Jivaro	Zapotec
Siriono	Trukese	Katab	
Yabarana		Ontong Javanese	
Zuni		Pawnee	
		Siamese	
		Timbira	

Based on Rosenblatt & Unangst (1979), p. 230.

As you can see from Table 6.1, if families had a serious financial stake in the couple's staying together, they were far more likely to "cement" marriages with elaborate wedding ceremonies.

Stella Ting-Toomey (1991) thought that couples in individualist and collectivist cultures would differ on the importance they attached to personal romantic commitments as opposed to family ties and obligations. In individualist cultures, she reasoned, young people expect their romantic affairs to fulfill most of their needs. Family and group ties are relatively weak. In collectivist cultures, young people are taught to expect less from love. Their affections are invested in their families and kin. To test this notion, she interviewed 781 men and women from the United States (a highly individualist country), France (a nation intermediate on individualism), and Japan (a country low in individualism). As predicted, students in the United States felt the most committed to their romantic partners. The French students were intermediate, and the Japanese students felt the least committed to their romantic partners.

The Icky Man Shuffle!

Jennifer Berman (1990).

In settled relationships, couples naturally wish that their love affair or marriage would last because they want it to last. Most cringe when they imagine being imprisoned in a loveless marriage. In *Money*, the English novelist Martin Amis (1984) described the sodden John Self's less than noble motivations for commitment. No one but Selina was interested in him:

I have been faithful to Selina Street for over a year, God damn it. Yes I have. I keep trying not to be, but it never works out. I can't find anyone to be unfaithful to her with. They don't want what I have to offer. They want commitment and candour and sympathy and trust and all the other things I seem to be really short of. They are past the point where they'll go to bed with somebody just for the hell of it. Selina is past that point also, long past. She used to be a well-known goer, true, but now she has her future security to think about. She has money to think about. Ah, Selina, come on. Tell me it isn't so. (p. 20)

Nonetheless, in many cultures, couples are kept together by external constraints. Once couples commit themselves to one another, often there are cultural, social, legal, religious, emotional, and/or economic barriers to separation. In most societies, of course, married couples have been forbidden to separate; even in the West, that so-called separating society, only recently was divorce sanctioned and made easy (Stone, 1990).

Feeling Understood and Accepted: Intimacy

What do most young couples mean by "intimacy"? Vicki Helgeson, Phillip Shaver and Margaret Dyer (1987) asked college men and women in North America to tell them about times when they felt most intimate with, or most distant from, someone they cared about. For most people, intimate relations were associated with feelings of affection and warmth, happiness and contentment, talking about personal things, and sharing pleasurable activities. What sorts of things put an impenetrable wall between couples? Distant relationships were associated with anger, resentment, and sadness as well as criticism, insensitivity, and inattention.

Men and women seemed to mean something slightly different by "intimacy." Women tended to focus primarily on love and affection and the expression of warm feelings when reliving their most intimate moments. They rarely mentioned sex. For men, a key feature of intimacy was sex and physical closeness. The threads of

Why Do We Have to Analyze Everything?

Marian Henley (1993).

intimacy—love and affection, trust, emotional expressiveness, communication, and sex—are so entwined that it is almost impossible to tease them apart.

Historical Perspectives on Intimacy

Earlier, we discussed the ideas of Lawrence Stone (1977) and his colleagues, who argued that in the West, until the Renaissance and the Enlightenment (1500 to 1800), intimacy was a scarce commodity. In describing the family pattern of the late medieval period and the sixteenth century (roughly 1400–1600) in England, Stone reminded us that the emphasis was necessarily on survival rather than on emotional communication.

> *There was no sense of domestic privacy, and interpersonal relations within the conjugal unit, both between husbands and wives and between parents and children were necessarily fairly remote, partly because of the ever-present probability of imminent death, partly because of cultural patterns which dictated the arranged marriage, the subordination of women, the neglect and early fostering out of children and the custom of harsh parental discipline. (pp. 408–409)*

Stone speculated that this family system, characterized by "psychological distance, deference" and a lack of privacy (p. 409), produced adults who were unequipped for intimate relationships—displaying "suspicion towards others, proneness to violence, and an incapacity to develop strong emotional ties to any one individual" (p. 409). A few critics have argued for a slightly brighter scenario (Gadlin, 1977; Ladurie, 1979; Taylor, 1989). The new social history is still in its infancy when it comes to the study of non-Western cultures. As a consequence, historians have not yet conducted the research necessary to tell us how common romantic and marital intimacy were in the past in those other societies. The suspicion is, however, that throughout history, the kind of intimacy that most people in modern societies demand today may have been a rare commodity.

Gender Differences in Intimacy

Men and women sometimes differ in how comfortable they feel about confiding in those they love. Traditionally, men were most at ease chatting about such things as politics, work, sports, money, sex, or their day-to-day activities. They tended to be less relaxed when discussing more intimate matters. Women were often more comfortable talking about such personal concerns. Zick Rubin and his colleagues (1980) asked dating couples what sorts of things they talked about with their steady dates. Men found it easy to talk about politics; women found it easy to talk about people. Men found it natural to talk about their strengths, women about their own fears and weaknesses. The more traditional the couples, the more stereotyped were their patterns of communication. Less traditional women and men were found to be fairly relaxed about discussing all sorts of personal matters—politics, friends, strengths and weaknesses. Similar results were secured by Christensen & Heavey, 1990; Roberts & Krokoff, 1990.

Most studies find that American men and women from a variety of ethnic groups differ in how willing they are to share their private thoughts and feelings with their casual and steady dates (Dindia & Allen, 1992). Elaine Hatfield and her students (1986), for example, interviewed 450 men and women from the University of Hawaii. Students were of Chinese American, European American, Filipino American, Hawaiian American, and Japanese American ancestry. College students were asked how they thought couples ought to deal with strong emotions. They were asked about such positive emotions as joy, love, and sexual excitement and such thorny emotions as anger, anxiety, depression, fear, frustration, grief, guilt and shame, hate, hurt, jealousy, loneliness, and resentment. What did they think was the best strategy? To exaggerate such feelings? Express them honestly? Play them down? In all ethnic groups, men and women had somewhat different ideas as to how honest people should be with those they loved. Everyone agreed that when couples were feeling loving, happy, or sexual, they should "tell it like it is." What they disagreed about was how negative feelings should be handled. Women believed that it was best to express such feelings tactfully but honestly. Men were more likely to stress emotional control; they insisted that such negative feelings should be played down.

A few researchers have speculated that African American couples might be better at communicating than are most couples. African Americans, they contend, have more tolerance for open, intense disclosure than do European Americans. One researcher, for example, observed: "Blacks respect those who communicate freely and clearly, expressing and sharing themselves. If people do not share, they must be made to, and manipulation of people is open, direct and more often verbal, rather than indirect as in most White families." (Aschenbrenner, 1975, p. 143)

Jean Oggins and her colleagues (Oggins, Veroff, & Leber, 1993) found some support for this hypothesis. They jotted down the names of 374 white and black Michigan couples who had applied for a marriage license. They got in touch with couples after they had been married five to eight months so that they could find out how well they were communicating. Could the newlyweds reveal their deepest feelings to their mates? Tell them exactly what they wanted? Talk about how things could be improved? Or was it easier to talk to almost anyone else about such things? They found that for the white couples, women were far better at disclosing their intimate feelings than were men. But such gender differences did not exist for black couples. Both men and women talked openly and easily with each other, about even the hardest issues.

Researchers find that after marriage, the gap between men's and women's interests in intimacy sometimes widens. Ted Huston, for example, interviewed 130 married couples at the University of Texas. For the wives, intimacy meant talking things over. The husbands, by and large, were more interested in action. They thought that if they did things (took out the garbage, for instance) and if they engaged in some joint activities, that should be enough. Huston found that during courtship men were willing to spend a great deal of time in intimate conversation. But after marriage, as time went on, they reduced the time for close marital conversation while devoting increasingly greater time to work or hanging around with their own friends. Huston observed:

> *Men put on a big show of interest when they are courting, but after the marriage their actual level of interest in the partner often does not seem as great as you would think, judging from the courtship. The intimacy of courtship is instrumental for the men, a way to capture the woman's interest. But that sort of intimacy is not natural for many men. (reported in Goleman, 1986, p. Y19)*

Not surprisingly, women often complain about men's "emotional stinginess" (Christensen & Heavey, 1990; Fishman, 1978; Roberts & Krokoff, 1990). Things have been found to be much the same in a variety of cultures—Finland (Øberg, Ruth, & Torstam, 1987), Norway (Thorsen, 1988), Sweden (Tornstam, 1992), and the United States (Hatfield & Rapson, 1993b). Lars Tornstam (1992) interviewed a sampling of 2,795 Swedish men and women who varied in age from 15 to 80. They asked them how much intimacy they expected in their love relationships: How important was it to trust each other completely? To talk openly about everything? To understand each other's innermost feelings? To have a feeling of mutual understanding? To be really interested in each others problems? When they looked at what young men and women expected from their relationships, they found an impasse at the gender gap. Women expected a great deal of intimacy from their love relationships. Men expected somewhat less. For example, 52 percent of women thought it was very important for romantic partners to be interested in one another's problems; only 38 percent of men considered it very important. As men and women get older, women's expectations diminish and the gender gap disappears. The authors noted: "Women, being socialized with a romantic view on relationships, start out with high expectations for intimacy, but are taught by real-life experiences to reduce these expectations during the life course" (p. 206).

In Japanese marriages, husbands and wives are rarely one another's best friends. Women's closest relationships are usually with their children, old classmates, and families. Men spend almost all their time with their colleagues (Roland, 1988). A similar situation exists in India (Kumar, 1991).

Cultural Perspectives on Intimacy

Stella Ting-Toomey (1991) suspected that young people in individualistic cultures (such as the United States) might differ from those in collectivist cultures (such as Japan) in how willing they were to share their thoughts and feelings with those they were interested in romantically. To find out, she asked men and women from the United States, France, and Japan to complete the *Disclosure Maintenance* scale. This scale includes such items as: "To what extent did you reveal or disclose very intimate things about yourself or personal feelings to this person?" As predicted, the American students talked the most intimately with their romantic partners. The French students were intermediate in intimacy, and the Japanese students were the least intimate with those they cared about.

She also hypothesized that romantic couples in individualist cultures would be more willing to openly acknowledge conflicts and to try to deal with them than would be couples in collectivist cultures, who would be more likely to flee from arguments and open conflict. To test this notion, she asked American, French, and Japanese men and women to think of someone of the opposite sex whom they cared about and to indicate how often they had arguments. The *Conflict Scale*, a five-item scale, contained such items as: "How often did you and this person argue with each other?" "To what extent did you communicate negative feelings toward this person (e.g., anger, dissatisfaction, frustration, etc.)?" She found, to her surprise, that French students were the most careful to avoid arguments. Both the Americans and the Japanese students were considerably more willing to risk conflict.

Several studies have found that although young people in the United States tend to assume that couples should communicate openly about relationship issues, in many Asian countries such as Japan and Korea young people assume that it is better to be subtle and discreet when confronting problems. As a consequence, couples in the United States tend to self-disclose more on a wider variety of intimate topics than do their Japanese counterparts (Barnlund, 1989; Gudykunst & Nishida, 1986) or their Korean counterparts (Won-Doornink, 1985).

There is, however, evidence that such cultural differences are rapidly eroding. Increasingly, men and women throughout the world are coming to expect both happiness and intimacy from marriage. Donna Castañeda (1993), for example, asked eighty-three Mexican American college students: "What qualities and characteristics are important in a love relationship to you?" She found that Mexican Americans, like Anglo Americans, emphasized the importance of trust, communication/sharing, mutual respect, shared attitudes/values, and honesty. Young people in China (Honig & Hershatter, 1988; Xu & White, 1990) and India (Honig & Hershatter, 1988; Yelsma & Athappilly, 1988) are increasingly beginning to require the same kinds of things from their relationships. Ge Gao (1991), for example, asked American and Chinese college students to tell him about their current romantic relationships. What sorts of things did they do together? How serious were they about one another? Did they think they would get married? In both the United States and China, Gao was surprised to discover, young people thought a close, intimate, satisfying relationship was a prerequisite for marriage. It was only when partners were deeply involved with one another (when they said such things as "[we do] basically everything; we see each other every day and do everything together"), when they found it easy to communicate ("we talk about everything; we've always shared our problems with each other; I don't usually hide anything from him"), when they knew each other so well that they could sense one another's feelings ("we can really understand each other without using words"), only then were they willing to consider getting married (pp. 105–109).

Sexual Excitement

One of the pleasures of passionate love, of course, is sexual joy and excitement, which we discussed in some detail in Chapters 4 and 5. Louise Erdrich (1988), a distinguished American Indian novelist, depicted in her novel *Tracks* Pauline Puyat's passionate fantasies about Napoleon Morrissey. Pauline was a Puyat Indian and Napoleon a Chippewa Indian and both were from North Dakota. For Pauline, sex is elemental. She imagines the two of them howling like cats, bucking like horses in heat. She thinks of snapping Napoleon in her beak "like a wicket-boned mouse." Alas, she can also imagine scampering mice, "running down with gossip."

Love and the Immune System

Donald Smith and Marianne Hoklund (1988) suspected that love, or at least *requited* love, is good for people. A famous case in point: The poet Elizabeth Barrett was a frail, sickly invalid. When she fell in love with the impassioned Robert Browning, her health somehow miraculously improved. Smith and Hoklund decided to test the hypothesis that love might promote good health. The authors interviewed sixty-four Danish college students. Were they in love? Were their feelings reciprocated? How happy were they? How healthy? When college students were in love and knew they were loved in return, they were at their best. They were self-confident, relaxed and happy, and unusually healthy (no sore throats or colds). When technicians drew blood samples and assayed natural killer cell (NK cell) activity, they found that lovers' NK cell activity was unusually low. The lovers' immune system was at full strength. On the other hand, when students were suffering the pangs of unrequited love, they were literally at risk. They reported feeling tense and depressed. They were especially prone to sore throats and colds. Many of them had been drinking (at least they displayed the tell-tale signs of a hang-over). More ominously, their natural killer cell activity was elevated—a sign that their immune system was trying to fight off disease. (Similar results were secured by Campbell, Sedikides, & Bosson, 1994.)

So far, we have focused on the delights of love. But the second sentence of our definition of passionate love reminds us that passion has a dark side as well: "Unrequited love (separation) is associated with emptiness, anxiety, or despair" (Hatfield & Rapson, 1993b, p. 5). Passionate lovers may panic when confronted with the prospect of dealing with someone they have idealized. They may suffer when they find their love is unrequited. They may discover they are extremely jealous. They may feel mortified, miserable, stung, and bruised. They may squabble; squabbles may escalate into sharp words and even violence.

The Agony of Passionate Love

> *We're not here to be happy. We're here to ruin ourselves, to break our hearts, to love the wrong people, and to die.*
>
> —*John Patrick Shanley*

Most of us would probably prefer to spend our time contemplating love's sweetness, rather than dwelling on love's thorns. In this chapter, we actually spend most of our time discussing love's dark side, however. There is little research on the sunny side of love but a great deal on its insanities. Perhaps love's problems are simply more interesting than love's *douceurs*. Leo Tolstoy (1918/1980) noted that "All happy families resemble one another, each unhappy family is unhappy in its own way" (p. 1). It is misery that is the stuff of novels. When a friend asks how your latest love affair or your marriage is going, for instance, there may be little to say once it has been noted that things are fine. But if things are *not* going so well . . . ! We are like the Ancient Mariner, clutching at the sleeves of strangers, longing to tell them Our Story. In the next section, we consider four common and transfixing problems: anxiety, unrequited love, jealousy, and violence.

Love, Fear, and Anxiety

> *The more a man loves, the more he suffers.*
> —Henri Frederic Amiel

Cairo author Naguib Mahfouz (1990), in *Palace Walk*, described the delicious blend of feelings Aisha Abd al-Jawad experienced when she looked out her window:

> *The mother left the balcony followed by Khadija, but Aisha tarried there till she was alone. Then she went to the side of the balcony overlooking Palace Walk. She peered out through the holes of the grille with interest and longing. The gleam in her eyes and the way she bit her lip showed she was expecting something to happen. She did not have long to wait, for a young police officer appeared from the corner of al-Khurunfush Street. He came closer, slowly making his way toward the Gamaliya police station. At that, the girl quickly left the balcony for the sitting room and headed for the side window. She turned the knob and opened the two panels a crack. She stood there, her heart pounding with a violence provoked by both fear and affection. When the officer neared the house, he raised his eyes cautiously but not his head, for in Egypt in those days it was not considered proper to raise your head in such circumstances. His face shone with the light of a hidden smile that was reflected on the girl's face as a shy radiance.*
>
> *She sighed and closed the window, fastening it nervously as though hiding evidence of a bloody crime. She retreated, her eyes closed from the intensity of the emotion. She let herself sink into a chair and leaned her head on her hand. She roamed through the space of her infinite sensations, experiencing neither sheer happiness nor total fear. Her heart was divided between the two emotions, each mercilessly trying to attract it. If she succumbed to the intoxication and enchantment of happiness, fear's hammer struck her heart, warning and threatening her. She did not know whether it would be better for her to abandon her adventure or to continue obeying her heart. Her love and fear were both intense. She lingered in her drowsy conflict for some time. Then the voices of fear and censure subsided, and during this truce she enjoyed an intoxicating dream. (p. 24)*

Numerous theorists including Sigmund Freud (1953), have proposed that passion and anxiety form an explosive combination. When we are ardently in love, it is natural to worry that we will say or do the wrong thing and spoil it all. Sometimes the alchemy between passion and anxiety produces too many sparks and things begin to fall apart. In *Passion*, the English novelist Jeanette Winterson (1987) lamented:

> *Lovers are not at their best when it matters. Mouths dry up, palms sweat, conversation flags and all the time the heart is threatening to fly from the body once and for all. Lovers have been known to have heart attacks. Lovers drink too much from nervousness and cannot perform. They eat too little and faint during their fervently wished consummation. They do not stroke the favoured cat and their face-paint comes loose. This is not all. Whatever you have set store by, your dress, your dinner, your poetry will go wrong. (p. 66)*

Yet, an array of theorists (Freud, 1953; Reik, 1972) have proposed that it is precisely when we are not at our best—when our self-esteem has been shattered, when we are anxious and afraid, when our lives are turbulent—that we are especially vulnerable to love. This makes some sense. After all, infants' early attachments, which motivate them to cling tightly to their mother's side when danger threatens and to go their own way when it is all safe, are thought to be the early prototype of love. Passionate love and consuming anxiety are also closely related both neuroanatomically and chemically (Hatfield & Rapson, 1993b).

A variety of researchers have demonstrated that individuals are especially prone to seek romantic ties when they are anxious. In a duo of studies, Elaine Hatfield and her students (1989), for example, found that teenagers who were either momentarily or habitually anxious were especially vulnerable to passionate love. Teenagers who varied in age from twelve to sixteen years of age, of Chinese, European, Japanese, Korean American, and mixed ancestry, were asked to complete either the *Child Anxiety Scale* or the *State-Trait Anxiety Inventory for Children*, which measures both state anxiety (how anxious teenagers happen to feel at the moment) and trait anxiety (how anxious they generally are). Teens who were either momentarily or habitually anxious were most likely to have experienced the raptures and languishings of passionate love.

Donald Dutton and Arthur Aron (1974) discovered a close link between fear and sexual attraction. The investigators compared the reactions of young men crossing two bridges in North Vancouver, Canada. The first, the Capilano Canyon suspension bridge, tilts, sways, and wobbles for 450 feet over a 230-foot drop to rocks and shallow rapids. The other bridge, a bit farther upstream, is a solid, safe structure. As each young man crossed the bridge, an attractive college woman approached him, explained that she was conducting a class project on the environment, and asked him to fill out a questionnaire for her. When the man had finished, she offered to explain her project in greater detail and wrote her telephone number on a small piece of paper so that the men could call her for more information. Which men called? Nine of the thirty-three men on the suspension bridge called her, but only two of the men on the solid bridge. Here, it appears that passion was intensified by the spillover of feeling from one realm to another.

Unrequited Love

> *Love requires absence, obstacles, infidelities, jealousy, manipulation, outright lies, pretend reconciliations, tantrums, and betrayals.*
>
> —*Diane Ackerman*

Recently, Roy Baumeister, Sara Wotman, and Arlene Stillwell (1993) asked college students at Case Western Reserve University to think about a time they had broken someone's heart or had their own hearts broken by unrequited love. Almost everyone could recall these powerful experiences: 95 percent of men and women had rejected someone who loved them; 93 percent had felt the sting of such rejection. The authors asked men and women to tell the story of their doomed love affairs. The would-be lovers and the lovelorn had very different stories to tell (See Table 6.2 on page 170).

The Stories of the Rejected
It is painful to be rejected. When David Lodge (1993) described Mark's rebuff of Clare's halting, lovestruck, overtures in *The Picturegoers*, readers all cringed:

> *Without warning, something gave inside her, like some part of a dam long under unsuspected strain. Emotion seemed to gush out of her eyes, nose, mouth, as she sighed, wept, mumbled between kisses, covering his face with spit, tears, lipstick and rain, clinging to him with the frantic strength of a drowning swimmer. But even in this tumult she felt that Mark was the sane, controlled life-guard, trying to calm her. She wanted to pull him down with her. She was seized with a desire to feel his hand on her breast again, as she had felt it for a fleeting second months ago. Seizing his hand, she kissed it, and thrust it under her raincoat and pressed it to her bosom. For a moment she felt his fingers cup her breast, then he snatched his hand away.*
>
> *"No, Clare."*
>
> *She was stunned by the rebuff. It wasn't until they were inside the dark hall, and Mark had taken off her coat and carefully hung it up, that shame and humiliation began to return to her numbed consciousness like the blood to her face. Then she ran soundlessly to her room. (pp. 153–154)*

Baumeister and his colleagues found, however, that for most broken-hearted lovers the experience of "fatal attraction" remained a surprisingly sweet memory. When they first fell in love, they had been filled with love and hope. They had focused almost entirely on their own needs, wants, and desires. They were convinced that the attraction had been mutual. Later, when things turned sour, they believed they had been led on, that the rejecter had never clearly communicated his or her disinterest. They felt that "all is fair in love and war." They viewed the beloved

TABLE 6.2 Would-Be Lovers and Those Who Reject Them

	Would-Be Lovers (percent)	Those Who Rejected Them (percent)
How did this affect your self-esteem?		
Raised	4.7	15.7
Lowered	49.2	1.4
What are your current feelings about this incident?		
Feel positive emotions	98.4	57.1
Feel negative emotions	43.8	70.0
Wish it had never happened	6.4	21.4
Would-be lover had feelings of preoccupation and longing	46.0	27.0
Would-be lover feared rejection	22.2	7.1
Rejecter felt flattered	1.6	23.5
Rejecter felt annoyed	3.1	51.4
Rejecter felt reluctant to deliver rejection	17.5	60.9
Guilt		
Respondent felt guilty	0.0	33.8
Unscrupulous tactics used by would-be lover	0.0	21.7
Unscrupulous tactics used by rejecter	14.1	5.7
Crucial Events		
Love was communicated	82.1	97.1
Feelings were initially reciprocated	35.5	19.1
Rejecter led the other on	54.8	24.2
Deny that rejecter led would-be lover on	15.6	38.6
Overt, explicit rejection	23.8	49.3
Would-be lover persisted	15.6	61.4
Perceptions of Other Person		
Praising statement about other	59.4	43.5
Critical statements about other	25.0	52.2
Would-be lover deceived self	18.8	40.6
Rejecter deceived self	3.1	4.3
Would be lover seemed mysterious to other	1.6	20.0
Rejecter seemed mysterious to other	39.1	2.9
Rejecter was considerate	37.7	55.9

Based on Baumeister, Wotman, & Stillwell (1993), pp. 382–385.

with incomprehension. How could he/she not love them when they loved so much? They cared little about the beloved's feelings. They were oblivious and indifferent to what the rejecting person was going through. Some seemed to enjoy wallowing in the drama of their misery. They blamed the other for not reciprocating their love; they felt angry, annoyed, and resentful at her/his stubbornness. And they remembered the infatuation afterward as a bitter-sweet affair despite the poison of disappointment at the current state of things.

Stories of Those Who Are Forced to Do the Rejecting

Contrary to conventional wisdom, it turned out that the loved were the ones who ended up suffering the most. At first, those who were loved beyond reason were flattered by the would-be lover's adoration. However, they soon found themselves caught up in an impossible situation. Whatever they did was wrong. It seemed cruel to reject someone who cared so much for them. It was even worse to lead someone on. They agonized over how to say "enough" without hurting feelings. But as the would-be lover persisted, guilt turned to annoyance, and then to rage. Eventually, the rejecters began to feel trapped and persecuted. What can be motivating him? Why won't she go away? Is he crazy? Doesn't she see she's driving me crazy?

In Tom Stoppard's play (1982) *The Real Thing*, Annie comments to her lover Henry on how irritating it is to be adored by someone when you no longer care two figs about them:

> *Annie: (Gleefully self-reproachful.) Isn't it awful? Max [her husband] is so unhappy and I feel so . . . thrilled. His misery just seems . . . not in very good taste. Am I awful? He leaves letters for me at rehearsal, you know, and gets me to come to the phone by pretending to be my agent and people. He loves me, and wants to punish me with his pain, but I can't come up with the proper guilt. I'm sort of irritated by it. It's so* tiring *and so* uninteresting. *You never write about that, you lot.*
>
> *Henry: What?*
>
> *Annie: Gallons of ink and miles of typewriter ribbon expended on the misery of the unrequited lover; not a word about the utter tedium of the unrequiting. It's a very interesting [thing]. . . . (p. 39)*

Table 6.2 summarizes the very different ways lovers and their reluctant beloved perceive things. It is clear from this tally that it is far better to have loved and lost than to have been loved.

Sometimes, the rejected lover's pursuit of the other turns into harassment. Leonard Jason and his colleagues (1984) defined harassment as "the persistent use of psychological or physical abuse in an attempt to begin or continue dating someone else after they have clearly indicated a desire to terminate a relationship" (p. 261). Romantic harassment included such behaviors as these: rejected lovers repeatedly telephoned late at night, they rang the bell and ran, watched, followed, repeatedly telephoned at home or work, besieged them with an avalanche of letters, sent flowers, jumped out of the bushes when the other returned home late at night from a date, insulted or physically attacked, or threaten to kill. The researchers found that a majority of college women (56 percent) had been romantically harassed at some time or another. Researchers haven't investigated how often men are harassed.

Interestingly enough, when harassers were interviewed, they generally did not think of such activities as harassment! They thought they were merely trying to establish a love relationship.

In attempting to combat men's harassment, women attempted a variety of strategies. Some did nothing. Some tried to "be nice" ("Can't we just be friends?")

and to reason with the men; some were direct or rude, saying or yelling "leave me alone!" Some changed their telephone number or moved. Some got boyfriends or parents to talk to or threaten the men; some filed harassment charges in civil court. Such harassment was painful for women. They experienced fear, anxiety, and depression. They suffered from stomachaches and nervous tics. In the short run, nothing worked terribly well; the lovers generally refused to give up. Today, of course, some communities have passed "anti-stalking laws" which help protect men and women who are victims of such fatal attraction.

Cultural Perspectives in Unrequited Love

There is, alas, no cross-cultural research to tell us whether people in various cultures suffer to the same extent from unrequited love. Anecdotal evidence, however, leads us to suspect that people are likely to be blinded by their desires, mortified by rejection, and frustrated by others' unwillingness to take no for an answer in all cultures. Some examples follow.

Louise Erdrich (1988), in *Tracks*, described the feelings of Pauline Puyat, the quick and brittle Puyat woman, blade-thin and awkward, for Eli Kashpaw, who casually rejects her ardent overtures. Pauline was drawn by Eli's face, his thick eyebrows, his flat strong nose, his seductive lips, and by the way he moved. But when she found that to him she was almost invisible, she "both turned from him and desired him, in hate." (p. 77)

William Jankowiak (1993) interviewed seventy-three Chinese men and women from a range of social, economic, and ethnic backgrounds. He concluded that men and women are especially vulnerable and fragile when it comes to romantic love. They have such idealistic notions about the nature of love that if their feelings are not reciprocated, they are left devastated and suicidal. One 35-year-old clerk discussed the terrors associated with Chinese courtship:

> You just don't understand Chinese customs. It is not like America. You cannot run around. You must stay with one girl. That girl is the center of your life. She is special. When I was in Lanzhou, I lived with four men. We annoyed each other. Then I met that dancer. She was pretty. She liked me. It was the first time I ever loved a girl. I wanted her; I desired her. I felt I must have her. When she left me for another man, I was crazy. I cried and cried, and I might have thought of killing myself. (p. 204)

Things are difficult for the rejecter as well. In China, for example, "politics is in command," in Mao's phrase. Love and sex have become entangled with politics, too. Since the government controls housing and jobs and restricts travel, the pressures on a person can be enormous. Consider the case of Lili, an exceptionally pretty Chinese teenager from Hangzhou (Butterfield, 1982). Her father was a senior general in the People's Liberation Army. Her family was rich, educated, and privileged. During the Cultural Revolution, however, her father was arrested on trumped-up charges, tortured, and killed. Her mother went mad and died. Because her father had been branded as a traitor, Lili and her sister, who was only twelve, were thrown out on the street; they were soon starving. Somehow, General Cao, an old friend of her father, heard of their plight and began to secretly send them small sums of money. They survived. Naturally Lili felt an enormous debt to General Cao.

There was one problem. General Cao wanted Lili to marry his son. Lili was repelled by the idea. She offered the excuse that she was too young to marry. The pressure continued:

> Then old Cao fell ill and Lili got a leave of absence to rush to Peking to be with him in the hospital. On his deathbed he pleaded with her to marry his son and let him die a happy man. Lili was distraught. She not only felt a great sense of obligation to Cao, but she was an orphan and had no relatives who could act as go-betweens in the traditional Chinese way to argue her case. Finally she spoke with the son, striking a deal. They would agree in front of Cao to be married, so he could die happily, but she would not marry him.
>
> But as soon as Cao was dead, the son "rushed all around Peking," Lili related, telling his relatives and friends that they were engaged. Lili ignored him, but he increased the pressure. He tried to kill himself, citing his loss of face when Lili reneged on her pledge. Cao's widow then went to the Party secretary of Lili's army danwei, charging her with improper conduct. She had agreed to the marriage, now she was backing out. Lili's Party leader called her in for investigation and "advised" her—it was tantamount to an order in the army—to marry the son since she had already committed herself.
>
> The son proposed what looked like a happy solution. "I'm losing too much face with things as they are," he said. Why not just go with him to the local civil affairs office and register their marriage—the official process for getting married in China today—and then they could forget it. She believed him and went to register. But that night he broke into the house where she was staying and, in her view, raped her, since she was unwilling. "I left a nice scar bite on his shoulder as evidence," she recalled. (pp. 130–131)

The power differentials of men over women in many traditional and not-so-traditional cultures constitutes a subtheme in some of these tales of passion gone awry.

Jealousy

> *A wife and a cooking vessel should always be carefully preserved, for they are consecrated by the touch of the owner and desecrated by the touch of others.*
> —An Indian Proverb

What is jealousy? Social commentators have argued that jealousy consists of two basic components: bruised pride and indignation at the violation of one's property rights.

Anthropologist Margaret Mead (1931) contended that jealousy is really little more than wounded pride. The shakier one's self-esteem, the more vulnerable one is to jealousy's pangs. Mead (1931) observed: "Jealousy is not a barometer by which depth of love can be read. It merely records the degree of the lover's insecurity. . . . it is a negative, miserable state of feeling, having its origin in the sense of insecurity and inferiority" (pp. 120–121). Researchers in the United States, Israel, and the Netherlands have found that people with low self-esteem *are* especially susceptible to jealousy (Bringle & Buunk, 1986; Nadler & Dotan, 1992; White & Mullen, 1989).

The French philosopher René Descartes, writing in the early seventeenth century, on the other hand, defined jealousy as "a kind of fear related to a desire to preserve a possession (cited in Davis, 1948/1977, p. 129). Researchers in several countries have also found that a loss—whether one thinks of one's romantic partner or mate as a beloved person or a mere possession—can stir up jealousy (White and Mullen, 1989). Researchers in Israel (Nadler & Dotan, 1992) and the Netherlands (Bringle & Buunk, 1986) have found that individuals experience the most jealousy and the most severe physiological reactions (trembling, increased pulse rate, nausea), when an affair poses a serious threat to their dating or marital relationship.

Ellen Berscheid and Jack Fei (1977) provided evidence that both factors (low self-esteem and the fear of loss) are important in fueling jealous passion. They found that the more insecure men and women are, the more dependent they are on their romantic partners and mates; and the more seriously their relationship is threatened, the more fiercely jealous they will be.

Gender Differences in Jealousy

In Chapters 1 to 3 we outlined the theory of evolutionary biologists such as David Buss (1992) who have argued that in the course of evolution men and women have been programmed to desire very different things in a love affair or marriage. It probably comes as no surprise to find that evolutionary theorists predict that men and women will also differ in the kinds of things that incite jealousy. Men, for example, can never know *for sure* that the children they think are theirs, and in which they choose to invest their all, are really their own. Thus, men should find the idea that their mates are having sex with a rival extremely threatening. Women, on the other hand, should be primarily concerned with ensuring that their mates provide continuing support for them and their offspring. Thus, they should not care much one way or another whether their mates are having a sexual liaison. What worries them is the possibility that their mates may be forming a deep, emotional attachment to a rival.

There is evidence that men tend to get most jealous when their wives are sexually involved with other men, whereas women get most jealous when their husbands spend time talking or sharing common interests with other women (Buss and Schmitt, 1993; Glass & Wright, 1985).

Researchers have also found that when men and women are jealous, they tend to react in somewhat different ways. In their review of the existing research on jealousy, Gordon Clanton and Lynn Smith (1987) found the following differences in the way men and women in the United States tend to respond when they are jealous:

Men are more apt to deny *jealous feelings; women are more apt to* acknowledge *them. Men are more likely than women to express jealous feelings through rage and even violence, but such outbursts are often followed by despondency. Jealous men are more apt to focus on the outside* sexual *activity of the partner and they often demand a recital of the intimate details; jealous women are more likely to focus on the* emotional *involvement between her partner and the third party. Men are more likely to* externalize *the cause of the jealousy, more likely to blame the partner, or the third party, or "circumstances." Women often* internalize *the cause of jealousy; they blame themselves. Similarly, a jealous man is more likely to display* competitive *behavior toward the third party while a jealous woman is more likely to display* possessive *behavior. She clings to her partner rather than confronting the third party.*

In general, we may say that male and female experiences and expressions of jealousy reflect male and female role expectations. (p. 11)

Israeli psychologists Arie Nadler and Iris Dotan (1992) found that jealous people may respond in two very different ways: (1) Some people focus on the threat to their feelings of self-esteem. Their reactions are designed to protect their own egos. For example, they berate their partners, beat them up, leave, or try to get even. (2) Some people focus on the threat to the present relationship. Their reactions are designed to try to improve their floundering relationship. They may try to make themselves more attractive, talk things out, or learn something from the experience. Nadler and Dotan concluded that men and women seem to respond quite differently to jealous provocation. In general, jealous men concentrate on shoring up their sagging self-esteem. Jealous women are more likely to try to do something to strengthen the relationship.

Jeff Bryson (1977) speculated that perhaps these male/female differences are due to the fact that most societies are patriarchal. It is acceptable for men to initiate relationships. Thus, when men are threatened, they can easily go elsewhere. Women may not have the same freedom. They therefore devote their energies to keeping the relationship from floundering. Nadler and Dotan (1992) pointed out that masculine and feminine sex roles are somewhat different. Men are taught to be concerned with power and status, whereas women are more concerned with intimacy and maintaining their relationships.

Studies in a variety of countries—including Israel (Nadler & Dotan, 1992) and the Netherlands (Buunk, 1982)—have found that these same gender differences exist in many parts of the world. Recently, Krystyna Stryzewski-Aune screened some videotapes that she and her colleague Beth Le Poire had captured "candid camera" style during an experiment on jealousy (Le Poire & Stryzewski-Aune, 1993). The scientists invited forty-four dating couples to participate in a communications experiment. Presumably, they were going to discuss a social-moral dilemma. In fact, what the scientists were interested in was the extent of jealousy in men's and women's nonverbal communication patterns with their sweethearts and their rivals. They did this in the following way: When couples arrived, a flustered experimenter and her "assistant" began to apologize profusely. Their video camera had just broken down (a frequent occurrence). Why didn't the two of them just sit and chat with her assistant for a moment while she tinkered with the camera. She was sure she could fix it. The trio sat chatting amiably for two minutes. Then, the assistant (A) (a charming, unusually good-looking young man or woman) made his or her move. In the control condition, "A" simply continued chatting amiably with the couple for four more minutes. In the jealousy condition, "A" (let us picture the assistant as a man) began flirting outrageously with the woman. "A" flattered her, gazed into her eyes, talked only to her, leaned toward her, and gently brushed his fingertips against her leg. Finally, "A" asked for her telephone number, so he could give her a call about a forthcoming experiment. After two minutes, he was called into the adjoining room and the couple was left "alone" for two more minutes. Unbeknownst to the couple, a video camera was secretly recording all of their movements and conversation during the warm-up period, the flirting incident, and their private chat when they were "alone" after "A" left the room. The tapes were startling. Initially, the scientists had been interested only in testing a simple hypothesis: Did jealous men and women react differently? The authors had expected jealous women to smile and pay special attention to their boyfriends while jealous men glared at their rival and paid careful attention to him, hoping to reestablish their "territorial rights." The tapes revealed much more than that, however.

Beginning with those whose partner was the object of the assistant's flirtation, jealous women kept smiling and speaking fairly pleasantly. Jealous men scowled and clammed up. Both genders began, as the assistant "came on," to focus their full attention on their partners. Both began to perform little actions designed to signal "he (she) is mine!" One woman licked her fingers, and smoothed down a nonexistent cowlick on her boyfriend's hair. Women brushed dandruff and lint off their boyfriend's jackets. They patted chests and rubbed backs. They put their legs on their boyfriends' laps. Men seemed to be a bit less frantic. Some plopped their legs across their girlfriends laps. One man hissed through clenched teeth: "I don't like him." "What?" she asked. "I don't like him," he repeated. "Don't give him your number." Then, scowling, he playfully (?) kicked her a time or two in the leg. "Ow," she complained. Both jealous men and women studiously ignored the romantic threat.

Their partners, those who were the objects of flirtation, tried to deal with the awkward situation as well. Men and women smiled politely to the advancing assistant and answered questions courteously. Sometimes they also turned to their partners and smiled at them, probably to reassure them that they weren't taking all this too seriously. Women seemed especially ill at ease. They kept glancing uneasily at their boyfriends. They tried to smooth things over. They joked with the jealous men, soothed them, babied them, patted their hair, attended to them. Men seemed somewhat less concerned with reassuring their partners.

Cultural Differences in Jealousy

Anthropologists, of course, have noted that cultures differ markedly in what sets off jealousy, in how jealous people get, and in whether or not they have the power to do anything about it (Hupka & Ryan, 1990; Hupka, 1991).

What Sparks Jealousy.   Men and women can use a number of clues to tell them that someone they love is drifting away. Ralph Hupka (1981) illustrated the point that cultures define very different things as threats to self-esteem, relationships, and property with this scenario:

> *On her return trip from the local watering well, a married woman is asked for a cup of water by a male resident of the village. Her husband, resting on the porch of their dwelling, observes his wife giving the man a cup of water. Subsequently, they approach the husband and the three of them enjoy a lively and friendly conversation into the late evening hours. Eventually the husband puts out the lamp, and the guest has sexual intercourse with the wife. The next morning the husband leaves the house early in order to catch fish for breakfast. Upon his return he finds his wife having sex again with the guest. The husband becomes violently enraged and mortally stabs the guest.*
>
> *At what point in the vignette may one expect the husband to be jealous? It depends, of course, in which culture we place the husband. A husband of the Pawnee Indian tribe in the 19th century bewitched any man who dared to request a cup of water from his wife. . . . An Ammassalik Eskimo husband, on the other hand, offered his wife to a guest by means of the culturally sanctioned game of "putting out the lamp." A good host was expected to turn out the lamp at night, as an invitation for the guest to have sexual intercourse with the wife. The Ammassalik, however, became intensely jealous when his wife copulated with a guest in circumstances other than the lamp game or without a mutual agreement between two families to exchange mates, and it was not unusual for the husband to kill the interloper.*
>
> *The Toda of Southern India, who were primarily polyandrous at the turn of the century . . . would consider the sequence of events described in the vignette to be perfectly normal. That is to say, the husband would not have been upset to find his wife having sexual relations again in the morning if the man were her* mokhthod-vaiol. *The Todas had the custom of* mokhthoditi *which allowed husbands and wives to take on lovers. When, for instance, a man wanted someone else's wife as a lover he sought the consent of the wife and her husband or husbands. If consent was given by all, the men negotiated for the annual fee to be received by the husband(s). The woman then lived with the man just as if she were his real wife. Or more commonly, the man visited the woman at the house of her husband(s).*
>
> *It is evident from these illustrations that the culture of a society is a more potent variable than characteristics of the individual in predicting which events someone will evaluate as a threat. (pp. 324–325)*

Bram Buunk and Ralph Hupka (1987) found that there are also cultural differences in the kinds of things that trigger jealousy in modern, industrialized nations. They interviewed 2,079 college students from seven industrialized nations—the United States, Hungary, Ireland, Mexico, the Netherlands, the former Soviet Union, and the former Yugoslavia. Students were asked to take a look at several statements: *flirting* ("It does not bother me when I see my lover flirting with someone else"); *kissing* ("When I see my lover kissing someone else my stomach knots up"); *dancing*

("When my lover dances with someone else I feel very uneasy"); *hugging* ("When somebody hugs my lover I get sick inside"); *sexual relationships* ("It would bother me if my partner frequently had satisfying sexual relations with someone else"); and *sexual fantasy* ("It is entertaining to hear the sexual fantasies my partner has about another person"). They were asked to indicate to what extent they agreed with each of these statements on a 7-point scale ranging from 1: strongly disagree, to 7: strongly agree.

There were some striking cross-national similarities in the kinds of things that people found threatening or nonthreatening. Behaviors such as dancing, hugging, and talking about sexual fantasies were taken in stride. Explicit erotic behavior—flirting, kissing, or having sexual relations with someone else—evoked strong jealousy.

There were some striking cultural differences in *exactly* what people found upsetting, however. U.S. citizens for example, took "hugging" for granted. They were about average in how upsetting they found the other activities to be. In the Netherlands, kissing, hugging, and dancing evoked less jealousy than in most other countries, but they got more upset by the idea of their partner having sexual fantasies about other people than did others. In Yugoslavia flirting evoked a more negative emotional response than in any other country, but they were least concerned about sexual fantasies or kissing. The Hungarians found both hugging and kissing most provoking. Those from the Soviet Union were upset by dancing and sexual relations.

Intensity of Jealousy.   Ralph Hupka and James Ryan (1990; Hupka, 1991) argued that a culture's social structure should have a marked impact on how vulnerable its members were to jealousy. Consider two tribes—the Ammassalik Eskimos (known for their extreme jealousy) and the Toda tribe of India (known for their startling lack of jealousy). The Ammassalik Eskimo family had to be completely self-sufficient (Mirsky, 1937). Each couple had to produce everything that they needed to survive—shelter, clothing, food, and utensils. Loners rarely survived the long, harsh Arctic winters. It is not surprising to discover that the Ammassalik were eager, if not desperate, to find a competent mate. No wonder that those who did had problems with jealousy. A passionate rival was literally a threat to survival.

The Todas of India, on the other hand, had a clan economy (Rivers, 1906). Marriage was a luxury, not a necessity. The most common form of marriage was fraternal polyandry: When a woman married, she became the wife of all her husband's brothers. Not surprisingly, people did not distinguish much between their own children and those of other tribesmen. Of course, men had no way of knowing who was the father of "their" children. Companions for friendship and for sex were easy to find. The clan worked together on most tasks and shared everything. The idea of "private" property did not really exist. Not surprisingly, in this society, jealousy was rare.

Hupka and Ryan argued that there was a simple explanation for such findings. In any culture, the more important marriage and private property are, the more jealous of potential romantic rivals will be the marital partners. To test this notion, the authors selected 150 tribal societies from those described in *The Human Relations Area Files*. The scientists then classified societies' political and economic customs: How important was it to be married? Was it, for example, necessary for survival? How easy was it to find sex outside of marriage? How important was private property? Was everything owned in common? Privately owned? Was theft punished? How important was it to have children?

Next, the authors coded the extent of jealousy in each society. In some, men generally didn't have any reaction when they heard their mates had been unfaithful. In others, such as the Maori of New Zealand (Mishkin, 1937), husbands demanded money or valuable property from their wives' lovers. If a Bakongo adulterer could not pay the compensation, he had to work the husband's fields as well as his own. This generally ensured that he would be too exhausted to chase women (White & Mullen, 1989). In other cultures, infidelity was cause for separation or divorce. In some, the adulterous spouse or rival was banished or killed. For example, the ancient Hebrews would stone to death a married woman and her lover if the affair took place in the city. In the country, it was assumed the woman had been raped but that no one had heard her screams; hence, there only the man was killed (Murstein, 1974).

The authors found that culture, and the severity of the threat that adultery posed in that culture, had a powerful impact on how men reacted to their wives' adultery. It was culture, not genes, that determined the nature of male response to news that their wives were having an affair. Would they react with a shrug, with indignation, or with murderous violence? Much depended on where they called home.

The data also highlighted the importance of power in determining how people respond to jealous provocations. In most tribes, women, who were usually physically weaker than men, had less political and economic power. Although neither men nor women liked infidelity, only the men were in a position to do much about it. In general, women were expected to respond to adultery with only the gentlest forms of aggression. They could express righteous indignation, cry, threaten to walk out, or divorce. The men were allowed to bring out the really big guns when offended: to banish or murder their mates.

How the Jealous React. Peter Salovey and Judith Rodin (1985) surveyed 25,000 heterosexual, bisexual, and homosexual Americans from a variety of ethnic groups. How did they react the last time they were jealous? These lovers described behavior that is familiar to all of us. Lovers became obsessed with painful images of their beloved in the arms of their rivals. They sought confirmation of their worst fears. They searched through their partner's personal belongings for unfamiliar names and telephone numbers. They telephoned their mates unexpectedly just to see if they were where they had said they would be. They listened in on their telephone conversations and followed them. They gave their mates the third degree about previous or present romantic relationships. Novelist Paul Theroux (1989), in *My Secret History*, described the reactions of Andre Parent, when he arrived home after four months of bitter travel through Vietnam and Siberia, to find that his wife Jenny had had a brief affair:

I believed that she too was leading two lives and that, unused to doing so, she would be careless. I could not wait for her to slip. I searched for proof.

First I looked in the house. There was her dressing table in the bedroom, full of drawers. All burglars and housebreakers go for the main bedroom and make straight for the dressing table: they know it contains everything. I sifted through and found foreign coins, hairpins, broken pens, her passport (she had not left the country in my absence), receipts for gas and electric bills, used checkbooks and jewelry. I recognized all the jewelry. So she had not been given that kind of present. I studied the check stubs—nothing there.

Her clothing was more revealing. Did the fact that she had brought quite a lot of new underwear mean something? I felt it did. But it was all I found. She seldom threw anything away. This meant her drawers and shelves were full. But it was junk, it meant nothing—it was old bus tickets, and out-of-date season tickets and timetables and broken pencils and cheap watches, and old clothes. Looking through this pitiful stuff only made me sad. (pp. 376–377)

Anthropologists find that people throughout the world engage in similar kinds of detective work. The Dobuan husband watches his wife while she works the fields and counts her footsteps if she goes into the bush. Too many footsteps mean a possibility of a secret sexual liaison (Mead, 1931). Apache men who leave their encampment generally ask their close blood relatives to spy on their wives (Goodwin, 1942).

At the same time that they are searching for clues that their mate is guilty, guilty, guilty, Gregory White and Paul Mullen (1989) noted that many jealous lovers seek constant reassurance that what they fear isn't so. They beg for repeated declarations of love. They need to be kissed, cuddled, held. The same lovers who are so suspicious and wily when they are searching for confirmation that their mates are having an affair often then believe the most fantastic excuses when they discover that their mates are, after all, having that affair. She will say, "I was so tired, I just fell asleep; we didn't sleep together the week we were together in Paris." And he will find that credible.

White and Mullen (1989) found that people try to cope with their jealous feelings, the threats to their self-esteem and their fears of loss in a variety of ways: Sometimes, as above, lovers refuse to see what they don't want to see. They deny there is a problem. ("They're just good friends. Very good friends.") Some jealous lovers focus on themselves. "What's wrong with me? What did I do wrong?" they ask. Once they spot "the problem," they set out to try to make themselves more appealing. They begin to wear more makeup or buy a new wardrobe. They start to work out more at the gym and eat fewer chocolate chip cookies.

Other people focus on controlling their mate. In medieval times, British and European nobility locked their wives up in chastity belts while they were off at the Crusades. Other cultures have relied on infibulation (stitching together the labia majora), vaginal plugs, and clitoridectomy (a form of female castration, designed to eliminate sexual pleasure), to keep women in check (Daly et al., 1982).

Other lovers focus on eliminating the rival. They may drop not so subtle hints about her appalling character ("Do you think she has AIDS? No? How about herpes?"). They point out that if their mates leave: They Will Pay. They try to make their mates feel guilty. ("I've given you the best years of my life.") They demand that their mates make a choice. ("It's him or me.") They track their mates to their new apartments and make scenes. They beat up their rivals.

When Andre Parent (Theroux, 1989), in *My Secret Life,* discovered his wife Jenny indeed had an affair with someone, he promised that he wouldn't make a scene if she would only tell him who it was. After weeks of pressure, she was exhausted. She admitted it was her boss, Terence Slee. Andre then spent his time fantasizing about ways to retaliate:

> *I imagined shooting him—suddenly opening fire, as he mounted the steps to his home; not killing him, but wounding him terribly, tearing an ear off, severing a hand, disfiguring his face, crippling him. He had a flat in a house in Islington. I sometimes loitered there. I thought of breaking all his windows, or setting the house on fire; pouring paint stripper over his car. I had heard of a man being able to bear severe persecution, even torture, and then breaking down completely when his dog was stolen. Slee had a cat. I had seen the creature at his window. I devised various ways of hanging the cat. (Theroux, 1989, p. 392)*

Eventually, most people give up. If the relationship really is over, they recognize it and try to get on with their lives. They call up old lovers and begin dating. They seek consolation. They try to spend more time with their family and friends. They buy a pet. They bury themselves in work.

Vengeance

Of course, some jealous lovers react more violently. In the seventeenth century, Robert Burton (1621/1827) wrote in *The Anatomy of Melancholy* that "those which are jealous proceed from suspicion to hatred; from hatred to frenzie; from frenzie to injurie, murder and despair" (p. 428). Historically, since men had the most power, they were allowed to let their "frenzie" lead to murder. Women had to be content with more tepid responses.

Arapaho (American Indian) men might beat their wives if they suspected they had been having sexual relations with anyone else:

> *Occasionally a suspicious man calmly sent his wife away, either to her paramour or to her home. More often he became angry and jealous. Usually he whipped her, and cut off the tip of her nose or her braids, or both. According to Kroeber . . . he also slashed her cheeks. This treatment of an unfaithful wife was conventional and neither her parents nor the tribe did anything about it. (Hilger, 1952, p. 212)*

The king of the Plateau tribes of Zimbabwe executed men caught with any of his wives. The wives were grossly mutilated (Gouldsbury & Sheane, 1911). In earlier times, Apache husbands also killed their rivals and mutilated their wives by cutting off the end of their noses; presumably that made them less appealing the next time (Goodwin, 1942).

In Western cultures, men are far more likely to beat or murder their girlfriends and wives than their rivals. Bullies usually attack "women and children first." (White & Mullen, 1989). Today in America, family peace centers report that about two-thirds of the wives who are forced to seek shelter do so because their husbands' excessive or unwarranted jealousy has led them to repeatedly assault the women (Gayford, 1979). Male jealousy is the leading cause of wife battering and homicide worldwide (Buss, 1992; Daly & Wilson, 1988a, 1988b). Most violent women admit that jealousy motivated their violence (Stets & Pirog-Good, 1987).

In the West such vengeance was approved or treated leniently until recently. The eighteenth-century English jurist Blackstone commented that killing in a situation where a man or woman is caught in the act "is of the lowest degree of manslaughter; . . . for there could not be a greater provocation" (quoted in Smith & Hogan, 1983, p. 288). Until 1972, under Article 1220 of the Texas Penal Code, a man could murder his wife and her lover if he found them in a "compromising position" and get away with it as "justifiable homicide." Women did not have equal shooting rights (Ivins, 1991, p. 169). To this day in Texas, if a man or woman intentionally kills his or her mate, the lover, or both, the crime is considered not murder but involuntary manslaughter (La Fave & Scott, 1972; Lewin, 1994). Late last year, legal experts, women's advocacy groups, and tabloid television shows fixed their attention on the case of a Chinese-American man, Dong Lu Chen, who beat his wife to death with a claw hammer after she confessed to adultery. Chen was granted five years' probation, based on the argument that his cultural background required him to kill his wife (Lewin, 1994).

In many countries, the courts have been sympathetic to such "crimes of passion." Traditionally, it was considered to be a man's right to defend his "honor." In Morocco, for example, the law excuses killing one's wife if she is caught in the act of adultery, but a woman would not be excused for killing her husband in the same circumstances (Greenhouse, 1994). In São Paulo (Brazil's most populous city), in 1980–1981, 722 men claimed "defense of honor" for murdering their wives. Brazilian women adopted the slogan "Lovers don't kill," and campaigned against allowing such a defense in murder trials. In 1991, a landmark case came before the Brazilian Supreme Court:

> In the coffee-processing town of Apucarana in Parana State, Joao Lopes became enraged in August 1988 when his wife, Teresa, announced that she was leaving him. Mr. Lopes searched the town for two days until he caught up with his wife and her lover, Jose Gaspar Felix, at a hotel.
>
> Bursting into the hotel room, Mr. Lopes knifed his rival to death on the spot, then caught up with his fleeing wife in the street and killed her with two knife blows.
>
> At the first trial, a jury of nine men accepted the argument that Mr. Lopes had killed to defend his honor.

An appeals court upheld the verdict. (Brooke, 1991, p. B9) The Supreme Court, however, ruled that men can no longer kill their wives and win acquittal on the grounds of "legitimate defense of honor." The Court ruled:

Homicide cannot be seen as a normal and legitimate way of reacting to adultery. Because in this kind of crime what is defended is not honor, but vanity, exaggerated self-importance and the pride of the lord who sees a woman as his personal property. (Brooke, 1991, p. B9)

Dating and Marital Violence

Of all the emotions, there is none more violent than love.
—Cicero

As we write this, we glance at *Ka Leo O Hawai'i*, the student newspaper of the University of Hawaii, and the headline states: "Love means abuse in some relationships. Morioka situation not rare among couples." The story goes on:

Nineteen-year-old UH student Sherry Morioka tried many times to break up with her boyfriend Abraham Fu. But Morioka's mother, Caroline, said Fu refused to let her daughter go.

Caroline said her daughter wanted to end the relationship because she didn't want to be choked, punched, shoved and slapped by Fu anymore.

Caroline said Fu wanted to know what her daughter did every minute, and even bought her a digital pager to keep tabs on her. She said Fu even got angry when her daughter spoke to male friends on the telephone.

After months of mental and physical abuse, Sherry finally got the strength to tell Fu that she didn't want the abuse—nor him, Caroline said.

Their relationship finally ended in May 1992, when Fu shot her in the head with a .357 magnum handgun. Morioka died after 10 days in a hospital.

Fu was convicted last Monday of manslaughter, a felony, and possession, use or threat to use a firearm in the commission of a felony. . . .

Fu will be sentenced Nov. 16 at 10 A.M. (Ablan, 1993, p. 1)

Abuse begins early in many love relationships. Couples may slap, shove, grab, bite, kick, or hit one another with their fists. They may threaten one another with knives or guns or beat one another (Marshall & Rose, 1987). Approximately 22 to 40 percent of dating couples and 38 percent of engaged couples report that they have had physically violent confrontations with their partners (Cate et al., 1982; Gryl et al., 1991). More than half the time (68 percent), both partners were abusive (Cate et al., 1982).

Frances Gryl and her colleagues (1991) asked 280 first-year college students who were in serious dating relationships how violent were those relationships. They asked students to complete Murray Straus's (1979) *Conflict Tactics Scale*. This scale asks couples to recall the time in the past year when they and their dates or mates had had a spat or fight. How had they and their partners reacted? The scale then listed nineteen tactics couples might have employed during a conflict. The list began with items from the Reasoning scale, such as "discussed issue calmly." It went on to the items on the Verbal Aggression scale, such as "Insulted or swore at the other," and ended with the Violence items. Couples were considered to have had a violent encounter if they admitted using physical force to get their way, including shoving, slapping, kicking, beating up, stabbing or shooting their sweethearts during a fight. For dating couples' replies, see Table 6.3.

As you can see from Table 6.3, in this study men and women were equally likely to inflict and sustain violence: 23 percent of the men and 30 percent of the women admitted that they had been violent; 39 percent of the men and 28 percent of the women reported that they had been the victims of violence. Most studies, however, find that men are far more aggressive than women. Men are more likely to punch, kick, choke, beat up, and threaten their lovers with knives or guns than are women. Their violence is also more likely to inflict serious emotional, sexual, and physical injury on their dating partners (Makepeace, 1986; Marshall & Rose, 1987).

Researchers have wondered whether gay, lesbian, and straight couples are equally likely to try to get their way by resorting to putdowns, throwing things, pushing, and violence. They find that they are (Metz, Rosser, & Strapko, 1994). In one study, for example, Caroline Waterman and her colleagues (1989) asked thirty-three gays and thirty-six lesbians to fill out the *Conflict Tactics Scale*. They found that 15 percent of gay men and 54 percent of lesbians admitted that they had reacted violently to their romantic partners. Twenty-one percent of gay men and 40 percent of gay women reported that they had been the victims of romantic violence. Often,

TABLE 6.3 Violence Inflicted and Sustained in Current Dating Relationship

Type of violence	Expressed violence		Suffered violence	
	Women % ever	Men % ever	Women % ever	Men % ever
Pushed, shoved or grabbed	19.9	11.3	19.9	18.5
Wrestled or pinned down	5.1	9.7	9.0	3.2
Threw an object at	7.1	4.0	3.8	15.3
Clawed, scratched, or bit	5.1	0.0	1.3	12.1
Slapped	17.9	8.9	7.7	21.8
Punched with fist	4.5	3.2	1.9	8.1
Hit with object	1.9	0.0	2.6	5.6
Kicked	3.2	2.4	1.9	7.3
Attempted to strangle	0.6	1.6	0.6	0.8
Used lethal weapon (knife, gun, etc.)	1.3	0.8	0.6	0.9

Based on Gryl et al. (1991), p. 254.

because men and women feel they have no other alternatives, couples decide to stay in these abusive relationships (O'Leary et al., 1986).

A study of more than 2,000 American married couples (Straus et al., 1980) found that more than 25 percent of them had engaged in some form of violence during their married life. Suzanne Steinmetz (1978) estimated that 3,300,000 American wives and 250,000 American husbands had been severely beaten by their mates. Women usually limited their attacks to making accusations, slapping, or throwing something. Men were far more violent. They were more willing to punch, kick, choke, beat up, and threaten their wives with a knife or a gun than were women. Since men are generally bigger than women, their violent acts do more damage. Not surprisingly, wives were more likely to be severely injured during such attacks than were husbands (Stets & Straus, 1990; Straus et al., 1980). Typical injuries ranged from cuts, bruises, black eyes, concussions, broken bones and miscarriages to permanent injuries, such as partial loss of hearing or vision; scars from burns, bites, or knife wounds; and damage to joints. And in far too many cases, death occurred (Browne, 1993).

After surveying more than 8,000 American families, Murray Straus (1990) concluded that the major causes of physical violence in the family are to be found in some basic characteristics of American society. The most important causes seemed to be patriarchal norms; sexist and racist social structures (which justify the use of violence to maintain the status quo; and the stresses caused by racism, sexism, and poverty. (See Straus and Gelles, 1990, for evidence in support of these contentions.)

Ethnic Differences in Abuse and Violence
African American essayist Pearl Cleage (1993), in *Deals With the Devil*, argues that African Americans are hardly immune to the violence that infects the rest of American society (see Box 6.1 on page 186).

Researchers have compared rates of violence in couples from African American, European American, and Hispanic backgrounds. As we might expect, they find that marital battering is too common in all these groups. Noel Cazenave and Murray Straus (1990), for example, compared African American and European American couples who had been interviewed in the National Family Violence Survey. On first glance, it looked as if black marriages were more violent than were those of other racial and ethnic groups. For example, black husbands were three times as likely as European American husbands to report reacting with severe violence during the previous year. Black women were twice as likely as European American women to have indulged in such mistreatment. A closer look at the data, however, made it clear that these differences seemed to have less to do with cultural and racial differences in attitudes toward violence than with couples' income and employment opportunities. When sociologists controlled for social class and the amount of social support couples had from family and friends, almost all of the differences disappeared. It seemed that it was not race but family income that was the critical determinant of how likely things were to spiral out of control. Black couples also seemed to get along best if they had family and friends nearby, who could provide social support and step in when arguments threatened to get out of hand.

BOX 6.1 Why I Write

Yesterday, as I was writing this, my neighbor, my sister, had to call the police to protect her from her husband, also my neighbor and my brother, who was threatening to douse them both with gasoline and light it in a murder/suicide if she did not stop divorce proceedings and come back to be his wife.

Last week after class, one of my students waited for me to confess softly that her boyfriend had been beating her and what should she do?

A month ago, a young friend who teaches preschool read to me from her journals a harrowing description of the night her former lover shot himself in the head after she escaped from his apartment following months of beating and torture.

My friend the corporate executive relates a story of leaping from a speeding car and running into some urban woods after her husband placed a gun to her temple while driving with her down a busy suburban street.

My friend the well-respected public servant comes to work with sunglasses to hide the two black eyes her husband gave her by beating her head against the wall while their children slept in the next room.

My sisterwriter with the three young children tells horror stories of being scalded with boiled water and forced to suck the barrel of a gun as if it was her husband's penis.

And my memory of my own nightmare as an undergraduate student at Howard University, listening to my boyfriend tell me I'd better not move as he tied my hands and feet and told me if he couldn't have me, nobody could.

But that's not all. I also remember the chorus of black male objections to Ntozake Shange's *For Colored Girls*. I hear the protests over Alice Walker's *The Color Purple,* and I remember the forums whining about negative images of black men in *The Women of Brewster Place,* and I wonder where those same black male voices are when black male violence is being condoned and taught and glamorized and ignored. I wonder when we are going to see the same commitment to fighting sexism in the work of our brotherwriters that we see to fighting racism. I wonder how much good all those poems about beautiful African queens can do in the face of a backhand slap across the mouth and a merciless rape in the bedroom of your own house. (pp. 3–4)

Murray Straus and Christine Smith (1990) compared Hispanic and European American couples who had been interviewed in the National Family Violence Survey. They found extremely high rates of violence among Hispanic couples. When European American couples were asked whether or not an argument had led to severe violence—if they had kicked, punched, bitten, or chocked their mate—3 percent of husbands and 4 percent of wives admitted that they had. Among Hispanic couples, 7 percent of husbands and 8 percent of wives admitted reacting with extreme violence. Once again, however, the higher rates of spouse abuse in Hispanic families reflected the youthfulness, urban residence, and economic deprivation of Hispanics. When those factors were controlled, again, these ethnic differences disappeared. It appears that the best way to promote American family values is to improve the quality of life in urban areas and to raise the socioeconomic level of poor families.

What about other ethnic groups? We were able to find only one study that explored the violence of men and women from various ethnic groups toward their parents, brothers, and sisters. Caroline and Robert Blanchard (1982) interviewed 620 college students at the Honolulu Community College. They asked men and women from five different ethnic groups—European, Chinese, Filipino, and Japanese Americans as well as Hawaiians and part Hawaiians—to look at a list of abusive activities (say, "You swore at or insulted a family member") and to indicate if they had ever done such a thing and, if so, how many times they had done it. Possible answers ranged from "0" to 20+ times. Their replies appear in Table 6.4.

In all cultures, men were slightly more combative, overall, than were women. The various ethnic groups also differed in how ready they were to resort to serious

TABLE 6.4   Number of Times Men and Women from Various Ethnic Groups Have Engaged in Various Violent Acts (Directed against Family Members)

Action	European American	Japanese American	Filipino American	Hawaiian and part Hawaiian	Chinese American
Men					
Swore at	8.8	6.5	5.5	8.2	3.9
Threatened to hit	2.7	1.7	1.1	5.2	2.4
Smashed something	2.3	1.8	1.6	2.6	2.9
Threw at	0.7	0.5	0.1	1.8	1.4
Pushed, grabbed, or shoved	1.3	1.1	1.6	4.0	2.1
Slapped	0.5	0.2	0.2	2.0	1.4
Kicked, bit, or hit with fist	1.4	0.7	0.6	2.3	1.3
Hit with object	0.2	0.2	0.4	0.7	1.1
Beat up	0.3	0.0	0.0	1.2	1.2
Used a weapon	0.0	0.1	0.0	0.0	0.0
Women					
Swore at	7.2	7.4	8.3	8.8	4.8
Threatened to hit	2.7	1.3	2.5	1.9	1.9
Smashed something	3.0	1.4	3.9	2.6	1.3
Threw at	1.6	0.8	2.0	0.8	0.0
Pushed, grabbed, or shoved	2.4	1.7	2.0	1.2	0.5
Slapped	2.3	1.5	2.7	1.2	0.9
Kicked, bit, or hit with fist	2.1	0.8	1.6	1.2	0.7
Hit with object	0.7	0.7	0.1	0.3	0.0
Beat up	0.4	0.0	0.1	0.1	0.0
Used a weapon	0.0	0.0	0.1	0.1	0.1

Based on Blanchard & Blanchard (1982), p. 180.

battering in family disagreements. When we look at men's reports, we find that Hawaiian or part Hawaiian and Chinese American men were generally the most violent; they were most likely to report having slapped, shoved, punched, or beat other family members. European American men were intermediate in their readiness to engage in serious violence. The Japanese American and Filipino American men were by far the least likely to engage in such serious violence. When we look at women's readiness to engage in serious battering, we find that Filipino American and European American women were most likely to push, slap, hit, and beat up other family members. Hawaiian and part Hawaiian and Japanese American women were intermediate in their levels of violence. Chinese American women were by far the least likely to engage in such violent activities.

Cultural Differences in Abuse and Violence

> *Beat a woman and a horse every three days.*
> —*Serbian saying*

> *Your abuse is the ring in my ear,*
> *Your blows are my toe-rings,*
> *If you kick me, it is my pulse and rice,*
> *The more you beat me with your shoes,*
> *The more we are united.*
> —*Muria Gond-India*

Cultures vary enormously in how violent couples are. In some societies, such as the Wape in New Guinea, as we shall see, violence is unknown. In others, such as Iran, India, Indo-Fiji, and Taiwan, wife-beating is very common (Counts, Brown, & Campbell, 1992). Chinua Achebe (1959), in *Things Fall Apart*, depicted the angry outburst of Okonkwo, a tribesman from Okonkwo (Africa) on the Feast of the New Yam:

> *The New Yam Festival was thus an occasion for joy throughout Umuofia. And every man whose arm was strong, as the Ibo people say, was expected to invite large numbers of guests from far and wide. Okonkwo always asked his wives' relations, and since he now had three wives his guests would make a fairly big crowd.*
>
> *But somehow Okonkwo could never become as enthusiastic over feasts as most people. He was a good eater and he could drink one or two fairly big gourds of palm-wine. But he was always uncomfortable sitting around for days waiting for a feast or getting over it. He would be very much happier working on his farm.*
>
> *The festival was now only three days away. Okonkwo's wives had scrubbed the walls and the huts with red earth until they reflected light. They had then drawn patterns on them in white, yellow and dark green. They then set about painting themselves with cam wood and drawing beautiful black patterns on their stomachs and on their backs. The children were also decorated, especially their hair, which was shaved in beautiful patterns. The three women talked excitedly about the relations who had been invited, and the children reveled in the thought of being spoiled by these visitors from motherland. Ikemefuna was equally excited. The New*

Yam Festival seemed to him to be a much bigger event here than in his own village, a place which was already becoming remote and vague in his imagination.

And then the storm burst. Okonkwo, who had been walking about aimlessly in his compound in suppressed anger, suddenly found an outlet.

"Who killed this banana tree?" he asked.

A hush fell on the compound immediately.

"Who killed this tree? Or are you all deaf and dumb?"

As a matter of fact the tree was very much alive. Okonkwo's second wife had merely cut a few leaves off it to wrap some food, and she said so. Without further argument Okonkwo gave her a sound beating and left her and her only daughter weeping. Neither of the other wives dared to interfere beyond an occasional and tentative, "It is enough, Okonkwo," pleaded from a reasonable distance. (pp. 39–41)

What determines whether or not a society is violent? David Levinson (1989) took a cross-cultural perspective on marital violence. He selected ninety preliterate and peasant societies from the *Human Relations Area Files*. The *HRAF* contains ethnographic materials on 330 societies from sixty major cultural/geographical regions around the world. From his analyses, Levenson concluded:

1. In most marriages throughout the world, verbal and physical abuse is common. In 84 percent of societies, angry husbands, wives, and co-wives slapped, shoved, cut, burned, dealt crushing blows, shot, and killed one another. Such violence was by no means universal however. In 16 percent of societies, marital violence was either unknown or very rare.

2. Husbands were far more likely than wives to beat their mates. Husband beat their wives in 84 percent of the societies sampled. Wives beat their husbands in 27 percent of samples. Husbands were also more violent than were wives. Their beatings sometimes caused scarring, broken bones, mutilation, or death.

3. Men beat women in huge numbers and with terrifying severity for a simple reason: they could get away with it. In most societies, men possessed the most status and power. Men had the final say in household decisions. They owned all the valuable property and the fruits of family labor. Wives could not escape from the marriage through divorce. In such societies, men commonly abused their wives. The Yugoslavian Serbs are a typical example of such a society:

The peasants consider, and so do their wives, that this is the husband's right as head of the family. If a woman does anything wrong and the husband does not give her a good beating, she begins to despise him, counts him a weakling and strives to assume his place in the home. . . . In the opinion of the village, the husband is absolute master in the home, who must see that there is order in the home, who has the right to punish the members of the family if they do anything very wrong. (Erlich, 1966, p. 270)

Many battered women try to kill themselves (see Counts, 1987).

Levenson found that other societies were more egalitarian. Women possessed relatively more status and power. They could own property and keep their own wages. Marriages were monogamous. The sexual double standard did not exist. Family and friends would step in to set limits as domestic disputes threatened to spiral out of control. Women formed strong, life-long bonds with one another. Both men and women could walk out or divorce if things got too bad. In such societies, there was little violence. Apparently, men thought twice before acting in ways that might force their wives to walk out. Typical of societies that were free of family violence were the Central Thai. Levinson concluded: "The central conclusion I reach from these findings is that family violence does not occur in societies in which family life is characterized by cooperation, commitment, sharing, and equality" (p. 104). Other anthropologists have secured similar results (Erchak & Rosenfeld, 1994). Many societies are beginning to confront the existence of such "loving" abuse and to try to devise ways to persuade couples to face and resolve their inevitable conflicts (Hatfield & Rapson, 1993b).

Passionate love is a powerful emotion. In the previous sections, we reminded ourselves that passionate affairs may be tossed by the cross-currents of delight and disappointment. In the next section, we will find that it is these very cross-currents that may give passionate love its peculiar power.

The Cross-Magnification Process

> *What do I understand of love? Once I used to think that love is the point where cruelty and compassion meet.*
>
> —Amos Oz

For most of us, passionate love is associated with a variety of emotions, pleasurable and painful. Elaine Hatfield (Carlson & Hatfield, 1992) argued that the most intense emotional experiences usually involve blends of emotions. This may not be pure coincidence. Perhaps emotions, especially positive emotions, have a better chance to rise to a fever pitch when several emotional units are activated. Love may be more intense than usual when it is kindled by fire and ice—by the impossible paradoxes of ecstasy *and* insecurity, jealousy and impatience, love and hate. The loss of a sweetheart may be especially hard to bear when combined with guilt about the way we treated him or her. Add grief and anger at the loss to that guilt, and the darkness deepens. There is considerable evidence that mixtures of emotions—good, bad, and neutral—can fuel passion (Hatfield & Rapson, 1993b).

The juxtaposition of passionate love with a spill of emotions, then, might not be entirely accidental. Passionate love's tender discoveries, sudden torments, and consuming desires may flourish when they are nurtured by a torrent of good experiences, and a sprinkling of unsettling, anxiety-producing, and even painful experiences. Although most people assume that we love the people we do *in spite of* the anxiety and anger they cause us, it may be that, in part, we love people *because* of the dangerously contradictory feelings they cause. Under the right conditions, anxiety and fear, insecurity, loneliness, frustration, jealousy, anger, and mixed emotions have all been found to be capable of fanning the flames of passion. Erotic passion demands physiological arousal and both pleasant and unsettling experiences are arousing (Hatfield & Rapson, 1993b).

In Chapter 3, we discussed the beginnings of love. We pointed out that people who endorse the various love schemas seem to expect very different things from passionate love and sexual desire. We noted that people in different cultures are, of course, provided with very different schemas concerning love. In this chapter, let us continue the discussion. We would argue that people who endorse the various love schemas might also be expected to differ in the highs and lows they experience in love. They might be expected to differ in how much difficulty they have in balancing commitment and intimacy with independence.

Love Schemas and the Highs and Lows of Love

Passionate lovers, regardless of how sensible or experienced they are, know that there are risks in any affair of the heart. Love is simply not predictable. Researchers have found considerable evidence that people's love profiles are linked to some extent to the pleasures and problems they encounter in passionate love affairs. It is easy to guess at the nature of the problems people with different agendas for love might expect to confront. Those who have a powerful desire for intimacy, at least some of the time, say, people who possess "secure," "clingy," or "fickle" love schemas, are powerfully drawn to love affairs. Those who possess a compelling desire for independence, at least some of the time, say, the "secure," "skittish," or "fickle," tend to shy away from too much involvement (Eidelson, 1983). We have detailed some of the likely advantages and disadvantages of each relationship style in Table 6.1.

Love Schemas and the Delights of Love

The delights of love are many. They have been mooned over in poetry, sentimentalized in movies and on television, commercialized in advertising, and trivialized in greeting cards. They have also been experienced by millions.

> *We float somewhere between love and self-absorption. . . . We play our cards close to our chests, then share, then become frightened and withdraw, then try to share again.*
>
> —Asa Baber

The Secure
Theoretically, the secure might be expected to do the best at navigating the shoals of passionate relationships.

Recently, Guy Bachman and his colleagues (1994) interviewed college men and women from a variety of American ethnic groups—African, Chinese, European, Filipino, Japanese, Korean, Pacific Islander, Hispanic, and Vietnamese. They asked students if they had ever been on the brink of making a serious commitment—thinking about, say, going steady, living together, becoming engaged, or married—and, if so, what kinds of thoughts had run through their minds. What sorts of emotional reactions had they experienced? They found that, as predicted, it was the secure, and only the secure, who were at ease when contemplating a serious commitment. It was they who were the most likely to endorse the following items: "I trusted that _____ was interested in me and only me." "I considered _____ to be a true friend as well as a lover." "I felt totally safe." "I was completely secure in my boyfriend's/ girlfriend's love." "I knew that I could tell my lover my personal thoughts and feelings, without fearing that he/she would think less of me . . . or even leave me." "It was easy for me to depend on my boyfriend/girlfriend for emotional support."

Secure people think of themselves as valuable and worthy of others' affection and concern. They assume their romantic partners are well-intentioned, trustworthy, reliable, and available; they wouldn't put up with them if that were not the case. They report that they find it easy to get close to others. They feel comfortable relying on others and being relied on by them in return. They rarely worry about being abandoned or smothered by others (Hazan & Shaver, 1987). They have happier, more positive relationships (Simpson, 1990). Their relationships involve more commitment, trust, satisfaction, intimacy, and interdependence (Singelis et al., 1995; Collins & Read, 1990; Hendrick & Hendrick, 1989; Levy & Davis, 1988; Simpson, 1990). They do better than most at negotiating companionate, stable, intimate love relationships (Hazan & Shaver, 1987; Mikulincer & Nachshon, 1991). For the secure, love poses few problems and promises great happiness if one has found a suitable and similarly secure partner. People with other personality types, of course, can experience many of these delights and provide comparable delights for their partners (see Table 6.5).

Love Schemas and the Pains of Love

We might expect people who possess the various love schemas to be particularly susceptible to certain kinds of problems (see Table 6.5). Once again, in the following sections, we depart from our usual format. We begin our discussion of each of the personality types by providing a literary example of the kinds of problems people who endorse the various schemas may encounter in their love affairs and the kinds of problems they may cause for those who are foolhardy enough to get involved with them. Then, we present the scientific evidence in support of these generalizations.

The Clingy
The clingy have low self-esteem. They have little confidence in themselves. They are frantic when they think their mates might not really love them. They are ambivalent about their lovers. On one hand, they idealize them. (The other could give

TABLE 6.5 Love Schemas: Their Strengths and Weaknesses

Love Schemas	Strengths and Weaknesses from the Point of View of:	
	Self	Partner
Strengths		
Secure	Good at closeness	Allows closeness
	Good at independence	Allows independence
Clingy	Good at closeness	Allows closeness
Skittish	Good at independence	Allows independence
Fickle	None	None
Casual	Good at independence	Allows independence
Uninterested	Good at independence	Allows independence
Weaknesses		
Secure	None	None
Clingy	Low self-esteem	Must endure complaints
	Feels unloved	Feels pressure to be more intimate
	Frustrated can't get closer	Feels smothered
	Feels insecure	Own desires for independence not recognized
	Worried about abandonment	Made to feel in the wrong
Skittish	Must endure complaints	Low self-esteem
	Feels pressured to be more intimate	Feels unloved
	Feels smothered	Frustrated can't get closer
	Own desire for independence not recognized	Feels insecure
	Made to feel in the wrong	Worried about abandonment
Fickle	Possesses the problems of *both* the clingy and the skittish. Also, of course, the fickle are maddeningly inconsistent.	
Casual	Potentially possesses the same problems as the skittish. They are less possessed, however, so problems are attenuated.	
Uninterested	If they got into a relationship, they would possess the same problems as the casual. Usually, they would not get involved, however, and neither they nor their nonexistent partners would experience problems. May be perceived to be frustrated, somewhat aloof/asexual.	

them so much, if only he or she would.) Yet they can't help but resent them for their reluctance to make a commitment, to get as close to them as they would like, and to take care of them. They worry that their romantic partners will abandon them. They stay so focused on what they themselves need that they are oblivious to their partners' very different feelings and needs. They are addicted to the relationship, careening dangerously into dependence. They ride on an emotional roller-coaster—elated one minute and anxious, frightened, and lonely the next. They have trouble finding a stable, committed, companionate relationship; their insatiable demands seem to drive others away. (For research in support of these propositions, see Bartholomew & Horowitz, 1991; Singelis et al., 1995; Collins & Read, 1990; Daniels & Shaver, 1991; Feeney & Noller, 1990; Hazan & Shaver, 1987, 1990; Hindy, Schwarz, & Brodsky, 1989; Kunce & Shaver, 1991; Levy & Davis, 1988; Mikulincer & Nachshon, 1991; Shaver & Hazan, 1993; Simpson, 1990).

In the study we described earlier, Guy Bachman and his colleagues (1994) found that the clingy tended to experience considerable anxiety when it seemed that they and their partners might make a serious commitment. They reported: "I tried desperately to win his/her approval." "I felt compelled to have sexual relations with my partner in order to keep him/her satisfied." "I wanted to spend every moment of my free time with my partner." "I became extremely anxious whenever _____ failed to pay enough attention to me." "I spent all my free time with my boyfriend/girlfriend." "I was constantly jealous." "I spent dramatically less time with my friends."

Many writers have detailed the problems of the clingy and desperate. Amy Tan (1989), in *The Joy Luck Club,* dramatized the marital problems of Rose Hsu Jordan (a Chinese American) and her husband Ted (a European American). When they were first married, Ted enjoyed having all the power, making all the decisions. He was the hero. She was the maiden in distress. Early in their marriage, they would stay up all night, discussing the choices they faced—where they wanted to live, where to go on vacation, whether or not to start a family. All the discussions ended the same way—with Rose's agreeable refrain: "Ted, you decide." Soon the discussions ended. Ted simply decided. In the end, however, Rose's clinging, dependent ways began to drive Ted crazy. Finally, he asked for a divorce. For Rose, the separation of yin and yang was obliterating.

If you have never been caught up in a relationship with a clingy person, it is easy to feel sorry for them. After all, all they are asking for is love and endless reassurance. But those who are swept up in relationships with the clingy suffer, too. French feminist Evelyne Sullerot (1979) observed that over the centuries:

> There is no weightier set of chains, no more paralyzing trap, than a woman "who has given all of herself," "who has totally surrendered" to a man. . . . Does not the book of Genesis, a tale from the man's point of view if ever there was one, tell us, in that curse that is called down on the head of the woman alone: "Thy desire shall be to thy husband, and he shall rule over thee" (and "In sorrow thou shalt bring forth children")? This is how a number of men conceive of the woman's way of experiencing love: as a creature who is dominated, driven by desire, eager to surrender herself totally. What would be a genuine revelation, perhaps, would be to show men such as this that even those women who play this game whose rules have been dictated by males are not really their willing servants, nor are they the willing servants of the couple. They escape their would-be masters by the very excess of the dependence forced upon them, seeing the world only through them, breathing all of nature in through them, using them to exist, feeding upon them, paralyzing them, devouring them. (pp. 30–31)

By granting a man utter responsibility for her fate, she shackles him with the ball and chain of a guilty conscience and imprisonment. Of course, clingy men smother and irritate their partners in exactly the same ways.

The Skittish

The skittish go to great lengths to avoid commitment. They fear romantic intimacy. In the study we described earlier, Bachman and his colleagues (1994) found that when the skittish were confronted with the necessity of making a serious commitment, they were likely to admit to two concerns: "I often worried that I was making a big mistake by getting so involved so soon." "I often felt trapped; I needed a lot more time to be alone." Not surprisingly, the fickle, casual, and uninterested expressed such concerns as well.

Israeli novelist Amos Oz (1991) rendered the anguished Yael's cry of "Leave me alone" when her self-centered and demanding ex-husband Fima began to pressure her to give him a second chance:

> *Don't come here anymore, Fima. You pretend you're living alone, but you're always clinging to other people. And I'm just the opposite; everybody clings to me, when the only thing I want really is to be left alone. Go away now, Efraim. I have nothing to give to you or to anyone. And I wouldn't even if I did. Why should I? I don't owe anyone anything. . . . You remember my father, dear devoted comrade Naftali Tsvi Levin, founding member of the historic settlement of Yavne'el? He's an old pioneer now, he's eighty-three and completely gaga. He sits in the old people's home in Afula staring at the wall all day, and if ever you ask him a question, like how are you feeling, what's new, what do you need, who are you, who am I, where does it hurt, he invariably replies with the same three-word question: 'In what sense?' He says it with a Yiddish lilt. Those three words are all he has left from the Bible, the Talmud, the Midrash, the Hasidic tales, the Haskalah, Bialik, and Buber, and all the other Jewish sources he knew by heart once. I'm telling you, Efraim, soon I too will have only three words left. Not 'In what sense?' but 'Leave me alone.' Leave me alone, Efraim. I'm not your mother. I have a project that's been dragging on for years now because a whole bunch of toddlers have been tugging at my sleeves to wipe their noses. Once, when I was little, my father the pioneer told me to remember that men are really the weaker sex. It was a joke of his. Well, shall I tell you something? . . . If I knew then what I know now, I'd have joined a nunnery. Or married a jet engine. I'd have passed on the weaker sex, with great pleasure. Give them a finger, they want your whole hand. Give them your whole hand, they won't even want the finger anymore. Just sit quietly over there, make the coffee, and don't interrupt. Don't draw attention to yourself. Do the washing and the ironing, provide sex, and shut up. Give them a rest from you, and after a week they're crawling back on all fours. . . . Go now, Efraim. I'm a woman of forty-nine, and you're no spring chicken yourself. The story's over. There's no replay. . . . Why do you keep coming back to mess me up, and everyone else too? What more do you want from me? Is it my fault you squandered everything you had, and everything*

you might have had, and what you found in Greece? Is it my fault that life goes by and time gnaws at everything? Is it my fault that we all die a little every day? What more do you want from me?" (pp. 261–263)

In therapy, we once saw Sam, a physician who managed a chain of neighborhood clinics. Sam was essentially a big, overgrown boy. The first time we saw him, he was faced with a dilemma. He was wildly, fatally attracted to Sandy, but they fought all the time. Should they get back together? When we saw Sam alone we found the story was a bit more complicated than that. A second girlfriend, Melissa, was arriving from California the next week, expecting to live with him. All he wanted from Sandy was one last passionate sexual encounter. We discontinued therapy.

Two years later, Sam returned again for therapy. Now his problem was Melissa. She was almost perfect. She experimented sexually in an exciting way. She arranged threesomes with other women. Perfect, yes, but . . . now she was pressuring him to marry. He could not marry because he was engaging in occasional dalliances. How occasional? With at least fifteen other women, all patients of his! What a wonderful system he had developed, we commented. He can't marry Melissa because of all the other women. He can't make any commitment to *them* because he is living with her. All this held together by a tissue of lies. Well, actually, truth be told, it's more complicated than that. He is still married to Sandy. "But it doesn't mean anything." Too insignificant to mention. A look at this case makes it clear how Sam differs from the casual dater. Here, the skittish person is intensely dedicated to keeping his freedom. There is nothing "casual" about his feelings.

Scientists find that the skittish are pessimistic about love. They see themselves as being aloof, emotionally distant, and skeptical about relationships. They prefer not to make any serious commitments. They prefer a series of uncommitted (though often intense) sexual relationships. They think of their lovers as overly eager to hurl themselves precipitously into long-term commitments. And they also regard the lovers as unreliable (Bartholomew & Horowitz, 1991).

The skittish avoid intimate social contacts. They are especially phobic about emotional confrontations. When their lovers try to talk over problems with them, they back away (Simpson et al., 1992). They prefer to focus their attention on their work or on nonsocial activities instead.

Men and women who get emotionally involved with the skittish naturally get frustrated. In the movie *Starting Over* (1979), Jill Clayburgh and Burt Reynolds discussed his inability to have a relationship:

Clayburgh: I understand. It's too much, it's too soon, or you don't like me enough, or you like me too much, or you're frightened or you're guilty, you can't get it up or out or in or what?!
    Reynolds: That just about covers it.

Not surprisingly, the romances of the skittish are generally not blissful. They rarely go well (Simpson, 1990). The work of a variety of researchers leads us to these gloomy conclusions (Bartholomew & Horowitz, 1991; Singelis et al., 1995; Collins & Read, 1990; Daniels & Shaver, 1991; Feeney & Noller, 1990; Hazan & Shaver, 1987, 1990; Hindy, Schwarz, & Brodsky, 1989; Kunce & Shaver, 1991; Mikulincer & Nachshon, 1991; Shaver & Hazan, 1992; Simpson, 1990).

The Fickle

In a letter, Julie De LesPinasse (1732–1776) expressed the torment of the fickle:

> *I cannot explain to myself the charm that binds me to you. You are not my friend, and you cannot become such: I do not trust you in the slightest; you have dealt me the most profound and painful hurt that can possibly be inflicted upon an honest soul and rend it asunder: at this moment, and perhaps forever, you are depriving me of the one consolation that heaven had granted me in these last days I have left to live; in short—how can I possibly tell you!—you have filled every moment of my life: the past, the present, and the future hold only pain, regrets, and remorse for me; in any event, my friend, I ponder, I consider all this, and I am drawn to you by an attraction, by a sentiment that I abhor, yet it has the power of a fateful malediction, of destiny itself. You do well not to take any notice whatsoever of me and of my lot: I have no right to demand anything of you; for my most passionate wish is that you come to mean nothing to me. What would you have to say of the state of mind of a miserable creature who for the first time would reveal herself to you thus, deeply perturbed, overwhelmed by feelings so diverse and so at odds with each other? You would pity her: your kind heart would be immediately touched; you would hasten to help, to succor such an unfortunate woman. Well, my friend, it is I who am this hapless creature; it is you who are the cause of this misfortune, and this soul on fire and in mortal pain is your creation. Ah! I still believe in you as I believe in God; you have every reason to bitterly repent your handiwork. (Sullerot, 1979, pp. 177–179)*

Guy Bachman and his colleagues (1994) proposed that since the fickle are plagued with the problems of both the clingy and the skittish (they desire what they don't have, but flee from what lies just within their grasp), one would expect them to behave like the clingy when trying to win another's love, but like the fickle once they were faced with an actual commitment. They found strong support for that hypothesis. Like the skittish, the fickle were wary of commitment. When asked to commit themselves to another, they felt trapped and worried that it was too much, too soon. (Similar results were secured by Singelis et al., 1995).

Back and forth, yes and no, here and gone, the fickle can drive their poor lovers nuts. Italian Novelist Pier Tondelli (1989) described the problems Thomas confronted in his on-again, off-again love affair with Leo:

> *Thomas tried not to catch his eye and said: . . . "I love you Leo. But . . . Sometimes there are terrible moments when you push me away. And others when, just as unexpectedly, you want my company.*

"You're unpredictable and I can't follow your moods. One minute you're here, then you're gone. And when you want me, because you've put the absurd idea into your own head that I should be on call, you arrive as if nothing at all happened during all those months. And I have to get used to the idea of you all over again. I have to love you, and then I have to stop loving you when you can't stand it any more. I have to be here for you, and then I have to vanish. If I need you just once, and come looking for you, and if my needing you doesn't coincide with the moment when you cry out for me, then I'm trespassing. And I can't do anything about it. I have either to go away or put up with being mistreated. I have to put up with your scorn and irony. Your insults. Leo, why don't you come to terms with your heart and accept the fact that you love me?" (pp. 155–156)

The fickle want what they do not have and they no longer want what they do have. When you want some privacy, they pursue you relentlessly. When you finally give your heart away, they flee or push you away. When you're away, they want you back. And so on, ad infinitum. They experience little joy in relationships. They are anxious during the affair and sad and angry once it is over. (For evidence in support of these contentions, see Choo et al., 1995; Bachman et al., 1994). Friendly advice to those involved with a fickle partner: run and don't look back.

The Casual

A most casual lover, the Vicomte de Valmont (played by John Malkovich) in the film *Les Liaisons Dangereuses* (Hampton, 1989) narrated his surprise when for a few flickering moments he experienced something more than his usual tepid reaction to love: "She was astonishing. So much so that I ended by falling on my knees and pledging her eternal love. And do you know that at that time and for several hours afterwards, I actually meant it" (p. 74). Before very long, Malkovich's character had returned to his usual detached and calculating mode.

If someone is foolish enough to try to seduce a casual lover into having a serious affair, he or she is bound to be frustrated. In Charles Baxter's (1993) novel *Shadow Play*, Alyse Schneider complained to her friend Wyatt Palmer about her boyfriend's casual attitude toward love. She had a theory:

"Once upon a time, the world was covered with forests and dragons. . . . People were in a minority compared to everything. . . . So when you, for example, went out in your armor on your steed and you fell in love with some damsel, it stuck, you follow me here? . . . If people are scarce, you love somebody because that person's all you're likely to get, and the person is precious, pure gold. You see? It was sort of supply-and-demand. . . . People were scarce and valuable and lovable. It was a seller's market.

. . . "But now," she said, "in the Age of the Renaissance Festival, you're not scarce, and neither am I. I'm nobody special and that goes for you, too. So, if you're using market theory in regard to humans, people are getting divorces and murdering each other enthusiastically for the same reason: supply. There's a big supply of the human being, so it's just passé to get interested and to stay interested in one of

them. So here's Dennis. He's gone all the time, he makes those phone calls. Sometimes he shows up, like last night. He takes off his clothes—I don't even know what time this is—and he's giving off an odor of unfaithfulness. I am in bed arranging my attitude toward all of this . . . So anyway here he is, and I'm wondering what happened to serial monogamy, so I turn to him and ask him where he's been, because you have to start a fight according to certain rules if it's going to be really satisfying, and then he says he has a theory. God. Everybody has a theory these days.

"He says, and he's sitting up now, not nearly as drunk as I was hoping he'd be, in fact not drunk at all, propping his head on his arm in that way that some guys have in bed that just really breaks my heart, that he loves me but that love shouldn't be dependency. That when people talk about love what they usually mean is dependency. He doesn't want me to depend on him, is what he means. And he doesn't want to depend on me, either. Well, you know, I didn't want to be crying during this scene, but, like, at least temporarily, I couldn't help it. So I asked him about all those things he said once, like how he loved me, how I was the most beautiful woman ever, how just the image of me walking got him through the day, how he'd love me until the collapse of time, and he said, and I quote, 'I meant it when I said it.'"

She smiled and pointed the pencil at Wyatt. "That was when I threw the ashtray at him." (pp. 139–140)

Many simply maintain detachment in the love affairs. They keep their feelings at bay. (For evidence in support of these contentions, see Choo et al., 1995; Bachman et al., 1994; Singelis et al., 1994). For some, this may be a pathology. For others, it is no more than a deliberate response to a world that offers varied and simpler pleasures than such a complex enterprise as a close relationship.

The Uninterested

The uninterested are not simply uninterested in relationships—they are barely aware that they exist. (For evidence in support of these contentions, see Singelis et al., 1995; Bachman et al., 1994). Amy Tan (1991), in *The Kitchen God's Wife* evoked Wen Fu's heartless treatment of his wife Jiang Weili. Wen Fu had no deep feelings for Jiang Weili as a person. He thought of her as a stone or a stick, that he could pinch or pound for his own entertainment.

Those who try to thaw out the uninterested are soon disillusioned. In *The Big Chill* (Kasdan, 1987), Meg lamented a more common problem—the emotional unavailability of many men:

If they're not married, they're gay. If they're not gay, they've just broken up with the most wonderful woman in the world or they've just broken up with a bitch who looked just like me. They're in transition from a monogamous relationship and they need more "space." Or they're tired of "space," but they just can't commit. They want to commit, but they're afraid to get close. They want to get close, but you don't want to get near them. (p. 80)

When Ted Singelis and his colleagues (1995) interviewed men and women from a variety of ethnic groups, he found that those people who classified themselves as "uninterested" in relationships also reported that they had rarely experienced *companionate love*. Only rarely had they felt committed to anyone or shared intimate moments with them.

Researchers are only just beginning to explore the correlates of the fickle, casual, or uninterested attachment styles. That work should be extremely important. For although the fickle are frequently pathological types, the casual and the uninterested are less likely to turn out to be as deranged. The years can be negotiated richly through work, friendships, and family, physical, aesthetic, artistic, and intellectual pursuits. Sex as recreation is more easily obtainable than at any time in the past 200 years. It is nowhere written that a lasting love relationship is a requisite for the decent life. Women and men who are casual or uninterested when it comes to romantic love may be quite passionate about other, equally valuable activities. We know too little about individuals with these love styles, and because they number in the hundreds of millions, if not billions, this yawning gap in our knowledge begs to be closed.

Conclusions

Just as we have much more to learn about the varied attachment styles, we know even less about the distribution of these profiles across the cultures. Are some of these personality types influenced by their temperament? Are those genetically predisposed to be anxious more likely to be found among the ranks of the clingy, skittish or fickle; are those predisposed to be depressed to be found among the ranks of the casual or disinterested? Or does culture play a major role in shaping one's attachment style? Or, most fruitfully perhaps, how does the interaction of biology and culture determine attachment styles? Are the Chinese more casual in love, on the whole, than the Italians? Or do attachment styles break up more along gender or class and economic lines than along national or regional lines? And has the distribution of these types changed through historical time? Can one anticipate future tendencies? And what, in the fullest sense, are the implications of one's attachment style for the individual, regardless of culture?

Lots of important questions, for which research currently offers few answers, need to be addressed by the scholars and thinkers of tomorrow. We have suggested here only the beginnings of such a fertile and nearly limitless research agenda.

$$Chapter \quad 7$$

Breaking Up and Starting Over

and every bed has been condemned
not by morality or law
but by time.

—Anne Sexton

People are well aware of the fragility of love. Sometimes love lasts only a few weeks. Frank Norris (1899/1965), in his novel *McTeague*, described McTeague's conquest of Trina Siepe. The moment McTeague won Trina, he realized he didn't really want her. His love endured, not a few weeks, but only a few seconds:

> *"Say, Miss Trina," said McTeague, after a while, "what's the good of waiting any longer? Why can't us two get married?"*
>
> *Trina still shook her head, saying "No" instinctively, in spite of herself.*
>
> *"Why not?" persisted McTeague. "Don't you like me well enough?"*
>
> *"Yes."*
>
> *"Then why not?"*
>
> *"Because."*
>
> *"Ah, come on," he said, but Trina still shook her head.*
>
> *"Ah, come on," urged McTeague. He could think of nothing else to say, repeating the same phrase over and over again to all her refusals.*
>
> *"Ah, come on! Ah, come on!"*
>
> *Suddenly he took her in his enormous arms, crushing down her struggle with his immense strength. Then Trina gave up, all in an instant, turning her head to his. They kissed each other, grossly, full in the mouth.*
>
> *A roar and a jarring of the earth suddenly grew near and passed them in a reek of steam and hot air. It was the overland, with its flaming headlight, on its way across the continent.*

The passage of the train startled them both. Trina struggled to free herself from McTeague. "Oh, please! Please!" she pleaded, on the point of tears. McTeague released her, but in that moment a slight, a barely perceptible, revulsion of feeling had taken place in him. The instant that Trina gave up, the instant she allowed him to kiss her, he thought less of her. She was not so desirable after all. But this reaction was so faint, so subtle, so intangible, that in another moment he had doubted its occurrence. Yet afterward it returned. Was there not something gone from Trina now? Was he not disappointed in her for doing that very thing for which he had longed? Was Trina the submissive, the compliant, the attainable just the same, just as delicate and adorable as Trina the inaccessible? Perhaps he dimly saw that this must be so, that it belonged to the changeless order of things—the man desiring the woman only for what she withholds; the woman worshiping the man for that which she yields up to him. With each concession gained the man's desire cools; with every surrender made the woman's adoration increases. But why should it be so? (pp. 61–63)

More often, romantic love lasts longer. It is only after both men and women have invested their hopes in the relationship that things fall apart.

When individuals are dizzyingly, wildly, in love, they are convinced that their passionate feelings will last forever. Yet, when we take an unflinching look at the many dismal relationships around us, it becomes clear that passion is often fleeting (Hatfield & Rapson, 1993b; Mathes & Wise, 1983[1]; Solomon, 1980). Perhaps this should not be surprising. Eric Klinger (1977) observed that highs "are *always* transitory. People experience deliriously happy moments that quickly fade and all attempts to hang on to them are doomed to fail" (p. 116). Theodor Reik (1972) warned that the best a couple intensely in love can hope for after several years of living together is a warm "afterglow."

In a series of studies, Hatfield and her colleagues (see Traupmann & Hatfield, 1981) interviewed dating couples, newlyweds, and older women, who had been married an average of thirty-three years; some had been married for as long as fifty-nine years. Unfortunately, older men were not interviewed. Over time, passionate love did seem to plummet (Figure 7.1). Couples started out loving their partners intensely. Both steady daters and newlyweds expressed "a great deal of passionate love" for their mates. But after many years of marriage, women reported that they and their husbands now felt only "some" passionate love for one another.

Other researchers have found that passionate love is equally fleeting in all kinds of love affairs—whether they are heterosexual, gay, or lesbian ones (McWhirter & Mattison, 1984).

The chances of companionate love's lasting a lifetime are somewhat greater. From the first, Hatfield and her colleagues found that couples' levels of companionate love were extremely high. Both steady daters and newlyweds expressed "a great deal" to "a tremendous amount" of companionate love for their partners. Although couples' companionate feelings also did seem to erode (but only a bit) with time, men and women still felt a great deal of love for one another even after thirty-three

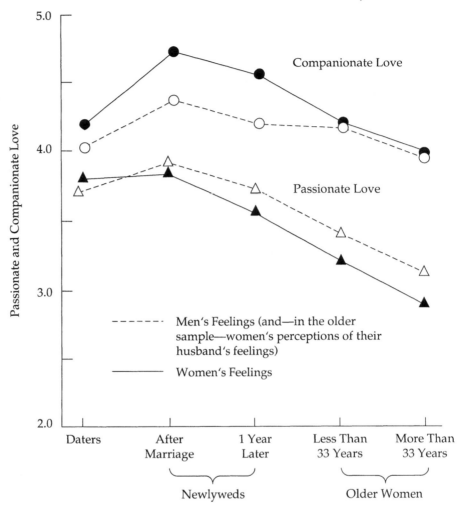

FIGURE 7.1 Dating Couples, Newlywed Couples, and Older Women's Passionate and Companionate Love for Their Partners

years of marriage. Typically, older women reported feeling "a great deal" of companionate love for their mates. Pessimists would point out that both passionate and companionate love continued to decline with time. Optimists might be cheered by the fact that companionate love was still so deep even after a long marriage (see Figure 7.1). In our view, the "flame" of passionate love is vastly overrated; the affection, warmth, contentment, comfort, and liberation of the "afterglow" is enormously underrated.

Robert Sternberg (cited in Goleman, 1985) pointed out that passionate and companionate love possess different trajectories (see Figure 7.2). He interviewed couples who had been married from one month to thirty-six years. Initially, it was passion that drew men and women to one another. As couples drew closer together, however, passion began to fade into the background. "Passion is the quickest to develop, and the quickest to fade," (p. 13) Sternberg observed. After a while, what

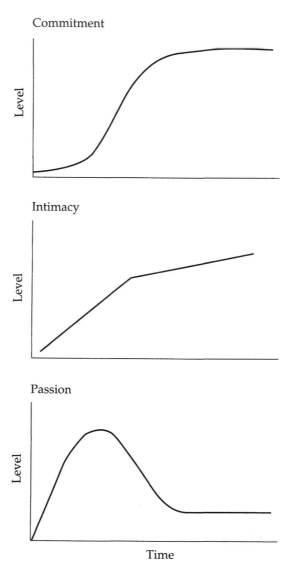

FIGURE 7.2   The Changing Ingredients of Love

Source: Robert Sternberg, Yale University. Appears in Hatfield & Rapson (1993b), p. 66.

mattered most was companionate love. It took longer for couples to feel fully committed to their marriages and to become intimate with one another, but these were the things that seemed to last. Figure 7.2 illustrates the time course of the various components of love.

Passionate Love in Other Cultures

> *I shall love you for three months. For me that will be an eternity.*
> —*Ninon De Lenclos*

Passion quickly burns itself out in all cultures. For example, anthropologist Marjorie Shostak (1981) and a !Kung (African) tribesman were observing a young married couple, running after each other:

> As I stood watching, I noticed the young man sitting in the shade of a tree, also watching. I said, "They're very much in love, aren't they?" He answered, "Yes, they are." After a pause, he added, "For now." I asked him to explain, and he said, "When two people are first together, their hearts are on fire and their passion is very great. After a while, the fire cools and that's how it stays." ... "They continue to love each other, but it's in a different way—warm and dependable." ... How long did this take? "It varies among couples. A few months, usually; sometimes longer. But it always happens." Was it also true for a lover? "No," he explained, "feelings for a lover stay intense much longer, sometimes for years." (p. 268)

Helen Fisher (1992) has argued that the transient nature of passionate love is a cultural universal. She believes that our *Homo Sapiens* ancestors experienced passionate love and sexual desire for very practical genetic reasons. Our hominid ancestors were primed to fall ardently, sexually, in love for about four years. This is precisely the amount of time it takes to conceive a child and take care of it until it is old enough to survive on its own. (In tribal societies, children are relatively self-sufficient by four years of age. By that time, they generally prefer to spend most of their time playing with other children.) Once our ancestors no longer had a practical reason to remain together, they had every evolutionary reason to fall out of love with their previous partner and to fall in love with someone new. Why were people programmed to engage in such serial pair bonding? Fisher maintained that serial monogamy produces maximum genetic diversity, which is an evolutionary advantage.

To test her hypothesis that, generally, love is fleeting, Fisher (1989) examined the divorce rates in collecting/hunting societies, agricultural, pastoral, fishing, and industrial societies, scouring ethnographic records and the *Demographic Yearbooks* of the United Nations. She found that, as predicted, throughout the world, couples most commonly divorced in their fourth year of marriage. She argues that today the same evolutionary forces that influenced our ancestors, shape the modern cross-cultural pattern of marriage/divorce/remarriage. Fisher's ideas are stimulating, but her exclusion of cultural forces, considering their omnipresence in nearly all matters related to love and sex, mandate a certain skepticism on the part of the reader.

The End of the Affair

> *What we call the beginning is often the end*
> *And to make an end is to make a beginning.*
> *The end is where we start from.*
> —T. S. Eliot

Warning Signs

Jennifer Berman (1988).

Hollywood notwithstanding, most love affairs end long before death does the lovers part. Alas, it is as important to understand breakups as it is the sweeter coming togethers.

Dating Relationships: Breaking Up

In one study, researchers (Hill, Rubin, & Peplau, 1979) tracked 231 young Boston couples, who were engaged, living together, or steadily dating, to find out how their love affairs would fare over a two-year period. By the end of the two years, 45 percent of the couples had broken up. More recently, Ellen Berscheid and her col-

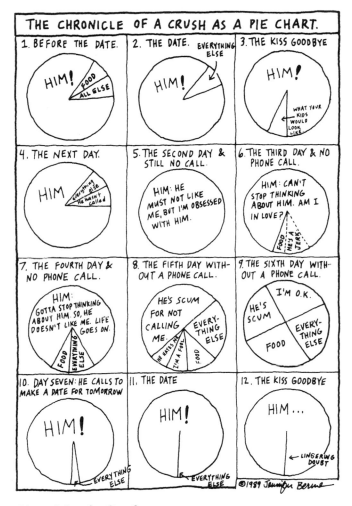

Chronicle of a Crush

Jennifer Berman (1989).

leagues (Berscheid et al., 1989) asked college students about their closest romantic relationship. In follow-up interviews three months later, they discovered that 34 percent of these love affairs had ended. By the end of nine months, 42 percent had dissolved. Susan Sprecher (1994) followed 101 Wisconsin couples, who were dating or engaged, over the four-year period from 1988 to 1992. After four years, she found that 58 percent of the couples had broken up.

Marriages: Divorce

> *Eddie Albert: Sixteen! How long were you married?*
> *Goldie Hawn: Oh God, it seemed like weeks.*
> —*Butterflies Are Free*

Most young people in most countries insist that they wouldn't marry someone unless they were in love. (We described this research in Chapter 2.) But what happens if love dies?

In her novel *Memories of Rain*, the Indian novelist Sunetra Gupta (1992) chronicled the love affair of Moni, a Calcutta schoolgirl, and the very English Anthony. Soon after their marriage, Anthony begins to take Moni for granted and to slip into a series of short-lived infatuations:

> *Many years ago, he had stood back, horrified, and watched his passion for her melt like candlewax, and he had rejoiced when a deep affection had come to take its place, he had held her small warm hands against his face with new joy, pressed his lips to the flesh that he no longer desired, placed his hand over the soft cage of bones that sheltered his child, he watched her tenderly as she drifted into gentle sleep beside him on the ferry, cradled her head on his chest, if they were to live on the memory of their love alone, that would be enough, for he had felt no greater sadness than to see their love pass, like wind through his fingers, he felt himself wiped clean of that rich emotion that had driven him through the wild heat to wait foolishly outside the stern gates of her college praying that she would emerge, he would gaze, disbelieving, at the unruffled fingers that had propelled him to such ecstasy by their mere touch upon his palm, he had bathed her swollen ankles with tears, on the first night that he returned with the smell of another woman deep within him, while she slept, he had wept at the foot of their bed . . . he had crept in beside her, and spilled heavy, sweet tears upon the field of hair that stretched across his pillow, in the darkness he had listened for the heartbeats of their child while the lingering scent of Anna's ivory flesh preyed upon sleep, and in his pain, he had reasoned that even if he had left her behind to the smoky Calcutta winters, he would have felt, even more sharply, that he was betraying their love, for he would not have tired of the memory of her eyes as quickly as he had become immune to their mystifying presence, he kneels among a pile of dead leaves, and for the first time in years, he mourns the death of their passion, the brittle shell of their tropical lust. (pp. 83–84)*

Should this loveless but companionable couple stay together or separate? Robert Levine and his colleagues (1994) asked young men and women in eleven cultures two questions:

1.   If love has completely disappeared from a marriage, I think it is probably best for the couple to make a clean break and start new lives.
2.   In my opinion, the disappearance of love is not a sufficient reason for ending a marriage, and should not be viewed as such.

College students were asked whether they agreed, disagreed, or were neutral about these two statements.

The authors predicted that only couples in Western, affluent nations would consider love to be critically important in a marriage. Couples in Eastern, collectivist, underdeveloped nations were expected to be less concerned with love and intimacy. In these cultures, couples were bound together by strong extended-family ties. There, love was seen as a suspect or disastrous basis for marriage. It was duty, family ties, and practicalities that were important. (Dion & Dion, 1993, would second their argument.)

The authors found no support for this hypothesis. Let us consider students' answers to Question 1, for example. (Students' answers to Question 2 would lead us to the same conclusion.) When students were asked if they thought couples should "make a clean break" if "love had completely disappeared from a marriage," students worldwide were in agreement that love was critically important to a marriage (see Table 7.1). It did not seem to matter how individualist/collectivist a

TABLE 7.1   Responses to the Statement: "If Love Has Completely Disappeared from a Marriage, I Think It Is Probably Best for the Couple to Make a Clean Break and Start New Lives."

Cultural Group	Response (percent)		
	Yes	Undecided	No
Australia	29.3	39.6	31.1
Brazil	77.5	9.9	12.7
England	44.6	32.1	23.2
Hong Kong	47.1	27.4	25.5
India	46.2	27.9	26.0
Japan	41.1	41.9	17.1
Mexico	51.7	20.3	28.0
Pakistan	33.0	17.4	49.6
Philippines	45.5	13.6	40.9
Thailand	46.9	21.0	32.1
United States	35.4	29.9	34.7

Based on Levine et al. (1994).

society was or how high the society's standard of living was. Students generally thought that love was the *sine qua non* of marriage.

Of course, once students are married, they may well discover that in fact marriages are held together by a sturdier cement than love.

How Common Is Divorce?

At any given time, 40 percent of American couples are likely to admit that they have considered leaving their partners (Gallup Poll, 1989). In fact, demographers Teresa Martin and Larry Bumpass (1989), on the basis of data from the U.S. Bureau of the Census, estimated that currently in the United States about two-thirds of all first marriages are likely to end in separation or divorce. How likely are couples from various ethnic groups to separate or divorce within the first five years of marriage? African Americans are slightly more likely to break up (36 percent are predicted to do so) than are either Mexican Americans (24 percent) or European Americans (22 percent). For most African Americans, once is enough. They are less likely than their peers to remarry after a divorce.

Although in America about 50 percent of first marriages in fact fail and in the future two-thirds of current marriages are predicted to fail, about 75 percent of men and women eventually decide to try again. About 50 percent of those remarriages will fail as well (Glick, 1989). Teresa Martin and Larry Bumpass (1989), based on data from the U.S. Census, point out that second marriages are actually slightly less likely to survive than are first marriages. This statistic may be a bit misleading. It does *not* suggest that most divorced people make an even poorer selection the second time around. Demographers point out that the first-marriage statistics naturally include many who, for religious or ideological reasons, have committed themselves never to divorce, regardless of how poorly things are going. Those people are absent from the second-marriage numbers. If divorce rate statistics are adjusted to take such realities into account, it becomes clear that some folks do learn from experience.

The various ethnic groups differ slightly in the likelihood of second marriages ending in separation or divorce after five years. Among African Americans, about 43 percent of second marriages are likely to end in separation or divorce. About 28 percent of Mexican American and 26 percent of European American marriages are likely to break up within five years. Margaret Mead once speculated that Western society is moving toward "serial monogamy." Couples pair, break up, and pair again, and again.

Divorce is also common throughout the world. Gwen Broude and Sarah Green (1983), for example, sampled 186 societies from the more than 1,000 preindustrial societies listed in the *Ethnographic Atlas*. They found that in most societies, divorce is fairly common (Table 7.2).

Generally, throughout the world, it is easier for men to divorce than for women to do so. Men can usually decide to divorce without being required to state their reasons for doing so. Women are more likely to be required to justify their actions. In Table 7.3, Brode and Greene tallied how easy it was for men and women to divorce in the 186 societies they surveyed.

TABLE 7.2 Frequency of Divorce

Frequency	Percent
Universal or almost universal	9
Common	37
A small minority of couples divorce	13
Frequent in first years of marriage and/or before children; rare thereafter	12
Rare, isolated instances, never	30

Based on Broude & Greene (1983), p. 275.

How common is divorce in various societies? Recently, William Goode (1993), in *World Changes in Divorce Patterns* examined divorce statistics worldwide. He found that different countries have very different divorce customs and laws. In the Arab world, until very recently, the Koran made it very easy for husbands to divorce their wives, but almost impossible for wives to divorce their husbands. In Tunisia, for example, men only had to recite "Talak" three times in front of two witnesses and they were free. Women could secure a divorce only if a *kadi* (a judge) ruled that their husbands had refused to provide shelter and food or had harmed their wives and children. In 1981 Tunisian law attempted to equalize men's and women's status, but the traditional practices often prevail over the new Code of Personal Status.

The Roman Catholic Church dictates the rules in many Latin American countries. In Chile divorce is forbidden, but "annulments" are very common. Argentina permits divorce by agreement. In Ireland, divorce is still forbidden. In the Northern European nations—such as Austria, Belgium, France, Germany, Netherlands, and Switzerland—divorce has been permitted for generations.

Goode concluded that in the last forty years major changes have occurred worldwide, and this seems likely to continue:

1. Divorce rates are rising not only in the Western countries, but almost everywhere. Some people view this trend as a sign of social progress. ("Millions of

TABLE 7.3 Grounds for Divorce

Grounds	For Men (percent)	For Women (percent)
No grounds (or justification) required for divorce	67	48
Grounds not absolutely necessary, but divorce is financially, legally, and/or socially easier with grounds	22	38
Divorce only with grounds	8	10
No divorce	3	5

Based on Broude & Greene (1983), p. 276.

people are now free from miserable domestic lives," endured often under repressive regimes. [p. xii]). Others see in this tendency an unmitigated disaster ("Changes in divorce patterns are creating social problems that are real, massive, and growing, and seem to require remedial action." [p. xii]). They see in it the decline of the family. But, for good or ill, the modern nations are likely to continue to be societies in which individuals seek their own happiness and interests rather than stay married for the sake of their children or because of societal constraints.

2. As a consequence, in many countries, there will be substantial increases in the number of people, especially women and children, who are economically devastated by divorce and need state support to survive.

3. Soon, modern societies will begin to spend less time in "moral hand-wringing and denunciation" (p. 327) and more time focusing on and trying to solve the problems associated with divorce. Goode suggests that perhaps the world can learn from the Nordic nations—Denmark, Norway, Sweden, and Finland—which have a high divorce rate but manage to protect couples and children from the most serious consequences of divorce. These countries have quietly taken collective responsibility for providing an adequate income, job opportunities, and child-care programs for families in transition.

For other information on this topic, see Fine & Fine, 1994.

In Table 7.4 we present divorce rates for the major nations of the West.

TABLE 7.4   Percent of Marriages Expected to End in Divorce in Various Countries

Country	Percentage of Marriages Ending in Divorce
United States[1]	50
Austria[2]	30
Belgium[2]	21
Denmark[2]	45
Federal Republic of Germany[3]	25
France[2]	31
Great Britain[2]	39
Netherlands[2]	32
Sweden[4]	36
Switzerland[2]	29
West Germany[2]	30

[1]Glick (1989).
[2]Goode (1993).
[3]Höhn & Otto (1984).
[4]Schoen & Baj (1984).

The United Nations (1992) routinely reports the number of divorces that occur throughout the world. In 1990, for example, the UN reported the number of couples divorcing per 1,000 population. It is difficult to interpret such statistics. In some countries, such as Ireland, divorce has been forbidden; those prohibitions are currently fading. Even where divorce remains illegal, people can still walk out and form other liaisons, although they still remain officially "married." In many Central American countries—such as El Salvador, the Dominican Republic, and Panama—the majority of couples may never marry. When these relationships end, they do not appear in the divorce statistics. In Russia, reports have often reflected ideology rather than reality; statisticians sometimes reported what they thought rates in a socialist state should be rather than the number of actual divorces. There are bigger problems. When we look at rates per 1,000, we must remember that in many countries a large percentage of the population—which after all includes, infants, children, and the elderly as well as those of marital age—that are not even married and thus are hardly "at risk" for divorce. Nonetheless, we are presenting these crude divorce rates because they remain instructive despite the above caveats (Table 7.5 on page 214).

It is almost impossible to underestimate the significance for societies as they move from making divorces nearly impossible to obtain to making them more readily accessible. Lawrence Stone (1990) in his history of English divorce, *Road to Divorce: England 1530–1987*, wrote:

> *The metamorphosis of a largely non-separating and non-divorcing society, such as England from the Middle Ages to the mid-nineteenth century, into a separating and divorcing one in the late twentieth, is perhaps the most profound and far-reaching social change to have occurred in the last five hundred years. (p. 422)*

That change in England and in most Western nations has been very recent in coming, but its implications for expanding individualist consciousness, particularly for women for whom separation was infinitely more difficult than men, has affected a huge range of institutional and psychological habits. "A gigantic moral, religious, and legal revolution," Stone went on, "has accompanied and made possible the shift from a system of marriage prematurely terminated by death to a system of marriage prematurely terminated by choice" (p. 422).

And now that revolution is spreading to the rest of the world. Historians are reluctant to engage in the simple moral debate that equates permissive divorce either with family and social breakdown or with the blessings of free choice. The permission for an individual to separate from relationships as a matter of personal choice has not taken place in a vacuum, but as a part of explosive and momentous social change. As Roderick Phillips (1988) concluded in his valuable study, *Putting Asunder: A History of Divorce in Western Society:*

> *Marriage stability, marriage breakdown, and divorce cannot be understood in isolation from their social context. It is fundamentally misleading and pointless to interpret the increase in marriage breakdown and divorce as evidence of the decline*

TABLE 7.5   Number of Divorces per 1,000 Population: 1990

Country	Rate of Divorce	Country	Rate of Divorce
Africa		*Europe*	
Egypt	1.64	Czechoslovakia	2.61
Tunisia	1.60	Denmark	2.95
		Finland	2.93
North America		France	1.90
Canada	3.05	Germany, Federal	
Cuba	3.56	Republic of	2.04
Mexico	0.63	Greece	0.87
Nicaragua	0.22	Hungary	2.36
Puerto Rico	3.89	Italy	0.44
United States	4.70	Netherlands	1.91
		Norway	2.18
South America		Poland	1.11
Brazil	0.23	Spain	0.57
Chile	0.42	Sweden	2.22
		Switzerland	1.94
Asia		United Kingdom	2.86
Hong Kong	0.96	Yugoslavia, Former	0.81
Indonesia	0.78		
Iran	0.65	*Oceania*	
Iraq	0.11	Australia	2.46
Israel	1.30	New Zealand	2.58
Japan	1.27	USSR, Former	3.39
Korea, Republic of	0.77		
Singapore	0.96		
Thailand	0.69		
Turkey	0.45		

Based on United Nations. (1992). *Demographic Yearbook: 1990.* (42nd issue). Department of International Economic and Social Affairs, Statistical Office. New York: United Nations Publication. pp. 752–756.

of matrimonial commitment or domestic morality. Marriage is integral to broad social, economic, demographic, and cultural processes, and it is entirely futile to expect marriage to remain constant or to have a consistent social meaning while social structures, economic relationships, demographic patterns, and cultural configurations have undergone the massive changes of the past centuries." (p. 640)

These changes are now global.

The replacement of arranged marriages by love marriages constitutes a cornerstone in the expansion of individual freedom around the world. But that expansion was sorely limited if love marriages could not be ended by lost-love separations and divorces. Today, at different speeds, in different forms, and not universally, we can see that in many societies love marriages and lost-love divorces now go together like a horse and carriage—for better or for worse.

Death

Half my heart is gone. Half my life is gone.
—*Reaction of 15-year-old Conchita Campfield
on hearing that her boyfriend was killed
by a stray bullet when leaving a house party*

Until the middle of this century, most marriages really fit the vow "till death do us part." This was because individuals had no choice. Now we increasingly think "till choice do us part." Many, however, choose never to part. And some who elect to take that path may even find themselves in harmonious and happy relationships. But even the most blissful relationship must eventually come to an end—in death. Italian author Pier Tondelli (1989) portrayed the desolate reaction of Leo to the death of his lover, Thomas, of AIDS:

Once alone, Leo sits on the bed and lifts Thomas's hand to his face.

"Squeeze my hand, please," Leo says. "Squeeze it hard."

"I've been so afraid of dying," Thomas whispers staring out in front of him.

Leo swallows. He feels how hot Thomas's skin is. And he feels how far away Thomas is, too. It is as if the enormity of what he has had to go through has already killed him. As if terror had completely numbed him—that terror that is relentlessly invading him hour after hour. Leo has seen that same look on other occasions. The look of a Palestinian child about to be killed. The look of a little African baby dying beside its mother's body, mangled by bombs. The imploring gaze of a small Amazonian Indian child watching his race being wiped out. The look of people dying and begging hopelessly for help that will not come. Children, children. . . .

Thomas's father comes back in. Leo realizes he should leave. In this last moment, Thomas is back in the family fold, with the very same people who brought him into the world. Now, with their hearts torn asunder by suffering, they are trying to help Thomas to die. There is no room for Leo in this parental reconciliation. Leo is not married to Thomas. He has not had children with him. Neither of them bears the other's name at the registry office, and there is not a single legal record on the face of the earth that carries the signatures of witnesses to their union. Yet for more than three years they have been passionately in love with one another. They have lived together in Paris and Milan, and they have traveled round Europe together. They have written together, played music together and danced together. They have quarreled and abused each other, and even hated each other. They have been in love . . .

He looks back at Thomas at the far end of the room and says good-bye. He says: "See you soon. Get better soon." But Thomas does not answer. He does not say a word to him. He looks at him with his huge, enormous dark eyes, clinging desperately, with dread and terror, to the figure who is about to walk out of his life forever. Leo cannot stand the sight of those gaping eyes a moment more. They are all he can see. The whole room is Thomas's eyes. He lowers his head and leaves, still muttering the odd word to suit the occasion. He knows full well that he will carry within him, for as long as he lives, that look from Thomas the manchild on his deathbed in his separate room. (pp. 26–28)

Explaining Breakups or Divorce

> *My first experience with a boyfriend taught me little, except, unconsciously,*
> *some of the subterfuges, self-deceptions, and brutal emotional economics of love.*
> —*P. D. James*

Who Had Control?

Generally, it is difficult to tell who decided to end a love affair or a marriage. Imagine this scenario. A man warns his girlfriend: "Unless you stop having an affair, I'm out of here." She refuses to abandon her lover. He walks out. Who chose to end the love affair? The man who finally took action? or the woman, who "drove him to it"? In long-term relationships, things get so complicated that it is often impossible to tell

In Love/Out of Love

Jennifer Berman (1990).

what is going on ("She drinks." "He would drive anyone to drink."), much less who *really* wanted out. Divorces tend to be made by thousands of interactions between the couple over a substantial body of time. Often, the person who officially asks for the divorce is simply completing a transaction made inevitable by years of trouble. Still, many individuals feel less guilty if the other "initiates" the separation and they may try to force that initiation out of their partner.

Despite this, dating couples generally agree about who initiated the breakup. Dating couples usually report that the breakup was not a mutual decision. In only 10 to 36 percent of dating break-ups was the decision thought to be a mutual one (Drigotas & Rusbult, 1992; Sprecher, 1993).

Nuran Hortacsu and Nuray Karanci (1987) interviewed Turkish college students whose dating relationships had just broken up. Only 32 percent of Turkish couples said the decision was mutual. Janice Gray and Roxane Silver (1990) interviewed forty-five couples in Ontario, Canada, who had recently filed for separation or divorce. They had been married, on the average, for thirteen years. They found that the reasons men and women gave for their breakups were remarkably self-serving. People tended to see themselves in a positive light: "He was the villain in the whole affair; I was the victim." "She was the one who bailed out; I was willing to try again."

"His" and "Her" Breakup: What Were the Reasons for the Breakup?

> *"Watch out for life," Obāsan used to say. "It's harder than it looks."*
> —*Cynthia Kadohata*

When Charles Hill, Zick Rubin, and Anne Peplau (1979) asked young Boston couples why their love affairs had ended, men and women gave different answers. Generally, women first recognized the relationship was in trouble and going nowhere. Women tended to be very sensitive to interpersonal problems. They could easily identify the specific difficulties that led to the breakup: "He wanted a traditional marriage; I didn't." "I was attracted to another man." Men tended to be less sure what caused the breakup. They tended to focus on an external problem: "We lived too far apart. It took an hour to get to her house." Couples rarely agreed on what caused the breakup or on how gradually (or abruptly) it came about. Other researchers have secured similar results (Baxter, 1984; Cupach & Metts, 1986).

What sorts of things cause the most problems for today's couples? Susan Sprecher (1994) asked 101 dating couples to take a look at twenty possible reasons for a breakup and to indicate how important each problem had been in shattering their affair. Table 7.6 on page 218 is a list of the ten problems couples said had caused them the most difficulty. In this study, men and women generally agreed about what had caused the breakup.

Lawrence Kurdek (1991) interviewed twenty-six gay and lesbian couples who had just split up. Why had they decided to separate? Kurdek concluded that the problems young couples face—whether straight, gay, or lesbian—are strikingly

TABLE 7.6   Reasons for the Breakup

Reasons Referring to the Self
   I desired to be independent.
   I became bored with the relationship.

Reasons Referring to the Partner
   My partner desired to be independent.
   My partner became bored with the relationship.
   My partner became interested in someone else.

Reasons Referring to the Couple's Interaction
   We had different interests.
   We had communication problems.
   We had conflicting sexual attitudes and/or problems.
   We had conflicting marriage ideas.
   We had different backgrounds.

Based on Sprecher (1994), p. 217.

similar. Couples complained that they just couldn't seem to communicate, that they had grown apart, that they were sexually incompatible, and so forth.

Similar studies have been conducted in non-Western countries with similar results. Hortacsu and Karanci (1987) observed that Turkey is in a transition to a "modern" society. In the traditional Turkish culture, dependency rather than autonomy, loyalty rather than independence, were valued. However, university students have become very modern. The authors interviewed 103 Turkish men and thirty-two Turkish women who were students at the Middle East Technical University and who had just broken off a romantic relationship. They asked why they had broken up. Students were allowed to list up to six reasons for the breakup. The principal reasons given for the separation were the partner's personality, incompatibility, and living too far apart. The authors were struck by the fact that students' reasons overlapped so greatly with the reasons students in Western countries give for their breakups. They noted only one exception: Turkish students rated as a reason for the separation "family and environmental [external] pressures" as slightly more important than did Western students.

Janice Gray and Roxane Silver (1990) interviewed forty-five couples in Ontario, Canada, who had recently filed for separation or divorce. They found that the reasons men and women gave for their breakups were remarkably self-serving. Consider these reports:

The husband, who left his wife for another woman [after 17 years of marriage], indicated that "I met another woman that I liked better than my spouse. . . . My new wife is younger and better looking. . . ." In contrast, his ex-spouse described the other woman as "a real bimbo" for whom "people were prone to using descrip-

tives such as 'the elevator doesn't go quite to the top.'" The husband of another couple blamed the breakup on his wife, indicating that "all she wanted was money to put in the bank. . . . She insisted I continue farming and working out." His ex-wife, on the other hand, wrote, "My husband seemed to be obsessed with making money, having two jobs most of the time." (p. 1188)

Couples saw their own and their mate's behavior "through a glass, darkly." He was the villain; she was the victim. Her affair was inconsequential; his was a real threat to the marriage. You could never get her back in that madhouse; he's dying to come back.

The Emotional Aftermath of Breakups and Divorce

> *The more a man loves, the more he suffers.*
> —Henri Frederic Amiel

People vary in the degree of pain and grief they feel when a dating or marital relationship ends. Some men and women are actually happy and relieved when it's over. Some care little one way or another. Others are devastated (Sprecher, 1993). One researcher (Stephen, 1987) found that after a breakup, 52 percent of men and women reported experiencing little distress, while 43 percent reported a great deal of distress. It is easy to guess the kind of things that make separation especially painful. The higher a person's self-esteem, the easier it is to survive a breakup. The more satisfied with their relationship, the closer they have been, and the longer they have been together, the worse will likely be the end. Breakups are also particularly upsetting if one fears that he or she will never find someone else to love and if one has few friends to provide social support (Berscheid, Snyder & Omoto, 1989; Frazier & Cook, 1993). These same factors have been found to determine how wrenching will be the experience in a variety of non-Western cultures as well, for example, in Turkey (Hortacsu & Karanci, 1987).

It is far less painful to think of oneself as leaving someone than to be the one who is left. The abandoned are likely to be stunned by the breakup and preoccupied with trying to figure out what went wrong. It takes them far longer to recover and get on with their lives (Frazier & Cook, 1993; Gray & Silver, 1990). This, too, has been found to be true in some non-Western cultures as well, such as Turkey (Hortacsu & Karanci, 1987).

Robert Weiss (1979) observed that, in serious relationships, most men and women experience intense and conflicting emotions after a breakup. They may, on one hand, feel euphoric and relieved *and*, on the other, feel anxious, depressed, and angry. The newly separated feel a whirlpool of emotions, and their feelings shift with such dizzying rapidity that it is difficult for them to deal with the turbulence. People in all cultures experience such floodtides of emotion.

Guilt

> *What deep wounds ever closed without a scar.*
> —Lord Byron

Janice Gray and Roxane Silver (1990) interviewed Canadian men and women who had just divorced. Those who had decided to divorce often felt guilty. Comments like these were typical:

- I have guilt, guilt—difficult to cope with.
- Almost unbearable guilt feelings.
- I'm the S.O.B. in everyone's eyes at this point; she is the injured party. (p. 1189)

Sadness and Depression

> *We are never so defenseless against suffering as when we love, never so forlornly unhappy as when we have lost our love object or its love.*
> —Sigmund Freud

Researchers asked college students who had just broken up to comment on their feelings (Means, 1991). Many still loved their partners. They wished things could have worked out, but they hadn't. Most were sometimes achingly sad. Two months after the break up, over 40 percent of the students were clinically depressed. (Depression was assessed via the *Beck Depression Inventory* [Beck, 1967.]) The Inventory classified 1 percent of the students as being "minimally depressed," 31 percent as "mildly to moderately depressed," 10 percent as "moderately to severely depressed," 2 percent as "severely" depressed, and 40 percent as clinically depressed.

When a love affair or marriage ends in death, the bereaved generally grieve for a very long time (Beach et al., 1990; Solsberry & Krupnick, 1984; Stroebe & Stroebe, 1987). Researchers have studied the stages in the grief process. The most common immediate reactions to a lover's or mate's death are shock, numbness, and disbelief. Eventually, in the hours or months following the death, numbness turn into an intense feeling of loss and pain. During this phase, searching behaviors—dreams in which the deceased still lives; seeing the deceased in the street; and other misperceptions, illusions, and hallucinations—are common. When the lost person fails to return, the lover begins to despair. People become sad, moody, guilty, angry, irritable, lonely, anxious, and restless. They have difficulty in concentrating. Offers of comfort and support are often spurned (Averill, 1968). Researchers find that one-third of all widowers are still sad, crying, and depressed more than a year after their wife's death (Clayton, 1982).

It used to be thought that people normally grieved only a year or two for those they loved and lost and then that was that. This turns out not to be true. Things *do* get better after a year or so, but if someone really meant a great deal to the bereaved, the survivors may continue to remember and to grieve for their lost sweethearts throughout their lives (Lehman, Wortman, & Williams, 1987). Eventually, however, most people form new attachments, develop new coping skills, go back to work, and begin to live again (Solsberry and Krupnick, 1984).

Anger and Bitterness

> *To think I have wasted years of my love, that I have longed for death, that the greatest love that I have ever known has been for a woman who did not please me, who was not my style.*
>
> *—Marcel Proust*

As relationships begin to deteriorate, couples often begin to fight. Sometimes when the newly separated think back on their relationship, a volcano of anger erupts. Some have suppressed their own feelings for decades in the interests of harmony. Now they realize how angry they had been for so much of the time. One young woman observed:

> *In separating from someone you discover in yourself things that you had never felt before in your life. That's one of the things that really freaks you out. I've always used my mind to keep down anything I didn't like. And now I discover, wow, I can hate! (Weiss, 1979, p. 208)*

Loneliness

Many newly separated and divorced couples suffer from intense loneliness. In *Oscar & Lucinda*, Peter Carey (1988) wrote of Lucinda's loneliness after the end of a relationship:

> *To know you will be lonely is not the same thing as being lonely. When Lucinda came down the Parramatta River in Sol Myer's boat she imagined her life would be a lonely one, and she felt strength through recognizing it. And yet what she imagined was not loneliness, which is boggy and sour, but something else which is bright and hard. The difference between what she imagined and what she finally experienced is the difference between a blade of a knife—an object of chilly beauty— and the chronic pain of an open wound. (p. 239)*

The lonely hunger for love, and in its absence they may also be angry, anxious, bored, or depressed (Perlman & Peplau, 1981). After a couple break up or divorce, or when a mate dies, people are especially forlorn (Lopata, 1969). Jenny de Jong-Gierveld (1986) asked 556 Dutch men and women, ranging in age from 25 to 75, how often they felt lonely. Those who were single, divorced, or widowed were the most lonely. Couples who were living together or married were far less likely to mention loneliness as a problem.

Cultural Differences in Loneliness

Cross-cultural psychologists (Triandis et al., 1988) have theorized that "idiocentric" individuals (who value individualism) will be more vulnerable to loneliness than "allocentric" individuals (who value collectivism). The researchers thought that when love went awry, the second group would be buffered by relatives and friends who could provide support. To test this hypothesis, they interviewed 200 college students in two very different cultures—the United States, a highly individualistic culture, and Puerto Rico, a collectivist culture (Hofstede, 1980). They assessed the extent of individualism via a seventy-two item idiocentrism-allocentrism scale. They also asked the students how often they felt lonely and how many friends and relatives they possessed who might be available to provide social support. As predicted, in both the United States and Puerto Rico, the higher the degree of individualism, the greater was the loneliness. The reason is clear. Individualists have little to rely on when love relationships fall apart.

Lars Tornstam (1992), interviewed a sampling of 2,795 Swedish men and women—single, married, divorced, and widowed—ranging in age from 15 to 80. As you might expect, it was the young, single individuals who were the loneliest. After the age of 40, people became less and less lonely. Apparently they learned to enjoy solitude or found ways to occupy their time by listening to music, reading, watching films, calling friends, taking long walks, or working.

Falling Ill

Couples who have broken up or divorced are unusually vulnerable to a host of mental and physical diseases. They have been found to have unusually high rates of alcoholism, diabetes, heart disease, tuberculosis, and cirrhosis of the liver. They are more likely to die from natural causes, twice as likely to commit suicide, and more likely to be murdered than when they were married (Bloom et al., 1979; Stroebe & Stroebe, 1987).

The consequences for those whose loved one has died are very serious. Bereavement has been found to increase people's vulnerability to mental illness (Stroebe & Stroebe, 1987). Sometimes the widowed constantly reproach themselves for things they have done or left undone. They cry. One moment they are agitated and restless, the next they can barely move. They can't sleep or they sleep all the time. They lack interest in the outside world and often give up the friends and activities they used to enjoy. They exist in pain. They may begin to eat excessively, drink, or take drugs (Beach et al., 1990). Bereavement may also spark a variety of physical symptoms, including migraines, headaches, facial pain, rashes, indigestion, peptic ulcers, weight gain or loss, heart palpitations, chest pain, asthma, infections, fatigue, and so forth. The death of a loved one also tends to aggravate existing illnesses, causes physical illness, and increases the likelihood of death (Stroebe & Stroebe, 1987; Traupmann & Hatfield, 1981).

Eventually, the bereaved can enter the resolution phase. In this final phase, they can recall the deceased without being overwhelmed by sadness and are at last ready to get reinvolved in the world (Bowlby, 1980).

We discussed the impact of love schemas on the beginnings and middles of relationships in Chapters 3 and 6. Let us complete the cycle by speculating about how people who endorse the various love schemas might be expected to react to the ending of a love affair.

Love Schemas and Reactions to Loss

People differ in how quickly they recover from the break-up of a love affair. Some mend quickly, whereas others appear never to recover fully. As one might expect, people with different love profiles seem to deal with loss in quite different ways. In Table 7.7, we describe some differences that we might expect. Let us consider these reactions in greater detail.

The Secure
Researchers have discovered that secure people with high self-esteem bounce back better from the loss of love than do others (Choo et al., 1995; Frazier & Cook, 1993; Harvey et al., 1989). They are less likely than others to try to cope with the end of a relationship by drinking or taking drugs than are others (Brennan & Shaver, 1995; Choo et al., 1995).

The French noblewoman Cécile Fournel had this sensible reaction to the end of her affair:

> *Dear Aglaé, I shall not tell you that when I next set eyes upon him, it will be with no suffering in my heart, no grief. I have given him too much and received from him too little for me not to feel a sort of heartbreak mingled with my pleasure at seeing him again after such a long separation. (Sullerot, 1979, p. 232)*

The Clingy
When the clingy contemplate breaking up, they may panic. Of course, their partners, who have been feeling increasingly smothered by their demands, may feel numb relief. In one recent study, Patricia Choo, Tim Levine, and Elaine Hatfield inter-

TABLE 7.7 The Reaction to Endings

Love Schema	The Lover's Expected Reaction
Secure	Somewhat upset
Clingy	Desperate
Skittish	Relieved
Fickle	Desperate/Relieved/Desperate/Relieved/ Desperate/Relieved
Casual	Ho-hum
Uninterested	Huh?

viewed young American men and women from the University of Hawaii, who came from diverse ethnic backgrounds: African, Chinese, European, Filipino, Hawaiian, Japanese, Korean, and mixed ethnic backgrounds. Subjects were asked if they had ever experienced being passionately in love, dating for awhile, and then breaking up. If so, how had they reacted? As predicted, the authors found that it was the clingy who suffered the most after a breakup. After a love affair ended, the clingy felt less joy and relief and more sadness, fear, and anger than did their peers. Students were also asked how they had tried to cope with their feelings and with the practical problems they faced in the week or two after the break-up. The scientists found that the clingy tended to blame themselves for breakups. The authors labeled their reaction *WhatHaveIDone?* The clingy were more likely than others to say they had done such things as these: "I spent a great deal of time trying to figure out what I might have done wrong; I spent a great deal of time trying to figure out what I could do to save our relationship; I spent a great deal of time talking to my friends, trying to figure out what I had done wrong; I spent a great deal of time talking to my friends, trying to figure out what had gone wrong;" and "I spent a great deal of time talking to my friends, trying to figure out if there was anything we could do to save the relationship."

In Charlotte Brontë's *Jane Eyre* (Brontë, 1847/1950), Jane, a governess, realizes that she must leave the man she loves passionately, the patrician owner of Thornfield Hall, Edward Fairfax Rochester. She clings:

> [Rochester]. "As for you,—you'd forget me."
> [Jane]. "That I never *should, sir: you know*"—impossible to proceed.
> "Jane, do you hear that nightingale singing in the wood? Listen!"
> In listening, I sobbed convulsively; for I could repress what I endured no longer; I was obliged to yield, and I was shaken from head to foot with acute distress. When I did speak, it was only to express an impetuous wish that I had never been born, or never come to Thornfield.
> "Because you are sorry to leave it?"
> The vehemence of emotion, stirred by grief and love within me, was claiming mastery, and struggling for full sway; and asserting a right to predominate: to overcome, to live, rise, and reign at last; yes,—and to speak.
> "I grieve to leave Thornfield: I love Thornfield:—I love it, because I have lived in it a full and delightful life,—momentarily at least. I have not been trampled on. I have not been petrified. I have not been buried with inferior minds, and excluded from every glimpse of communion with what is bright and energetic, and high. I have talked, face to face, with what I reverence; with what I delight in—with an original, a vigorous, an expanded mind. I have known you, Mr. Rochester; and it strikes me with terror and anguish to feel I absolutely must be torn from you for ever. I see the necessity of departure; and it is like looking on the necessity of death."
> (p. 273)

Rochester expresses equal dismay at the idea of being separated from Jane Eyre:

"Are you anything akin to me, do you think, Jane?"

I could risk no sort of answer by this time: my heart was full.

"Because," he said, "I sometimes have a queer feeling with regard to you—especially when you are near me, as now: it is as if I had a string somewhere under my left ribs, tightly and inextricably knotted to a similar string situated in the corresponding quarter of your little frame. And if that boisterous channel, and two hundred miles or so of land come broad between us, I am afraid that cord of communion will be snapt: and then I've a nervous notion I should take to bleeding inwardly." (p. 272–273)

The Skittish

When the skittish break up, they may feel simple relief. In the study we described earlier (Choo et al., 1995), it was the skittish who were most likely to say that after a break-up they felt joy and relief. Choo and her colleagues also assessed the extent to which people blamed themselves (asking *WhatHaveIDone?*) versus their partners (saying *ThatJerk*) after a break-up. We described the *WhatHaveIDone?* kind of reaction in the previous section. *ThatJerk* comprised such items as "I spent a great deal of time thinking about how badly my partner had treated me; I spent a great deal of time talking to my friends—almost all of them agreed that my partner was really the one who had problems;" and "I told myself: 'I'm lucky to have gotten out of that relationship.'" Choo found that the skittish were less likely than others to blame either themselves *or* their partners after a break-up. What they (and the fickle) tend to do is drink or take drugs. (The authors labeled this reaction *Let'sParty*.) It is probably not too encouraging for men and women, who go to singles' bars in the hope of finding someone to love, to realize that they may well bump into the skittish and the fickle, recovering from their last blighted love affair. (Similar results were secured by Brennan & Shaver, 1995).

Israeli novelist Amos Oz (1991), in *Fima*, described the reaction of the elderly Baruch Nomberg, who has trouble getting really close to anyone. He walled himself off even from his wife's death:

[When his wife died], Baruch Nomberg, in his usual impetuous way, did not wait even a week: the weekend after the funeral he hurled all her belongings into boxes and crates, all her dresses and shoes and books, and her dressing table with the round Russian mirror, and the bed linen embroidered with her initials. He hastily donated the lot to the leper hospice in Talbiyeh. He erased every trace of her existence, as though her death had been an act of betrayal. As though she had run away with another man. But he did have her graduation photograph enlarged, and hung it over the sideboard, from where she looked down on the two of them all those years with a wistful, skeptical smile and with shyly down-turned eyes, as though she admitted her fault and repented of it. (pp. 151–152)

Their partners may suffer more at abrupt dismissals. In one study of dating couples, Jeffry Simpson (1990) found that after a break-up, men who were secure or clingy in their love styles suffered far more than did the skittish.

The Fickle

One of our best friends is the prototype of a fickle lover. He is quite self-mocking and that is a good thing because we tease him mercilessly. He is fifty-seven years old and desperate to marry. Yet, the women he chooses are obviously impossible. He is an elegant academic. His latest love affair is a young, very young, New Age type. He is a theater buff. She likes literature of the people. He is a restaurant reviewer, a *haute cuisine* chef, and a gourmet. She is a special type of vegetarian, who doesn't eat any animal or fish that possesses eyes! Recently, he visited us and read selected correspondence from three years of their courtship. He expected that his literate letters would melt our hearts. As he read, both of us got more and more furious . . . at him. When she loved him, he was scornful. Everything she did was wrong. But when finally she had had enough, left, and eventually made plans to marry someone else, he "suddenly" realized how much he loved and needed her. His letters begged her to come back, demanded that she do so; he cajoled and threatened. Because she had hurt him, he had the right, the *duty*, to disrupt her wedding and to trash her house. But he loved her desperately, and so on and on.

Not surprisingly, such fickle lovers often drive their partners nuts. People are naturally enraged at being "jerked around" again and again. Ninon De Lenclos (1620–1705) wrote an irritated letter to her fickle lover:

> Your conduct reveals more and more of the truth to me, and you show yourself to be not at all clever: You have given up everything for me since the beginning of our liaison, you tell me. But that is what a man always does, not only for the woman he loves, but for the one he merely desires; he makes sacrifices for the woman he wishes to possess, and ceases to make them for the woman who adores him. If her heart suffers, if her health is affected, he relies on time to heal her. This is behavior worthy of the fickle men whom you resemble. I have long been aware of this; there was no need to fill up four pages telling me this yet again. . . . Since you are capable of such cold reasoning, this reply will serve to prove to you how inappropriate your letter was. Keep your sublime ideas to yourself henceforth, and should you be still capable of making a sacrifice in my behalf, I pray you to spare me your icy sermons. (Sullerot, 1979, p. 135)

> Men have died from time to time and worms have eaten them, but not for love.
> —William Shakespeare

The Casual

Casual romances can be a great deal of fun—just so long as there is truth in advertising, so long as everyone understands that this affair is just for fun. In English novelist Muriel Spark's (1963) *The Girls of Slender Means*, the narrator comments on the unthinking casualness of girls' attachments to servicemen in World War II:

> The weeks had passed, and since in the May of Teck Club they were weeks of youth in the ethos of war, they were capable of accommodating quick happenings and reversals, rapid formations of intimate friendships, and a range of lost and discov-

ered loves that in later life and in peace would take years to happen, grow and fade. The May of Teck girls were nothing if not economical. Nicholas, who was past his youth, was shocked at heart by their week-by-week emotions.

"I thought you said she was in love with the boy."

"So she was."

"Well, wasn't it only last week he died? You said he died of dysentery in Burma."

"Yes I know. But she met this naval type on Monday, she's madly in love with him."

"She can't be in love with him," said Nicholas.

"Well, they've got a lot in common she says."

"A lot in common? It's only Wednesday now." (pp. 116–117)

Sometimes, of course, lovers who thought there was more to a love affair than there really is get irritated or hurt. In Carrie Fisher's film *Postcards from the Edge* (1987), Meryl Streep discusses love with Dennis Quaid. She merely gets sarcastic:

Streep: You said you loved me.
Quaid: I meant it at the time.
Streep: What is it, a viral love? Kind of a twenty-four hour thing?

In Oscar Hijuelos' (1993) novel *The Fourteen Sisters of Emilio Montez O'Brien*, he describes the passionate involvement of the love-besotted Emilio for a touring actress, Spring Mayweather:

Her youthfulness, his strength, her softness, his ardor, her naughtiness, her compliance, his reckless thousand kisses, his large "bone," the scent of her hair, her quivering and sweet femininity, saliva, kisses, the churning of hips and cries.

They were inseparable for the next three days, his father vaguely aware of the young lady's presence, Emilio reluctant to hang around to help, walking about in a delirium of love, his every thought on Spring: not his sisters, his actorly ambitions, or Errol Flynn, or Cuba or Ireland or anything else. She was good to him; whenever they could get away, they'd meet and go off to their tranquil spot and she was tender and affectionate. . . . on their last afternoon, with Emilio swearing that he had fallen in love with her and on the verge of declaring his intentions, she said: "Well, I guess this is our last time together."

"Last?"

"Well, we're off to a few more towns this month, and then we go to Ohio, and from there we just keep on going."

"Will you come back?"

"I don't know. I'll write you. Maybe we can figure something out."

His handsome features drooping in consternation, his expression sad: "But I thought we had something going."

"My goodness, don't you know I can't get tied down. In any case, you're too young to get all tangled."

And when he was silent, she added, "For crying out loud, men do this kind of thing all the time to women, especially these days. Now, can't we just enjoy ourselves?"

They made love for a last time on a hot Sunday evening and in the days that followed, his spirits were so low that he loathed himself—and this would get him in trouble over the years—for a tendency to feel easy attractions and to fall in love too quickly. (pp. 242–243)

The Uninterested

Of course, the uninterested have no interest in a relationship. They would barely notice were their mythical relationship to end. Earlier, we described a study by Choo and her colleagues (1995). The scientists found that after a breakup, those who said they were uninterested in relationships were more likely to feel simple joy and relief and were less likely to feel guilty than were others. The uninterested were also less likely than others to ask *WhatHaveIDone?* (to blame themselves) after a breakup.

Anton Chekhov (1912), described the deadened reactions of Ivanoff when the doctor warned him that unless he began to attend to his wife Anna, who had consumption, she would die:

Ivanoff. *What you say is true, true. I must be terribly guilty, but my mind is confused. My will seems to be paralysed by a kind of stupor; I can't understand myself or anyone else. . . . Anna is a splendid, an exceptional woman. She has left her faith, her parents, and her fortune for my sake. If I should demand a hundred other sacrifices, she would consent to every one without the quiver of an eyelid. Well, I am not a remarkable man in any way, and have sacrificed nothing. However, the story is a long one. In short, the whole point is, my dear doctor—[Confused] that I married her for love and promised to love her forever and now after five years she loves me still and I—[He waves his hand] Now, when you tell me she is dying, I feel neither love nor pity, only a sort of loneliness and weariness. (p. 82)*

Dealing with Loss

After a breakup, separation, divorce, or the death of a partner, many people need to mourn for a while before reentering the social world. People try different strategies to deal with loss. Oscar Hijuelos (1989) recounted the story of Cesar and Nestor Castillo, the Mambo Kings. Here, the author describes how they attempted to deal with the depression they felt when their love affairs, marriages, or work went wrong:

Cubans then (and Cubans now) didn't know about psychological problems. Cubans who felt bad went to their friends, ate and drank and went out dancing. Most of the time they wouldn't think about their problems. A psychological problem was part of someone's character. Cesar was un macho grande; *Nestor,* un infeliz. *People who hurt bad enough and wanted cures expected these cures to come immediately. Cesar was quite friendly with some* santeras, *really nice ladies who had come from Oriente Province and settled on 110th Street and Manhattan Avenue. And whenever Cesar felt bad about anything, if he felt depressed about the fact that he still had to work in a meat-packing plant to maintain his flamboyant life-style, or when he felt guilty about his daughter down in Cuba, he would go see his friends for a little magical rehauling. These* santeras *liked to listen to the radio all day, loved to have children and company around them. If he felt bad, he would just go in there and drop a few dollars into a basket, lie on his stomach on a straw mat on the floor, ring a magic bell (which symbolized his goddess, Caridad, or charity) and pay homage to the goddess Mayari, for whom these women were intermediaries. And pssssst! his problems would lift away. Or they would lay hands on him. Or he would just go over to 113th and Lenox, to a* botanica, *and get himself a "cleaning"—the saint pouring magic herbs over him—guaranteed to do the trick. Going to confession at the Catholic church did the same job: a heartfelt opening of the heart and an admission of sins; then the cleansing of the soul. (And no death-bed confession either, no admission to heaven because of last rites. These Cubans died as they lived, and a man who would not confess his sins at age twenty-five was not going to do so at seventy.)*

Nestor went with Cesar and was cleaned, paid obeisance, and felt better for a few days. Then the feeling came back to him, and he was unable to move. (pp. 114–115)

Gender Differences in Dealing with Loss

Historically, women have been stereotyped as the more emotional gender, especially in their close relationships (Broverman et al., 1972; Sprecher & Hatfield, 1987). Stephen Kern (1992), in *The Culture of Love* gave examples of the way Victorian artists dramatized the ending of a love affair:

> *The Victorians were well aware that many women and men loved secretly and in vain, but most of them embellished those sufferings and defeats with the pathos of high drama distinctive to their age. . . .*
>
> *Victorians show the rejected woman in conventional melodramatic poses—holding her broken heart, slumping in a chair, clutching a letter, lying in a crumpled heap, wasting away in despair, or contemplating suicide (generally by drowning). Less frequent images of the jilted man are equally melodramatic, although the man assumes different postures. Men hold their heads rather than their hearts, stand or sit stiffly rather than slump or collapse, drink themselves into oblivion rather than waste away, and kill themselves with ropes or guns rather than by drowning. Briton Riviere's* Jilted! *. . . shows a man who thinks he knows why he has been rejected, for he clutches the letter with the bad news. . . .*

Riviere glamorizes his stalwart man dressed in a stylish riding outfit. The man is hurting, but he will bounce back and rejoin the "hunt" like a good sport. His spurred boots splay out in defeat, but the rest of his pose indicates a will to deal with the situation. His strong jaw is set; his brow is knitted in concentration. He is a model of determination in the face of bitter disappointment. (p. 381)

In fact, the evidence from real life suggests just the opposite. It is men, not women, who are most emotionally upset when dating relationships or marriages end (Hill, Rubin, & Peplau, 1979; Stroebe & Stroebe, 1987). Men are more likely to rely on their sweethearts and wives for everything than are women. Most men's only confidante is their mate. Women usually have a variety of confidantes (Caldwell & Peplau, 1982). Men are less likely to have maintained close ties to family and friends, who can provide social support in times of stress (Barbee, Gulley, & Cunningham, 1990; Duck, 1991). Thus, they suffer more when their primary relationship ends.

Researchers have also contended that today's men and women may cope with stressful life events in very different ways. Men generally ignore adversity, and distract themselves from what they are feeling. They may exercise, take drugs, drink, or lose themselves in their work. Women tend to brood about problems. They try to figure out if they were to blame and to sort out exactly what went wrong. They talk to other people to get their ideas. They try to set things right (Ingram et al., 1988; Nolen-Hoeksema, 1987). These are the stereotypes. Recent research suggests, however, that at least in the area of love, men and women are not so different as they have been purported to be (see Box 7.1).

Cultural Differences in Dealing with Loss

Personal accounts remind us of the universality of the suffering that accompanies the end of an affair. French writer Annie Ernaux (1993) in *Simple Passion* painstakingly depicted her obsessive love for A, even after their affair had ended:

He left France and went back to his own country six months ago. I shall probably never see him again. At first, when I woke up at two o'clock in the morning, I didn't care whether I lived or died. My whole body ached. I would have liked to tear out the pain but it was everywhere. I longed for a burglar to come into my bedroom and kill me. During the day I tried desperately to find things to do, so as not to remain idle, otherwise I felt I would be lost (the meaning of the word was vague: to have a nervous breakdown, to start drinking, and so on).

. . . I wanted to remember his body with all my being—from his hair down to the tips of his toes. I could conjure up, vividly, his green eyes, the lock of hair falling over his forehead, the curve of his shoulders. I could feel his teeth, the inside of his mouth, the shape of his thighs, the texture of his skin. . . .

For many weeks:

BOX 7.1 Gender Differences in Dealing with Loss

Lisa Orimoto and her colleagues (1993) interviewed 237 University of Hawaii students. The students were representative of Hawaii's multicultural background and came from a variety of ethnic backgrounds: African, European, Chinese, Filipino, Hawaiian, Japanese, Korean, Samoan, South Asian, and mixed. The researchers asked the subjects how they felt after a recent break-up and how they tried to cope with the situation. The authors found that men's and women's emotional reactions differed surprisingly little. Both were usually devastated by the breakup. They felt a kaleidoscope of emotions—love, anger and, grief, as well as occasional relief that things were finally over.

How did they deal with their feelings and with the practical problems they faced following the separation? Women were more likely to try to focus on the problems and try to figure out what had happened and whether they could make improvements next time around. In the main, however, both men and women used similar strategies. Both men and women felt that they should have coped better than they actually did.

1. *Women paid attention to the problem.* They were more prone to cry, to talk to their friends, to read self-help books and magazines, and to

see therapists in an effort to better understand the workings of love.

Men and women were equally likely to use the other techniques:

2. *Both men and women sometimes tried to play things down.* They tried to hide their feelings so others wouldn't know what they were going through. They binged. They drank or took drugs (tranquilizers, sleeping pills, marijuana). They went out of their way to avoid bumping into the one they loved. They avoided going places or doing things that had been part of their lives together. They stayed in bed.

3. *Both used cognitive techniques to manage their feelings.* They talked to themselves like a Dutch uncle. "Who needs him (or her) anyway"? "It's his (her) loss!" "There are lots of good fish in the sea." "I'm lucky to have gotten out of that relationship." "You've learned a valuable lesson."

4. *Both tried to distract themselves from their loss.* They did things to improve their looks or sex appeal (got a haircut, bought clothes, or went on a diet). They kept themselves busy with sports, schoolwork, or career. They engaged in physical activities (they jogged, played basketball, or went swimming.)

I would wake up in the middle of the night, and remain in a confused state until morning, awake, incapable of thinking. I wanted to lose myself in a deep sleep but he continued to hover above me.

I didn't want to get up. I would see the day stretch ahead of me, with no plans. I felt that time was no longer taking me anywhere, it only made me grow old. . . .

I would make wishes: if he calls me before the end of the month, I'll give five hundred francs to a charity. I imagined that we had met in a hotel, at an airport, or that he had sent me a letter. I replied to words he had never spoken, sentences he would never write. (pp. 41, 43, 44–45)

Amazingly, we have been unable to find any research on cultural differences in dealing with romantic loss. This is surely a topic that subsequent researchers might be expected to address.

Starting Over: Dating and Remarriage

> *A girl must marry for love, and keep on marrying until she finds it.*
> —Zsa Zsa Gabor

Gender Differences in Remarriage

Gender Differences in the United States

In America, most men and women who have been divorced or widowed eventually remarry. Almost all men remarry shortly after divorce. Whether or not women remarry at all depends on their age. Lenore Weitzman (1985) observed:

> *If she is under thirty, she has a 75 percent chance of remarrying. But her chances diminish significantly as she grows older: between thirty and forty, the proportion is closer to 50 percent, and if she is forty or older, she has only a 28 percent chance of remarriage. (p. 204)*

What accounts for this discrepancy? When men and women are in their teens and early twenties, there are slightly more eligible men than women. After 25, however, increasingly there are too many women for too few men (Kennedy, 1989). Men begin to fall ill and die. Those that are still healthy tend to remain interested in younger women. This produces a "marriage squeeze" for women. The squeeze is not so great as the popular media suggest, but it is a problem for women nonetheless.

On the average, most divorced people remarry within two years (National Center for Health Statistics, 1987). In America, there are a variety of reasons why it is easier for men to remarry than for women to do so.

Gender Differences in Other Societies

In most tribal societies (78 percent) divorced men and women were allowed to marry again. Those that restricted remarriage (22 percent), were almost always harder on women than on men (Frayser, 1985). Public opinion, for example, prevented Khalka Mongol women from remarrying if they were at fault in the divorce, particularly if the couple had children. Husbands who were responsible for precipitating the divorce, on the other hand, were not discouraged from remarrying (Vreeland, 1953).

In past centuries, in many societies—China, Egypt, Greece, and even the Scandinavian nations (today's symbols for progressivism)—men could generally remarry after divorcing or being widowed, but women were forbidden to do so (Upreti & Upreti, 1991). For women there was no "second chance" in these and many other places.

Historians H. C. and Nandini Upreti (1991), for example, explained the Indian *The Myth of Sati*. Originally, the word *sati* (or suttee) meant "a good and virtuous woman" or "a chaste wife." The ideal wife was supposed to be sweet, innocent, pure, self-sacrificing, and self-effacing. She was loyal and faithful. In medieval India, the notion that the virtuous woman lived only for her husband began to take on a darker coloring. It meant that when he died she was expected to throw herself on his funeral pyre or to be buried with him. If the widow resisted, his family forced her to submit. A family had a great deal to gain from the practice of *suttee*. The widow's death meant that they, not the widow, inherited the couple's property. They were also spared an enormous economic burden. Families were responsible for supporting widows. (If a man had taken a child bride, or several brides, the family might have to maintain them for decades.) Widows were forbidden to have sexual relations or remarry. Until the nineteenth century, many women were forced to *sati*. The British (a colonial power) and some Indian groups began to discourage the practice. In 1987, a newlywed burned herself in Deorala in Sikar (Rajasthan). Indian women's organizations protested the custom as well as the generally low status of Indian women. Parliament passed a law forbidding *sati*.

Today, however, in many Indian communities, widows are still forbidden to marry and are treated very badly. Rajput widows, for example, are supposed to live a life devoid of joy. Their heads are sometimes shaved. They are given revolting food to eat and must wear rags. They are required to stay indoors. They are forbidden to attend religious ceremonies. They must sleep on the ground. They are treated by the family and the rest of society as unclean and polluting.

In China, during the Ming and Qing dynasties (1368–1912), the State gave awards to "virtuous widows," women of exemplary character, who retired from the world and resisted remarriage throughout their lifetimes. The stories of the virtuous sound strange to modern ears. One young widow, Lingnü, cut off her hair, both her ears and her nose to demonstrate to her parents that she was resolved not to marry. Another honored widow killed herself to avenge the defilement of her husband's memory. (The defilement? She *heard* ruffians in the street utter coarse words.) Li cut off her "defiled" hand with an axe. (The cause? Li and her young son were marooned at nightfall at an inn in Kaifeng, as she was taking her husband's body home for burial. The innkeeper refused to provide lodging for them and dragged her out of the inn by the arm. She severed the dishonored part from her body, in honor of her husband.) Honored widows often confined themselves in a single room, never leaving that room until the day of their death. Widows could also display their virtue by starving themselves to death or committing suicide (Elvin, 1984).

When William Good (1993) surveyed practices in Europe, the Anglo countries, Latin America, Japan, Malaysia, and the Arab world, he concluded that currently:

> *In the West both marriage and remarriage rates have dropped among both men and women, though men, with their usual economic advantage, have continued to remarry at a higher rate than women. Moreover, in the marriage market men are "worth more" than women of the same age for almost any age beyond thirty years. In addition, women have added still more years to their life expectancy than have men.*

> *As a consequence, with each passing year, a divorced woman will find fewer*
> *men in the marriage pool available to her. . . . Her market prospects are less rosy.*
> *(p. 323)*

Goode found such differences to exist throughout the world. In one study, for example, researchers asked a sampling of Japanese men and women who had been divorced if they wanted to remarry. If men and women were young (20–29 years of age), 64 percent of men and 41 percent of women hoped to remarry. If men and women were a little older (30–39), they were less eager to remarry. Although 58 percent of men still wanted to marry, only 24 percent of women were willing to do so. By age 50–59, although 42 percent of men wished to remarry, only 11 percent of women were willing to do so (Cornell, 1989). In any case, in Japan 50 to 75 percent of divorced men and 45 to 70 percent of divorced women eventually do remarry (Tsubouchi, 1984). Japanese men are more likely to remarry than are Japanese women. The older people get, the greater is the discrepancy between a man's and a woman's chances of ever remarrying.

Finally, the same general pattern—that men are more likely to remarry *sooner* after divorce than are women, especially if men and women are older—has been found to exist not only in America but in Japan (Cornell, 1989) and West Germany (Klein, 1990) as well. As men and women become more similar, particularly in economic power, we might expect such gender differences to begin to diminish.

How Happy Are Second Marriages?

After being kicked around in the quirky world of love, many people become wiser. Amy Tan (1991), in *The Kitchen God's Wife* described the two marriages of Jiang Weili (Winnie Louie). Winnie's first husband was cruel and abusive. But her second husband, Jimmie Louie loved her beyond all reason. Winnie's two marriages could not have been more different.

One researcher (Albrecht, 1979) found that 88 percent of remarried couples stated that their present marriage was "much better" than the former marriage that had ended in divorce and 65 percent felt that the experience gained in the earlier marriage helped them in adjusting to the present one. Another study asked couples which was happiest—their first marriage or their current one? They generally agreed that their second marriage was better (Albrecht, 1979). Researchers concluded that "the second marriage usually benefits by comparison to the first. It is as if individuals moved from a dreary, unpleasant job to a better one" (Furstenberg & Spanier, 1984, p. 84).

Not everyone learns from experience, however. In America, remarriages are somewhat more likely to end in divorce than are first marriages. About 49 percent of first marriages end in divorce. About 61 percent of men and 54 percent of women who have remarried experience redivorce as well (Glick, 1984). Of course, as we explained earlier, this statistic may be inflated since those people most opposed to divorce would not appear in this sample.

Conclusions

Yale historian Robin Winks once said that writing history is "like nailing jelly to the wall." But, he added "someone must keep trying" (Kamisar, 1993, p. 12). Trying to describe sweeping historical trends and then to predict future trends is even more difficult. But let us, in a playful and modest spirit, make the effort.

The global village created by worldwide communication, computers and satellites, information exchange, travel, and trade will most certainly continue to reduce cultural differentiation and augment homogenization. While we can anticipate that the world of the future might combine something of East and West, there can be little question that for the short term the influence of the West over the East will be far greater than the reverse. For some, that is an appealing vision. They equate Westernization with freedom, equality, democracy, and higher living standards. For others, that is a nightmare vision, an image of selfishness, rampant greed, and materialism—made in the West. African American novelist John Wideman (1990) sketched a stark portrait of American greed:

> *You hate to watch Old Greed stirring around down in his ugly pocket and you damned sure avoid looking at his fingers when he draws out the little piece of change you're begging for. You know good and well the nasty place it's coming from but you ain't hardly refusing what he holds out, blood, vomit, shit, piss, pus and all.*
>
> *Answer's always yes. Yes, I'll take the money. Don't care how much blood's on it. Don't care if it's my blood. Yours. I wasn't the one responsible. I'd prefer clean money but till clean drops down from heaven this will do. Yes. I'll take it. Somebody will take it. Mize well be me. Money's money. None of it's clean.*
>
> *See, to me, man, that's the bottom line. No matter how you cut it, human nature gets down to a simple fact. You want yours and I want mine, don't matter whose blood on the money, yes, we'll take it. World operates the way it does because that's the bottom line. Survival's the bottom line. (p. 84)*

But are greed, selfishness, and materialism really strictly Western ideas? Certainly Wideman doesn't think so. Historians and political pundits remind us that all of human history has been marked by such failings.

At this point we must address a most difficult conundrum that underlies every moral issue in this book. In the West today, two critically important ideas have gained popularity. Unfortunately, sometimes these two ideals contradict one another.

First comes cultural sensitivity. Those in Western countries are urged to be less arrogant and judgmental (less Eurocentric), more appreciative of cultural diversity, and to adopt a respectful stance of moral relativism when judging societies very different from our own. A few angry anti-Western critics carry this admonition to its extreme. They contend that the West has been such a dark force throughout modern history that it has forfeited any and all right to judge other civilizations. In their view, "Westernization" means material greed, selfishness, imperialism, aggression, intolerance, unbelief, drugs, crime, and violence. While there clearly is a Western "style" to these afflictions, we would remind readers that all societies have been and are ethnocentric and murderous. The story of human history *is* the story of selfishness, greed, violence, and cruelty. The little shoots of peace, freedom, and tolerance that push into the world are very tender. They are easily trampled by self-righteousness, anger, and hate.

The idea of cultural sensitivity is not always congruent, however, with a second popular ideal—the idea of universal human rights. This concept asserts that, whatever their cultural sources, certain practices are abhorrent: infanticide, genocide ("ethnic cleansing"), and torture to name just a few. The human rights agenda calls for the condemnation and elimination of these grisly practices. This idea places certain serious limitations on cultural tolerance.

Whatever one thinks of Westernization, individualism, democracy, capitalism, and materialism *in general*, we suspect that when it comes to the topics we discuss in this book, we will find greater consensus in how these two values should be balanced than one might expect. For here we are not dealing with the culture as a whole but only with *love and sex*. And in these realms, "Westernization" assumes a considerably less malign cast, particularly when seen from the point of view of 51 percent of the global population: the women of the world.

The Westernization model in the frame of passion and sex seems to be built on three notions—notions that, our data suggest, are spreading at differential rates into all corners of the world and will continue to do so *if* existing historical trends are not reversed (a substantial "if.")

We may see people throughout the world approaching this revolutionary trio of powerful ideas: first, a belief in the equality of women and members of minority groups; second, a belief that in life the pursuit of happiness and the avoidance of pain are desirable goals; and third, a belief that change and improvement in life are attainable and that action toward those ends may be preferable to resignation and passive acceptance of age-old traditions, whatever their value.

These ideals may seem self-evident and even banal to some Western readers, but non-Westerners will recognize the awesome changes that would be brought about in their societies when and if these ideals fully take hold. Even in the West, they are far from having fully been embraced. In the area of passionate love and sexual desire, we might expect societies to stop regarding passionate love and sexual desire as evil and to end the punishment of those who feel those emotions. Cultures would reduce their opposition to sexual and gender equality. The double standard would continue to erode. The shift from arranged marriage to free marriage would accelerate. We might see greater acceptance of heterosexuality, bisexuality, or homosexuality as a choice; increased sexual permissiveness; and divorce made easier. These tendencies will be deplored (and celebrated) by many, and the moral issues behind them are not simple. But tendencies they unmistakably are and because of that they require from us a closer scrutiny as this book draws to a close.

From Male Supremacy to Gender Equality

No social tendency surpasses in significance that of the women's movement. Although its sources lie in the West, this study of love, sex, and marriage time and again has noted its spread around the world, particularly in the three arenas of egalitarianism, the pursuit of happiness, and the belief in the possibility of change and improvement. Yet, this extraordinary journey has just begun; as we approach the end of the twentieth century, male supremacy continues to be the rule worldwide—even in the West, where enormous progress has occurred. Recently, Geraldine Ferraro (1993) reported that in 1993 Western and developing-world women joined together to speak at United Nations human rights conferences in Vienna and in Geneva. They won recognition from the world community that abuses of women's rights—which include female infanticide, genital mutilation, the sale of brides, dowry murders, *suttee* or widow burning (in India, widows are still sometimes required to immolate themselves on their husbands' funeral pyres: see Upreti & Upreti, 1991), and discriminatory laws against women's civic, social, and legal equality—are abuses of human rights. The Global Campaign for Women's Human Rights also received a commitment from 183 countries to move toward eliminating all forms of discrimination against women. Ferraro argued that tradition and culture can no longer be cited to justify repression of half the world's population (p. A12).

In 1994, in Cairo, the International Conference on Population and Development focused on the rights of women worldwide for the first time. They achieved an unparalleled consensus (Crossette, 1994). Also in 1994, the State Department focused on the treatment of women in its annual human rights report. Its report on 193 countries painted a grim picture of day-to-day discrimination and abuse: In Burma and Thailand very young girls were still routinely coerced into prostitution. Girls are ritually mutilated in the Sudan and Somalia. In Saudi Arabia and Kuwait, household maids are often beaten and raped. In China, women are subject to forced abortions and sterilizations. In many countries, boys are given the best food and medical attention; girls are neglected (Greenhouse, 1994).

In India in 1992, despite a 32-year-old statute banning dowries (the money and gifts given by the bride's parents to the groom), government statistics indicated that husbands killed 4,785 brides because their parents were unable to pay a large enough dowry (Gargan, 1993). Typically, young brides who cannot pay the money their husbands demand for motor scooters or houses are doused with kerosene and set alight, pushed into swelling rivers, or driven to suicide (see Kumari, 1989).

In many African, Far Eastern, and Middle Eastern societies, boys' and girls' genitals are ritually mutilated during tribal initiation rites. Edgar Gregersen (1982) observed:

> *People in many different societies have felt and still feel that the genitals should be altered in one way or another by cutting, piercing, hacking, or slicing, or by inserting objects. (p. 100)*

During initiation rites, boys may have the foreskin of their penis slit or removed or the underside of the penis may be split lengthwise down to the urethra. Demographers estimate that from 80 to 100 million girls and women, primarily on the African continent, have been genitally mutilated in traditional rituals (Rosenthal, 1993; Walker, 1992). African leaders' attitudes toward these initiation rites are mixed. In part, there is a desire to uphold tribal traditions. Women, however, pay the terrible price for such "traditions." Young girls are held or tied down. Traditional circumcisers often perform the operations with crude instruments—dull sawtooth knives, shards of unwashed glass, the lid of a tin can, razor blades, or rusty razors. Tribal doctors may slice off the hood of the clitoris, cut out the entire clitoris, excise the *labia minora* and part of the *labia majora,* or sew together the sides of the vulva with catgut or with thorns. (In the latter case, women must urinate and menstruate through a tiny hole that is allowed to remain in the scarred tissue. When women marry, the man must sometimes force his penis through the small opening, painfully enlarging it. Supporters of these rites insist that potential wives must endure such operations for two reasons. First, they permit husbands the certainty that their potential brides (whose sexual openings have been sewn tight) are virgins. Genital mutilations also ensure that women, because they have no clitoris, will feel little or no sexual pleasure. Hence, they will never be tempted to commit adultery. The 84 million African women who have undergone such mutilations typically suffer a series of serious side effects from such operations (Hosken, 1982). Many suffer serious infection and scarring. They are left with chronic pain when they menstruate or urinate. Sexual relations are not to be enjoyed but endured, because they are at best neutral and at worst extremely painful. Of course, women no longer experience orgasm. Women may also suffer from urinary infections and childbirth complications. Many women die during the operation or from complications afterward.

The African American novelist, Alice Walker (1992), who is a leader in the fight to end these practices, has recounted the story of Tashi, an African American woman herself, in *Possessing the Secret of Joy.* Wishing to honor the ancient traditions of the Olinkas, the tribe of her birth, Tashi returns to Africa to ask M' Lissa, the tribal *tsunga,* to scar her face with Olinka tribal markings and to cut out the "unclean" parts of her body. The operation is a disaster. Tashi's mind, spirit, and body remain scarred by the operation.

> *Tashi is convinced that the little girls who are dying, and the women too, are infected by the unwashed, unsterilized sharp stones, tin tops, bits of glass, rusty razors and grungy knives used by the* tsunga, *who might mutilate twenty children without cleaning her instrument. There is also the fact that almost every act of intercourse involves tearing and bleeding, especially in a woman's early years. The opening that is made will never enlarge on its own, but must always be forced. Because of this, infections and open sores are commonplace. (p. 248)*

Suddenly Tashi recognizes that she has denounced white oppression only to submit willingly to traditional black male oppression. She recognizes the link between male power, the enslavement of women, and women's genital mutilation.

In a different sort of example, *The New York Times* on July 29, 1991, relayed a harrowing story. It told of a group of young teenage Kenyan boys at St. Kizito's School rampaging wild through an adjacent girls' dormitory to rape seventy-one teen-age schoolgirls and kill nineteen other girls. "'This tragedy has underscored the abominable male chauvinism that dominates Kenyan social life,' wrote Hilary Ng'Weno, editor in chief of *The Weekly Review,* the nation's most widely read magazine. 'The lot of our women and girls is lamentable. We treat them as second-class beings, good only for sexual gratification or burdensome chores. We bring up our boys to have little or no respect for girls.'" The deputy principal of the school "told President Daniel arap Moi when he visited the destroyed dormitory: 'The boys never meant any harm against the girls. They just wanted to rape.'" (Perlez, 1991, p. A4.)

In Islamic Pakistan, women who dare to accuse someone of rape risk imprisonment. The Hudood Ordinance declares that in the case of a disagreement, men's testimony must be assumed to be more credible than women's. In addition, often only the man is allowed to testify in court. Thus, a few of the few women who dared to complain of rape actually ended up being prosecuted for adultery themselves (a crime for women) while their attackers went scot free (Schork, 1990).

In another recent *New York Times* piece (Kristof, 1991a, July 21) readers were reminded that in contemporary China, continuing a long tradition (and despite Mao's attempts to reverse it), men and boys are still considered more valuable than women and girls. Until about a century ago in rural areas, Chinese girls were not even given names. They were simply called "eldest daughter," "No. 2 daughter," and so on. Even the mother of Deng Xiaoping, China's 88-year-old senior leader, never had a given name. As a child she was called "eldest kid," and later she was known simply by her surname, Dan, and called "Dan, wife of Deng." These days girls all get names (Kristof, 1993, p. A4).

Today, however, when asked to name their children and grandchildren, many peasants still do not bother to count girls. When asked how many children he had, one Beijing father, for example, said "one"—a son. When asked if he had any other children, he said, "No." However, when asked if his son had any sisters, he remembered: "Yes, one elder sister" (Kristof, 1993, p. A4).

This preference for boys dies hard. In former times in China, Korea, and India, for example, parents often practiced infanticide. Infant girls were exposed to the elements, thrown down wells, or killed. Today in China technology has speeded up the process. Couples bribe a doctor to tell them the results of routine ultrasound scan. If women are going to have a boy, the pregnancy proceeds. If they are expecting a girl, many arrange to have an abortion. As a consequence, sex ratios (of boys to girls) have become increasingly skewed. Normally, women would give birth to 103.8 to 104.9 boys for every 100 girls. In China, in 1992, a whopping 118.5 boys were reported born for every 100 girls. It is estimated that approximately 1.7 million Chinese girls were either aborted or killed. Authorities have begun to warn that in twenty years there may be bachelor villages—populated entirely by men, the girls and women having long since been destroyed.

The problem is not limited to China. According to demographers (Kristof, 1991b) nearly 1.6 million girls and women are "missing" in Bangladesh; 600,000 in Egypt; 23 million in India; 200,000 in Nepal; and 3 million in Pakistan. Infants may be victims of infanticide, starvation, or neglect. Parents may view an infant daughter with diarrhea, for example, as a nuisance, even though they view the same problem in a boy as a medical crisis that requires the intervention of a doctor (Rathus, Nevid, & Fichner-Rathus, 1993, p. 302).

Yet, male chauvinism is fading. In her memoir *The Woman Warrior*, Maxine Hong Kingston (1975) wittily illustrated the changing role of Chinese women, in China as well as in America:

> . . . . *Quite often the big loud women came shouting into the house, "Now when you sell this one, I'd like to buy her to be my maid." Then they laughed. They always said that about my sister, not me because I dropped dishes at them. I picked my nose while I was cooking and serving. My clothes were wrinkled even though we owned a laundry. . . .*
>
> *But if I made myself unsellable here, my parents need only wait until China, and there, where anything happens, they would be able to unload us, even me—sellable, marriageable. So while the adults wept over the letters about the neighbors gone berserk turning Communist ("They do funny dances; they sing weird songs just syllables. They make us dance; they make us sing"), I was secretly glad. As long as the aunts kept disappearing and the uncles dying after unspeakable tortures, my parents would prolong their God Mountain [American] stay. We could start spending our fare money on a car and chairs, a stereo. Nobody wrote to tell us that Mao himself had been matched to an older girl when he was a child and that he was freeing women from prisons, where they had been put for refusing the businessmen their parents had picked us as husbands. Nobody told us that the Revolution (the Liberation) was against girl slavery and girl infanticide (a village-wide party if it's a boy). Girls would no longer have to kill themselves rather than get married. May the Communists light up the house on a girl's birthday.*
>
> *I watched our parents buy a sofa, then a rug, curtains, chairs to replace the orange and apple crates one by one, now to be used for storage. Good. At the beginning of the second Communist five-year plan, our parents bought a car. But you could see the relatives and the villagers getting more and more worried about what to do with the girls. We had three girl second cousins, no boys; their great-grandfather was the old man who lived with them, as the river-pirate great-uncle was the old man who lived with us. When my sisters and I ate at their house, there we would be—six girls eating. The old man opened his eyes wide at us and turned in a circle, surrounded. His neck tendons stretched out. "Maggots!" he shouted. "Maggots! Where are my grandsons? I want grandsons! Give me grandsons! Maggots!" He pointed at each one of us, "Maggot! Maggot! Maggot! Maggot! Maggot! Maggot!" Then he dived into his food, eating fast and getting seconds. "Eat, maggots," he said. "Look at the maggots chew."*
>
> *"He does that at every meal," the girls told us in English.*
>
> *"Yeah," we said. "Our old man hates us too. What assholes." (pp. 222–223)*

There are signs around the world that these assumptions of the worthlessness of women (and the absolute rights of men to have their way over them) may not be immutable doctrines. The changes of modernism sweeping around the world are making their way into some of the sanctuaries of the most deeply entrenched male-dominated societies. These dramatic transformations in the role of women are occurring in many unexpected corners of the planet. A variety of researchers provide evidence that this revolution has begun to reach into many of the Arab countries (Shaaban, 1991), China (Chu & Ju, 1993; Tsui, 1989; Zhangling, 1983), Japan (Fuku-take, 1981; Kumagai, 1984), Mexico (Greenhouse, 1994); Morocco (Davis & Davis, 1994), Russia (Imbrogno & Imbrogno, 1989; Kerblay, 1983), Saudi Arabia (Sasson, 1992), Turkey (Greenhouse, 1994); and a variety of other countries (Lewin, 1995).

And what about the moral debate over the toleration of cultural diversity versus universal human rights? We believe in the importance of such toleration and the need for Westerners to be very careful about making ethnocentric judgments. But toleration cannot always be absolute, and the cruel examples above illustrate some of those limits. Girl infanticide and genital mutilation should not be tolerated by the world community. And who speaks for the cultures that still engage in such practices? We do not much hear the voices of the victims. Have they no say in what their culture inflicts on them? The world looks different from the point of view of the victim than that of the victimizer.

In the Sicilian documentary film *Children of Fate* (1992), which compared the lives of certain individuals in 1961 and then again in 1991, one of them, Luigi, mercilessly beat his wife every night, was drunk all the time, took food out of his children's mouths, had no job, and eventually went to prison—a despicable man. His wife left him in 1984 and remembered her years with Luigi as a hideous nightmare. But in 1991, Luigi, then out of prison, reminisced with his drinking partners about how grand the old days were compared with his current single days and told the filmmakers: "We talk about the old times in Cortile Cascino [a bad Palermo slum]. How nice it was. How life was better then. We were one big family."

It may also be useful to remember Karen Horney's famous attack on male chauvinism in general (and Freud's in particular). In 1930 she cautioned against the tendency to assume that our way is the only way, an argument that cut against both cultural imperialism and self-justifying cultural ideology:

> *At any given time, the more powerful side will create an ideology . . . to help maintain its position and to make this position acceptable to the weaker one. In this ideology the differences of the weaker one will be interpreted as inferiority, and it will be proven that these differences are unchangeable, basic, or God's will. It is the function of such an ideology to deny or conceal the existence of a struggle." [That is one reason} why we have so little awareness of the fact that there is a struggle between the sexes. It is in the interest of men to obscure this fact; and the emphasis they place on their ideologies has caused women, also, to adopt these theories. (Cited in Quinn, 1988, p. 228.)*

The Pursuit of Happiness and the Avoidance of Pain

Underlying the women's movement, and perhaps the most far-reaching and subversive notion behind all modernization, is one practically taken for granted because it runs so deep. This is the simple idea that in life we are entitled to pursue happiness and avoid pain. The alternative asks us to accept what is given, to resign ourselves to inevitability and not try to change things, and to repress individual desire. The alternative has been a staple of many religions, including many branches of Christianity and most varieties of Hinduism and Buddhism, hoping to stem the tide of individualism and self-interest. Authoritarians, political and religious, have worked hard to sell these propositions to their constituencies; they have not been uninterested, sometimes quite cynically, in maintaining order and keeping down the unwashed masses.

Although the validation of the pursuit of happiness returned to currency only in the eighteenth-century Enlightenment, after a very long absence, there is evidence of growing acceptance of it now in many countries of the world. As it relates to our issues, we have seen enlarging validation for passionate love and sexual desire, a growth in premarital sexual activity, an increase in sexual permissiveness, a growing acceptance of birth control, and a belief that individuals should be permitted to terminate unhappy marriages by divorce in China (Tsui, 1989) and Russia (Imbrogno & Imbrogno, 1989; Kerblay, 1983). The engine of individualism is the belief in personal and social progress.

A Belief That Things Can Change for the Better

Godwin Chu and Yanan Ju (1993), in *The Great Wall in Ruins,* provided some more solid evidence that in China things have begun to change. They observed that "Fatalism used to be strong among the Chinese people. When the hardship of life became almost unbearable, Chinese people generally blamed it on fate and accepted it as unalterable. Social injustice was thus not actively contested" (p. 259). What about today? Chu and Ju interviewed 2,000 randomly selected people from metropolitan Shanghai, from two towns in the Qingpu area, and from twenty rural villages. They asked, "If someone does not do well all his life, do you think this is because (1) he does not work hard enough, or (2) he is treated unfairly by others, or (3) it is his fate?" Today, they found that most people (72 percent) blamed the person himself for his failures. Some (15 percent) were willing to blame other people. Only a few (14 percent) blamed fate.

When the popular magazine *China Youth* asked readers whether or not they agreed with the statement that "it is best to leave our life to fate," they received 7,600 replies. Only 12 percent of readers agreed with the statement; 88 percent of readers disagreed (Bai & Wang, 1988). When viewing these changes, Chu and Ju (1993) lamented that "the cultural Great Wall is crumbling. It seems to lie in ruins, waiting for a modern miracle to resurrect it and imbue new life to the Chinese society it has traditionally defended" (p. 271).

BOX 7.2 Dirty Dancing

A recent article in the *India Tribune Magazine* complained about the revolution that was happening in Indian films. The culprit, the writer insisted, was "the import of foreign values through MTV (especially on shows like MTV grind)." He complained:

"In *Aankhen*, the raunch 'n' roll superhit of the year, oomph princess, Shilpa Shirodkar croons the sexually audacious 'Aangan mein hamae baba' while standing with her legs akimbo and pounding masalas with a long pole. In case Govinda doesn't get the message, she pushes his head within the folds of her ghagra for good measure. In *Khalnaaikaa*, after Jeetendra has let her know that her choli hides his 'cheez manpasand,' Varsha finds her tight choli in a tight spot. So she throws open her dupatta, does a mammary jiggle and screeches, "Tabahi hai, tabahai hai, tabahai."

In the yet-to-be-released-but-seen-ad-nauseum-on-Zee-TV song from *Pehchaan*, Saif Khan lies atop Shilpa Shirodkar in bed and the only rhythm method followed in their unremitting undulation is to the beat of the song they're both ludicrously singing. Even before the censors came into the picture, the makers themselves saw the light and are reshooting the song thankfully. In Parampara ("it should have been named Pump-ra," complains one movie reader), a rain-drenched Ramya pushes her bosom into a passion-drenched Vinod Khanna's face—in the climax of the song! After a point you do begin to empathise with Vinod's numb look . . . Sex on music . . . or dirty dancing? Just what is happening around here?" (*India Tribune Magazine*, 1993, pp. 16–17).

The historian, even without knowing much about cholis and dupattas, might timidly whisper "Westernization!" The message still manages somehow to get through.

Modernism has wrought its most far-reaching change with its onslaught on fatalism (Heilbroner, 1994; Manchester, 1992). Whether this is to be lamented or praised presents us with one of the most profound questions of our historical moment.

And what of fatalist, timeless India? Romantics often stereotype India as a land where people think in terms of generations rather than weekends, a place where people try to learn not to care about their lot rather than changing their circumstances. Yet history has breached the frontier of the Indian subcontinent as well (see Box 7.2).

Coda: The Demise of Passionate Love and Marriage?

The world is a dangerous place, its future threatened by overpopulation, resource depletion, environmental deterioration, and, worst of all, nuclear annihilation. Ethnic, religious, and national hatreds have risen to cast a chill on the good news provided by the end of the Cold War. Violence and poverty cast their shadow on all of us.

Yet, in writing about passion and marriage, the changes sweeping over the world exhibit a more positive cast. Most readers may feel hope about the spread of the three ideas that appear to be globally reshaping the private lives of so many of our sisters and brothers: gender equality, personal freedom, and the possibility of betterment.

But it would be misleading to end this book on a note of triumphalism, however muted. The future cannot be predicted by anyone; history works in odd and quirky ways and rarely is it linear. The historian of the 500-year rise of affective individualism, Lawrence Stone (1977), ended his pathbreaking work in a cautionary way:

> *Despite its many virtues, the rise in the West of the individualistic, nuclear, child-oriented family which is the sole outlet of both sexual and affective bonding is thus by no means always an unmixed blessing. This intense affective and erotic bonding is no more permanent a phenomenon than were the economic ties of property and interest that united families in the past, even if this is the rough general direction in which Western society has been moving over the last three hundred years. Today parents can expect to live twenty or thirty years beyond the departure of the children from the home, the number of children is declining fast, and the number of mothers with small children who go out to work is rapidly growing. The separate economic preoccupations of each parent are beginning to detach them both from the home and from their dependence on each other. Already, moreover, the peer-group is almost as important as the family in the social life of the children. It therefore seems possible that a new, more loosely structured, less emotionally and sexually cohesive, and far more temporary family type is already being added to the number of options available. . . . Furthermore, the historical record suggests that the likelihood of this period of extreme sexual permissiveness continuing for very long without generating a strong back-lash is not very great. (p. 427)*

Stone wrote that last sentence before the outbreak of the AIDS epidemic, which has rendered many of the young very wary in the sexual marketplace. As if she had read Stone's admonitory speculations and decided to take it to the next step, Katha Pollitt recently (1993) commented on the fact that, in America, increasing numbers of well-educated career women are choosing to remain single—even when they decide to have children. She asked:

> *What if instead of trying to bully women to the altar, we ask why they're no longer running up the aisles?*
>
> *Maybe marriage no longer serves women very well. Historically, lucky women married for love and still do—I'm sure that most of today's unwed employed moms would be pleased to tie the knot with a diaper-changing Mr. Right—but beneath the hearts and flowers, middle-class marriage was an economic bargain. He supported her; she minded the house and children.*
>
> *With rare exceptions, marriage was the only path to female adulthood: a home of one's own, community standing, a sex life, children. Barred from professional training and good jobs, threatened with disgrace and the loss of her baby if she got*

pregnant, mocked as a spinster if she stayed unwed past her early 20's, a woman was pushed into marriage by just about every social institution: family, religion, neighbors, custom, law, school, the workplace, doctors of soul and body.

None of this is true today. If women can support themselves, they don't need to marry for what was politely called security but was, to put it bluntly, money. If single women can have sex, their own homes, the respect of friends and interesting work, they don't need to tell themselves that any marriage is better than none. Why not have a child on one's own? Children are a joy; many men are not. To take care of a child makes sense: Children cannot cook their own meals, make their own doctor's appointments, do their own laundry. To take care of a husband after working all day makes much less sense, but most men still seem to expect it. All around them, single women see divorced women, raising their kids, often with little or no child support, and hear married moms say that they might as well be single for all the help they get from their mates. If single women increasingly see marriage and motherhood as separate commitments, perhaps the reason is that they are.

The collapse of the traditional middle-class marriage bargain has left both sexes bewildered, and is a major cause of the much-discussed open hostility between men and women. But how can you make the sexes act as if they needed each other to survive when they don't? All they need each other for is love, and love is hard to find. That is the nettle the family-values proponents refuse to grasp. They keep talking as if women can be corralled into marriage by appeals to morality and self-sacrifice or punitive social policies. But the futility of their cause is shown by the feeble measures they propose: deglamorizing single motherhood, emphasizing fatherhood, stigmatizing single moms or their kids.

. . . . There isn't any way, in our modern, secular society, to reconnect marriage and maternity. We'd have to bring back the whole 19th century: Restore the cult of virginity and the double standard, ban birth control, restrict divorce, kick women out of decent jobs, force unwed pregnant women to put their babies up for adoption on pain of social death, make out-of-wedlock children legal nonpersons.

None of this will happen, so why not come to terms with reality? Instead of trying to make women—and men—adapt to an outworn institution, we should adapt our institutions to the lives people actually live. Single mothers need paid maternal leave, day care, flexible schedules, child support, pediatricians with evening hours. Most of all, they need equal pay and comparable worth. What they don't need is sermons. (p. A19)

Interestingly enough, the challenges to marriage are not limited to the West. Ian Timaeus and Wendy Graham (1989) recounted a similar story when attempting to explain why in Botswana and Lesotho (Africa), in a traditional, male-dominated, polygamous society, women are beginning to refuse to marry. Traditionally, men were supposed to provide for their families. Yet, in southern Africa, this has been difficult. Locally, there have been few jobs. Farming has failed in the wake of recurring droughts and cattle disease. To make a living, men have signed year-long contracts to work in the gold mines in the Republic of South Africa. While their husbands have been gone, married women have had to run the farms and find some way to support their children. Husbands and wives, long separated, frequently have had extramarital affairs. As a consequence, over the years, marriage patterns have changed. Women are being granted the power to possess their own farms and to control their own wealth. Increasingly, men and women are choosing not to marry at all or to marry late, even when children are involved. Polygynous unions are now rare. Divorce is common. The authors have speculated that, in the near future, most men and women may find it more profitable to live together for a time than to embark on a permanent alliance. (A similar speculation has been made by Solway, 1990.) Recent research indicates that throughout the world, in rich and poor countries alike, the structure of family life is undergoing profound changes—perhaps as a consequence of women's changing social and economic status. First, marriages are dissolving (through separation, abandonment, divorce, or death) more frequently than ever before. Second, more women are the heads of households than in the past. Third, out-of-wedlock births are increasing. And, fourth, mothers now carry increasing economic responsibility for children. (Lewin, 1995)

The global story of transformations in love, sex, and marriage is one of the most arresting and far-reaching to be told, and the research is just beginning. But it is also an elusive tale. If much of the world is replaying in fifty years the epochal revolution launched by the West over the past five centuries, we must remember that the revolution is ongoing, with destinations unknown and moral consequences uncertain. We will better keep our bearings—intellectually, culturally, and personally—if we spread our study beyond narrow disciplinary confines and beyond the West, if only because the revolution itself is no longer bound by academic specialization or geographical frontiers.

Endnote

1. Although the authors, themselves, argue that passionate love does not decline with time, we are forced to conclude just the opposite. Our studies found that passionate love was higher when couples were dating exclusively, fell a bit once they were committed, and declined even more once they married. This does not seem encouraging.

References

Ablan, J. (1993, October 4). Love means abuse in some relationships. *Ka Leo O Hawai'i*, p. 1.

Abu-Lughod, L. (1986). *Veiled sentiments: Honor and poetry in a Bedouin society*. Berkeley: University of California Press.

Achebe, C. (1959). *Things fall apart*. New York: Astor-Honor.

Acton, W. (1865). *The functions and disorders of the reproductive organs in youth, in adult age, and in advanced life: Considered in their physiological, social, and psychological relations* (4th ed.). London: John Churchill.

Adams, A. (1993). *Almost perfect*. New York: A. A. Knopf.

Ahmed, L. (1992). *Women and gender in Islam*. New Haven, CT: Yale University Press.

Ainsworth, M. D. S. (1967). *Infancy in Uganda: Infant care and the growth of love*. Baltimore: Johns Hopkins University Press.

Ainsworth, M. D. S. (1989). Attachments beyond infancy. *American Psychologist, 44,* 709–716.

Ainsworth, M. D. S., Blehar, M. C., Waters, E., & Wall, S. (1978). *Patterns of attachment: A psychological study of the strange situation*. Hillsdale, NJ: Lawrence Erlbaum Associates.

Albrecht, S. L. (1979). Correlates of marital happiness among the remarried. *Journal of Marriage and the Family, 41,* 857–867.

Aldhous, P. (1992). French venture where U.S. fears to tread. *Science, 257,* 25.

Allen, G. (1895). *The woman who did*. Boston: Roberts Bros.

Allgeier, E. R., & Wiederman, M. W. (1991). Love and mate selection in the 1990s. *Free Inquiry, 11,* 25–27.

Alzate, H. (1984). Sexual behavior of unmarried Colombian university students: A five-year follow up. *Archives of Sexual Behavior, 13,* 121–132.

Alzate, H. (1989). Sexual behavior of unmarried Colombian university students: A follow up. *Archives of Sexual Behavior, 18,* 239–250.

Amis, M. (1984). *Money: A suicide note*. New York: Viking Penguin.

Ammar, H. (1954). *Growing up in an Egyptian village: Silwa, Province of Aswan*. London, England: Routledge & Kegan Paul.

Ariès, P. (1962). *Centuries of childhood*. New York: Random House.

Ariès, P. (1985). Thoughts on the history of homosexuality. In P. Ariès & A. Béjin (Eds.), *Western sexuality: Practice and percept in past and present times* (pp. 62–75). New York: B. Blackwell.

Aron, A., & Rodriguez, G. (1992, July 25). Scenarios of falling in love among Mexican-, Chinese-, and Anglo-Americans. Sixth International Conference on Personal Relationships, Orono, ME.

Asayama, S. (1975). Adolescent sex development and adult sex behavior in Japan. *The Journal of Sex Research, 11,* 91–112.

Asayama, S. (1976). Sexual behavior in Japanese students: Comparisons for 1974, 1960, and 1952. *Archives of Sexual Behavior, 5,* 371–390.

Aschenbrenner, J. (1975). *Lifelines: Black families in Chicago.* New York: Holt, Rinehart, & Winston.

Atwood, M. (1989). *Cat's eye.* New York: Doubleday.

Auden, W. H. (1980). *Collected poems.* (E. Mendelson, Ed.), Franklin Center, PA: The Franklin Library.

Averill, J. R. (1968). Grief: Its nature and significance. *Psychological Bulletin, 70,* 721–748.

Axtell, J. L. (1981). *The European and the Indian: Essays in ethnohistory of colonial North America.* New York: Oxford University Press.

Azuma, H., Kashiwagi, K., & Hess, R. (1981). *Hahaoya no taido koudou to kodomo no chiteki hattatsu* [The influence of maternal teaching style on the cognitive development of children]. Tokyo: University of Tokyo Press.

Bachman, G., Levine, T., Muto, K., & Hatfield, E. (1994). *Love schemas* and commitment. Unpublished manuscript. The University of Hawaii, Honolulu, HI.

Backhouse, E., & Bland, J. O. P. (1914). *Annals & memoirs of the court of Peking: From the 16th to the 20th century.* New York: AMS Press.

Bai, N. & Wang, X. (1988). *The social psychology of reform: Changes and choices.* Chengtu: Sichuan People's Publishing House.

Bailey, B. L. (1988). *From front porch to back seat: Courtship in twentieth-century America.* Baltimore: Johns Hopkins.

Bailey, D. S. (1955). *Homosexuality and the Western Christian tradition.* London, England: Longmans, Green, & Co.

Banner, L. W. (1983). *American beauty.* Chicago: The University of Chicago Press.

Barbee, A. P., Gulley, M. R., & Cunningham, M. R. (1990). Support seeking in personal relationships. *Journal of Social and Personal Relationships, 7,* 531–540.

Barclay, A. M. (1969). The effect of hostility on physiological fantasy responses. *Journal of Personality, 37,* 651–667.

Barnes, J. (1985). *Flaubert's parrot.* New York: Alfred A. Knopf.

Barnlund, D. (1989). *Communicative styles of Japanese and Americans: Images and realities.* Belmont, CA: Wadsworth.

Bartholomew, K., & Horowitz, L. M. (1991). Attachment styles among young adults: A test of a four-category model. *Journal of Personality and Social Psychology, 61,* 226–244.

Baucom, D. H., & Adams, A. N. (1987). Assessing communication in marital interaction. In D. D. O'Leary (Ed.), *Assessment of marital discord* (pp. 139–181). Hillsdale, NJ: Erlbaum.

Baumeister, R. F., Wotman, S. R., & Stillwell, A. M. (1993). Unrequited love: On heartbreak, anger, guilt, scriptlessness, and humiliation. *Journal of Personality and Social Psychology, 61,* 377–391.

Baxter, C. (1993). *Shadow play.* New York: W. W. Norton & Co.

Baxter, L. A. (1984). Trajectories of relationship disengagement. *Journal of Social and Personal Relationships, 1,* 29–48.

Beach, S. R. H., Sandeen, E. E., & O'Leary, K. D. (1990). *Depression in marriage.* New York: The Guilford Press.

Beck, A. (1967). *Depression: Clinical, experimental, and theoretical aspects.* New York: Hoeber.

Belcastro, P. A. (1985). Sexual behavior differences between black and white students. *The Journal of Sex Research, 21,* 56–67.

Bell, A. P., Weinberg, M. S., & Hammersmith, S. (1981). *Sexual preference: Statistical appendix.* Bloomington, IN: Indiana University Press.

Beller, E. K., & Pohl, A. (1986, April). *The Strange Situation revisited.* Paper presented at the International Conference on Infant Studies, Beverly Hills, CA.

Bellew-Smith, M., & Korn, J. H. (1986). Merger intimacy status in adult women. *Journal of Personality and Social Psychology, 50,* 1186–1191.

Bem, S. L. (1993). *The lenses of gender.* New Haven, CT: Yale University Press.

Bendix, R. (1964). *Nation-building and citizenship: Studies of our changing social order.* New York: Wiley.

Berry, J. W., Poortinga, Y. H., Segall, M. H., & Dasen, P. R. (1992). *Cross-cultural psychology: Research and applications.* Cambridge, England: Cambridge University Press.

Berscheid, E. (1993). Foreword. In A. E. Beall & R. J. Sternberg (Eds.), *The psychology of gender* (pp. vii–xvii). New York: Guilford Press.

Berscheid, E., & Fei, J. (1977). Romantic love and sexual jealousy. In G. Clanton & L. G. Smith

(Eds.), *Jealousy* (pp. 101–114). Englewood Cliffs, NJ: Prentice-Hall.

Berscheid, E., Snyder, M., & Omoto, A. (1989). The Relationship Closeness Inventory: Assessing the closeness of interpersonal relationships. *Journal of Personality and Social Psychology, 57,* 792–807.

Bhatia, J. (1986, February 27). Taboos: Lifting India's fig-leaf prudery. *Far Eastern Economic Review,* p. 37–38.

Blackwood, E. (1986). Breaking the mirror: The construction of lesbianism and the anthropological discourse on homosexuality. *The many faces of homosexuality: Anthropological approaches to homosexual behavior* (pp. 1–17). New York: Harington Park Press.

Blanchard, D. C., & Blanchard, R. J. (1982). Hawaii: Violence, a preliminary analysis. In A. P. Goldstein & M. H. Segall (Eds.), *Global perspectives on aggression* (pp. 159–192). New York: Pergamon Press.

Bleier, R. (1984). *Science and gender: A critique of biology and its theories on women.* New York: Pergamon Press.

Blood, R. O., Jr. (1967). *Love match and arranged marriage.* New York: Free Press.

Blood, R. O., & Wolfe, D. M. (1960). *Husbands and wives: The dynamics of married living.* New York: Free Press.

Bloom, B. L., White, S. W., & Asher, S. J. (1979). Marital disruption as a stressful life event. In G. Levinger & O. C. Moles (Eds.), *Divorce and separation* (pp. 184–200). New York: Basic Books.

Blumstein, P., & Schwartz, P. (1983). *American couples.* New York: Morrow.

Bolton, R. (1994). Sex, science, and social responsibility: Cross-cultural research on same-sex eroticism and sexual intolerance. *Cross-Cultural Research, 28,* 134–190.

Bowlby, J. (1969). *Attachment and loss: Vol 1. Attachment.* New York: Basic Books.

Bowlby, J. (1973). Affectional bonds: Their nature and origin. In R. Weiss (Ed.), *Loneliness: The experience of emotional and social isolation* (pp. 38–52). Cambridge, MA: MIT Press.

Bowlby, J. (1979). *The making and breaking of affectional bonds.* London: Tavistock Publications.

Bowlby, J. (1980). *Attachment and loss: Vol 3. Sadness and depression.* New York: Basic Books.

Braudel, F. (1984). *The perspective of the world.* (S. Reynolds, Trans.). New York: Harper & Row.

Breakwell, G. M., & Fife-Schaw, C. (1992). Sexual activities and preferences in a United Kingdom sample of 16–20 year olds. *Archives of Sexual Behavior, 21,* 271–293.

Brenner, M. (1991). Erotomania. *Vanity Fair, 54,* 188–195.

Bressler, L. C., & Lavender, A. D. (1986). Sexual fulfillment of heterosexual, bisexual, and homosexual women. *Journal of Homosexuality, 12,* 109–122.

Briffault, R. (1927). *The mothers: A study of the origins of sentiments and institutions* (Vol. 1). London, England: George Allen & Unwin.

Bringle, R. G., & Buunk, B. (1986). Examining the causes and consequences of jealousy: Some recent findings and issues. In R. Gilmour & S. Duck (Eds.), *The emerging field of personal relationships* (pp. 225–240). Hillsdale, NJ: Erlbaum.

Britton, D. M. (1990). Homophobia and homosociality: An analysis of boundary maintenance. *Sociological Quarterly, 3,* 423–439.

Brontë, C. (1950). *Jane Eyre.* New York: The Modern Library.

Brooke, J. (1991, March 29). "Honor" killing of wives is outlawed in Brazil. *The New York Times,* Sec. B, p. 16.

Broude, G. J. & Green, S. J. (1983). Cross-cultural codes on husband-wife relationships. *Ethology, 22,* 273–274.

Broverman, I., Vogel, S., Broverman, D., Clarkson, F., & Rosenkrantz, P. (1972). Sex role stereotypes: A current appraisal. *Journal of Social Issues, 28,* 59–78.

Brown, D. E. (1991). *Human universals.* Philadelphia, PA: Temple University Press.

Browne, A. (1993). Violence against women by male partners: Prevalence, outcomes, and policy implications. *American Psychologist, 48,* 1077–1087.

Bryson, J. B. (1977, August). Situational determinants of the expression of jealousy. In H. Sigall (Chair), *Sexual jealousy.* Symposium presented at the 85th meeting of the American Psychological Association, San Francisco, CA.

Bullough, V. L. (1990). History and the understanding of human sexuality. *Annual Review of Sex Research, 1,* 75–92.

Bumroongsook, S. (1992). *Conventions of mate selection in twentieth-century central Thailand*. Unpublished Masters thesis. Department of History, University of Hawaii, Honolulu, HI.

Burton, R. (1621/1927). *The anatomy of melancholy*. London: Longman.

Burton, S. (1990, May 14). Straight talk on sex in China. *Time*, p. 82.

Buss, D. M. (1985). Human mate selection. *American Scientist, 73*, 47–51.

Buss, D. M. (1988a). Love acts: The evolutionary biology of love. In R. J. Sternberg & M. L. Barnes (Eds.), *The psychology of love* (pp. 100–118). New Haven: Yale University Press.

Buss, D. M. (1988b). The evolution of human intrasexual competition: Tactics of mate attraction. *Journal of Personality and Social Psychology, 54*, 616–628.

Buss, D. M. (1989). Sex differences in human mate preferences: Evolutionary hypotheses tested in 37 cultures. *Behavioral and Brain Sciences, 12*, 1–49.

Buss, D. M. (1992). Sex differences in jealousy: Evolution, physiology, and psychology. *Psychological Science, 3*, 251–255.

Buss, D. M. (1994). *The evolution of desire*. New York: Basic Books.

Buss, D. M. and 49 colleagues. (1990). International preferences in selecting mates: A study of 37 cultures. *Journal of Cross-Cultural Psychology, 21*, 5–47.

Buss, D. M., & Barnes, M. (1986). Preferences in human mate selection. *Journal of Personality and Social Psychology, 50*, 559–570.

Buss, D. M., & Schmitt, D. P. (1993). Sexual strategies theory: An evolutionary perspective on human mating. *Psychological Review, 100*, 204–232.

Butterfield, F. (1982). Sex without joy love and marriage. *China: Alive in the bitter sea* (pp. 129–161). New York, NY: Times Books.

Buunk, B. P. (1980). Extramarital sex in the Netherlands: Motivations in social and marital context. *Alternative Lifestyles, 3*, 11–39.

Buunk, B., & Hupka, R. B. (1987). Cross-cultural differences in the elicitation of sexual jealousy. *Journal of Sex Research, 23*, 12–22.

Byrne, D., Clore, G. L., & Smeaton, G. (1986). The attraction hypothesis: Do similar attitudes affect anything? *Journal of Personality and Social Psychology, 51*, 1167–1170.

Byrne, D., Gouaux, C., Griffitt, W., Lamberth, J., Murakawa, N., Prasad, M., Prasad, A., & Ramirez, M. III. (1971). The ubiquitous relationship: Attitude similarity and attraction—a cross-cultural study. *Human Relations, 24*, 201–207.

Caldwell, M. A., & Peplau, L. A. (1982). Sex differences in same-sex friendship. *Sex Roles, 8*, 721–732.

Call, V. R. A., Sprecher, S., & Schwartz, P. (in press). The frequency of marital sex. *Journal of Marriage and the Family*.

Campbell, J. (1964). *Honour, family, and patronage: A study of institutions and moral values in a Greek mountain community*. Oxford: Clarendon Press.

Campbell, W. K., Sedikides, C., & Bosson, J. (1994). Romantic involvement, self-discrepancy, and psychological well-being: A preliminary investigation. *Personal Relationships, 1*, 399–404.

Campos, J. J., Barrett, K., Lamb, M. E., Goldsmith, H. H., & Stenberg, C. (1983). Socioemotional development. In M. M. Haith & J. J. Campos (Eds.), *Handbook of child psychology: Vol. 2. Infancy and psychobiology* (pp. 783–915). New York: Wiley.

Camus, A. (1989). *The stranger*. (M. Ward, Trans.), New York: Vintage Books.

Capellanus, A. (1174/1941). *The art of courtly love* (J. J. Parry, Trans.). New York: Norton.

Cappella, J. N., & Palmer, M. T. (1990). Attitude similarity, relational history, and attraction: The mediating effects of kinesic and vocal behaviors. *Communication Monographs, 57*, 161–183.

Carey, P. (1988). *Oscar & Lucinda*. New York: Harper & Row.

Carlson, J. G., & Hatfield, E. (1992). *Psychology of emotion*. Fort Worth, TX: Harcourt, Brace, Jovanovich.

Carns, D. E. (1973). Talking about sex: Notes on first coitus and the double sexual standard. *Journal of Marriage and the Family, 35*, 677–688.

Carstairs, J. M. (1956). Hinjra and Jiryan: Two derivatives of Hindu attitude to sexuality. *British Journal of Medical Psychiatry, 29*, 128-138.

Castañeda, D. M. (1993). The meaning of romantic love among Mexican-Americans. *Journal of Social Behavior and Personality, 8*, 257–272.

Cate, R. M., Henton, J., Koval, J., Christopher, F. S., & Lloyd, S. A. (1982). Premarital abuse: A social psychological perspective. *Journal of Family Issues, 3*, 79–90.

Cate, R. M., & Lloyd, S. A. (1992). *Courtship*. Newbury Park, CA: Sage.

Caudill, W., & Weinstein, S. (1969). Maternal care and infant behavior in Japan and America. *Psychiatry, 32*, 12–43.

Cazenave, N. A., & Straus, M. A. (1990). Race, class, network embeddedness, and family violence: A search for potent support systems. In M. A. Straus & R. J. Gelles (Eds.), *Physical violence in American families* (pp. 321–339). New Brunswick, NJ: Transaction Publishers.

Chan, D. W. (1990). Sex knowledge, attitudes, and experience of Chinese medical students in Hong Kong. *Archives of Sexual Behavior, 19*, 73–93.

Chang, C-s. (1928/1968). *Sex histories: China's first modern treatise on sex education.* (H. S. Levy, Trans.), Yokohama: Hakuen Sha.

Chekhov, A. P. (1912). Ivanoff. (M. Fell, Trans.), *Plays of Anton Tchekoff* (pp. 73–153). New York: Charles Scribner's Sons.

Chenault, K. (1992, October 29). China's rigid anti-homosexuality attitude bends a bit. Honolulu, HI: *Star Bulletin*, p. A-17.

Choo, P., Levine, T., & Hatfield, E. (1995). *Gender, Love schemas, and reactions to romantic break-ups. Unpublished manuscript. University of Hawaii, Honolulu, HI.*

Christensen, A., & Heavey, C. L. (1990). Gender and social structure in the demand/withdraw pattern of marital conflict. *Journal of Personality and Social Psychology, 59*, 73–81.

Christensen, H. T. (1973). Attitudes toward marital infidelity: A nine-cultural sampling of university student opinion. *Journal of Comparative Family Studies, 4*, 197–214.

Chu, G. C. (1985). The changing concept of self in contemporary China. In A. J. Marsella, G. DeVos, & F. L. K. Hus (Eds.), *Culture and self: Asian and Western perspectives* (pp. 252–277). London, England: Tavistock.

Chu, G. C., & Ju, Y. (1993). *The great wall in ruins.* New York: State University of New York Press.

Cisneros, S. (1992). One holy night. In F. B. Evans, B. Gleason, & M. Wiley (Eds.), *Cultural tapestry: Readings for a pluralistic society* (pp. 112–117). New York: HarperCollins.

Clanton, G., & Smith, L. G. (Eds.) (1987). *Jealousy.* Lantham, MA: University Press of America.

Clark, R. D., III, & Hatfield, E. (1989). Gender differences in receptivity to sexual offers. *Journal of Psychology and Human Sexuality, 2*, 39–55.

Clayton, P. J. (1982). Bereavement. In E. S. Paykel (Ed.), *Handbook of affective disorders* (pp. 403–415). New York: The Guilford Press.

Clayton, R. R., & Bokemeier, J. L. (1980). Premarital sex in the seventies. *Journal of Marriage and the Family, 40*, 9–21.

Cleage, P. (1993). *Deals with the devil and other reasons to riot.* New York: Ballantine.

Clement, U., Schmidt, G., & Kruse, M. (1984). Changes in sex differences in sexual behavior: A replication of a study on West German students (1966–1981). *Archives of Sexual Behavior, 13*, 99–120.

Cohen, S. (1976). *Social and personality development in childhood.* New York: Macmillan.

Cohen, Y. (1969). Ends and means to political control: State organizations and the punishment of adultery, incest, and violation of celibacy. *American Anthropologist, 71*, 658–687.

Coleman, E. M., Hoon, P. W., & Hoon, E. F. (1983). Arousability and sexual satisfaction in lesbian and heterosexual women. *The Journal of Sex Research, 19*, 58–73.

Collier, J. F., & Rosaldo, M. Z. (1981). Politics and gender in simple societies. In S. B. Ortner & H. Whitehead (Eds.), *Sexual meanings. The cultural construction of gender and sexuality* (pp. 275–329). Cambridge: Cambridge University Press.

Collins, N. L., & Read, S. J. (1990). Adult attachment, working models, and relationship quality in dating couples. *Journal of Personality and Social Psychology, 58*, 644–663.

Coontz, S. (1988). *The social origins of private life: A history of American families, 1600–1900.* London, England: Verso.

Cornell, L. L. (1989). Gender differences in remarriage after divorce in Japan and the United

States. *Journal of Marriage and the Family, 51,* 457–463.

Counts, D. A. (1987). Female suicide and wife abuse: A cross-cultural perspective. *Suicide and Life-Threatening Behavior, 17,* 194–204.

Counts, D. A. (1991). "All men do it": Wife beating in Kaliai, Papua New Guinea. In D. A. Counts, J. K. Brown, & J. C. Campbell, (Eds.), *Sanctions and sanctuary: Cultural perspectives on the beating of wives* (pp. 63–76). Boulder, CO: Westview Press.

Counts, D. A., Brown, J. K., Campbell, J. C. (1992). *Sanctions & sanctuary: Cultural perspectives on the beating of wives.* Boulder, CO: Westview Press.

Crittenden, P. M. (1988). Relationships at risk. In J. Belsky & T. Nezworski (Eds.), *Clinical implications of attachment* (pp. 136–174). Hillsdale, NJ: Erlbaum.

Crossette, B. (1994, September 14). Population debate: The premises are changed. *The New York Times International,* p. A3.

Cunningham, M. R. (1991). *A psycho-evolutionary, multiple-motive interpretation of physical attractiveness.* Speech delivered at the 99th meeting of the American Psychological Association, San Francisco, CA.

Cunningham, M. R., Barbee, A. P., & Pike, C. L. (1990). What do women want? Facialmetric assessment of multiple motives in the perception of male facial physical attractiveness. *Journal of Personality and Social Psychology, 59,* 61–72.

Cupach, W. R., & Metts, S. (1986). Accounts of relational dissolution: A comparison of marital and non-marital relationships. *Communication Monographs, 53,* 311–334.

Daly, M., & Wilson, M. (1988a). Evolutionary social psychology and family homicide. *Science, 242,* 519–524.

Daly, M., & Wilson, M. (1988b). *Homicide.* Hawthorne, NY: Aldine.

Daly, M., Wilson, M., & Weghorst, S. J. (1982). Male sexual jealousy. *Ethology and Sociobiology, 3,* 11–27.

Daniels, T., & Shaver, P. R. (1991). *Attachment styles and power strategies in romantic relationships.* Unpublished manuscript, Department of Psychology, State University of New York at Buffalo.

Darling, C. A., & Davidson, J. K. (1986). Coitally active university students: Sexual behaviours, concerns, and challenges. *Adolescence, 21,* 403–419.

Darling, C. A., Davidson, J. K., & Cox, R. P. (1991). Female sexual response and the timing of partner orgasm. *Journal of Sex and Marital Therapy, 17,* 3–21.

Darling, C. A., Kallen, D. J., & Van Dusen, J. E. (1984). Sex in transition, 1900–1980. *Journal of Youth and Adolescence, 13,* 385–399.

Darnton, R. (1984). *The great cat massacre.* New York: Basic Books.

Darwin, C. (1871). *The descent of man and selection in relation to sex.* London: Murray.

Davis, D. A., & Davis, S. S. (1994). Sexual values in a Moroccan town. In W. J. Lonner & R. Malpass (Eds.), *Psychology and culture* (pp. 225–230). Boston, MA: Allyn & Bacon.

Davis, J. A., & Smith, T. W. (1991, July). *General social surveys, 1972–1991.* Chicago: National Opinion Research Center: University of Chicago.

Davis, K. (1948/1977). Jealousy and sexual property. In G. Clanton & L. G. Smith (Eds.), *Jealousy* (pp. 129–135). Englewood Cliffs, NJ: Prentice-Hall.

Davis, K. E., & Todd, M. J. (1982). Friendship and love relationships. In K. E. Davis (Ed.), *Advances in descriptive psychology* (Vol. 2, pp. 79–122). Greenwich, CT: JAI.

DeBuono, B. A., Zinner, S. H., Daamen, M., & McCormack, W. M. (1990). Sexual behavior of college women in 1975, 1986, and 1989. *New England Journal of Medicine, 322,* 821–825.

Defoe, D. (1727). *Conjugal lewdness: Or, matrimonial whoredom.* London: T. Warner.

Degler, C. N. (1978). What ought to be and what was: Women's sexuality in the nineteenth century. In M. Gordon (Ed.), *The American family in social-historical perspective* (2nd ed.). (pp. 403–425). New York: St. Martin's Press.

Degler, C. N. (1980). *At odds: Women and the family in America from the revolution to the present.* New York: Oxford University Press.

deJong-Gierveld, J. (1986). Loneliness and the degree of intimacy in interpersonal relationships. In R. Gilmour & S. Duck (Eds.), *The emerging field of personal relationships* (pp. 241–249). Hillsdale, NJ: Earlbaum.

DeLamater, J. (1987). Gender differences in sexual scenarios. In K. Kelley (Ed.), *Females, males, and sexuality: Theories and research* (pp. 127–139). Albany, NY: SUNY Press.

DeLamater, J., & MacCorquodale, P. (1979). *Premarital sexuality: Attitudes, relationships, behavior.* Madison, WI: University of Wisconsin Press.

DeLillo, D. (1988). *Libra.* New York: Viking.

D'Emilio, J., & Freedman, E., (1988). *Intimate matters: A history of sexuality in America.* New York: Harper & Row.

De Mente, B. (1989). *Everything Japanese.* Lincolnwood, IL: Passport Books.

deRougemont, D. (1940). *Love in the Western world* (M. Belgion, Trans.). New York: Harcourt, Brace & World.

de Sade, Marquis. (1797/1963). *Histoire de Juliette,* in *Oeuvres complètes du marquis de Sade* (Vol. 9). Paris, France: Cercle du Livre Précieux.

Dewaraja, R., & Sasaki, Y. (1991). Semen-loss syndrome: A comparison between Sri Lanka and Japan. *American Journal of Psychotherapy, 45,* 14–20.

Diamond, M. (1993). Homosexuality and bisexuality in different populations. *Archives of sexual behavior, 22,* 291–310.

Dilman, I. (1987). *Love and human separateness.* Oxford, England: Basil Blackwell.

Dindia, K., & Allen, M. (1992). Sex differences in self-disclosure: A meta-analysis. *Psychological Bulletin, 112,* 106–124.

Dion, K. K., & Dion, K. L. (1993). Individualistic and collectivistic perspectives on gender and the cultural context of love and intimacy. *Journal of Social Issues, 49,* 53–69.

Dixon, B. W., Streiff, E. J., & Brunwasser, A. H. (1991). Pilot study of household survey to determine HIV seroprevalence. *Morbidity and Morality Weekly Report, 40,* 1–5.

Doherty, R. W., Hatfield, E., Thompson, K., & Choo, P. (1994). Cultural and ethnic influences on love and attachment. *Personal Relationships, 1,* 391–398.

Doi, L. T. (1963). Some thoughts on helplessness and the desire to be loved. *Psychiatry, 26,* 266–272.

Doi, L. T. (1973). *The anatomy of dependence* (J. Bester, Trans.). Tokyo: Kodansha International.

Donnelly, D. A. (1993). Sexually inactive marriages. *Journal of Sex Research, 30,* 171–179.

Drigotas, S. M., & Rusbult, C. E. (1992). Should I stay or should I go? A dependence model of breakups. *Journal of Personality and Social Psychology, 62,* 62–87.

Duben, A., & Behar, C. (1991). *Istanbul households.* Cambridge, England: Cambridge University Press.

Duberman, M. B. (1989). "Writhing bedfellows" in antebellum South Carolina: Historical interpretation and the politics of evidence. In M. B. Duberman, M. Vicinus, & G. Chauncey, Jr. (Eds.), *Hidden from history: Reclaiming the gay and lesbian past* (pp. 153–168). Markam, Ontario, Canada: New American Library.

Duberman, M. B., Vicinus, M., & Chauncey, G. Jr. (1989). *Hidden from history: Reclaiming the gay and lesbian past.* Markam, Ontario, Canada: New American Library.

Duck, S. (1991). *Personal relationships and social support.* London: Sage Publications.

Dunn, J. (1989). *Modern revolutions: An introduction to the analysis of a political phenomenon.* Cambridge, England: Cambridge University Press.

Dutton, D., & Aron, A. (1974). Some evidence for heightened sexual attraction under conditions of high anxiety. *Journal of Personality and Social Psychology, 30,* 510–517.

Eibl-Eibesfeldt, I. (1971). *Love and hate.* New York: Holt, Rinehart & Winston.

Eidelson, R. J. (1983). Affiliation and independence issues in marriage. *Journal of Marriage and the Family, 45,* 683–688.

Ellis, B. J., & Symons, D. (1990). Sex differences in sexual fantasy: An evolutionary psychological approach. *The Journal of Sex Research, 27,* 527–555.

Ellrich, R. J. (1985, May). Modes of discourse and the language of sexual reference in eighteenth-century French fiction. In R. P. Maccubin (Ed.), *Unauthorized sexual behavior during the Enlightenment,* a special issue of *Eighteenth-Century Life, 9,* p. 222.

Elvin, M. (1984). Female virtue and the state in China. *Past and Present, 104,* 111–152.

Erchak, G. M., & Rosenfeld, R. (1994). Societal isolation, violent norms, and gender relations: A reexamination and extension of Levinson's model of wife beating. *Cross-Cultural Research, 28,* 111–133.

Erdrich, L. (1988). *Tracks*. New York: Harper and Row.

Erikson, E. H. (1959). Identity and the life cycle. *Psychological Issues, 1*, Monograph 1.

Erikson, E. H. (1982). *The life cycle completed: A review.* New York: Norton.

Erlich, V. St. (1966). *Family in transition: A study of 300 Yugoslav villages*. Princeton, NJ: Princeton University Press.

Ehrlichman, H., & Eichenstein, R. (1992). Private wishes: Gender similarities and differences. *Sex Roles, 26*, 399–421.

Ernaux, A. (1993). *Simple passion*. (Tanya Leslie, Trans.). New York: Four Walls Eight Windows.

Evola, J. (1983). *The metaphysics of sex*. New York: Inner Tradition.

Ewart, A. (1967). *The great lovers*. New York: Hart.

Family Planning Association of Hong Kong. (1987). *Adolescent sexuality study 1986*. Hong Kong: Family Planning Association.

Fausto-Sterling, A. (1986). *Myths of gender*. New York: HarperCollins.

Feeney, J. A., & Noller, P. (1990). Attachment style as a predictor of adult romantic relationships. *Journal of Personality and Social Psychology, 58*, 281–291.

Fehr, B. (1988). Prototype analysis of the concepts of love and commitment. *Journal of Personality and Social Psychology, 55*, 557–579.

Fehr, B. (1993). How do I love thee? Let me consult my prototype. In S. Duck (Ed.). *Individuals in relationships: Understanding Relationship Processes Series*, Vol 1. (pp. 87–120). Newbury Park, CA: Sage.

Fehr, B., & Russell, J. A. (1991). Concept of love viewed from a prototype perspective. *Journal of Personality and Social Psychology, 60*, 425–438.

Ferraro, G. A. (1993, August 11). U.N. needs to act on rights of women. *The New York Times*, A12.

Fine, M. A., & Fine, D. R. (1994). An examination and evaluation of recent changes in divorce laws in five Western countries: The critical role of values. *Journal of Marriage and the Family, 56*, 249–263.

Fischer, K. W., Shaver, P. R., & Carnochan, P. (1990). How emotions develop and how they organize development. *Cognition and Emotion, 4*, 81–127.

Fisher, C. (1987). *Postcards From the Edge*. New York: Simon & Schuster.

Fisher, H. E. (1989). Evolution of human serial pair-bonding. *American Journal of Physical Anthropology, 78*, 331–354.

Fisher, H. E. (1992). *Anatomy of love: The natural history of monogamy, adultery, and divorce*. New York: W. W. Norton.

Fisher, S. (1980). Personality correlates of sexual behavior in black women. *Archives of Sexual Behavior, 9*, 27–35.

Fishman, P. M. (1978). Interaction: The work women do. *Social Problems, 25*, 397–406.

Fitness, J., & Fletcher, G. J. O. (1993). Love, hate, anger, and jealousy in close relationships: A prototype and cognitive appraisal analysis. *Journal of Personality and Social Psychology, 65*, 942–958.

Foa, U. G., Anderson, B., Converse, J. Jr., Urbansky, W. A., Cawley, M. J. III, Muhlhausen, S. M., & Tornblom, K. Y. (1987). Gender-related sexual attitudes: Some crosscultural similarities and differences. *Sex Roles, 16*, 511–519.

Ford, C. S., & Beach, F. A. (1951). *Patterns of sexual behavior*. New York: Harper & Row.

Ford, K., & Norris, A. E. (1993). Urban hispanic adolescents and young adults: Relationship of acculturation to sexual behavior. *Journal of Sex Research, 30*, 316–323.

Forrest, J. D., & Singh, S. (1990). The sexual and reproductive behavior of American women, 1982–1988. *Family Planning Perspectives, 22*, 206–214.

Frayser, S. G. (1985). *Varieties of sexual experience: An anthropological perspective on human sexuality*. New Haven, CT: HRAF Press.

Frazier, P. A., & Cook, S. W. (1993). Correlates of distress following heterosexual relationship dissolution. *Journal of Social and Personal Relationships, 10*, 55–67.

Freud, S. (1933/1953). Contributions to the psychology of love: A special type of choice of objects made by men. In E. Jones (Ed.), *Collected papers* (Vol. 4) (pp. 192–202). London, England: Hogarth Press.

Friday, N. (1973). *My secret garden*. New York: Pocket Books.

Fukutake, T. (1981). *Japanese society today*. (2nd Ed.). Tokyo: University of Tokyo Press.

Fukuda, N. (1991). Women in Japan. In L. L. Adler (Ed.), *Women in cross-cultural perspective.* (pp. 205–219). Westport, CT: Praeger.

Furstenberg, F. F. Jr., & Spanier, G. B. (1984). *Recycling the family: Remarriage after divorce.* Beverly Hills, CA: Sage Publications.

Gadlin, H. (1977). Private lives and public order: A critical view of the history of intimate relationships in the United States. In G. Levinger & H. L. Rausch (Eds.), *Perspectives on the meaning of intimacy* (pp. 33–72). Amherst, MA: University of Massachusetts Press.

Gadpaille, W. (1975). *The cycles of sex.* New York: Charles Scribner's Sons.

Gagnon, J. H. (1977). *Human sexualities.* Glenview, IL: Scott, Foresman.

Gagnon, J. H., & Simon, W. (1987). The sexual scripting of oral-genital contacts. *Archives of Sexual Behavior, 16,* 1–25.

Gallup Poll. (1989). *Marriage satisfaction.* Los Angeles: Los Angeles Times Syndicate.

Gangestad, S. W. (1993). Sexual selection and physical attractiveness: Implications for mating dynamics. *Human Nature, 4,* 205–236.

Gangestad, S. W., Thornhill, R., & Yeo, R. A. (1994). Facial attractiveness, developmental stability, and fluctuating asymmetry. *Ethnology and Sociobiology, 15,* 73–85.

Gao, G. (1991). Stability of romantic relationships in China and the United States. In S. T. Toomey & F. Korzenny (Eds.), *Cross-cultural interpersonal communication,* (Vol. 15), (pp. 99–115). London: Sage Publications.

Gargan, E. A. (1993, December 30). Bangalore journal: For many brides in India, a dowry buys death. *The New York Times International,* A5.

Gay, J. (1986). "Mummies and babies" and friends and lovers in Lesotho. In E. Blackwood (Ed.), *The many faces of homosexuality: Anthropological approaches to homosexual behavior* (pp. 97–116). New York: Harrington Park Press.

Gay, P. (1984). *The Bourgeois experience: Victoria to Freud. Education of the senses.* (Vol. 1). New York: Oxford University Press.

Gay, P. (1986). *The Bourgeois experience: Victoria to Freud. The tender passion.* (Vol. 2). New York: Oxford University Press.

Gayford, J. J. (1979). Battered wives. *British Journal of Hospital Medicine, 22,* 496, 503.

Gebhard, P. H., & Johnson, A. B. (1979). *The Kinsey data: Marginal tabulations of the 1938–1963 interviews conducted by the Institute for Sex Research.* Philadelphia: Saunders.

Geertz, C. (1960). *The religion of Java.* Chicago: University of Chicago Press.

Ghose, Z. (1984). *The beautiful empire.* Woodstock, NY: The Overlook Press.

Gil, V. E. (1992). Clinical notes: The cut sleeve revisited: A brief ethnographic interview with a male homosexual in mainland China. *The Journal of Sex Research, 29,* 569–577.

Gilligan, C. (1982). *In a different voice.* Cambridge, MA: Harvard University Press.

Gillis, J. R. (1985). *For better, for worse: British marriages, 1600 to the present.* New York: Oxford University Press.

Glass, S. P., & Wright, T. L. (1985). Sex differences in type of extramarital involvement and marital dissatisfaction. *Sex Roles, 12,* 1101–1120.

Glass, S. P., & Wright, T. L. (1992). Justifications for extramarital relationships: The association between attitudes, behaviors, and gender. *Journal of Sex Research, 29,* 361–387.

Glick, P. C. (1984). Marriage, divorce, and living arrangements: Prospective changes. *Journal of Family Issues, 5,* 7–26.

Glick, P. C. (1989). Remarried families, stepfamilies and stepchildren: A brief demographic profile. *Family Relations, 38,* 24–37.

Goleman, D. (1985, September 10). Patterns of love charted in studies. *The New York Times,* p. Y13.

Goleman, D. (1986, April 1). Two views of marriage explored: His and hers. *The New York Times,* p. Y19.

Golod, S. (1993). Sex and young people. In I. Kon & J. Riordan (Eds.), *Sex and Russian society* (pp. 135–151). Bloomington, IN: Indiana University Press.

Goode, W. J. (1959). The theoretical importance of love. *American Sociological Review, 24,* 38–47.

Goode, W. J. (1963). *World revolution and family patterns.* New York: Free Press.

Goode, W. J. (1993). *World changes in divorce patterns.* New Haven, CT: Yale University Press.

Goodwin, G. (1942). *The social organization of the Western Apache.* Chicago: University of Chicago Press.

Goossens, F. A. (1986). *The quality of attachment relationships of two-year-old children of working and nonworking mothers and some associated factors (Doctoral dissertation, University of Leiden, Netherlands).*

Gorer, G. (1938). *Himalayan village.* London, England: Michael Joseph.

Gould, L. (1970). *Such good friends.* New York: Random House.

Gouldsbury, C., & Sheane, H. (1911). *The Great Plateau of Northern Rhodesia.* London: Edward Arnold.

Gray, J. D., & Silver, R. C. (1990). Opposite sides of the same coin. Former spouses' divergent perspectives in coping with their divorce. *Journal of Personality and Social Psychology, 59,* 1180–1191.

Greeley, A. M. (1991). *Faithful attraction: Discovering intimacy, love, and fidelity in American marriage.* New York: Doherty.

Greenblat, C. S. (1983). The salience of sexuality in the early years of marriage. *Journal of Marriage and the Family, 45,* 289–299.

Greenhouse, S. (1994, February 3). State dept. finds widespread abuse of world's women. *The New York Times, 143,* 1A–6A.

Gregersen, E. (1982). *Sexual practices: The story of human sexuality.* New York: Franklin Watts.

Griffitt, W., & Hatfield, E. (1985). *Human sexual behavior.* Glenview, IL: Scott, Foresman.

Gross, J. (1993, September 25). Combating rape on campus in a class on sexual consent. *The New York Times,* pp. A1, Y7.

Grossmann, K. E., Grossmann, K., Huber, F., & Wartner, U. (1981). German children's behavior toward their mothers at 12 months and their fathers at 18 months in Ainsworth's Strange Situation. *International Journal of Behavioral Development, 4,* 157–181.

Gryl, F. E., Stith, S. M., & Bird, G. W. (1991). Close dating relationships among college students: Differences by use of violence and by gender. *Journal of Social and Personal Relationships, 8,* 243–264.

Gudykunst, W., & Nishida, T. (1986). The influence of cultural variability on perceptions of communication behavior associated with relationship terms. *Human Communication Research, 13,* 147–166.

Guisinger, S., & Blatt, S. J. (1994). Individuality and relatedness: Evolution of a fundamental dialectic. *American Psychologist, 49,* 104–111.

Gupta, S. (1992) *Memories of rain.* New York: Grove Press.

Gupta, U. & Singh, P. (1982). An exploratory study of love and liking and type of marriage. *Indian Journal of Applied Psychology, 19,* 92–97.

Halpern, D. M. (1990). *One hundred years of homosexuality and other essays on Greek love.* New York: Routledge.

Hammerstein, O. II. (1945). *Carmen Jones.* New York: Alfred A. Knopf.

Hampton, C. (1989). *Les liaisons dangereuses.* Hollywood, CA: Script City Publishers.

Handy, E. S. C. (1923). The native culture of the Marquesas. *Bulletin-Bernice P. Bishop Museum* No. 9. Honolulu, HI.

Harlow, H. F. (1975). Lust, latency and love: Simian secrets of successful sex. *Journal of Sex Research, 11,* 79–90.

Harlow, H. F., Harlow, M. K., & Suomi, S. J. (1971). From thought to therapy: Lessons from a primate laboratory. *American Scientist, 59,* 539–549.

Harris Poll (1988). *Survey for Project Hope.* Louis Harris & Associates, New York.

Harrison, D. E., Bennett, W. H., Globetti, G., & Alsikafi, M. (1974). Premarital sexual standards of rural youth. *Journal of Sex Research, 10,* 266–277.

Hart, D. M. (1976). *The Aith Waryaghar of the Moroccan Rif.* Tucson: University of Arizona Press.

Hart, D. V. (1968). Homosexuality and transvestism in the Philippines. *Behavioral Science Notes, 3,* 211–248.

Harvey, J., Agostinelli, G., & Weber, A. (1989). Account-making and the formation of expectations about close relationships. In C. Hendrick (Ed.), *Review of personality and social psychology,* (Vol. 10), (pp. 39–62). Newbury Park, CA: Sage.

Hatano, Y. (1991). Changes in the sexual activities of Japanese youth. *Journal of Sex Education and Therapy, 17,* 1–14.

Hatfield, E. (1993, October 16). Passion and its enemies. Paper delivered at the Society for Experimental Social Psychology meetings, Santa Barbara, CA.

Hatfield, E., Brinton, C., & Cornelius, J. (1989). Passionate love and anxiety in young adolescents. *Motivation and Emotion, 13,* 271–289.

Hatfield, E., Cacioppo, J., & Rapson, R. L. (1994). *Emotional contagion.* Cambridge, England: Cambridge University Press.

Hatfield, E., & Rapson, R. L. (1987a). Gender differences in love and intimacy: The fantasy vs. the reality. In W. Ricketts & H. L. Gochros (Eds.), *Intimate relationships: Some social work perspectives on love* (pp. 15–26). New York: Hayworth Press.

Hatfield, E., & Rapson, R. L. (1987b). Passionate love: New directions in research. *Advances in Personal Relationships, 1,* 109–139.

Hatfield, E., & Rapson, R. L. (1987c). Passionate love/sexual desire: Can the same paradigm explain both? *Archives of Sexual Behavior, 16,* 259–278.

Hatfield, E., & Rapson, R. L. (1992a, July 25). *Ethnic differences in passionate love.* Paper presented at the International Conference on Personal Relations, Orono, Maine.

Hatfield, E., & Rapson, R. L. (1992b). Similarity and attraction in close relationships. *Communication Monographs, 59,* 209–212.

Hatfield, E., & Rapson, R. (1993a). Historical and cross cultural perspectives on passionate love and sexual desire. *Annual Review of Sex Research, 4,* 67–98.

Hatfield, E., & Rapson, R. L. (1993b). *Love, sex, and intimacy: Their psychology, biology, and history.* New York: HarperCollins.

Hatfield, E., Schmitz, E., Cornelius, J., & Rapson, R. L. (1988). Passionate love: How early does it begin? *Journal of Psychology and Human Sexuality, 1,* 35–52.

Hatfield, E., Schmitz, E., Parpart, L., & Weaver, H. B. (1986). *Ethnic and gender differences in emotional experience and expression.* Unpublished manuscript. University of Hawaii, Honolulu, HI.

Hatfield, E., & Sprecher, S. (1986a). Measuring passionate love in intimate relations. *Journal of Adolescence, 9,* 383–410.

Hatfield, E., & Sprecher, S. (1986b). *Mirror, mirror: The importance of looks in everyday life.* Albany, NY: SUNY Press.

Hatfield, E., & Sprecher, S. (in press). Men's and women's mate preferences in the United States, Russia, and Japan. *Journal of Cross-Cultural Psychology.*

Hatfield, E., Sprecher, S., Pillemer, J. T., Greenberger, D., & Wexler, P. (1988). Gender differences in what is desired in the sexual relationship. *Journal of Psychology and Human Sexuality, 1,* 39–52.

Hatfield, E., Traupmann, J., Sprecher, S., Utne, M., & Hay, J. (1984). Equity and intimate relations: Recent research. In W. Ickes (Ed.), *Compatible and incompatible relationships* (pp. 1–27). New York: Springer-Verlag.

Hatfield, E., & Walster, G. W. (1978). *A new look at love.* Lanham, MD: University Press of America.

Hazan, C., & Shaver, P. (1987). Romantic love conceptualized as an attachment process. *Journal of Personality and Social Psychology, 52,* 511–524.

Hazan, C., & Shaver, P. R. (1990). Love and work: An attachment-theoretical perspective. *Journal of Personality and Social Psychology, 59,* 270–280.

Hazan, C., & Zeifman, D. (in press). Sex and the psychological tether. *Advances in personal relationships* (Vol. 5).

Hedges, C. (1994, October 21). Kuwait Journal: War's passion spent, love's in the air. *The New York Times International,* p. A4.

Heibroner, R. (1994). *Visions of the Future: The Distant Past, Yesterday, Today, and Tomorrow.* New York: Oxford University Press.

Heiman, J. R. (1977). A psychophysiological exploration of sexual arousal patterns in females and males. *Psychophysiology, 14,* 266–274.

Helgeson, V. S., Shaver, P., & Dyer, M. (1987). Prototypes of intimacy and distance in same-sex and opposite-sex relationships. *Journal of Social and Personal Relationships, 4,* 195–233.

Hendrick, C., & Hendrick, S. S. (1986). A theory and method of love. *Journal of Personality and Social Psychology, 50,* 392–402.

Hendrick, C., & Hendrick, S. S. (1989). Research on love: Does it measure up? *Journal of Personality and Social Psychology, 56,* 784–794.

Hendrick, S. S., & Hendrick, C. (1987a). Love and sex attitudes: A close relationship. In W. H. Jones & D. Perlman (Eds.), *Advances in personal relationships, 1,* (pp. 141–169). Greenwich, CT: JAI.

Hendrick, S. S., & Hendrick, C. (1987b). Love and sexual attitudes, self-disclosure, and sensation-seeking. *Journal of Social and Personal Relationships, 4,* 281–297.

Henton, J., Cate, R., Koval, J., Lloyd, S., & Christopher, F. S. (1983). Romance and violence in dating relationships. *Journal of Family Issues, 4,* 467–482.

Herek, G. M. (1984). Attitudes toward lesbians and gay men: A factor-analytic study. *Journal of Homosexuality, 10,* 39–52.

Herodotus (1942). Persian wars, book 1. *The Greek historians. The complete and unabidged historical works of Herodotus, Thucydides, Xenophon, and Adrian.* New York: Random House.

Hessellund, H. (1976). Masturbation and sexual fantasies in married couples. *Archives of Sexual Behavior, 5,* 133–147.

Hijuelos, O. (1989). *The Mambo Kings play songs of love.* New York: Harper Perennial.

Hijuelos, O. (1993). *The fourteen sisters of Emilio Montez O'Brien.* New York: Farrar, Straus & Giroux.

Hilger, M. I. (1952). *Arapaho child life and its cultural background.* Washington, DC: Government Printing Office.

Hill, C. T., Rubin, Z., & Peplau, L. A. (1979). Breakups before marriage: The end of 103 affairs. In G. Levinger & O. C. Moles (Eds.), *Divorce and separation* (pp. 64–82). New York: Basic Books.

Hindy, C. G., Schwarz, J. C., & Brodsky, A. (1989). *If this is love why do I feel so insecure?* New York: The Atlantic Monthly Press.

Hinsch, B. (1990). *Passions of the cut sleeve: The male homosexual tradition in China.* Berkeley, CA: University of California Press.

Ho, D. Y. F. (1982). Asian concepts in behavioral science. *Psychologia, 25,* 228–235.

Hodgson, J. W., & Fischer, J. L. (1979). Sex differences in identity and intimacy development. *Journal of Youth and Adolescence, 8,* 37–50.

Hoebel, E. A. (1940). The political organization and law-ways of the Comanche Indians. *Memoirs of the American Anthropological Association, 54,* 1–149.

Hofman, A. (1984). Contraception in adolescence: A review. 1. Psycholosocial aspects. *Bulletin of the World Health Organization, 62,* 151–162.

Hofstede, G. (1980). *Culture's consequences: International differences in work-related values.* Beverly Hills, CA: Sage.

Hofstede, G. (1983). National culture revisited. *Behavior Science Research, 18,* 285–305.

Höhn, C., & Otto, J. (1984). Bericht über die demographische Lage in der Bundesrepublik und über die Weltbevölkerungstrends. *Zeitschrift fur Bevölkerungswissenschaft, 4,* 445–518.

Holmes, K. K. (1993, July 1). *Sexually transmitted disease seroprevalence related to general knowledge, attitudes, beliefs, and practices among the general population in Lima, Peru.* Paper presented at the International Academy of Sex Research, 19th Annual Meeting, Pacific Grove, CA.

Honig, E., & Hershatter, G. (1988). *Personal voices: Chinese women in the 1980s.* Stanford, CA: Stanford University Press.

Hortacsu, N., & Karanci, A. N. (1987). Premarital breakups in a Turkish sample: Perceived reasons, attributional dimensions and affective reactions. *International Journal of Psychology, 22,* 57–64.

Hosken, F. P. (1982). *The Hosken report: Genital and sexual mutilation of females.* Lexington, MA: Women's International Network News.

Howell, N. (1979). *Demography of the Dobe !Kung.* New York: Academic Press.

Hrdy, S. B. (1981). *The woman that never evolved.* Cambridge, MA: Harvard University Press.

Hsu, F. L. K. (1971). Psychosocial homeostasis and jen: Conceptual tools for advancing psychological anthropology. *American Anthropologist, 73,* 23–44.

Hsu, F. L. K. (1953). *Americans and Chinese: Passage to difference* (3rd ed.). Honolulu: University Press of Hawaii.

Hsu, F. L. K. (1985). The self in cross-cultural perspective. In A. J. Marsella, G. DeVos, & F. L. K. Hsu (Eds.), *Culture and self: Asian and Western perspectives* (pp. 24–55). London, England: Tavistock.

Huang, K., & Uba, L. (1992). Premarital sexual behavior among Chinese college students in the United States. *Archives of Sexual Behavior, 21,* 227–240.

Hudson, W. W., & Ricketts, W. A. (1980). A strategy for the measurement of homophobia. *Journal of Homosexuality, 5,* 357–372.

Hunt, M. (1959). *The natural history of love*. New York: Grove Press.

Hunt, M. (1974). *Sexual behavior in the 1970s*. Chicago: Playboy Press.

Hupka, R. B. (1977, August). Societal and individual roles in the expression of jealousy. In H. Sigall (Chair), *Sexual jealousy*. Symposium presented at the meetings of the American Psychological Association (pp. 7–9), San Francisco.

Hupka, R. B. (1981). Cultural determinants of jealousy. *Alternative Lifestyles, 4*, 310–356.

Hupka, R. B. (1991). The motive for the arousal of romantic jealousy: Its cultural origin. In P. Salovey (Ed.), *The psychology of jealousy and envy* (pp. 252–270). New York: Guilford Press.

Hupka, R. B., & Ryan, J. M. (1990). The cultural contribution to jealousy: Cross-cultural aggression in sexual jealousy situations. *Behavior Science Research, 24*, 51–71.

Hyde, J. S. (1990). *Understanding human sexuality*. New York: McGraw-Hill.

Imbrogno, S., & Imbrogno, N. (1989). Soviet woman and the autonomous family. *International Journal of Sociology of the Family, 19*, 1–20.

India Tribune Magazine (1993, September 25). Dirty dancing—sex on music crosses all borders to kiss vulgarity, pp. 16 and 18.

Ingram, R. E., Cruet, D., Johnson, B. R., & Wisnicki, K. S. (1988). Self-focused attention, gender, gender role, and vulnerability to negative affect. *Journal of Personality and Social Psychology, 55*, 967–978.

Iwawaki, S., & Eysenck, H. J. (1978). Sexual attitudes among British and Japanese students. *Journal of Psychology, 98*, 289–298.

Iwawaki, S., & Wilson, G. D. (1983). Sex fantasies in Japan. *Personality and Individual Differences, 4*, 543–545.

Ivins, M. (1991). *Molly Ivins can't say that, can she?* New York: Random House.

Iyer, P. (1988). *Video night in Kathmandu and other reports from the not-so-far-East*. New York: Alfred A. Knopf.

Jahoda, G. (1980). Theoretical and systematic approaches in cross-cultural psychology. In H. C. Triandis & W. W. Lambert (Eds.), *Handbook of cross-cultural psychology: Vol. 1. Perspectives* (pp. 69–141). Boston: Allyn & Bacon.

James, W. H. (1981). The honeymoon effect on marital coitus. *Journal of Sex Research, 17*, 114–123.

Jankowiak, W. R. (1993). *Sex, death, and hierarchy in a Chinese city: An anthropological account*. New York: Columbia University Press.

Jankowiak, W. R., & Fischer, E. F. (1992). A cross-cultural perspective on romantic love. *Ethology, 31*, 149–155.

Jason, L. A., Reichler, A., Easton, J., Neal, A., & Wilson, M. (1984). Female harassment after ending a relationship: A preliminary study. *Alternative Lifestyles, 6*, 259–269.

Jones, J. C., & Barlow, D. H. (1987, November). *Self reported frequency of sexual urges, fantasies, and masturbatory fantasies in heterosexual males and females*. Paper presented at the annual meeting of the Association for the Advancement of Behavior Therapy.

Jones, D., & Hill, K. (1993). Criteria of facial attractiveness in five populations. *Human Nature, 4*, 271–296.

Joseph, R., & Joseph, T. B. (1987). *The rose and the thorn*. Tucson, AZ: University of Arizona Press.

Kâğitçibaşi, C. (1990). In J. J. Berman (Ed.), Family and socialization in cross cultural perspective: A model of change. *Nebraska Symposium on Motivation: 1989: Cross-Cultural Perspectives, 37*, (pp. 136–200). Lincoln: University of Nebraska Press.

Kakar, S., & Ross, J. M. (1986). *Tales of love, sex and danger*. Delhi, India: Oxford University Press.

Kama Sutra of Vatsyayana, The. (1st–4th century A.D./1963). (Sir R. Burton & F. F. Arbouchnot, Trans.). New York: Putnam.

Kamisar, Y. (1993, September 26). Why the bad guys keep winning. *The New York Times Book Review, 7*, 11–12.

Kaplan, H. S. (1987). *The illustrated manual of sex therapy*. New York: Brunner/Mazel.

Karnad, G. (1975). *Hayavadana*. Calcutta, India: Oxford University Press.

Kasdan, L. (1987). *The big chill*. New York: St. Martin's Press.

Kato, K., & Markus, H. (1992). *Interdependence and culture: Theory and measurement*. Unpublished manuscript. The University of Michigan, Ann Arbor, MI.

Kelley, K. (1984–1985). Sexual fantasy and attitudes as functions of sex of subject and content of erotica. *Imagination, Cognition, and Pesonality,* *4,* 339–347.

Kennedy, R. (1989). *Life choices* (2nd ed.). New York: Holt, Rinehart & Winston.

Kenrick, D. T., & Keefe, R. C. (1989). Time to integrate sociobiology and social psychology. *Behavioral and Brain Sciences, 12,* 24–25.

Kenrick, D. T., Sadalla, E. K., Groth, G. E., & Trost, M. R. (1990). Evolution, traits, and the stages of human courtship: Qualifying the parental investment model. *Journal of Personality, 58,* 97–117.

Kephart, W. M. (1967). Some correlates of romantic love. *Journal of Marriage and the Family, 29,* 470–479.

Kerblay, B. (1983). *Modern Soviet society.* (R. Swyer, Trans.). New York: Pantheon Books.

Kermoian, R., & Leiderman, H. (1982). *The infant's role in maintenance of attachment security: Evidence from a study of African infants.* Paper presented at the International Conference of Infant Studies, Austin, TX.

Kern, S. (1992). *The culture of love: Victorians to moderns.* Cambridge, MA: Harvard University Press.

King, P. (1993, August 6–8). "I will not be a loser." *USA Weekend.* pp. 4–6.

Kingston, M. H. (1975). *The woman warrior.* New York: Vintage Books.

Kinsey, A. C., Pomeroy, W. B., & Martin, C. E. (1948). *Sexual behavior in the human male.* Philadelphia: Saunders.

Kinsey, A. C., Pomeroy, W. B., Martin, C. E., & Gebhard, P. H. (1953). *Sexual behavior in the human female.* Philadelphia: Saunders.

Kite, M. E., & Deaux, K. (1986). Attitudes toward homosexuality: Assessment and behavioral consequences. *Basic and Applied Social Pschology, 7,* 137–162.

Klassen, A. D., Williams, C. J., & Levitt, E. (1981). *American sexual standards.* Unpublished manuscript. Alfred C. Kinsey Institute for the Study of Sex, Gender and Reproduction, Bloomington, IN.

Klein, T. (1990). Wiederheirat nach scheidung in der bundesrepublik: Eine empirische uberprufung bisland vorliegender theorieansetz aus der perspektive des lebensverlaufs. *Kolner-Zeit-schrift-fur-Soziologie-und-Sozialpsychologie, 42,* 50–80.

Klinger, E. (1977). *Meaning and void: Inner experience and the incentives in people's lives.* Minneapolis, MN: University of Minnesota Press.

Knafo, D., & Jaffee, Y. (1984). Sexual fantasizing in males and females. *Journal of Research in Personality, 18,* 451–462.

Knoth, R., Boyd, K., & Singer, B. (1988). Empirical tests of sexual selection theory: Predictions of sex differences in onset, intensity, and time course of sexual arousal. *Journal of Sex Research, 24,* 73–89.

Kobayashi, K. (1993, March 26). Ganal defense: Filipino culture. *The Honolulu Advertiser,* p. 1.

Kon, I. (1993). Sexuality and culture. In I. Kon & J. Riordan (Eds.), *Sex and Russian society* (pp. 15–43). Bloomington, IN: Indiana University Press.

Konner, M. (1982). *The tangled wing: Biological constraints on the human spirit.* New York: Henry Holt.

Kontula, O. (1993, November 4–7). *Sexual behavior changes in Finland during the last 20 years.* Meetings of the Society for the Society for the Scientific Study of Sex, Chicago, IL.

Kontula, O., & Haavio-Mannila, E. (1995). *Sexual pleasures: Enhancement of sex life in Finland, 1991–1992.* Brookfield, VA: Dartmouth.

Kramer, H., & Sprenger, J. (1486/1971). (Reverend M. Summers, Trans.). *The Malleus Maleficarum.* New York: Dover Publications.

Kristof, N. D. (1991a, July 19). A peek through the keyhole at a new China. *The New York Times,* pp. A1, A7.

Kristof, N. D. (1991b, November 5). Stark data on women: 100 million are missing. *The New York Times,* pp. C1, C12.

Kroeber, A. L. (1902). *The Arapho.* New York: Knickerbocker Press.

Kumagai, F. (1984). The life cycle of the Japanese family. *Journal of Marriage and the Family, 46,* 191–204.

Kumar, U. (1991). Life stages in the development of the Hindu woman in India. In L. L. Adler (Ed.), *Women in cross-cultural perspective* (pp. 142–158). New York: Praeger.

Kumari, R. (1989). *Brides are not for burning: Dowry victims in India.* New Delhi, India: Radiant Publishing.

Kunce, L. J., & Shaver, P. R. (1991). *An attachment-theoretical approach to caregiving in romantic relationships.* Unpublished manuscript, Psychology Department, State University of New York at Buffalo.

Kurdek, L. A. (1991). The dissolution of gay and lesbian couples. *Journal of Social and Personal Relationships, 8,* 265–278.

LaBeff, E. E., & Dodder, R. A. (1982). Attitudes toward sexual permissiveness in Mexico and the United States. *The Journal of Social Psychology, 116,* 285–286.

Ladurie, E. L. R. (1979). *Montaillou: The promised land of error.* (B. Bray, Trans.), New York: Vintage Books.

La Fave, W. R., & Scott, A. W. (1972). *Handbook on criminal law.* New York: West.

Lamb, M. E., Hwang, C. P., Frodi, M., & Frodi, M. (1982). Security of mother- and father-infant attachment and its relation to sociability with strangers in traditional and non-traditional Swedish families. *Infant Behavior and Development, 5,* 355–367.

Langlois, J. H., & Roggman, L. A. (1990). Attractive faces are only average. *Psychological Science, 1,* 115–121.

Lateef, S. (1990). Rule by the *Danda:* Domestic violence among Indo-Fijians. *Pacific Studies, 13,* 43–62.

Lauman, E. O., Gagnon, J. H., Michael, R. T., & Michaels, S. (1994). *The social organization of sexuality: Sexual practices in the United States.* Chicago, IL: University of Chicago Press.

Lawson, A. (1988). *Adultery: An analysis of love and betrayal.* New York: Basic Books.

Lawson, A., & Samson, L. (1988). Age, gender, and adultery. *British Journal of Sociology, 39,* 409–440.

Leamer, L. (1986). *As time goes by.* New York: Harper & Row.

Lebra, T. S. (1976). *Japanese patterns of behavior.* Honolulu, HI: University of Hawaii Press.

Lee, G. R., & Stone, L. H. (1980). Mate-selection systems and criteria: Variation according to family structure. *Journal of Marriage and the Family, 42,* 319–326.

Lee, J. A. (1973). *The colors of love: An exploration of the ways of loving.* Don Mills, Ontario, Canada: New Press.

Lehman, D. R., Wortman, C. B., & Williams, A. F. (1987). Long term effects of losing a spouse or child in a motor vehicle crash. *Journal of Personality and Social Psychology, 52,* 218–231.

Leigh, B. C. (1989). Reasons for having and avoiding sex: Gender, sexual orientation, and relationship to sexual behavior. *Journal of Sex Research, 26,* 199–209.

LePoire, B. A., & Aune, K. S. (1993). *Viva la similaritie! The lack of gender differences in the nonverbal reactions to a romantic threat.* Unpublished manuscript. Texas A & M University, College Station, TX.

Levine, D. (1968). The flexibility of traditional culture. *Journal of Social Issues, 24,* 129–141.

Levine, R., Sato, S., Hashimoto, T., & Verma, J. (1994). *Love and marriage in eleven cultures.* Unpublished manuscript. California State University, Fresno, CA.

Levinger, G. (1979). A social psychological perspective on marital dissolution. In G. Levinger & O. C. Moses (Eds.), *Divorce and separation* (pp. 37–60). New York: Basic Books.

Levinson, D. (1989). *Family violence in cross-cultural perspective. Frontiers of anthropology* (Vol. 1). Newbury Park, CA: Sage Publications.

Levy, M. B., & Davis, K. E. (1988). Lovestyles and attachment styles compared: Their relations to each other and to various relationship characteristics. *Journal of Social and Personal Relationships, 5,* 439–471.

Lewin, T. (1994, October 21). Outrage over 18 months for man who killed his wife in 'heat of passion.' *The New York Times National,* p. A9.

Lewin, T. (1995, May 30). The decay of families is global, study says. *The New York Times International Edition,* p. A5.

Lidegaard, Ø., & Helm, P. (1990). Seksualvaner blandt 15–54 årige kvinder. *Nordisk Sexologi, 8,* 124–136.

Lieh-Mak, F., O'Hoy, K. M., & Luk, S. L. (1983). Lesbianism in the Chinese of Hong Kong. *Archives of Sexual Behavior, 12,* 21–30.

Li-Repac, D. C. (1982). *The impact of acculturation on the child-rearing attitudes and practices of Chinese-American families: Consequences for the attach-*

ment process. Doctoral dissertation, University of California, Berkeley, CA.

Liskin, L. (1992, November-December). Youth in the 1980s: Social and health concerns. *Population Reports, 13*, M-349–M-388.

Liu, D. L. (1991). *National sex civilization survey*. Shanghai, China: Sex Sociological Research Center.

Liu, D. L., Ng, M. L., & Chou, L. P. (1992). *Sexual behavior in modern China: A report of the nationwide 'sex civilisation' survey on 20,000 subjects in China*. Shanghai: San Lian Bookstore Publishers.

Lodge, D. (1993). *The picturegoers*. London, England: Penguin Books.

Lopata, H. Z. (1969). Loneliness: Forms and components. *Social Problems, 17*, 248–261.

Lütkenhaus, P., Grossmann, K. E., & Grossmann, K. (1985). Infant-mother attachment at twelve months and style of interaction with a stranger at the age of three years. *Child Development, 56*, 1538–1542.

Lykken, D. T., & Tellegen, A. (1993). Is human mating advantageous or the result of lawful choice? A twin study of mate selection. *Journal of Personality and Social Psychology, 65*, 56–68.

Mace, D., & Mace, V. (1980). *Marriage: East and West*. New York: Dolphin Books.

Mahfouz, N. (1990). (W. M. Hutchins & O. E. Kenny, Trans.), *Palace walk*. New York: Doubleday.

Main, M. & Hesse, E. (1990). Parents' unresolved traumatic experiences are related to infant disorganized status: Is frightened and/or frightening parental behavior the linking mechanism? In M. T. Greenberg, D. Cicchetti, & E. M. Cummings (Eds.), *Attachment in the preschool years* (pp. 161–184). Chicago: University of Chicago Press.

Main, M., & Solomon, J. (1990). Procedures for identifying infants as disorganized/disoriented during the Ainsworth strange situation. In M. T. Greenberg, D. Cicchetti, & E. M. Cummings (Eds.), *Attachment in the preschool years* (pp. 121–160). Chicago: University of Chicago Press.

Makepeace, J. M. (1986). Gender differences in courtship violence victimization. *Family Relations: Journal of Applied Family and Child Studies, 35*, 383–388.

Manchester, W. (1992). *A world lit only by fire*. Boston: Little Brown.

Margolin, L. (1989). Gender and the perogatives of dating and marriage: An experimental assessment of a sample of college students. *Sex Roles, 20*, 91–102.

Markus, H. R., & Kitayama, S. (1991). Culture and self: Implications for cognition, emotion, and motivation. *Psychological Review, 98*, 224–253.

Márquez, G. G. (1990). *Collected novellas*. New York: HarperCollins.

Marshall, L. L., & Rose, P. (1987). Gender, stress and violence in the adult relationships of a sample of college students. *Journal of Social and Personal Relationships, 4*, 299–316.

Marston, P. J., Hecht, M. L., & Robers, T. (1987). "True love ways": The subjective experience and communication of romantic love. *Journal of Social and Personal Relationships, 4*, 387–407.

Martin, T. C., & Bumpass, L. L. (1989). Recent trends in marital disruption. *Demography, 26*, 37–51.

Masters, W. H., & Johnson, V. E. (1966). *Human sexual response*. Boston: Little, Brown.

Masters, W. H., & Johnson, V. E. (1970). *Human sexual inadequacy*. Boston: Little, Brown.

Masters, W. H., & Johnson, V. E. (1979). *Homosexuality in perspective*. Boston: Little, Brown.

Mathes, E. W., & Wise, P. S. (1983). Romantic love and the ravages of time. *Psychological Reports, 53*, 839–846.

Maykovich, M. K. (1976). Attitudes versus behavior in extramarital sexual relations. *Journal of Marriage and the Family, 38*, 693–699.

McNeill, W. H. (1963). *The rise of the West: A history of the human community*. Chicago: University of Chicago Press.

McWhirter, D. P., & Mattison, A. M. (1984). *The male couple: How relationships develop*. Englewood Cliffs, NJ: Prentice-Hall.

Mead, M. (1931). Jealousy: Primitive and civilized. In S. D. Schmalhausen & V. F. Calverton (Eds.), *Woman's coming of age* (pp. 35–48). New York: Horace Liveright.

Mead, M. (1935/1969). *Sex and temperament in three primitive societies*. New York: Dell Publishing.

Mead, M. (1969). *Sex and temperament in three primitive societies*. New York: Dell Publishing.

Means, J. (1991). Coping with a breakup: Negative mood regulation expectancies and depression following the end of a romantic relationship. *Journal of Personality and Social Psychology, 60,* 327–334.

Melikian, L., & Prothro, E. T. (1954). Sexual behaviour of university students in the Arab Near East. *Journal of Social Psychology, 49,* 59–64.

Melikian, L., & Prothro, E. T. (1967). Social change and sexual behavior of Arab university students. *Journal of Social Psychology, 73,* 169–175.

Metz, M. E., Rosser, B. R. S., & Strapko, N. (1994). Differences in conflict resolution styles between heterosexual, gay, and lesbian couples. Submitted to *Journal of Sex Research, 31,* 293–307.

Meyer, J. J. (1930). *Sexual life in ancient India.* New York: E. P. Dutton.

Meyer, M. (1987). *Strindberg.* Oxford, England: Oxford University Press.

Meyers, S. M., Ridge, R. D., & Berscheid, E. (1991). *"Love" vs. "in love."* Unpublished manuscript. University of Minnesota, Department of Psychology, Minneapolis, MN.

Mhloyi, M. M. (1990). Perceptions on communication and sexuality in marriage in Zimbabwe. Special issue: Women's mental health in Africa. *Women and Therapy, 10,* 61–73.

Michael, R. T., Laumann, E. O., Gagnon, J. H., & Smith, T. W. (1988). Number of sex partners and potential risk of sexual exposure to human immunodeficiency virus. *Morbidity Mortality Weekly Report, 37,* 565–567.

Mikulincer, M., Florian, V., & Tolmacz, R. (1990). Attachment styles and fear of personal death: A case study of affect regulation. *Journal of Personality and Social Psychology, 58,* 273–280.

Mikulincer, M., & Nachshon, O. (1991). Attachment styles and patterns of self-disclosure. *Journal of Personality and Social Psychology, 61,* 321–331.

Minturn, L., Grosse, M., & Haider, S. (1969). Cultural patterning of sexual beliefs and behavior. *Ethnology, 8,* 301–313.

Mintz, S., & Kellogg, S. (1988). *Domestic revolutions: A social history of American family life.* New York: Free Press.

Mirsky, J. (1937). The Eskimo of Greenland. In M. Mead (Ed.), *Cooperation and competition among primitive peoples* (pp. 51–86). New York: McGraw-Hill.

Mishkin, B. (1937). The Maori of New Zealand. In M. Mead (Ed.), *Cooperation and competition among primitive peoples* (pp. 428–457). New York: McGraw-Hill.

Miyake, K., Chen, S-J., & Campos, J. J. (1985). Infant temperament, mother's mode of interaction, and attachment in Japan: An interim report. In I. Bretherton & E. Waters (Eds.), *Growing points of attachment theory and research* (pp. 276–297). Chicago: University of Chicago Press.

Money, J. (1977). Peking: The sexual revolution. In J. Money & H. Musaph (Eds.), *Handbook of Sexology* (pp. 543–550). Amsterdam: Excerpta Medica.

Money, J. (1980). *Love and love sickness.* Baltimore, MD: Johns Hopkins University Press.

Moore, B., Jr. (1966). *Social origins of dictatorship and democracy: Lord and peasant in the making of the modern world.* Boston: Beacon Press.

Morens, D. M., & Polloi, H. (in preparation). Sexual experience and health risk in the Republic of Palau.

Morioka, K. (1987). A Japanese perspective on the life course: Emerging and diminishing patterns. *Journal of Family History, 12,* 243–260.

Muehlenhard, C. L., & Quackenbush, D. M. (1988, November). *Can the sexual double standard put women at risk for sexually transmitted diseases? The role of the double standard in condom use among women.* Paper presented at the Annual Meeting of the Society for the Scientific Study of Sex, San Francisco, CA.

Murstein, B. I. (1974). *Love, sex, and marriage through the ages.* New York: Springer.

Murstein, B. I. (1986). *Paths to marriage.* Beverly Hills, CA: Sage.

Murstein, B. I., & Holden, C. C. (1979). Sexual behavior and correlates among college students. *Adolescence, 14,* 625–639.

Nadler, A., & Dotan, I. (1992). Commitment and rival attractiveness: Their effects on male and female reactions to jealousy arousing situations. *Sex Roles, 26,* 293–310.

Napier, A. Y. (1977). *The rejection-intrusion pattern: A central family dynamic.* Unpublished manuscript, School of Family Resources, University of Wisconsin, Madison, WI.

National Center for Health Statistics. (1987). *Advance Report on Final Divorce Statistics, 1985,*

Monthly Vital Statistics Report 36. Hyattsville, MD: Public Health No. (PHS) 88-1120.

Nave-Herz, R. (1989). Childless marriages. *Marriage and Family Review, 14,* 238–250.

Needham, G. B. (1951, May). Mrs. Manley: An eighteenth-century wife of bath. *Huntington Library Quarterly, 14,* 259–284.

Nevid, J. S., Fichner-Rathus, L. F., & Rathus, S. A. (1995). *Human sexuality in a world of diversity.* (2nd Ed.), Boston: Allyn & Bacon.

Ng, M. L., & Lau, M. P. (1990). Sexual attitudes in the Chinese. *Archives of Sexual Behavior, 19,* 373–388.

Nolen-Hoeksema, S. (1987). Sex differences in unipolar depression: Evidence and theory. *Psychological Bulletin, 101,* 259–282.

Norikoshi, K. (1990). Love: A primatological approach. *Japanese Psychological Review, 33,* 304–318.

Norrgard, L. (1990). Opening the Hong Kong closet. *Out/Look (National Gay Lesbian Quarterly), 2,* 56–61.

Norris, F. (1899/1965). *McTeague.* New York: Holt, Rinehart, and Winston.

Øberg, P., Ruth, J. E., & Tornstam, L. (1987). Ensamhetsupplevelser hos de äldre; I: Sociala föhållanden, *Gerontologia, 2,* 44–55.

Oggins, J., Veroff, J., & Leber, D. (1993). Perceptions of marital interaction among black and white newlyweds. *Journal of Personality and Social Psychology, 65,* 494–511.

O'Leary, K. D., Arias, I., Rosenbaum, A., & Barling, J. (1986). *Premarital physical aggression.* Unpublished manuscript. State University of New York at Stony Brook.

O'Leary, K. D., Barling, J., Arias, I., Rosenbaum, A., Malone, J., & Lyree, A. (1989). Prevalence and stability of physical aggression between spouses: A longitudinal analysis. *Journal of Consulting and Clinical Psychology, 57,* 263–268.

Oliver, M. B., & Hyde, J. S. (1993). Gender differences in sexuality: A meta-analysis. *Psychological Bulletin, 114,* 29–51.

Orimoto, L., Hatfield, E., Yamakawa, R., & Denney, C. (1993). *Gender differences in emotional reactions and coping strategies following a break-up.* Unpublished manuscript. University of Hawaii, Honolulu, HI.

Orlofsky, J. L., & Ginsburg, S. D. (1981). Intimacy status: Relationship to affect cognition. *Adolescence, 16,* 91–100.

Oz, A. (1991). (Trans. N. De Lange). *Fima.* New York: Harcourt Brace & Co.

Pa, Chin. (1972). *Family.* New York: Doubleday. (Originally published 1933)

Padilla, E. R., & O' Grady, K. E. (1987). Sexuality among Mexican Americans: A case of sexual steroptyping. *Journal of Personality and Social Psychology, 52,* 5–10.

Peplau, L. A. (1981, March). What homosexuals want in a relationship. *Psychology Today,* 28–38.

Peristiany, J. G. (Ed.), (1966). *Honour and shame: The values of Mediterranean society.* Chicago: University of Chicago Press.

Perlez, J. (1991, July 29). Kenyans do some soul-searching after the rape of 71 girls. *The New York Times,* pp. A1, A4.

Perlman, D., & Peplau, L. A. (1981). Toward a social psychology of loneliness. In S. Duck & R. Gilmour (Eds.), *Personal relationships. 3: Personal relationships in disorder* (pp. 31–56). London: Academic Press.

Phillips, R. (1988). *Putting asunder: A history of divorce in Western society* (pp. 630–640). New York: Cambridge University Press.

Plato (5th century B.C./1950). Symposium. (B. Jowett, Trans.), *The portable Plato* (pp. 121–187). New York: Viking Press.

Plutchik, R. (1980). *Emotion: A psychoevolutionary synthesis.* New York: Harper & Row.

Pollak, S., & Gilligan, C. (1982). Images of violence in thematic apperception test stories. *Journal of Personality and Social Psychology, 42,* 159–167.

Pollitt, K. (1993, July 22). Bothered and bewildered. *The New York Times,* p. A19.

Popenoe, D. (1987). Beyond the nuclear family: A statistical portrait of the changing family in Sweden. *Journal of Marriage and the Family, 49,* 173–183.

Prakasa, V. V., & Rao, V. N. (1979). Arranged marriages: An assessment of the attitudes of the college students in India. In G. Kurian (Ed.), *Cross-cultural perspectives of mate-selection and marriage* (pp. 11–31). Westport, CT: Greenwood Press.

Prather, J. E. (1990). "It's just as easy to marry a rich man as a poor one!" Students' accounts of parental messages about marital partners. *Mid-American Review of Sociology, 14*, 151–162.

Quinn, N. (1977). Anthropological studies on women's status. *Annual Review of Anthropology, 6*, 181–225.

Quinn, S. (1988). *A mind of her own: The life of Karen Horney.* New York: Addison-Wesley.

Rapson, R. L. (1988). *American yearnings: Love, money, and endless possibility.* Lanham, MD: University Press of America.

Rathus, S., Nevid, J. S., & Fichner-Rathus, L. (1993). *Human sexuality in a world of diversity.* Boston: Allyn and Bacon.

Reber, A. S. (1985). *The Penguin dictionary of psychology.* New York: Viking.

Regan, P. C. (1994). *The perceived impact of sexual desire upon romantic love and romantic relationships: An experimental examination of what Grandma always knew (but social psychologists sometimes forget).* Unpublished manuscript. University of Minnesota, Department of Psychology, Minneapolis, MN.

Regan, P. C., & Berscheid, E. (in press). Gender differences about the causes of male and female sexual desire. *Personal Relationships.*

Reik, T. (1972). *A psychologist looks at love.* New York: Holt, Rinehart and Winston.

Reinisch, J. M., Sanders, S. A., & Ziemba-Davis, M. (1988). The study of sexual behavior in relation to the transmission of human immunodeficiency virus: Caveats and recommendations. *American Psychologist, 43*, 921–927.

Reiss, I. L. (1967). *The social context of premarital sexual permissiveness.* New York: Holt, Rinehart & Winston.

Reiss, I. L. (1989) Society and sexuality: A sociological explanation. In K. McKinney & S. Sprecher (Eds.), *Human sexuality: The societal and interpersonal context* (pp. 3–29). Norwood, NJ: Ablex.

Reiss, I. L., Anderson, R. E., & Sponaugle, G. C. (1980). A multivariate model of the determinants of extramarital sexual permissiveness. *Journal of Marriage and the Family, 42*, 395–411.

Reiss, I. L., & Lee, G. R. (1988). *Family systems in America* (4th ed.). New York: Holt, Rinehart, & Winston.

Rivers, W. H. R. (1906). *The Todas.* London: Macmillan.

Roberts, J. M. (1976). *History of the world.* New York: Knopf.

Roberts, L. J., & Krokoff, L. L. (1990). A time-series analysis of withdrawal, hostility, and displeasure in satisfied and dissatisfied marriages. *Journal of Marriage and the Family, 52*, 95–105.

Robey, B., Rutstein, S. O., & Morris, L. (1992, December). The reproductive revolution: New survey findings. *Population Reports, Series M, No. 11*, 1–29.

Roland, A. (1988). *In search of self in India and Japan.* Princeton, NJ: Princeton University Press.

Rosenbaum, M. E. (1986). The repulsion hypothesis: On the nondevelopment of relationships. *Journal of Personality and Social Psychology, 51*, 1156–1166.

Rosenblatt, P. C. (1967). Marital residence and the function of romantic love. *Ethnology, 6*, 471–480.

Rosenblatt, P. C., & Anderson, R. M. (1981). Human sexuality in cross-cultural perspective. In M. Cook (Ed.), *The bases of human sexual attraction* (pp. 215–250). London, England: Academic Press.

Rosenblatt, P. C., & Unangst, D. (1979). Marriage ceremonies: An exploratory cross-cultural study. In G. Kurian (Ed.), *Cross-cultural perspectives of mate-selection and marriage* (pp. 227–242). Westport, CT: Greenwood Press.

Rosenblum, L. A. (1985, September 18) *Discussant: Passionate love and the nonhuman primate.* Paper presented at the International Academy of Sex Research meetings, Seattle, WA.

Rosenthal, A. M. (1993, July 27). The torture continues. *The New York Times*, A13.

Ruan, F. F. (1991). *Sex in China: Studies in sexology in Chinese culture.* New York: Plenum.

Ruan, F. F., & Bullough, V. L. (1992). Lesbianism in China. *Archives of Sexual Behavior, 21*, 217–226.

Rubin, L. B. (1990). *Erotic wars: What happened to the sexual revolution?* New York: HarperCollins.

Rubin, Z., Hill, C. T., Peplau, L. A., & Dunke-Schetter, C. (1980). Self-disclosure in dating couples: Sex roles and the ethic of openness. *Journal of Marriage and the Family, 42*, 305–317.

Rushton, J. P. (1988). Genetic similarity, mate choice, and fecundity in humans. *Ethology and Sociobiology, 9*, 329–335.

Rushton, J. P. (1989). Epigenesis and social preference. *Behavioral and Brain Sciences, 12,* 31–32.

Sagi, A., Lamb, M. E., Lewkowicz, K. S., Shoham, R., Dvir, R., & Estes, D. (1985). Security of infant-mother, father, and metapelet attachments among kibbutz-reared Israeli children. *Monographs of the Society for Research in Child Development, 50,* 257–275.

Saikaku, I. (1956). *Five women who loved love* (W. T. De Bary, Trans.). Rutland, VT: Charles E. Tuttle.

Salovey, P., & Rodin, J. (1985, September). The heart of jealousy. *Psychology Today, 19,* 22–29.

Samshasta [or Xiao Mingxiong, pseudonym]. (1989). *Tungxing'ai wenti sanshijang [Thirty questions about homosexuality],* Hong Kong: Yiuwo.

Samson, J-M., Lévy, J. J., Dupras, A., & Tessier, D. (1991). Coitus frequency among married or cohabiting heterosexual adults: A survey in French-Canada. *Australian Journal of Marriage and Family, 12,* 103-109.

Sasson, J. P. (1992). *Princess: A true story of life behind the veil in Saudi Arabia.* New York: William Morrow.

Schmidt, G., & Sigusch, V. (1970). Sex differences in response to psychosexual stimulation by films and slides. *Journal of Sex Research, 6,* 268–283.

Schmidt, C., Sigusch, V., & Schafer, S. (1973). Responses to reading erotic stories: Male-female differences. *Archives of Sexual Behavior, 2,* 181–199.

Schoen, R., & Baj, J. (1984). Cohort marriage and divorce in five Western countries. In R. F. Tomasson (Ed.), *Comparative Social Research, 7,* 197–229.

Schork, K. (1990, August 19). The despair of Pakistan's women: Not even Benazir Bhutto could stop the repression. *Washington Post,* Sec. C, p. 4.

Schover, L. R. & Jensen, S. B. (1988). *Sexuality and chronic illness: A comprehensive approach.* New York: Guilford.

Schwartz, S. H. (1993, June). *Toward explanations of national differences in value priorities.* Invited address delivered at the XXIV Congress of the InterAmerican Society of Psychology. Santiago de Chile.

Schwartz, S. H. (1994). Beyond individualism-collectivism: New cultural dimensions of values. In U. Kim, H. C. Triandis, C. Kâğitçibaşi, C., S.- C. Choi, & G. Yoon (Eds.), *Individualism and collectivism: Theory, method, and applications, Cross Cultural Research and Methodology, 18,* (pp. 85–122). London, England: Sage.

Seltzer, R. (1992). The social location of those holding antihomosexual attitudes. *Sex Roles, 26,* 391–398.

Shaaban, B. (1991). *Both right and left handed: Arab women talk about their lives.* Bloomington, IN: Indiana University Press.

Shapurian, R., & Hojat, M. (1985). Sexual and premarital attitudes of Iranian college students. *Psychological Reports, 57,* 67–74.

Shaver, P., & Hazan, C. (1988). A biased overview of the study of love. *Journal of Social and Personal Relationships, 5,* 474–501.

Shaver, P. R., & Hazan, C. (1993). Adult romantic attachment: Theory and empirical evidence. In D. Perlman & W. Jones (Eds.), *Advances in personal relationships* (Vol. 4) (pp. 29–70). Greenwich, CT: JAI Press.

Shaver, P. R., Wu, S., & Schwartz, J. C. (1991). Cross-cultural similarities and differences in emotion and its representation: A prototype approach. In M. S. Clark (Ed.), *Review of personality and social psychology,* (Vol. 13) (pp. 175–212). Beverly Hills, CA: Sage Publications.

Shlapentokh, V. (1984). *Love, marriage, and friendship in the Soviet Union: Ideals and practices.* New York: Praeger.

Shostak, M. (1981). *Nisa: The life and words of a !Kung woman.* Cambridge, MA: Harvard University Press.

Simpson, J. A. (1990). Influence of attachment styles on romantic relationships. *Journal of Personality and Social Psychology, 59,* 971–980.

Simpson, J. A., Campbell, B., & Berscheid, E. (1986). The association between romantic love and marriage: Kephart (1967) twice revisited. *Personality and Social Psychology Bulletin, 12,* 363–372.

Simpson, J. A., & Gangestad, S. W. (1992). Sociosexuality and romantic partner choice. *Journal of Personality, 60,* 31–50.

Simpson, J. A., Rholes, W. S., & Nelligan, J. S. (1992). Support seeking and support giving within couples in an anxiety-provoking situation: The role of attachment styles. *Journal of Personality and Social Psychology, 62,* 434–446.

Singelis, T., Choo, P., & Hatfield, E. (1995). *Love schemas* and romantic love. *Journal of Social Behavior and Personality, 10*, 15–36.

Sittitrai, W., Brown, T., & Virulrak, S. (1992). Patterns of bisexuality in Thailand. In R. Tielman, M. Carballo, & A. Hendricks (Eds.), *Bisexuality and HIV/AIDS* (pp. 97–117). Buffalo, NY: Prometheus Books.

Skocpol, T. (1979). *States and social revolutions: A comparative analysis of France, Russia, and China.* New York: Cambridge University Press.

Smith, D. F., & Hokland, M. (1988). Love and salutogenesis in late adolescence: A preliminary investigation. *Psychology: A Journal of Human Behavior, 25*, 44–49.

Smith, J. C., & Hogan, B. (1983). *Criminal law* (5th ed.). London: Butterworths.

Smith, P. B., & Bond, M. H. (1994). *Social psychology across cultures: Analysis and perspectives.* Boston: Allyn & Bacon.

Smith, P. K., & Noble, R. (1987). Factors affecting the development of caregiver-infant relationships. In L. W. C. Tavecchio & M. H. van IJzendoorn (Eds.), *Attachment in social networks. Contributions to the Bowlby-Ainsworth attachment theory* (pp. 93–134). Amsterdam: Elsevier Science.

Smith, T. W. (1991). Adult sexual behavior in 1989: Number of partners, frequency of intercourse and risk of AIDS. *Family Planning Perspectives, 23*, 102–107.

Sneddon, I., & Kremer, J. (1992). Sexual behavior and attitudes of university students in Northern Ireland. *Archives of Sexual Behavior, 21*, 295–312.

Solomon, R. L. (1980). The opponent-process theory of acquired motivation: The costs of pleasure and the benefits of pain. *American Psychologist, 35*, 691–712.

Solsberry, V., & Krupnick, J. (1984). Adults' reactions to bereavement. In M. Osterweis, F. Solomon, & M. Green (Eds.), *Bereavement: Reactions, consequences, and care* (pp. 47–68). Washington, DC: National Academy Press.

Solway, J. S. (1990). Affines and spouses, friends and lovers: The passing of polygny in Botswana. *Journal of Anthropological Research, 46*, 41–66.

Sommer, V. (1993, November 13). *Primate origins: The hardware of human sexuality.* Meetings of the

Society for the Scientfic Study of Sex, San Diego, CA.

Sonenstein, F., Pleck, J., & Ku, L. (1989). Sexual activity, condom use, and AIDS awareness among adolescent males. *Family Planning Perspectives, 21*, 152–158.

Sorensen, R. C. (1973). *Adolescent sexuality in contemporary America.* New York: World Book.

Spanier, G. B., & Margolis, R. L. (1983). Marital separation and extramarital sexual behavior. *The Journal of Sex Research, 19*, 23–48.

Spark, M. (1963). *The girls of slender means.* New York: Alfred A. Knopf.

Specter, M. (1995, July 8). Gay Russians are 'free' now but still stay in fearful closet. *The New York Times National Edition*, p. A1.

Spielberger, C. D., Gorsuch, R. L., & Lushene, R. E. (1970). *STAI manual for the State-Trait Inventory.* Palo Alto, CA: Consulting Psychologist Press.

Sponaugle, G. C. (1976, April). *Correlates of attitudes toward extramarital sexual relations.* Paper presented at the 1976 meeting of the Midwest Sociological Society, St. Louis, MO.

Sponaugle, G. C. (1989). Attitudes toward extramarital relations. In K. McKinney & S. Sprecher (Eds.), *Human sexuality: The societal and interpersonal context* (pp. 187–209) Norwood, NJ: Ablex.

Sprecher, S. (1989). Premarital sexual standards for different categories of individuals. *Journal of Sex Research, 26*, 232–248.

Sprecher, S. (1994). Two sides to the breakup of dating relationships. *Personal Relationships, 1*, 199–222.

Sprecher, S., Aron, A., Hatfield, E., Cortese, A., Potapova, E., & Levitskaya, A. (1994). Love: American style, Russian style, and Japanese style. *Personal Relationships, 1*, 349–369.

Sprecher, S., Barbee, A., & Schwartz, P. (1995). "Was it good for you too?": Gender differences in first sexual intercourse experiences. *The Journal of Sex Research, 32*, 3–15.

Sprecher, S., & Chandak, R. (1992). Attitudes about arranged marriages and dating among men and women from India. *Free Inquiry in Creative Sociology, 20*, 1–11.

Sprecher, S., & Hatfield, E. (1987). *Gender differences in emotional experience and expression in close re-*

lationships. Unpublished manuscript, University of Wisconsin, Madison, WI.

Sprecher, S., & Hatfield, E. (1995, November). Premarital sexual standards among U.S. college students and a comparison with those of Russian and Japanese students. *Archives of Sexual Behavior.*

Sprecher, S., & McKinney, K. (1993). *Sexuality.* Newbury Park, CA: Sage.

Sprecher, S., McKinney, K., Walsh, R., & Anderson, C. (1988). A revision of the Reiss Premarital Sexual Permissiveness Scale. *Journal of Marriage and the Family, 50,* 821–828.

Staples, R. E. (1978). *The black woman in America.* Chicago: Nelson-Hall.

Stavrianos, L. S. (1981). *Global rift: The Third World comes of age.* New York: Morrow.

Steig, W. (1951). *The rejected lovers.* New York: Alfred A. Knopf.

Steinmetz, S. K. (1978). Violence between family members. *Marriage and Family Review, 1,* 1–16.

Stephen, T. (1987). Attribution and adjustment to relationship termination. *Journal of Social and Personal Relationships, 4,* 47–61.

Stephens, W. N. (1963). *The family in cross-cultural perspective.* New York: Holt, Rinehart and Winston.

Sternberg, R. J. (1986). *Construct validation of a triangular theory of love.* Unpublished manuscript, Yale University, New Haven, CT.

Sternberg, R. J. (1988). Triangulating love. In R. J. Sternberg & M. L. Barnes (Eds.), *The psychology of love* (pp. 119–138) New Haven, CT: Yale University Press.

Stets, J. E., & Pirog-Good, M. A. (1987). Violence in dating relationships. *Social Psychology Quarterly, 50,* 237–246.

Stets, J. E., & Straus, M. A. (1990). Gender differences in reporting of marital violence and its medical and psychological consequences. In M. A. Straus & R. J. Gelles (Eds.), *Physical violence in American families: Risk factors and adaptation to violence in 8,145 families* (pp. 151–165). New Brunswick, NJ: Transaction.

Stone, L. (1977). *The family, sex, and marriage: In England 1500–1800.* New York: Harper & Row.

Stone, L. (1990). *Road to divorce: England 1530–1987.* New York: Oxford University Press.

Stoppard, T. (1982). *The real thing.* London: Farber and Farber.

Straus, M. A. (1979). Measuring intrafamily conflict and violence: The Conflict Tactics (CT) scale. *Journal of Marriage and the Family, 41,* 75–88.

Straus, M. A. (1990). The national family violence surveys. In M. A. Straus & R. J. Gilles (Eds.), *Physical violence in American families: Risk factors and adaptions to violence in 8,145 families* (pp. 3–16). New Brunswick, NJ: Transaction.

Straus, M. A., & Gelles, R. J. (1990). *Physical violence in American families: Risk factors and adaptions to violence in 8,145 families.* New Brunswick, NJ: Transaction.

Straus, M. A., Gelles, R. J., & Steinmetz, S. K. (1980). *Behind closed doors: Violence in the American family.* New York: Anchor/Doubleday.

Straus, M. A., & Smith, C. (1990). Violence in Hispanic families in the United States: Incidence rates and structural interpretations. In M. A. Straus & R. J. Gelles (Eds.), *Physical violence in American families* (pp. 341–367). New Brunswick, NJ: Transaction Publishers.

Stroebe, W., & Stroebe, M. S. (1987). *Bereavement and health: The psychological and physical consequences of partner loss.* New York: Cambridge University Press.

Sue, D. (1979). Erotic fantasies of college students during exams. *The Journal of Sex Research, 15,* 299–305.

Sue, D. (1982). Sexual experience and attitudes of Asian-American students. *Psychological Reports, 51,* 401–402.

Suggs, D. N., & Miracle, A. W. (1993). *Culture and human sexuality.* Pacific Grove, CA: Brooks/Cole.

Suggs, R. C. (1966). *Marquesan sexual behavior.* New York: Harcourt, Brace, & World.

Sullerot, E. (1979). *Women on love: Eight centuries of feminine writing.* (H. R. Lane, Trans.) Garden City, NY: Doubleday.

Sundet, J. M., Magnus, P., Kvalem, I. L., Samuelsen, S. O., & Bakketeig, L. S. (1992). Secular trends and sociodemographic regularities of coital debut age in Norway. *Archives of Sexual Behavior, 21,* 241–252.

Svevo, I. (1949). (B. De Zoete, Trans.), *As a man grows older.* New York: New Directions.

Swartz, M. J., & Jordan, D. K. (1980). *Culture: The anthropological perspective.* New York: Wiley.

Symons, D. (1979). *The evolution of human sexuality.* New York: Oxford University Press.

Takahashi, K. (1986). Examining the Strange-Situation procedure with Japanese mothers and 12-month-old infants. *Developmental Psychology, 22,* 265–270.

Tan, A. (1989). *The joy luck club.* New York: G. P. Putnam's Sons.

Tan, A. (1991). *The kitchen god's wife.* New York: G. P. Putnam's Sons.

Tannahill, R. (1980). *Sex in history.* New York: Stein & Day.

Tavris, C., & Offir, C. (1984). *The longest war: Sex differences in perspective* (2nd ed.). New York: Harcourt, Brace, Jovanovich.

Taylor, C. (1989). *Sources of the self: The making of the modern identity.* Cambridge, MA: Harvard University Press.

Tesch, S. A., & Whitbourne, S. K. (1982). Intimacy and identity status in young adults. *Journal of Personality and Social Psychology, 43,* 1041–1051.

Theroux, P. (1983). *The kingdom by the sea.* New York: Penguin Books.

Theroux, P. (1989), *My secret history.* New York: G. P. Putnam's Sons.

Thomas, K. (1959). The double standard. *Journal of the History of Ideas, 20,* p. 202.

Thompson, A. P. (1983). Extramarital sex: A review of the research literature. *The Journal of Sex Research, 19,* 1–22.

Thompson, A. P. (1984). Emotional and sexual components of extramarital relations. *Journal of Marriage and the Family, 46,* 35–42.

Thomson, B. (1908). *The Fijians: A study of the decay of custom.* London, England: William Heinemann.

Thornhill, R., & Gangestad, S. W. (1993). Human facial beauty: Averageness, symmetry, and parasite resistance. *Human Nature, 4,* 237–270.

Thorsen, K. (1988). *Ensomhet som opplevelse og utfordring. En studie av ensomhet blant eldre.* Oslo: Norsk Gerontologisk Institutt.

Timaeus, J. & Graham, W. (1989). Labor circulation, marriage, and fertility in Southern Africa. In R. J. Lesthaeghe (Ed.), *Reproduction and social organization in sub-saharian Africa* (pp. 365–400). Berkeley, CA: University of California Press.

Ting-Toomey, S. (1991). Intimacy expressions in three cultures: France, Japan, and the United States. *International Journal of Intercultural Relations, 15,* 29–46.

Tissot, S. A. D. (1766/1985). *Onanism.* New York: Garland Publishing.

Tolstoy, L. (1918/1980). (L. and A. Maude, Trans.), *Anna Karenina.* Oxford, England: Oxford University Press.

Tondelli, P. V. (1989). (S. Pleasance, Trans.). *Separate rooms.* New York: Serpent's Tail.

Tong, S. (1993). (M. S. Duke, Trans.). *Raise the red lantern: Three novellas.* New York: William Morrow.

Toobey, J. & Cosmides L. (1990). The past explains the present: Emotional adaptations and the structure of ancestral environments. *Ethology and Sociobiology, 11,* 375–424.

Topley, M. (1975). Marriage resistance in rural Kwangtung. In M. Wolf & R. Witke (Eds.), *Women in Chinese society* (pp. 67–88). Stanford, CA: Stanford University Press.

Tornstam, L. (1992). Loneliness in marriage. *Journal of Social and Personal Relationships, 9,* 197–217.

Toynbee, A. J. (1962). *A study of history.* New York: Oxford University Press.

Traupmann, J., & Hatfield, E. (1981). Love and its effect on mental and physical health. In R. Fogel, E. Hatfield, S. Kiesler, & E. Shanas (Eds.), *Aging: Stability and change in the family* (pp. 253–274). New York: Academic Press.

Travis, C. B., & Yeager, C. P. (1991). Sexual selection, parental investment, and sexism. *Journal of Social Issues, 47,* 117–129.

Trawick, M. (1990). *Notes on love in a Tamil family.* Berkeley, CA: University of California Press.

Triandis, H. C. (1980). Introduction. In H. C. Triandis, & W. W. Lambert. (Eds.), *Handbook of cross-cultural psychology: Perspectives* (Vol. 1). (pp. 1–14). Boston: Allyn & Bacon.

Triandis, H. C. (1994). *Culture and social behavior.* New York: McGraw-Hill.

Triandis, H. C., Bontempo, R., Villareal, M. J., Asai, M., & Lucca, N. (1988). Individualism and collectivism: Cross-cultural perspectives on self-ingroup relationships. *Journal of Personality and Social Psychology, 54,* 323–338.

Triandis, H. C., McCusker, C., & Hui, C. H. (1990). Multimethod probes of individualism and collectivism. *Journal of Personality and Social Psychology, 59*, 1006–1020.

Tsubouchi, Y. (1984). Nupitality. In United Nations, Economic and Social Commission for Asia and the Pacific (Ed.), *Population of Japan. Country Monograph Series No. 11 ST/ESCAP269.* New York: United Nations.

Tsui, M. (1989). Changes in Chinese urban family structure. *Journal of Marriage and the Family, 51*, 737–747.

Turner, C., Anderson, P., Fitzpatrick, R., Fowler, G., & Mayon-White, R. (1988). Sexual behavior, contraceptive practice and knowledge of AIDS of Oxford University students. *Journal of Biosocial Science, 20*, 445–451.

Tyler, P. E. (1994, November 27). Sex is all the talk in China along with banking. *The New York Times International,* Y3.

Tylor, E. B. (1871/1958). *The origins of culture.* New York: Harper Torchbooks.

Udry, J. R. (1980). Changes in the frequency of marital intercourse from panel data. *Archives of Sexual Behavior, 9*, 319–325.

United Nations. (1992). *Demographic yearbook: 1990.* (42nd issue). Department of International Economic and Social Affairs, Statistical Office. New York: United Nations Publication.

Upreti, H. C., & Upreti, N. (1991). *The myth of sati: Some dimensions of widow burning.* Bombay: Himalaya Publishing House.

Van De Castle, R. L. (1971). *The psychology of dreaming.* New York: General Learning.

van den Boom, D. C., Broekema, A., Leonard, S., & Kellenaers, C. J. J. (1987). *Individual differences in attachment behavior in a Dutch sample: Stability and its relationship to changing life circumstances.* Leiden, The Netherlands: Department of Psychology, University of Leiden.

van IJzendoorn, M. H., & Kroonenberg, P. M. (1988). Cross-cultural patterns of attachment: A meta-analysis of the strange situation. *Child Development, 59*, 147–156.

Vogel, E. (1963). *Japan's new middle class.* Berkeley, CA: University of California Press.

Vreeland, H. H. (1953). *Mongol community and kinship structure.* New Haven, CT: Human Relations Area Files.

Walker, A. (1992). *Possessing the secret of joy.* New York: Harcourt, Brace, Jovanovich.

Wallen, K. (1989). Mate selection: Economics and affection. *Behavioral and Brain Sciences, 12*, 37–38.

Wallerstein, I. M. (1974). *The modern world-system.* New York: Academic Press.

Wallen, K. (1989). Mate selection: Economics and affection. *Behavioral and Brain Sciences, 12*, 37–38.

Walsh, R. H. (1989). Premarital sex among teenagers and young adults. In K. McKinney & S. Sprecher (Eds.), *Human sexuality: The societal and interpersonal context* (pp. 162–186). Norwood, NJ: Ablex.

Waterman, C. K., Dawson, L. J., & Bologna, M. J. (1989). Sexual coercion in gay male and lesbian relationships: Predictors and implications for support services. *The Journal of Sex Research, 26*, 118–124.

Weiler, S. J. (1981). Aging and sexuality and the myth of decline. In J. Marsh & S. Kiesler (Eds.), *Stability and change in the family* (pp. 317–327). New York: Academic Press.

Weinberg, M. S., Swensson, R. G., & Hammersmith, S. K. (1983). Sexual autonomy and the status of women: Models of female sexuality in U.S. sex manuals from 1950–1980. *Social Problems, 30*, 312–324.

Weinberg, M. S., & Williams, C. J. (1988). Black sexuality: A test of two theories. *The Journal of Sex Research, 25*, 197–218.

Weiss, R. S. (1979). The emotional impact of marital separation. In G. Levinger & O. C. Moles (Eds.), *Divorce and separation* (pp. 201–210). New York: Basic Books.

Weitzman, L. J. (1985). *The divorce revolution.* New York: Free Press.

Wellings, K., Field, J., Wadsworth, A. M., Johnson, A. M., Anderson, R. M., & Bradshaw, S. A. (1990). Sexual lifestyles under scrutiny. *Nature, 348*, 276–278.

Wen, J. K. (1973). Social attitudes toward homosexuality. National Taiwan University. College of Medicine thesis, Taipei.

Wen, J. K. (1978). Sexual attitudes of college students. *Green Apricot* (Taipei), *46*, 106–107.

Werebe, M. J. G., & Reinert, M. (1983). Attitudes of French adolescents toward sexuality. *Journal of Adolescence, 6*, 145–159.

Whitam, F. L., & Mathy, R. M. (1986). *Male homosexuality in four societies: Brazil, Guatemala, the Philippines, and the United States.* New York: Praeger.

White, G. L., & Mullen, P. E. (1989). *Jealousy: Theory, research, and clinical strategies.* New York: Guilford Press.

White, K. M., Speisman, J. C., Jackson, D., Bartis, S., & Costos, D. (1986). Intimacy maturity and its correlates in young married couples. *Journal of Personality and Social Psychology, 50,* 152–162.

Whitley, B. E. (1988, August). *College students' reasons for sexual intercourse: A sex role perspective.* Paper presented at the 96th meeting of the American Psychological Association, Atlanta.

Wickler, W. (1972). *The sexual code.* Garden City, NY: Doubleday.

Wideman, J. E. (1990). *Philadelphia fire.* New York: Henry Holt.

Wiederman, M. W., & Allgeier, E. R. (1992). Gender differences in mate selection criteria: Sociobiological or socioeconomic explanations? *Ethology and Sociobiology, 13,* 115–124.

Wilson, G. D., & Lang, R. J. (1981). Sex differences in sexual fantasy. *Personality and Individual Differences, 2,* 343–346.

Winterson, J. (1987). *Passion.* New York: Vintage International.

Wittfogel, K. A. (1957). *Oriental despotism: A comparative study of total power.* New York: Yale University Press.

Won-Doornik, M. (1985). Self-disclosure and reciprocity in conversation: A cross-national study. *Social Psychology Quarterly, 48,* 97–107.

Wu, S., & Shaver, P. R. (1992, July 23–28). Conceptions of love in the United States and the People's Republic of China. Paper presented at the Sixth Conference of the International Society for the Study of Personal Relationships, Orono, ME.

Wyatt, G. E. (1989). Reexamining factors predicting Afro-American and white American women's age at first coitus. *Archives of Sexual Behavior, 18,* 271–298.

Wyatt, G. E. (1993, July 27). *Sociocultural influences on sexuality.* Invited address at the 19th Annual Meeting of the International Academy of Sex Research, Pacific Grove, CA.

Wyatt, G. E., Newcomb, M. D., & Riederle, M. H. (1993). *Sexual abuse and consensual sex.* Newbury Park, CA: Sage.

Xia Zhengnong. (Ed.). (1980) *Cihai (The sea of words).* Shanghai: Cishu Cubanshe.

Xu, X. & Whyte, M. K. (1990). Love matches and arranged marriages: A Chinese replication. *Journal of Marriage and the Family, 52,* 709–722.

Yamaguchi, S. (1990a). *Personality and cognitive correlates of collectivism among the Japanese: Validation of collectivism scale.* Paper presented at the 22nd International Congress of Applied psychology, Koyoto, Japan.

Yamaguchi, S. (1994). Collectivism among the Japanese: A perspective from the self. In U. Kim, H. C. Triandis, C. Kâğitçibaşi, S.-C. Choi, & G. Yoon (Eds.), *Individualism and collectivism: Theory, method, and applications cross cultural research and methodology, 18,* (pp. 175–189). London, England: Sage.

Yang, C. K. (1959). *The Chinese family in the communist revolution.* Cambridge, MA: MIT Press.

Yang, K. S. (1988). Will societal modernization eventually eliminate cross-cultural psychological differences? In M. H. Bond (Ed.), *The cross-cultural challenge to social psychology* (pp. 67–85). Newbury Park, CA: Sage.

Yap, P. M. (1965). Koro—a culture-bound depersonalization syndrome. *British Journal of Psychiatry, 111,* 43–50.

Yelsma, P., & Athappilly, K. (1988). Marital satisfaction and communication practices: Comparisons among Indian and American couples. *Journal of Comparative Family Studies, 19,* 37–54.

Zelnik, M. & Kantner, J. (1980). Sexual activity, contraceptive use and pregnancy among metropolitan-area teenagers: 1971–1979. *Family Planning Perspectives, 12,* 230–237.

Zessen, G. van & Sanfort, T. (1991). *Seksualiteit in Nederland.* Amsterdam, The Netherlands: Swets & Zeitlinger.

Zhangling, W. (1983). Chinese family problems: Research and trends. *Journal of Marriage and the Family, 45,* 943–948.

Credits

Page 9 From *Video night in Kathmandu* by Pico Iyer. Copyright © 1988 by Pico Iyer. Reprinted by permission of Alfred A. Knopf, Inc.

Page 12 From *Interdependence and culture: Theory and measurement* by Kato Kazuo and Hazel Markus. Unpublished manuscript. Reprinted by permission.

Page 14 From "National culture revisited" by Geert Hofstede, in *Behavior Science Research, 18,* 285–305. Copyright © 1993 by Geert Hofstede. Reprinted by permission of Sage Publications, Inc.

Page 16 Quoted by permission of the author, Dr. Godwin C. Chu. Original material contained in Godwin C. Chu (1985), "The changing concept of self in contemporary China," in Anthony J. Marsella, George De Vos, and Francis L. K. Hsu (Eds.), *Culture and self: Asian and Western perspectives* (pp. 252–277). London, England: Tavistock.

Page 26 by Jennifer Berman. Copyright © 1989 by Jennifer Berman. Reprinted with permission.

Page 27 From "International preferences in selecting mates: A study of 37 cultures" by David M. Buss, in *Behavioral and Brain Sciences, 12,* pp. 1–49. Copyright © David M. Buss. Reprinted with the permission of Cambridge University Press.

Page 28 From "Sex differences in human mate preferences: Evolutionary hypotheses in 37 cultures" by David M. Buss et al., in *Journal of Cross-Cultural Psychology, 21,* pp. 5–47. Copyright © by David M. Buss. Reprinted with permission.

Page 31 From "Love and marriage in eleven cultures," by R. Levine, S. Sato, T. Hashimoto, and J. Verma. Unpublished manuscript. Reprinted with permission.

Page 32 From Douglas T. Kenrick, Edward K. Sadalla, Gary Groth, and Melanie R. Trost, "Evolution, traits, and the stages of human courtship: Qualifying the parental investment model," *Journal of Personality 58:1,* pp. 97–116. Copyright © Duke University Press, 1990. Reprinted with permission.

Page 34 by Jennifer Berman. Copyright © 1990 by Jennifer Berman. Reprinted by permission.

Page 38 by Jennifer Berman. Copyright © 1991 by Jennifer Berman. Reprinted by permission.

Page 38 From *Such good friends* by Lois Gould. Copyright © 1970 by Lois Gould. Reprinted by permission of Random House, Inc.

Pages 42–43 Foreword by Ellen Berscheid. In Anne E. Beall and Robert J. Sternberg (Eds.), 1993. *The psychology of gender* (pp. vii–xvii). New York: Guilford Press.

Page 46 From *Collected novellas* by Gabriel García Márquez. Copyright © 1990 by Gabriel García Márquez.

Page 48 From "Cross-cultural codes on husband-wife relationships" by G. J. Broude and S. J. Green. With the kind authorization of Blackwell Wissenschafts-Verlag GmbH, Berlin, taken from *Ethology, 22,* pp. 273–274, 1983.

Page 50 From "Love matches and arranged marriages: A Chinese replication" by X. Xu and M. K. Whyte, in *Journal of Marriage and the Family, 52,* pp. 709–722. Reprinted by permission. Martin King Whyte is Professor of Sociology at the University of Michigan.

Pages 54-55 From "Attitudes about arranged marriages and dating among men and women from India" by S. Sprecher and R. Chandak, in *Free Inquiry in Creative Sociology, 20,* pp. 1–11. Reprinted by permission.

Page 56 From "Love matches and arranged marriages: A Chinese replication" by X. Xu and M. K. Whyte, in *Journal of Marriage and the Family, 52,* pp. 709–722. Reprinted by permission. Martin King Whyte is Professor of Sociology at the University of Michigan.

Page 61 From *At odds: Women and the family in America from the Revolution to the present* by Carl N. Degler. Copyright © 1980. Oxford University Press. Citing *Young Ward's diary* by B. J. Stern. Copyright © 1935. G. P. Putnam's Sons.

Page 61 From "How emotions develop and how they organize development" by Kurt W. Fisher. Philip R. Shaver, and Peter Carnochan, in *Cognition and Emotion, 4,* pp. 8–127 (Fig. 2, p. 90). Copyright © 1990. Reprinted by permission of the authors and Lawrence Erlbaum Associates Ltd., Hove, UK.

Page 62 From "Sally Forth" by Howard and Macintosh. Copyright © 1994 by Howard and Macintosh. Reprinted by permission of King Features Syndicate.

Page 63 From "Measuring passionate love in intimate relations" by Elaine Hatfield and Susan Sprecher, in

Journal of Adolescence, 9, pp. 383–410. Reprinted by permission of Academic Press Ltd., London, England.

Page 64 From Sternberg, R. J. (1988). Companionate Love Scale. In R. J. Sternberg & M. L. Barnes (Eds.), *The psychology of love* (pp. 119–138). New Haven: Yale University Press. Copyright © 1988 by R. J. Sternberg. Reprinted by permission of Yale University Press.

Page 65 From *Downstown* by Tim Downs. Copyright © 1993 by Tim Downs. Reprinted by permission of Universal Press Syndicate.

Page 66 From Sternberg, R. J. (1988). Triangulating love. In R. J. Sternberg & M. L. Barnes (Eds.), *The psychology of love* (pp. 119–138). New Haven: Yale University Press. Copyright © 1988 by R. J. Sternberg. Reprinted by permission of Yale University Press. •

Pages 68–69 From *McTeague* by Frank Norris. Copyright © by Frank Norris. Published by Holt, Rinehart & Winston.

Pages 74–75 From "Romantic love conceptualized as an attachment process" by Cindy Hazan and Phillip Shaver, in *Journal of Personality and Social Psychology,* 52, pp. 511–524. Copyright © 1987 by the American Psychological Association. Reprinted with permission.

Pages 81–82 Reprinted from *Shadow play* by Charles Baxter, with the permission of W. W. Norton & Company, Inc. Copyright © 1993 by Charles Baxter.

Pages 82–83 From *Cat's eye* by Margaret Atwood. Copyright © 1989 by Margaret Atwood. Published by Doubleday, a division of Bantam Doubleday Dell Publishing Group Inc.

Page 84 by Jennifer Berman. Copyright © 1991 by Jennifer Berman. Reprinted with permission.

Page 83–84 From *Almost perfect* by Alice Adams. Copyright © 1993 by Alice Adams. Published by Alfred A. Knopf, Inc.

Page 85 From *Hidden from history: Reclaiming the gay and lesbian past* by M. Duberman, M. Vicinus, and G. Chauncey, Jr. Copyright © 1989. Published by New American Library.

Page 86 From *Inside the helmet* by Peter King. Copyright © 1993 by Peter King. Reprinted by permission of Simon & Schuster, Inc.

Page 87 From *Strindberg* by Michael Meyer. Copyright © 1987 by Michael Meyer. Published by Oxford University Press.

Pages 90, 91 From *At odds: Women and the family in America from the Revolution to the present* by Carl N.

Degler. Copyright © 1980. Oxford University Press. Citing *Young Ward's diary* by B. J. Stern. Copyright © 1935. G. P. Putnam's Sons.

Page 92 by Jennifer Berman. Copyright © 1992 by Jennifer Berman. Reprinted with permission.

Page 93 From "One holy night" by Sandra Cisneros. In *Cultural tapestry: Readings for a pluralist society.* Copyright © 1992 by Sandra Cisneros. Published by HarperCollins Publishers.

Pages 97, 98, 99, 100 From *Sex in China* by Fang-fu Ruan. Copyright © 1991 by Fang-fu Ruan. Reprinted by permission of Plenum Publishing.

Page 101 From *China: Alive in the bitter sea* by Fox Butterfield. Copyright © 1982 by Fox Butterfield. Reprinted by permission of Times Books, a division of Random House, Inc., and by Hodder & Stoughton Ltd., Kent, UK.

Page 102 From *Video night in Kathmandu* by Pico Iyer. Copyright © 1988 by Pico Iyer. Reprinted by permission of Alfred A. Knopf, Inc.

Page 107 Excerpt from *The great cat massacre and other essays in French cultural history* by Robert Darnton. Copyright © 1984 by Basic Books, Inc. Reprinted by permission of Basic Books, a division of HarperCollins Publishers, Inc.

Pages 107, 108 Excerpts from *The family, sex and marriage: England 1500–1800* by Lawrence E. Stone. Copyright © 1977 by Lawrence E. Stone. Reprinted by permission of HarperCollins Publishers, Inc., by Weidenfeld and Nicolson, London, UK, and by permission of the author.

Page 112 Reprinted by permission of the publisher from Bleier, Ruth, *Science and gender.* (New York: Teachers College Press, © 1984 by Teachers College, Columbia University. All rights reserved.) p. 166.

Page 118 From *Separate rooms* by Pier V. Tondelli, translated by S. Pleasance. English translation copyright © 1989 by S. Pleasance. Reprinted by permission of Serpent's Tail.

Page 118 From "Attitudes toward homosexuality: Assessment and behavioral consequences," by Mary E. Kite and Kay Deaux, 1986, *Basic and Applied Social Psychology,* 7, pp. 137–162.

Page 124 From "Mate selection: Economics and affection," by Kim Wallen. Reprinted with the permission of K. Wallen and Cambridge University Press, from *Behavioral and Brain Sciences 12,* 37–39, 1989.

Copyright © Hachette 1974. Reprinted by permission of the publisher.

Page 195 Excerpts from *Fima* copyright © 1991 by Amos Oz and Maxwell-Macmillan-Keter Publishing Ltd. English translation copyright © 1993 by Nicholas de Lange. Published in the U.K. by Chatto & Windus Ltd. and in the U.S. by Harcourt Brace & Company. Reprinted by permission.

Pages 198–199 Reprinted from *Shadow play* by Charles Baxter, with the permission of W. W. Norton & Company, Inc. Copyright © 1993 by Charles Baxter.

Page 204 From *Love, sex, and intimacy: Their psychology, biology, and history* by Elaine Hatfield and Richard L. Rapson. Copyright © 1993 by E. Hatfield and R. Rapson. Reprinted by permission of HarperCollins Publishers.

Page 206 by Jennifer Berman. Copyright © 1988 by Jennifer Berman. Reprinted with permission.

Page 207 by Jennifer Berman. Copyright © 1989 by Jennifer Berman. Reprinted with permission.

Page 209 From "Love and marriage in eleven cultures," by R. Levine, S. Sato, T. Hashimoto, and J. Verma. Unpublished manuscript. Reprinted with permission.

Page 211 From "Cross-cultural codes on husband-wife relationships" by G. J. Broude and S. J. Green. With the kind authorization of Blackwell Wissenschafts-Verlag GmbH, Berlin, taken from *Ethology, 22,* pp. 273–274, 1983.

Page 214 From *Demographic yearbook: 1990* (42nd issue), by the Department of International Economic and Social Affairs, Statistical Office. New York: United Nations Publication. Copyright © 1992 by the United Nations. Reprinted by permission.

Page 215 From *Separate rooms* by Pier V. Tondelli, translated by S. Pleasance. English translation copyright © 1989 by S. Pleasance. Reprinted by permission of Serpent's Tail.

Page 216 by Jennifer Berman. Copyright © 1990 by Jennifer Berman. Reprinted with permission.

Page 218 From *Personal relationships* (in press) by Susan Sprecher. Reprinted by permission of the author.

Page 221 Excerpts from *Oscar & Lucinda* by Peter Carey. Copyright © 1988 by Peter Carey. Reprinted by permission of HarperCollins Publishers, Inc.

Page 223 From *Women on love: Eight centuries of feminine writing* by Evelyne Sullerot, translated by H. R. Lane. Copyright © Hachette 1974. Reprinted by permission of the publisher.

Page 224 From *Jane Eyre* by Charlotte Brontë.

Page 225 Excerpts from *Fima* copyright © 1991 by Amos Oz and Maxwell-Macmillan-Keter Publishing Ltd. English translation copyright © 1993 by Nicholas de Lange. Published in the U.K. by Chatto & Windus Ltd. and in the U.S. by Harcourt Brace & Company. Reprinted by permission.

Pages 227–228 Excerpt from *The fourteen sisters of Emilio Montez O'Brien* by Oscar Hijuelos. Copyright © 1993 by Oscar Hijuelos. Reprinted by permission of Farrar, Straus & Giroux, Inc.

Pages 228-229 Excerpt from *The Mambo Kings play songs of love* by Oscar Hijuelos. Copyright © 1989 by Oscar Hijuelos. Reprinted by permission of Farrar, Straus & Giroux, Inc.

Page 229 From *The culture of love* by Stephen Kern. Copyright © 1992 by Stephen Kern. Published by Harvard University Press.

Pages 230–231 Reprinted by permission from *Simple passion* by Annie Ernaux. Copyright © 1991 Editions Gallimard. Reprinted by permission of Four Walls Eight Windows.

Pages 240 From *The woman warrior* by Maxine Hong Kingston. Copyright © 1975, 1976 by Maxine Hong Kingston. Reprinted by permission of Alfred A. Knopf, Inc. Maxine Hong Kingston is the author of *The woman warrior, China men, Hawai'i one summer, and Tripmaster monkey–his fake book.*

Page 244 Excerpts from The family, sex and marriage: England 1500–1800 by Lawrence E. Stone. Copyright © 1977 by Lawrence E. Stone. Reprinted by permission of HarperCollins Publishers, Inc., by Weidenfeld and Nicolson, London, UK, and by permission of the author.

Pages 244–245 From "Bothered and Bewildered," by Katha Pollitt, July 22, 1993, Op-Ed. Copyright © 1993 by The New York Times Company. Reprinted by permission.

Author Index

Subject Index

Page numbers of illustrative and boxed material are in *italic* type.